ISRAEL

IN PROPHECY

ISRAEL
IN PROPHECY

A CHRONOLOGY

DR. RICHARD HILL

XULON PRESS

Xulon Press
2301 Lucien Way #415
Maitland, FL 32751
407.339.4217
www.xulonpress.com

Printed in the United States of America.

ISBN-13: 978-1-54564-255-9

Acknowledgments

First and foremost, all the blessing, honor, glory, dominion, and thanks go to my Adonai Yeshua HaMeshiach (Lord Jesus the Messiah). He is my everything, and without Him this book would never have been written! I hope and pray He will use it for His glory.

My wife Oanh and children, Stephanie, Rebekah, and Isaak, whom I love very much. Oanh is the epitome of a Proverbs 31 wife, who had to deal with a husband working our ministry unto the Lord into the late hours of the night. She is a true tireless servant of the Lord; I am a blessed man for having such a wonderful helpmate. My children are a great help in the ministry, too. They have lived their whole lives working for the Lord. They also had to learn great patience and perseverance from the Lord as we traversed this great country of ours, preaching the good news message of Yeshua and teaching the Jewish roots in the congregations.

Dr. Arnold Fruchtenbaum, who is the Messianic Jewish movement's foremost theologian. He was selected by the Lord to pave the way for Messianic Jewish eschatology and theology (what he has termed "Israelology"). He developed a sequencing of Messianic Jewish eschatology events. If you do not own a copy of *The Footsteps of the Messiah*, then you are truly missing out on understanding eschatology in its God-intended Jewish form. *Footsteps* is a comprehensive commentary on the book of Revelation. Much of his theology and eschatology is used in this book.

The Complete Biblical Library by Thoralf and Tor Inge Gilbrant. This set is a comprehensive interlinear Bible that gives the scholar and layperson everything one would need for Bible study. All the Hebrew and Greek definitions noted in this book come from the *Complete Biblical Library*'s Hebrew-English or Greek-English dictionaries.

FOREWORD

The title clearly identifies the goal and purpose of this work and provides the content of the book. The author begins with the present State of Israel and continues into the Eternal Order.

Starting with the principal of using literal interpretation unless the text indicates otherwise, he concludes with a dispensational frame of reference and defends a pre-tribulational and pre-millennial understanding of Bible prophecy. Furthermore the author clearly shows the role of Israel in the plan of God in connection with all the facets of God's plan in the present and the future.

This does not mean that all in the same theological perspective will agree with all the details. The author graciously commends my own work, *The Footsteps of the Messiah: A Study of the Sequence of Prophetic Events,* and readers of both works will note a number of differences. The reader therefore should become a Berean and do their own study and then come to their own conclusions.

In spite of our differences, this work is highly recommended.

Arnold G. Fruchtenbaum, Th.M; Ph.D

Preface

I like writing the preface of my books after the book is already written. This gives me a much broader picture of the whole book. It certainly was a labor of love with lots of highs and lots of lows. When the highs come, writing is awesome, and I feel really close to the Lord, but when the lows creep in, they make for very tough writing, and I feel very frustrated.

This reminds me of our relationships with our loved ones, acquaintances, and especially our Lord. I have drawn closer to the Lord as I have written this book. But as I draw closer, I recognize how wretched I truly am. I understand what Paul was saying in Romans 7:24, "Miserable man that I am!" Folks like to debate about whether Paul was talking about himself when he was an immature believer or when he was a mature believer. But actually, this does not matter. What matters is that he came to the reality that he was completely and utterly wretched before a holy, righteous, and just God! Humankind needs to come to this reality as well.

This is the reason why the Scripture says that all our righteous deeds are seen by God as filthy garments (Isaiah 64:6). If we human beings perform good deeds in our flesh without having a personal relationship with Him, then God sees these good deeds as filthy rags. The issue is that He is so holy, righteous, pure, and just that we cannot approach Him in our sinful state. So, whatever we think is good in our sinful state is truly evil in His eyes because the good is tainted with evil. It is as simple as that. God cannot and will not receive anything from us that is evil. So, what is the answer to the human problem? As Paul stated in the rest of the verse—Yeshua (Jesus)!

Coming to terms with our sin is coming to Yeshua for the answer. He gives us salvation through His love. He does not just want us to be saved from our sin and saved from going to Sheol (Hell), although this is extremely important. He wants a personal love relationship with us right now. He definitely wants us to worship Him as the one and only God. But He also wants us to love Him back and follow Him because He first loved us. The one and only Almighty Creator God of the universe wants to have a special personal love relationship with you! This love of God transcends all the evil, filthy rags that we have performed in our lives. He loves us no matter what we have done to Him or to others. He loves us while we are still in our sin. He will forgive all of our sin if we just repent and believe in Yeshua. This is God's love for all of humanity.

Now let's take this concept and apply it to Israel. God loves Israel, the Jewish people, with all His heart. This love does not falter because of Israel's sins. God does not take His love away from Israel because of whatever evil she has done! Yes, there certainly have been ups and downs in their relationship. There was even a divorce, but reconciliation occurred as well. The Lord has a plan for Israel! He called Abraham as the first Hebrew and created the Jewish people through Isaac and Jacob. He called the Jewish people to be His own people out of all the nations of the world. He chose the Jewish people to be His representatives on Earth to let the pagan world know of the one and only God! More important to this book is that God made promises and covenants to Abraham, Isaac, and Jacob and the Jewish people that cannot be canceled! He is a faithful and truthful God who can never lie. He does what He says He will do. Sometimes, the ultimate conclusion of that promise will occur thousands of years later, but the point is that God's promises *will be ultimately fulfilled!* He cannot change His mind about His promises.

Many of God's promises to the Jewish people have yet to be completely fulfilled. That's why this book needs to be written, and more importantly, needs to be read and studied! Many believers today do not know that God has a plan for Israel! We all certainly need to know God's truth concerning Israel. He has a plan for Israel that includes regathering to the Land of Israel, judgment, salvation, and restoration. Much of this plan is still future. Understanding Israel in prophecy is essential to understanding biblical prophecy!

This plan also includes a glorious future with the Lord, and all believers need to know about it. Why? Because the Lord loves the Jewish people! If He loves the Jewish people, then we need to love the Jewish people, too. But as my former boss Barry Berger used to say, "The good news message of Yeshua needs to go to the Jewish people first, as Romans 1:16 says, but sad to say, the Jewish people are not hearing the good news first nor last, but not at all!"

Paul's love for the Jewish people is dramatically revealed in his great desire for the good news to be shared with them in Romans 1:16, "For I am not ashamed of the Good News, for it is the power of God for salvation to everyone who trusts—to the Jew first and also to the Greek." The reason why the Jewish people are not even hearing the good news message of Yeshua is because we are not loving the Jewish people like the Lord loves the Jewish people! Most of the time the Jewish people are not even an afterthought. And yet the Lord tells us to love them by sharing Yeshua with them first. Not second. Not last. But first! Barry used to tell all believers, "The greatest form of anti-Semitism is not sharing the love of God to the Jewish people in the form of the good news message of Yeshua."

With this in mind, the purpose of this book is five-fold:

1. To introduce and teach believers the subject of "Israel in Prophecy."
2. To introduce a chronology of prophetic events that focus on Israel.
3. To warn Jewish people of the coming prophetic events, including the future holocaust.
4. To encourage believers to share the good news message of Yeshua HaMeshiach with Jewish people.
5. To encourage believers to live godly lives unto the Lord.

First, I cannot stress how important it is for most believers to change their mind concerning Israel and Israel in prophecy. There is so much teaching on TV and radio today that contradicts this book, teaching that Israel has no future, that Israel is apostate, and that God is done with Israel because of her sin and that He replaced her with the Body of Messiah. This is not good teaching, plain and simple! These teachers will be appropriately judged by the Lord. But the most unfortunate thing that is happening today is that many believers are being way too easily swayed into accepting this teaching! I am utterly shocked over the flock's lack of discernment regarding this type of teaching. It is time for critical thinking, critical studying of the Scriptures, and discernment. Israel in prophecy is so important to God that He wrote many Scriptures about it! If it's so important to God, then it absolutely needs to be important to us, too!

Second, putting the study of *Israel in Prophecy* in a biblical chronology is not an easy thing to do. We really cannot be 100 percent sure that any sequence is fully correct. Why? Because we do not have sufficient biblical information. However, we can be 100 percent sure that all these events will take place in the future. The issue is that it may not be in the exact order I present them. I have put this order together in the power and will of the Ruach (the Holy Spirit) as He has led me over the last twenty-four-plus years of studying His Word. The joy comes from doing your own study and being directed by the Lord to find out how He will lead you in ordering these events. I certainly believe we need much more critical study and literature on this topic. I hope and pray this book will inspire others onward.

Third, if you had the ability to heal all people of cancer, would you share it with the world? Of course, you would. But if you absolutely know the truth of the future of Israel and how bad the future is going to be, would you warn them? The Jewish people need to heed the warnings of the Scriptures, and we are the "watchmen" to tell them. So, we need to be about the Lord's work, watching out for Israel!

Fourth, would you also then share the good news message of Yeshua with the Jewish people so they can be saved today and not have to go through the future holocaust? My hope and prayer are that this book will help to light a fire in believers to share the good news of Yeshua with the Jewish people.

Knowing that two-thirds of the Jewish people living in the Land of Israel will die in Jacob's Trouble (the Tribulation Period) should inspire us to share the good news message of Yeshua with them! If they die without Yeshua, they will certainly be judged by the Lord and end up in Sheol. The "apple of God's eye" ending up in Sheol is not an idea that I am happy with. We all need to be prepared to share Yeshua with the Jewish people first! Knowing their future should exhort us to action.

Fifth, studying prophecy is certainly exciting and fun. However, one of the purposes of prophecy is to encourage us to live godly lives right now! If we know our future and the blessings that will be bestowed upon us, then this should help to take the pressure off of us and to live our lives today for the Lord in His power, in His will, and in His Spirit! I truly hope and pray that you are greatly blessed by reading this book!

And never forget a great command of the Bible for all believers found in Psalm 122:6, "*Pray for the peace of Jerusalem: May they prosper who love you.*" Shalom!

Dr. Richard Hill
Las Vegas, NV
March, 2018

Contents

Chapter 1

INTRODUCTION

God has a prophetic plan for Israel. Most believers of Yeshua (Jesus) do not know that Israel is God's timepiece for prophecy. Why? Most pastors either do not know it themselves, or if they do know it, they are not preaching it from their pulpits. Unfortunately, more than 50 percent of all Bible-believing believers today ascribe to amillennialism. This is the belief that Yeshua has been ruling from His throne in heaven since the ascension and will not rule in a 1,000-year Messianic Kingdom on Earth. They believe that all of Bible prophecy was fulfilled by AD 70. Amillennialists come to their conclusions through the hermeneutical technique of spiritualizing the biblical text rather than taking a more literal approach. Israel is certainly the missing link for most students of prophecy as we shall see in our study.

Actually, Israel is the key to all end-times prophecy. The Psalms speak of Arab nations constantly attacking Israel throughout her history. Ezekiel writes of a future war of a confederacy of nations attacking Israel. The One-World Order is an extension of Daniel's fourth beast. This is the Roman Empire coming back to life to rule and dominate the world, including Israel.

The seven-year Tribulation Period is a time of God's judgment for the world. But for Israel this timeframe is called

"Jacob's Trouble." It is a time where the Lord calls Israel back to Him through His judgment for her sin. The one-world religion in the first half of Jacob's Trouble will attack and kill Jewish and Gentile believers of Yeshua. The second half of Jacob's Trouble sees the Anti-messiah and his evil ones trying to destroy all Jewish people around the world. The Anti-messiah focuses his attention on this holocaust of Jewish people. Even the Rapture is considered Jewish because some of Israel will participate in it. Additionally, the Rapture is Jewish because it beautifully pictures the ancient Jewish wedding ceremony and fulfills the Jewish Feast of Trumpets (Yom Teruah, aka Rosh Hashanah).

Not all of Israel's future is bad news. The Bible predicts a third and fourth temple will be built. Israel will have a seven-year peace treaty with the world (although it will be broken by the Anti-messiah). At the end of Jacob's Trouble, Israel will be saved! That is, all the Jewish people who make it through Jacob's Trouble alive will be saved by the Lord. They will believe in Yeshua as their Jewish Messiah.

Then the Lord will return in His Second Coming to destroy all the enemies of the Jewish people. These are the millions of soldiers who attack the city of Jerusalem at the end of the Tribulation Period. Their purpose will be to wipe out all the rest of the Jewish population in Israel before the end of Jacob's Trouble. Messiah Yeshua will come back just in time to prevent this from happening. Yeshua will deliver His chosen people, the Jewish believers from annihilation at the hands of the Anti-messiah. He will then establish the Messianic Millennial Kingdom. He will rule and reign over the entire world for 1,000 years from His fourth Jewish temple built on the razed Jewish temple mount in the Jewish Land of Israel! Life in Israel during the Messianic Millennial Kingdom will be a Messianic Jewish lifestyle for 1,000 years.

After this, HaSatan (the Satan) will perform the last anti-Semitic attack against the Lord and His chosen ones at the city of

Jerusalem. After the Lord wipes out the Jewish people's enemies, He will then create new heavens and a new earth for all eternity. The city in which He has decided to live out eternity is called the "New Jerusalem." It will be the eternal home for all believers from all of history. Our eternal home will be the New Jerusalem that descends from heaven to the new earth. It will be from this eternal home that all believers will continue to worship and serve Yeshua and the Father in a Jewish way!

With all this Jewish flavor to prophecy, it is a wonder why many believers do not know or understand this. That is what this book, *Israel in Prophecy*, is all about. We shall be studying all the Scriptures of the Bible that cover this topic, and there are many! But first, before we can study Israel in the future, we need to understand why it seems that the whole world hates Israel in the present.

Chapter 2

ISRAEL TODAY: THE ENMITY

Israel is in dire straits! It seems that the whole world is growing in its hatred of Israel and the Jewish people. More and more European countries are joining in the United Nations (UN) rhetoric against Israel as the religion of Islam increases in these countries. Anti-Semitic atrocities are increasing against the Jewish people around the world. The BDS (Boycott, Divestment, Sanctions) movement against Israel is gaining ground, not only around the world, but in America's college campuses. Even the United States (Israel's last real friend and big brother) during the eight years of President Obama's administration, dramatically diverted its support from Israel. Israel realized that they were all alone on Planet Earth.

However, under President Trump, America's support for Israel has returned with great leaps and bounds. But, our next Democratic president could very easily turn the policy back against Israel. So why all this conflict and hostility over the little tiny nation of Israel? After all, it's only 263 miles long, 71 miles at its widest width and 9 miles at its shortest. It's home to less than 7 million Jewish people. So, again I ask, "Why all this hatred directed at Israel and the Jewish people?

Biblically speaking, there are at least two answers. First, is what many believers of Yeshua often forget about—the big picture! HaSatan is in a war against God! He is trying to oust

God by usurping God's chosen people, the Jews. He hates everything that God loves, and God loves the Jewish people. God loves the Jewish people so much that He made wonderful promises to them through His covenants. One of those promises is to ultimately bring the redeemed nation of Israel, led by her Messiah Yeshua, into the Messianic Jewish Kingdom (the Millennial Kingdom). If Satan can thwart just one of God's promises to the Jewish people, then he can declare victory over God and claim to be the supreme being of the universe.

Now, we know this can never happen; however, HaSatan continues to try. His plan is to energize the world in its hatred of the Jewish people and eventually try to destroy Israel and completely wipe out all of the Jewish people. The Bible clearly reveals this evil through Israel's history and especially in the future Jacob's Trouble (the Tribulation Period).

The second reason why the world hates Israel is because it has always hated Israel! The biblical history of Israel clearly shows that, even from her beginning, there was turmoil and hatred toward her. The hatred of the Jewish people has passed from generation to generation right up to the present time, and it will continue until Yeshua returns in His Second Coming. To be able to understand Israel's current troubles in the world, we must go back to the beginning of the Jewish people's history. We must go back to Israel's ancient past.

Israel in the Past

Israel's history has been described as the paradox of the world's history. Philosophers and historians have confessed that, while they understand the history of the world, the history of the Jewish people is an enigma they cannot solve. That's primarily because they don't read and believe in the Bible. The Bible tells us of Israel's history. The Lord does not include all of Israel's history but what is necessary for all believers to know and understand her past and future.

Genesis 16:1–6

1 Now Sarai, Abram's wife, had not borne him children. But she had an Egyptian slave-girl—her name was Hagar. 2 So Sarai said to Abram, "Look now, *ADONAI* [LORD] has prevented me from having children. Go, please, to my slave-girl. Perhaps I'll get a son by her." Abram listened to Sarai's voice. 3 So Sarai, Abram's wife, took her slave-girl Hagar the Egyptian—after Abram had lived ten years in the land of Canaan—and gave her to Abram her husband to be his wife. 4 Then he went to Hagar and she became pregnant. When she saw that she was pregnant, in her eyes her mistress was belittled.

5 So Sarai said to Abram, "The wrong done to me is because of you! I myself placed my slave-girl in your embrace. Now that she saw that she became pregnant, so in her eyes I am belittled. May *ADONAI* judge between you and me!"

6 Abram said to Sarai, "Look! Your slave-girl is in your hand. Do to her what is good in your eyes."

So Sarai afflicted her, and she fled from her presence.

This is the story of how Ishmael came into being. It's an intriguing account of Abraham (Abram), Sarah (Sarai), and Hagar and the beginning of the hatred between them and their descendants. In verses 1–2, Sarah declared to Abraham that she is unable to bear children for him and that he should take Hagar as her surrogate. Abraham listened to Sarah and took Hagar as his second wife. Verse 3 gives us the timing of the story. It was ten years after Abraham and Sarah entered into Canaan (which would later be the Land of Israel).

Shortly after they arrived, the Lord gave Abraham a promise that He would give the Land to his seed (Genesis 12:7). But it was about ten years later and the Lord had not provided them a son as He promised. I think too many believers sell Abraham and Sarah short in this account. Abraham and Sarah actually waited on the Lord for ten years before deciding to act on their own! How many of today's believers would wait on the Lord for ten years? So, after all this time, they concluded on their own that they needed to take action. Unfortunately, this action would have devastating consequences for the Jewish people for their entire history!

In verse 4, we find that Hagar has conceived and then has "belittled" Sarah. "Belittled" (*kalal*) means "to be small, to be light." The issue here is that Hagar looked down upon Sarah when she was able to conceive and while Sarah was still barren. In biblical times, it was absolutely imperative for women to be married and to have children. This was their primary goal in life and the way to preserve human life on earth. Not only was this important for the life of the clan/family, but for the preservation of the Jewish people as a whole. Sarah must have been heartbroken over this whole affair. Certainly, a slave such as Hagar would not expect to get away with this kind of behavior unless she believed that she was now elevated in status above Sarah because of her ability to conceive.

Sarah blamed Abraham in verse 5 for this wrongdoing. She even asked God to judge between her and Abraham! This dramatic deferment to the Lord must have made Abraham quite nervous. Abraham's reaction in verse 6 is perhaps one of the wisest responses any husband can give his wife. He basically said that, as Hagar was her slave, she should punish her as she wished. Although Hagar was a wife, she was still a slave. With Abraham's answer, he defused the situation. God did not need to judge between them any longer since Sarah was content that judgment had been given over to her hands. Abraham also did not have to make any difficult decisions between Sarah and Hagar. Sarah then harshly punished Hagar, and Hagar promptly fled.

Genesis 16:7–12

> 7 Then the angel of *ADONAI* found her by the spring of water in the wilderness, next to the spring on the way to Shur. 8 He said, "Hagar, Sarai's slave-girl, where have you come from and where are you going?"
> She said, "I am fleeing from the presence of my mistress Sarai."
> 9 The angel of *ADONAI* said, "Return to your mistress and humble yourself under her hand." 10 Then the angel of *ADONAI* said to her, "I will bountifully multiply your seed, and they will be too many to count." 11 Then the angel of *ADONAI* said to her,
> Behold, you are pregnant
> and about to bear a son,
> and you shall name him Ishmael—
> for *ADONAI* has heard your affliction.
> 12 He will be a wild donkey of a man.
> His hand will be against everyone,
> and everyone's hand against him,
> and away from all his brothers will he dwell.

Hagar obviously did not like Sarah's treatment, so she decided to run away. The Angel of the Lord found her by the spring on the way to Shur (verse 7). On the way to Shur is on the way back to Egypt! Hagar was originally from Egypt and may have been headed back there. In verses 8–9, the Angel of the Lord reminded Hagar that she was Sarah's slave and that she should submit herself to Sarah's authority as mistress. This is the second issue identified between these two. Hagar first despised Sarah and now she thought too highly of herself and would not submit to Sarah's authority. These sorts of issues breed contempt and hatred unless they are dealt with on a godly level. There is nothing like living with scorned women in a clan or household.

Despite all these fleshly issues getting in the way of household harmony, the Angel of the Lord blessed Hagar with a tremendous promise of multiplying her descendants (verse 10). He even stated that there would be too many to count. In verse 11, the Angel of the Lord proclaimed to Hagar that she was pregnant with a son and that she should call his name "Ishmael," which means "God hears." The Lord heard her cry for help and gave heed to her affliction. Muslims around the world count Ishmael, Hagar's son, as an important prophet and a patriarch of Islam. They recognize Ishmael as the forefather of several prominent Arab tribes. They also believe their prophet Mohammed was a descendent of Ishmael who would help to bring this promise about and also establish a great nation. Most of the almost 2 billion Muslims around the world trace their physical and spiritual roots to Ishmael and his father Abraham. Hagar would then be the matriarch of the movement.

In verse 12, the Angel of the Lord continues his proclamation with what I call the "four conflict prophecies." The first conflict prophecy states that Ishmael will be like "a wild donkey of a man." This metaphor shows Ishmael's rough and rugged character mixed with his *meshugenah* (mad or crazy) demeanor. Wild donkeys and even domestic ones can and will fly off the handle for no apparent reason at all. One moment they are docile and the next moment they are kicking and braying out of control as if their life depended on it. This is what Ishmael's character trait is like: he will be wild and out of control. Not only is this Ishmael's trait, but I believe it is a general character trait passed on down the line to his descendants, as well. Of course, not every descendant possesses this trait.

The second conflict prophecy states Ishmael's "hand will be against everyone." He will be aggressive, full of hostility, and war-like in his behavior toward all people. This type of behavior brings about constant upheaval in one's life.

The third conflict prophecy proclaims that "everyone's hand will be against him." When a person is war-like and aggressive toward their fellow man, their fellow man usually responds with aggression and war-like behavior. The old saying, "What goes around, comes around" is correct. People who like to fight will eventually find someone to fight against.

The fourth conflict prophecy states that Ishmael will live "away from all his brothers." "Away" is comprised of two Hebrew words (*al panim*). *Al* means "upon, over, concerning or against." *Panim* means "face, countenance or presence." In the context of conflict, it is better to translate this phrase as, Ishmael "will live/dwell against the face of all his brothers." Since Ishmael is already prophesied as being aggressive and war-like against everyone, he will definitely be hostile toward his brothers as well. His brothers include all the Muslims, Arabs, and Persian peoples plus (we must not forget) the Jewish people! Ishmael and Isaac were blood brothers, and there should have been love between them and their seed. However, instead of loving one another as brothers, there has been a whole lot of anger and hatred between them as enemies.

Genesis 21:8–13

> 8 The child grew and was weaned—Abraham made a big feast on the day Isaac was weaned. 9 But Sarah saw the son of Hagar the Egyptian whom she had born to Abraham—making fun. 10 So she said to Abraham, "Drive out this female slave and her son, for the son of this female slave will not be an heir with my son—with Isaac."
>
> 11 Now the matter was very displeasing in Abraham's eyes on account of his son. 12 But God said to Abraham, "Do not be displeased about the boy and your slave woman. Whatever Sarah says to you, listen to her voice. For through Isaac shall your seed be called. 13 Yet I will also make the son of the slave woman into a nation, because he is your seed."

In this scripture passage, Isaac has made it on to the scene, and Abraham is having a great feast in celebration of his weaning. Sarah caught Ishmael "making fun" of Isaac. "Making fun" (*tsachaq*) means "to laugh, to jest, to play and to mock." Ishmael's mocking of Isaac was so serious and severe that Sarah wanted Hagar and Ishmael to have no part in the inheritance. They were to leave the clan, and they were to leave immediately. Sarah discerned Ishmael's evil intentions concerning Isaac's inheritance, and she reacted in God's will. Isaac, not Ishmael, was the promised seed of Abraham. God would make a nation through Ishmael because he was the seed of Abraham, but he had no claim to the inheritance—that was Isaac's!

Galatians 4:28–30

> 28 Now you, brothers and sisters—like Isaac, you are children of promise. 29 But just as at that time the one born according to the flesh persecuted the one born according to the *Ruach* [Spirit], so it is now. 30 But what does the Scripture say? "Drive out the slave woman and her son, for the son of the slave woman shall not inherit with the son of the free woman.

Galatians 4:28–30 confirms that this "making fun" was a lot more serious in nature. At the time of the great feast (and probably before that time as well), Isaac was persecuted by Ishmael. So, the mocking in Genesis is described as persecution in Galatians. Is it any wonder that Sarah reacted so harshly against Ishmael? Verse 30 uncovers the timing of the persecution just prior to Abraham sending Hagar and Ishmael away. Further, the phrase "so it is now" at the end of verse 29 reveals that this persecution not only occurred in the past when Isaac was a young boy, but that the persecution continued on through their descendants into Paul's present time. Scripture and history show that this persecution of the Muslims, Arabs, and Persians against the Jewish people continues to our present day and will continue right up to Yeshua's Second Coming!

Genesis 27:35, 36, 41; 28:6–9

> 35 Then he said, "Your brother came deceitfully and took your blessing."
> 36 He said, "Is this why he was named Jacob—since he's tricked me twice already? My birthright he's taken. Look! Now he's taken my blessing!" Then he said, "Haven't you saved a blessing for me?" (Genesis 27:35, 36)
> 41 So Esau bore a grudge against Jacob because of the blessing with which his father had blessed him, and Esau said in his heart, "Let the time for mourning my father draw near, so that I can kill my brother Jacob!" (Genesis 27:35, 36, 41)
>
> 6 Now Esau saw that Isaac blessed Jacob when he sent him to Paddan-aram to take for himself a wife from there, when he blessed him and commanded him saying, "Don't take a wife from the daughters of Canaan." 7 Jacob listened to his father Isaac and to his mother and went toward Paddan-aram. 8 Then Esau saw that the daughters of Canaan were contemptible in his father Isaac's eyes. 9 So Esau went to Ishmael and took Mahalath, the daughter of Ishmael Abraham's son, Nebaioth's sister for his wife, besides his other wives. (Genesis 28:6–9)

The narrative continues with the children of Isaac. Jacob supplanted Esau by taking his blessing as the eldest brother from their father, Isaac (verse 35). In verse 36, Esau wrongly accuses Jacob of stealing his birthright. But, Esau actually sold his birthright for a bowl of lentil soup (Genesis 25:32–33). So, Esau trumped up half the charges against Jacob, although he was truthful about Jacob stealing his blessing. In verse 41, Esau revealed his true feelings toward Jacob. He had borne a grudge against Jacob and hated him enough to want to kill him after his father's death. Soon after this discovery, Jacob escaped to Haran with Isaac's blessing. With Jacob out of the picture, Esau became vindictive and disobedient toward his father Isaac, partly because he despised his birthright (Genesis 25:34).

In Genesis 28:6–9, we see Esau's attitude continue to change for the worse. He knew Isaac blessed Jacob on his departure and told him not to marry the daughters of Canaan. So, Esau then married a daughter of Ishmael! He knew this was wrong and against his father's wishes, but he did it anyway. It is this kind of vindictive and disobedient behavior that continued in his life and in his descendants' lives. However, many years later, Jacob came back to the Land, and Esau was the first to greet him. They made up for the past and somewhat lived in harmony for the rest of their lives (Genesis 33). However, the damage had been done; the stories of hatred and conflict were told throughout their generations, and the hatred continued to spread.

Esau dwelt in the land of Edom, which is south of Moab and south east of the Dead Sea. Today that land is the south-west portion of Jordan. All modern Muslim, Arab, and Persian nations are descendants from either Esau or Ishmael.

These few biblical examples show the hatred between the Muslims and the Jews began with the discord between Hagar and Sarah, Ishmael and Isaac, and Esau and Jacob. The question arises: how is this hatred for the Jewish people passed down through the generations? The answer is a spiritual one.

Exodus 20:5

> 5 Do not bow down to them, do not let anyone make you serve them. For I, *ADONAI* your God, am a jealous God, bringing the iniquity of the fathers upon the children to the third and fourth generations of those who hate Me.

Within God's declaration for the Jewish people not to worship any other gods, He proclaims a dreadful curse on those who hate Him. The sins of the fathers who hate Him will be passed down the lineage to their children up to the third and fourth generation! This is a dramatic announcement against most of humanity, let alone the Muslims, Arabs, and Persians of the world! Most people do not know who their great-grandfather was, let alone who their great-great-grandfather was. And yet their sins will be passed on down the line to their grandchildren and great-grandchildren. What exactly does this mean?

I believe it means the descendants of the haters of God have a spiritual propensity to behave in the same way their forefathers did. So, if their forefathers were anti-Semitic, hating Israel and the Jewish people, then they will have a natural spiritual tendency to fall into the same sin. Therefore, the hatred for the Jewish people is passed down through the generations, never to be broken. The reason why we continue to see this hatred toward the Jewish people today is because it is passed on down the descendants' line without any human agent to break it. Hatred breeds hatred. However, there is one way to break this diabolic chain of hatred. The answer is Yeshua! If a person were to receive Yeshua, then the generational curse can be broken.

At this point, it is very important to distinguish between nations and individuals. Not all Muslims, Arabs, or Persians hate Israel and the Jewish people. However, when the Scriptures speak of the Ishmaelite's and Edom's (for example) hatred for the Jewish people, it is talking about how the leadership and most of the people of that nation hate the Jewish people. Not every single person falls into this category of enmity. Today, not all the Muslims, Arabs, Persians and Palestinians who live in Israel hate the Jewish people. There are many who do not ascribe to the hate-mongering and want to live in peace with the Jewish people.

There are also many who believe in Yeshua and have set a great standard of God's love by worshiping Yeshua together with Jewish believers. Some have even built and shared congregations with these Jewish believers. These groups are showing the world that there can be *shalom* (peace) in the Land when Yeshua is in the center of the equation.

<u>Numbers 20:14–21</u>

> 14 Moses sent messengers from Kadesh to the king of Edom. "Thus says your brother, Israel:
> 'You know all the hardship that came on us. 15 Our forefathers went down to Egypt, so we lived there for a very long time. The Egyptians mistreated us, and our fathers. 16 But we cried out to *ADONAI,* He heard our cry, sent an angel and brought us out of Egypt. See now, we are at Kadesh, a town on the frontier of your territory. 17 Permit us to pass through your territory. We will not cross through any field or vineyard or drink water of any well. But we will travel on the king's highway. We will not deviate to the right or left until we will have passed through your territory.'"
> 18 But Edom said to him, "You may not pass through me—or I will march out against you with the sword."
> 19 *Bnei-Yisrael* [Children of Israel] then said to him, "We will travel on the main road, and if we or our livestock even drink any of your water, we will pay its price. It's nothing, just to pass through on foot!"
> 20 He answered, "You may not pass through!" Yet Edom came out to oppose them with a large and well-armed

> people. 21 Since Edom refused to permit Israel to cross through her territory, Israel turned away from them.

Here is another example of the disdain for the Jewish people by her blood brother. It is approximately 600 years after Abraham, and Israel has left Egypt in the Exodus. They are now traveling northward to enter Israel from the east. Israel's desire was to travel through Edom to get to Moab, but Edom said no.

In verse 14, we pick up the story with Moses sending messengers to the king of Edom with a message for his kindred, his "blood brother." Israel only wanted to pass through, not even drinking water from any wells they found. They just wanted to travel though Edom on the king's highway, which was created for such travel.

However, the king of Edom responded with a resounding "No" (verses 15–18). The Jews were not allowed to travel through, and if they did, Edom would attack them (verses 19–20). In verse 21, Israel then turned away from Edom. What a great opportunity Edom had to forge a loving and gracious relationship with her blood brother who was enslaved in Egypt for over 400 years. What had Israel done to her in the last 400 years? Absolutely nothing! So, why didn't they want a relationship with Israel? They obviously had listened to the hate-filled stories that were passed down from generation to generation and kept that hatred locked up in their hearts until such a time they were ready to act upon it.

Ezekiel 35:1–15

> 1 The word of *ADONAI* came to me saying: 2 "Son of man, set your face against Mount Seir and prophesy against it. 3 Say to it, thus says *ADONAI Elohim* [LORD God]: 'Behold, I am against you, Mount Seir. I will stretch out My hand over you and make you utterly

desolate. 4 I will lay your cities waste. You will be devastated. So you will know that I am *ADONAI*.
5 "Because you have a long-standing hatred and have delivered *Bnei-Yisrael* to the power of the sword in the time of their calamity, in the time of their final punishment, 6 therefore, as I live'—it is a declaration of *ADONAI*—'I will destine you for blood, and bloodshed will pursue you. Since you did not hate bloodshed, therefore bloodshed will pursue you. 7 I will make Mount Seir an utter desolation. I will cut off from it all who come and go. 8 I will fill its mountains with its slain; on your hills, your valleys and all your streams those slain by the sword will fall. 9 I will make you everlasting desolations; your cities will not be inhabited. Then you will know that I am *ADONAI*.
10 "Because you said: 'These two nations and these two lands will be mine! We will possess them'—though *ADONAI* was there—11 "therefore, as I live"—it is a declaration of *ADONAI*—"I will deal with you with the same anger and envy that you had because of your hatred against them. I will make Myself known among them, when I judge you. 12 You will know that I, *ADONAI*, have heard all your blasphemies that you uttered against the mountains of Israel saying: "They are laid desolate—they are given for us to devour!" 13 You have magnified yourselves against Me with your mouth. You multiplied your words against Me. I heard it."
14 Thus says *ADONAI Elohim:* "When the whole earth rejoices, I will make you desolate. 15 As you rejoiced over inheriting the house of Israel, because it was desolate, so I will do to you. You will be desolate, Mount Seir and all Edom—all of it. Then they will know that I am *ADONAI*."

Ezekiel sealed the deal on our understanding about this extended enmity toward Israel from other nations (though this passage is specifically speaking of Edom). In verses 1–4, we find the Lord's declaration against Mount Seir. He will make Mount Seir and its cities a wasteland and a desolation. One reason why the Lord would destroy Mount Seir is so that they would know that He is the Lord! God works in mysterious ways and sometimes works through devastating judgment to try and bring repentance to a people or nation. I believe this is exactly what He's doing here. It does not mean this nation will automatically become believers of Yeshua when the destruction comes, but it does mean they will at a minimum understand that the God of Israel is judging them.

The question comes to mind: "Who is Mount Seir? Verse 15 tells us the answer. Mount Seir represents the whole nation of Edom! Remember, today Edom is located on the southwest side of Jordan. This area is thriving today with many cities and a combined population of more than 200,000 people. At the end of verse 15, God declares a second time that they will know that He is the Lord through this terrible destruction.

Many believers ask me the question, "Hasn't Edom already been judged?" Yes, it has been judged, but not to the extent that is described in this scripture. In verse 7, the Lord declared once again that Edom will be a waste and a desolation. In verse 8, the slain of the Edomites will fill their mountains, hills, valleys, and even in its ravines! This means the dead will be strewn all over the country. Verse 9 profoundly states their cities will not be inhabited, and Edom will be an everlasting desolation! These specific judgments have not occurred in history and are similar to the events of Yeshua's Second Coming.

"Everlasting" (*olam*) means "forever." There is an obvious starting point for this forever destruction of Edom, but there is not an ending point. Forever is a very long time! Therefore, since there are Jordanians still living in this ancient country, the prophecy has yet to be fulfilled. If the prophecy has yet to be completely fulfilled in the past or the present, when shall it be fulfilled? Definitely in the future!

Now let us look at other reasons why God is going to utterly destroy Edom. In verse 5, the Lord proclaims the everlasting destruction of Edom will come about because of their everlasting hatred for Israel! As stated earlier, the Edomites are descendants of Esau who hated his brother Jacob. Since this hatred is everlasting, it had a beginning with the forefather of Edom, and it was shared with all the Edomites on a continuous basis throughout their years. All modern Arab, Muslim, and Persian nations are descendants from either Esau or Ishmael and thus share this hatred toward Israel. It is also clear Edom's (and many other Muslim, Arab and Persian countries') actions toward Israel reveal this hatred.

Another example of a nation having everlasting hatred toward Israel is found in Ezekiel 25. The Lord says He will pour out His wrath on Ammon, Moab, Edom, and Philistia because of their everlasting hatred and actions toward Israel. Ezekiel 25:15 specifies concerning Philistia: "Thus says ADONAI Elohim: "Because the Philistines have acted in revenge and have taken severe vengeance with scornful soul, destroying in *unending hatred*"" (emphasis mine). Here the Lord specifically singled out the Philistines for having "unending hatred" toward Israel. This enmity goes back to the beginning when Israel moved into the land of Canaan. Obviously, this hatred continued with the Philistines down through their bloodline to Ezekiel's days.

In Ezekiel 35:6, the Lord also declares that bloodshed will pursue Edom until its destruction. The Lord will not even allow people to travel to and from Edom (verse 7), causing it to become completely isolated. The reason for this judgment is found in verse 11. It states that the Lord will deal with Edom according to their own anger, envy and hatred toward the Jewish people. It is clear from history that this judgment has yet to happen. This prophecy is then still future.

Obadiah 8–16

8 In that day,"—declares *ADONAI*—
"will I not destroy the wise men from Edom
and understanding from the hill country of Esau?
9 Then your mighty men, O Teman, will be shattered—
so everyone will be cut off from the hill country of Esau by slaughter.
10 "Because of your violence to your brother Jacob, shame will cover you, and you will be cut off forever.
11 On the day that you stood aloof—on the day that strangers carried away his wealth, while foreigners entered his gates and cast lots for Jerusalem—you were just like one of them.
12 You should not look down on your brother
on the day of his disaster, nor should you rejoice over the children of Judah in the day of their destruction. You should not speak proudly
in the day of their distress.
13 Do not enter the gate of My people
In the day of their disaster.
Yes, you. Do not gloat over their misery in the day of their disaster. Yes, you—do not loot their wealth in the day of their calamity.
14 Do not stand at the crossroad to cut down his fugitives, and do not imprison his survivors in the day of distress.
15 "For the day of *ADONAI* is near against all the nations. As you have done, it shall be done to you. Your dealing will return on your own head.
16 For just as you have drunk on My holy mountain, so all the nations shall drink continually. Yes, they will drink and gulp down,
and then be as though they had never existed.

Obadiah repeats the Lord's desire to destroy Edom. However, Obadiah provides us with specific information for the reasons why and gives us a timetable for when this will happen. Verse 8 begins with the phrase "in that day." This speaks of the Day of the Lord as we see in verse 15. The context of the destruction of Edom is when the Lord will destroy all the nations in the Day of the Lord! In verses 8–9, the Lord declares He will destroy the wise and understanding men of Edom because of their arrogance (verse 3). All the Edomites will be cut off and slaughtered.

The reason why God is going to do this is because of Edom's violence toward his brother Jacob (verse 10). The Lord here reminds the Edomites that they are blood brothers with Israel and should be loving them instead of hating them. But because of their evil violence against Israel, they will be cut off forever! Verses 11–14 reveal the specific violent acts performed against Israel when she was attacked by foreigners. Edom stood aloof and did not help, acted just like the stealing invaders, rejoiced over Israel's demise, killed any fugitives, and imprisoned any survivors fleeing the carnage. Rather than helping their blood brothers, Edom helped the enemies of the Jewish people and approved of their evil deeds against Israel.

For these and many other reasons, the Lord will judge all the nations (including Edom) in the Day of the Lord (verse 15)! When the Lord's destruction against the world comes, it will be like these nations did not even exist (verse 16)!

Jeremiah emphatically states that this destruction will be immense in the Day of the Lord (Jeremiah 25:30–33). The slain will be strung out on the face of the Earth from one nation to another nation! No one will be left to lament, gather, or bury them! The devastation will be like no other in history, nor will there be another after it.

Paul's profound statement in Galatians 6:7 comes to mind, "Do not be deceived—God is not mocked. For whatever a man sows, that he also shall reap." If people sow hatred and violence, then they shall reap hatred and violence in their lives! Ultimately, the Lord is the One who will bring about this judgment, and specifically, as Obadiah verse 15 states, it will occur in the Day of the Lord.

Psalm 83:1–9

1 A song: a psalm of Asaph.
2 God, do not keep silent.
Do not hold Your peace, O God.
Do not be still.
3 For look, Your enemies make an uproar.
Those who hate You lift up their head.
4 They make a shrewd plot against Your people,
conspiring against Your treasured ones.
5 "Come," they say, "let's wipe them out as a nation!
Let Israel's name be remembered no more!"
6 For with one mind they plot together.
Against You do they make a covenant.
7 The tents of Edom and the Ishmaelites,
Moab and the Hagrites,
8 Gebal, Ammon and Amalek,
Philistia with the inhabitants of Tyre,
9 even Assyria has joined them,
becoming a strong arm for Lot's sons. *Selah*

Until this point, we have only seen that the Scriptures show the Ishmaelites, Edomites, and Philistines eternally hate the Jewish people. But Psalm 83 reveals in dramatic fashion many more nations that hate Israel. This psalm of Asaph is a cry to God for action against the evil ones and their enmity against the Jewish people (verse 2). In verse 3, we see the enemies of our Lord also revealing their hatred of God by "lift[ing] up their head." This means these evil ones are exalting themselves in their own pride against the Lord. So how are they going to show their hatred?

Verse 4 shows the enemies of the God of Israel making shrewd plans and conspiring against "Your people" and "Your treasured ones." God's people and God's treasured ones are most certainly the Jewish people. The Jewish people were chosen by God out of all the peoples of the world to be His people (Deuteronomy 7:6). Verse 5 reveals there is no doubt that the enemies of the God of Israel are the enemies of the Jewish people! They are even quoted as saying that they want to "wipe them out as a nation" and "let Israel's name be remembered no more!" How many hundreds of times over the years have *meshugenah* world leaders clearly expressed these very sentiments?

We have heard it time and time again from leaders like Yasser Arafat, Mahmoud Ahmadinejad, Adolf Hitler, Benito Mussolini, and many others, who have publicly stated their desire to destroy all the Jewish people. Verse 6 is very telling. They even have conspired together in unity and made a covenant against God! Making a covenant against the God of Israel is showing a very strong commitment against the Lord and one that is not easily broken! They have bound themselves in this covenant to come against the Lord and His chosen people. The question comes to mind, "Who are these nations and peoples who hate the Lord and Israel so much that they bound themselves in a covenant to destroy them?" Verses 7–9 identify their ancient names, and I will reveal their modern names.

Verse 7 begins with Edom. Edom is Esau, and he migrated to the southeast of the Dead Sea. Today this area is southwest Jordan. It is interesting to note that Jordan signed a peace treaty with Israel in 1994 and has kept peace with the Jewish people. But peace treaties can be easily broken. Note that under President Mohamed Morsi, radical Muslims in Egypt in 2012–2013 were calling for Morsi to abolish Egypt's peace treaty with Israel. This did not happen since Morsi was deposed from office by the Egyptian military.

Next on our list is the Ishmaelites. Ishmael dwelt in the wilderness of Paran and his mother took a wife for him from Egypt (Gen. 21:21). It is believed that this area was just east of Egypt in the Sinai Peninsula and the southern desert of Israel. Ishmael's twelve sons settled in this area east of Egypt as well (Gen. 25:18). These twelve princes gave rise to the "Twelve Tribes of Ishmael". The early Muslims were descended from these Arab tribes. Evidently, the Ishmaelites settled in or expanded to Gilead, which is to the east of the Sea of Galilee (Gen. 37:25). Today, this area is northwest Jordan.

All Muslims, Arabs and Persians descend from either Ishmael or Esau. So, any nation that has a physical line with Ishmael can be included as an Ishmaelite, such as Saudi Arabia and Iran. There have been recent talks about Saudi Arabia's desire to join the peace treaty between Israel and Egypt. Saudi Arabia is friendly with Israel, but this could change at a moment's notice.

Moab lived to the east of the Dead Sea and north of Edom. Today that would be west-central Jordan. The Hagrites were an Arab Bedouin tribe living to the east of Gilead. During the reign of King Saul, the tribe of Reuben, Gad and half-tribe of Manasseh made war with them and conquered them (1 Chron. 5:10, 18-20). Today, this area is northwest Jordan.

Verse 8 continues the list of the enemies of the Jewish people with Gebal. Gebal was a coastal city in Lebanon. So Gebal, then, refers to Lebanon. Israel had a war with Hezbollah in 2006. Although Hezbollah is stationed in Lebanon, Israel's war was not against Lebanon. However, since then, Lebanon's citizens have voted Hezbollah leaders into its government. Once this happened, Israel declared that if a war broke out against Hezbollah, then Israel would attack Lebanon, as well.

Ammon lived to the north of Moab. Today, this area is northwest Jordan. So, all of the western side of today's Jordan are identified as enemies of the Lord and Israel. This, then, would include the whole nation of Jordan. Amalek lived in the area between Judah and Egypt. Today it is called the Sinai Peninsula. The Sinai Peninsula is part of Egypt. However, there was a time between 1967 and 1981 when Israel owned the Sinai Peninsula. But she gave it back to Egypt in 1981 as a part of the peace treaty. Not only did she give back the land in exchange for peace, but all the developmental buildings, equipment, etc. used for drilling oil and natural gas was given to Egypt for the sake of peace, too.

Philistia was in the southwest corner of Canaan. Today that land is called the Gaza Strip. Yasser Arafat tried to make a historical connection between the Palestinians and the Philistines. However, the scientific community of the world struck down this notion. It is interesting to note that peoples from this small plot of land would be enemies and haters of the Jewish people and attack Israel! This is exactly what we see today. I believe this Scripture shows that the Gaza Strip would continue to be a thorn in Israel's side. In 2005, Israel gave the Palestinian Authority the Gaza Strip in exchange for peace. The very same day Israel left that strip of land was the day the Palestinians blasted missiles into Israel. This is in fulfillment of this Scripture.

Tyre is a city along the southern coast of Lebanon. Today's Tyre is the fourth largest city in Lebanon. Just as Gebal represents Lebanon, Tyre also represents Lebanon.

And finally, we have Assyria. Assyria was located along the Tigris River in the Upper Mesopotamia area. Today, that would be Iraq and some of eastern Syria. After the second Gulf War of 2003, Saddam Hussein was hunted down, tried in a court of law, found guilty, and sentenced to death by hanging in 2006. After his death, instead of ushering in the intended peaceful transition to a quasi-democratic free nation, Iraq experienced a conundrum of political chaos. These events have ushered in a war by the new fanatical Islamic group known as the Islamic State of Iraq and Syria (ISIS). They have taken control over about half of Iraq and half of Syria as of 2016. From their strongholds in both nations, they have also threatened Israel with complete and utter destruction. However, by the end of 2017, ISIS's stronghold over this land has faltered dramatically. Syria has been in a state of war since ISIS and the rebels attacked. Russia and Iran have helped Syria and built military bases for their own soldiers, some of which are very close to the Golan Heights border with Israel. This certainly is a precarious position that could explode at any time.

Some believers think that Psalm 83 is speaking of a specific war. However, the context of the psalm indicates that the hatred and violent plans against the Jewish people are a continuous action in the present. Let's take a look at some of Israel's recent history that proves this point.

Some Jewish History

After 6 million Jewish people died in World War II, the UN voted 33-13 on Nov. 29, 1947, to partition the land called the British Mandate of Palestine into two parts: one part for the Arabs (which became what is now called Jordan) and one for the Jews (Israel). The Jews reluctantly agreed, but the Arabs fiercely rejected the offer because they could not fathom being next to a Jewish state!

On May 14, 1948, when the British withdrew from Israel, the Jews proclaimed an independent state of Israel. The very next day, Israel was attacked by Iraq, Lebanon, Syria, Jordan, and Egypt. These five Muslim nations, united in their hatred for Israel, planned and conspired together to attack and try to wipe out God's chosen people. All five of these nations are identified in Psalm 83! How foolish is it to think that anyone can completely destroy the Jewish people when Jeremiah 31:35–37 profoundly states:

35 Thus says ADONAI, who gives the sun as a light by day and the fixed order of the moon and the stars as a light by night, who stirs up the sea so its waves roar, ADONAI-Tzva'ot [LORD of Hosts] is His Name: 36 "Only if this fixed order departs from before Me"—it is a declaration of ADONAI—"then also might Israel's offspring cease from being a nation before Me—for all time."
37 Thus says ADONAI: "Only if heaven above can be measured and the foundations of the earth searched out beneath, then also I will cast off the offspring of Israel—for all they have done. It is a declaration of ADONAI.

It would be better for these peoples and nations to try and destroy the sun, moon, and stars first! Better yet, maybe they should try to measure the heavens or search out the foundations of the earth first—they would have a better chance of succeeding. The Lord does not slumber or sleep when it comes to the enemy's efforts in trying to wipe out the Jewish people. He promised to watch over, keep, and protect Israel, and she will never be completely destroyed!

In 1967, Egypt closed the straits of Tiran to Israeli shipping. This exploit was considered to be an act of war. What ensued is called the Six Day War. Israel attacked Egypt (including the Sinai Peninsula), Jordan, and Syria and captured the West Bank, the Gaza Strip, the Golan Heights, the Sinai Peninsula, and East Jerusalem. All three of these nations are mentioned in Psalm 83 as enemies of God and Israel. In today's negotiations with Israel, we always hear that Israel needs to revert back to pre-1967 borders. What these and other nations are really saying is that Israel needs to give up all the land they won in the Six Day War for the sake of peace. Israel already has already given the Sinai Peninsula back to Egypt and the Gaza Strip to the Palestinians. For them to give up the Golan Heights and the West Bank as well would be military suicide! Both these areas are considered by Israel's military to be necessary for Israel's safety and security.

In 1973, an Arab coalition of Syria and Egypt launched a surprise attack against Israel on the most holy day of the year for Jewish people. Hence, the war is called the Yom Kippur War (Day of Atonement). The fighting mostly took place in the Golan Heights and Sinai Peninsula. Within days, Israel repelled both armies back to the pre-war ceasefire lines.

In 2000, the Palestinians began what is known as the Second Intifada. Intifada means uprising, resistance and rebellion. The Palestinians started this violent uprising against Israel because Ariel Sharon visited the Temple Mount. They thought this visit was provocative and therefore responded with violence. Since 2000, they have bombarded Israel with missiles and performed bus bombings.

In 2014, the Palestinians starting using new ways to kill Jewish people and called this the Third Intifada. They dug underground tunnels (American tax money helped pay for the costs of supplies) to infiltrate Israel. They have called their *jihadis* to rebel against Israel by using guns to shoot, knives to stab, and cars to run over Jewish people. They are calling these aggressive acts to kill and injure Jewish people as "lone wolf" attacks. Instead of a battle between armed forces, these attacks are performed by individuals or small groups of terrorists. Thus, Israel's response and wrath cannot be against all of the Palestinians, but only against the assailants.

All of this history (and there is much more Israeli history) is to show proof of how Psalm 83 has been fulfilled in the recent past and will continue to be fulfilled in the future as more terror will be perpetrated by these nations against Israel. Through the propaganda machine and the recent Syrian refugee movement to Europe and the United States, we are seeing a dramatic increase of this anti-Semitic spirit and belief system.

I believe this will continue to grow and will ultimately be the foundation for the Ezekiel War and Jacob's Trouble (the

Tribulation Period). This is the big-picture scenario that I believe most believers are missing. Believers are in a spiritual war. HaSatan, the Adversary, is attacking us and the Jewish people. He certainly hates all the people of the world, but he hates Jewish people and believers with a passion.

Therefore, HaSatan is energizing the world to hate Israel and the Jewish people and conform to his plan of destroying God's chosen people. If Satan can completely destroy Israel, then he will have defeated God because the Lord has an awesome plan for Israel, which He continuously is working out. If HaSatan can defeat God, then he can claim to be like God and try to replace Him—which was his downfall from the beginning (Isaiah 14:12–17; Ezekiel 28:12–19). So, what is God's plan for Israel today?

Chapter 3

ISRAEL TODAY: THE REGATHERING

Most believers do not know that God has a plan for Israel, nor do they know what that plan is. God loves the Jewish people and chose them to be a kingdom of priests and a holy nation (Exodus 19:4–6). He called them through Abraham and desired to bless the world through them with the good news message of the Messiah (Genesis 12:1–3). He additionally said that He would bless anyone who blessed the Jewish people and curse those who curse the Jewish people (verse 3). Since the first-century diaspora (dispersion) of the Jewish people around the world, God has been working with Israel.

Ezekiel 36:22–28

> 22 "Therefore say to the house of Israel, thus says *ADONAI Elohim:* 'I do not do this for your sake, house of Israel, but for My holy Name, which you profaned among the nations wherever you went. 23 I will sanctify My great Name, which has been profaned among the nations—which you have profaned among them. The nations will know that I am *ADONAI*'"—it is a declaration of *ADONAI*—"'when I am sanctified in you before their eyes.'"

> 24 "'For I will take you from the nations, gather you out of all the countries and bring you back to your own land. 25 Then I will sprinkle clean water on you and you will be clean from all your uncleanness and from all your idols. 26 Moreover I will give you a new heart. I will put a new spirit within you. I will remove the stony heart from your flesh and give you a heart of flesh. 27 I will put My *Ruach* [Spirit] within you. Then I will cause you to walk in My laws, so you will keep My rulings and do them. 28 Then you will live in the land that I gave to your fathers. You will be My people and I will be your God.

This scripture passage has one of the most profound declarations concerning Israel's present situation. Ezekiel wrote to his Jewish people in a "thus saith the Lord" scenario. God spoke directly to Israel and He said He was about to act on her behalf, but not for her sake (verse 22). He was acting so that His name would be glorified. He would prove His name to be holy among all the world (verse 23). The Lord is going to work a marvelous miracle through Israel so that the whole world will see and know that the Lord is God! What is He going to do?

Verse 24 shows us that the Lord is going to gather the Jewish people from around the world into the Land of Israel! Ezekiel wrote this prophecy between 593 and 563 BC, but it was not until the late 1800s and early 1900s that it began to be fulfilled. It was during this time that Jewish organizations were allowed to buy land in Israel. More and more Jewish people started moving into the Land, and in 2018, there are almost 7 million Jewish people living in the Land!

This prophecy has been fulfilled and continues to be fulfilled in the present every time a Jewish person makes *aliyah* (immigrates to Israel to become a citizen). This prophetic Israeli Jewish event is called *the regathering*. This worldwide regathering of the Jewish people is additionally emphasized in Ezekiel 37:1–14. The Lord gave Ezekiel another vision of a valley of dry bones that represented the whole nation of Israel. In the diaspora (dispersion), the Jewish people felt they were spiritually dead and had no hope. But God encouraged the Jewish people that He is their hope. He will bring them back to life and back to the Land of Israel. This has now been occurring for the last 100 years.

It is interesting to note how the Jewish people will be regathered from around the world. God says in verse 24, "I will take you from the nations" around the world. *He* will do the regathering! The Lord also says He will bring them back to "*your* own land" (emphasis mine). Who owns the land? Ultimately, it is the Lord's! But here in verse 24, He says that the Land is the Jewish people's! So why are so many Palestinians and Muslims claiming the Land to be their own?

In verse 25, the Lord will cleanse the nation of Israel of all its filthiness and idol worship. Although verse 24 is currently being fulfilled, verse 25 has yet to be fulfilled. Israel is still swimming in its sin and idol worship. Israel is a microcosm of the United States where spiritual freedom reigns, and people may worship anyone or anything they want. Thus, there are a myriad of religions in the Land, and many gods are worshipped. Their sin and filthiness is ever before them, and sometime in the future the Lord will cleanse them. I believe this cleansing judgment will occur during Jacob's Trouble.

God is going to cleanse Israel in the future through tribulation. Zechariah 13:1–2 warns that in the Day of the Lord, a fountain will be opened for Israel to be cleansed of sin and unrighteousness. The names of the idols will not even be remembered anymore. The Lord will even remove the false prophets and the spirit of uncleanness from the Land. The Lord will accomplish this through the whole seven years of Jacob's Trouble. In the end, Messiah Yeshua will come and wipe out the enemies of the Jewish people and set up His Kingdom!

Verse 26 can be perplexing; however, I believe there is a simple answer to understanding this dilemma. God is going to give Israel a new heart and a new spirit to prepare them for receiving the Ruach Kodesh (Holy Spirit) in verse 27. Unfortunately, in general, the Jewish people are a stiff-necked people, and this verse proclaims they have a hardened heart of stone, not open to the Lord's Ruach. So, the Lord is going to give them a new heart and spirit in the time of Jacob's Trouble so that they will be prepared to receive Yeshua as their Messiah, Lord, and Savior.

The Lord is very clear here in that He will put His Ruach within the Jewish people! This signifies that the nation of Israel at one point in time will all become believers of Yeshua, have their names written in the Book of Life, become born again, and receive the Ruach Kodesh. I believe this takes place just prior to Yeshua's Second Coming, which occurs at the end of Jacob's Trouble. Ezekiel 37:14 reiterates this sentiment. The Lord will put His Spirit within the regathered nation of Jewish people. They will come to life just as the dry bones became human; then they will live in their own Land and personally know that the God of Israel is Adonai. Zechariah 13:8–9 also confirms that one-third of the Jewish people will be brought through the tribulation fire of Jacob's Trouble, receive the Spirit of God, and finally be saved.

At the end of verse 27, there is an interesting phrase explaining that God will cause the Jewish people to walk in the Ruach after they have received the Ruach Kodesh. However, He actually states they will walk in His statutes and obey His rules. The Lord is talking about Israel living in the Messianic Millennial Kingdom under Messiah's kingship and what I call His "new and improved" Torah (the Law).

Finally, in verse 28, we see the promise that the Lord gave to Moses and the Jewish people a long time ago will be fulfilled! In Exodus 6:7-8, the Lord promised Moses that He would bring the enslaved Jewish people out of the land of Egypt into the Promised Land of Israel. God also swore to Abraham, Isaac, and Jacob that their seed would live in the Land. But the important point here is that a saved Israel will live in the Land with Yeshua as her King for a thousand years and "*you shall be My people and I will be your God*." The Jewish people will finally be God's people and God will finally be their God!

To summarize this section, God is regathering all the Jewish people into the Land of Israel (verse 24) to bring judgment through Jacob's Trouble (verse 25). This, in turn, will bring salvation to Israel at the end of Jacob's Trouble (verse 26–27); and finally, they shall dwell in the Land as God's chosen people under Yeshua's reign for a thousand years (verse 28).

Ezekiel 37:20–28

> 20 The sticks that you write on will be in your hand before their eyes.
> 21 "Then say to them, thus says *ADONAI Elohim:* 'Behold, I will take *Bnei-Yisrael* from among the nations, where they have gone. I will gather them from every side and bring them into their own land. 22 I will make them one nation in the land, on the mountains of Israel, and one king will be king to them all. They will no longer be two nations and never again be divided into two kingdoms. 23 They will never again be defiled with their idols, their detestable things or with any of their transgressions. I will save them out of all their dwellings in which they sinned. I will purify them. Then they will be My people and I will be their God. 24 My servant David will be king over them. They will all have One Shepherd. They will walk in My ordinances and observe My rulings and do them. 25 They will live in the land that I gave to My servant Jacob, where your ancestors lived. They will live there—they, their children and their children's children, forever, and My

servant David will be their prince forever. 26 I will cut a covenant of *shalom* with them—it will be an everlasting covenant with them. I will give to them and multiply them. I will set up My Sanctuary among them forever. 27 My dwelling-place will be over them. I will be their God and they will be My people. 28 Then the nations will know that I am *ADONAI* who sanctifies Israel, when My Sanctuary is in their midst forever.'"

This scripture portion speaks of the famous two-stick story of Ezekiel. The Lord told Ezekiel to take the two sticks and bind them together into one. The two sticks represented the two divided kingdoms of Israel: the northern kingdom (which was called Israel) and the southern kingdom (which was called Judah). The Lord's point here was to encourage the Jewish people of Ezekiel's time that there will come a day in the future when the two kingdoms shall become one nation.

In verses 20–21, the Lord proclaimed a second time that He will regather the Jewish people from the nations of the world and bring them back into the Land of Israel. When the Lord regathers Israel, it is for the purpose of having a unified nation under one king, not two kingdoms (verse 22). He obviously does not want a divided Israel to continue to fight against one another. A divided kingdom only brings destruction (Matthew 12:25). Then they shall not defile themselves anymore with their idol worship and sins. Although this is a wonderful promise, it has yet to be fulfilled! Israel today is very much like the United States and allows for religious freedom. The problem with this freedom is that it brings with it idol worship and the Land becomes defiled before the Lord.

After the Lord makes them one nation, He will cleanse and save them (verse 23). Remember, this cleansing aspect involves God's judgment against Israel (this occurs during Jacob's Trouble). In the end, they shall finally be saved and truly become God's people, and He shall be their God!

In verses 24–25, the Lord prophesies that Israel will then live and walk in His ordinances and statues. In the Messianic Millennial Kingdom, Israel will live under what I call Yeshua's "new and improved" Torah (Law). We do not know much about this new Torah. However, it is documented in Ezekiel 40–48. In this scripture passage, there are many new rules and regulations concerning how Jewish and Gentile believers are going to live in the Land during the Millennial Kingdom! Yes, there are going to be animal sacrifices for sin, too!

In verse 25, God gives us a clue as to how long Israel will live in the Land. Forever! *Olam*, as we already mentioned, means "forever." However, it also means "for a long period of time, like an age." The long period of time here would be the full length of the Messianic Millennial Kingdom, which is 1,000 years. After Yeshua's thousand-year reign in the Land, the Lord will create a new heaven and a new earth. On this new earth, He will place the New Jerusalem, which is the City of God. This is where all believers will live with God the Father and the Lord Yeshua forever.

In verses 26–28, we find out that the Lord will make an everlasting covenant of peace with Israel. They will be His people, living in the Land in peace, and God Himself will dwell with them. I believe this is speaking of Yeshua ruling and reigning as their King fulfilling the Abrahamic and Davidic covenants in the Messianic Kingdom! The Lord here uses the word "forever" to describe how long: (1) They will live in the Land; (2) His covenant of peace will last; (3) He will set His sanctuary in their midst; and (4) David His servant will rule.

There are at least two understandings concerning His servant David reigning forever as the prince/king of Israel. Some theologians believe this is in reference to the actual David who ruled as Israel's second king over Israel. The resurrected David will have another opportunity to reign over Israel as king in the Millennium. Other theologians believe the phrase "His servant

David" is in reference to the Messiah. He will reign as King over Israel forever. (more is written on this issue in Chapter 17).

Isaiah 43:3–7

3 For I am ADONAI your God,
the Holy One of Israel, your Savior.
I have given Egypt as your ransom,
Ethiopia and Seba in your place.
4 Since you are precious in My eyes, honored,
because I love you,
I will give a man in exchange for you,
and other peoples for your life.
5 Do not fear, for I am with you.
I will bring your offspring from the east
and gather you from the west.
6 I will say to the north, 'Give them up!'
and to the south, 'Do not hold them back.'
Bring My sons from far
and My daughters from the ends of the earth.
7 Everyone who is called by My Name,
whom I created for My glory.
I formed him—yes, I made him!"

If there was any doubt that this regathering of the Jewish people was a worldwide regathering, then this next scripture reading should help. Isaiah was writing at a time when the northern kingdom was already taken captive to Assyria. Judah, the southern kingdom, was following in the ungodly ways of the northern kingdom and hence would be judged as well if they did not repent.

In Isaiah 43, the Lord encouraged Israel that He would redeem them and would continue to watch over and bless them. In verses 3–4, the Lord declared to Israel that He is their Savior and that He loves them. Other nations will be judged in her place, but she would live! Verse 5 began the regathering stage that will be worldwide. The Lord declared He would gather their "offspring" (*zera*) from the east and the west. This reveals the regathering is not in Isaiah's day but in the future since it would be with the Jewish people's descendants!

But that's not all; the Lord continues to regather from the north and the south. He stated that He would bring them from afar and from the ends of the earth (verse 6). However, up until this point, the Lord spoke in generalities. In verse 7, He clarifies exactly who of the Jewish people would be regathered. Everyone who would be called by His name, whom He created for His glory. These are the Jewish believers in Yeshua who will make it through Jacob's Trouble alive and were scattered all over the world. Yeshua's angels will help them to be regathered back to the Land for entrance into the Kingdom.

<u>Jeremiah 32:36–42</u>

> 36 Now therefore thus says *ADONAI*, the God of Israel, concerning this city, about which you say, "It is handed over to the king of Babylon by the sword, famine, and pestilence.
> 37 "See, I will gather them out of all the countries, where I have driven them in My anger, My fury, and great wrath, and I will bring them back to this place and cause them to dwell securely. 38 They will be My people, and I will be their God. 39 I will give them one heart and one way, so they may fear Me forever; for their good and for their children after them.
> 40 I will make an everlasting covenant with them: I will never turn away from doing good for them. I will put My fear in their hearts, so that they will not depart from Me.
> 41 "Yes, I will delight in doing good for them, and with all My heart and all My soul I will in truth plant them in this land."

> 42 For thus says *ADONAI:* "Just as I have brought all this great evil on this people, so I will bring on them all the good that I have promised them.

Jeremiah was writing at a time when King Nebuchadnezzar was besieging Jerusalem. It was just prior to the fall of Jerusalem in 586 BC. Jeremiah was fearful that Jerusalem would be lost. In verse 36, Adonai spoke, but did not address this issue. Rather, He encouraged Jeremiah that He would regather all the Jewish people from all the lands where He was driving them (verse 37). The Lord would perform a worldwide regathering of the Jewish people! This part of the prophecy has and is still being fulfilled. God is in the midst of drawing all His Jewish people back to the Land! He started this process back in the late 1800s and early 1900s. When they all finally come back, He will make them dwell in safety (verse 37). I don't think anyone on Earth right now would say Israel is dwelling in safety with all the current threats of war occurring all around them and within the Land!

In verse 38, God repeats His promise that He gave to Moses about the Jewish people: "*They will be My people, and I will be their God.*" After the regathering, the Jewish people will be God's people in a personal relationship. This fulfillment occurs when Yeshua sets up the Messianic Millennial Kingdom with all Messianic Jews and Gentiles. Jeremiah affirms this wonderful relationship in 30:22–31:1. Here, the Lord declared twice that He will be the Jewish people's God, and they shall be His people. The Lord connects this declaration to the "latter days." After His fierce anger and wrath punish all the evil ones in Jacob's Trouble, He then will set up the Kingdom with Israel finally being His people.

The Lord will then give them one heart and one way to live so that they and their children will always fear the Lord (verse 39). This verse is currently not being fulfilled in Israel today. Not every Jewish person is fearing the Lord. On the contrary, most Jewish people are not walking with the Lord. "Forever" is for a long time and reveals this is speaking of the Kingdom age!

The Lord will also cut a new covenant with them after they return (verse 40). This covenant is an everlasting covenant that guarantees a personal, loving relationship between God and His people forever! This is the New Covenant that Yeshua will cut with His people once He sets up the Messianic Millennial Kingdom (Jeremiah 31:31-34)!

The Lord will rejoice over this newfound covenant and faithfully plant the Jewish people in the Land (verse 41). This will once again fulfill His promises to Abraham and David concerning the Jewish people living in the Land forever! How will this happen? The Lord says He is faithful to keep His promises (verse 42). He will be the One to make it happen! So how can replacement theologians believe that God can go back on His promises to Abraham and the Jewish people and think they have replaced Israel in these promises, especially when Adonai Himself says right here in verse 42 that He will faithfully fulfill these promises to the Jewish people! All I can say is, "Oy vey!" Repent from this teaching!

Chart

The Israel in Prophecy chart simply reveals how Israel is doing today. There are going to continue to be Israeli-Arab wars, just as there have always been in the past. The everlasting hatred coming from the Muslims, Arabs, and Persians of the world will continue. However, that hatred will also spread around the world and will ultimately help to lead all nations to do battle against Jerusalem. No American president or any other president or king will be able to negotiate peace in the Middle East. Why is this? None of these leaders are dealing with the real issue of hatred these people have toward the Jewish people. One cannot appease hatred with material things or deals. There is only one who can deal with their hatred—that is Yeshua!

The effects of these wars and the accompanying hatred are at least three-fold: (1) the increasing desire of the Jewish people to make *aliyah* and be regathered back to the Land that likely will continue through to the middle of Jacob's Trouble; (2) talk of a peace treaty with Israel will dramatically increase as time moves forward; and (3) the desire to build the third temple will increase among the Jewish people. The current plan for the Temple Mount Faithful group is to periodically try to set the cornerstone in place to force an issue to rebuild the temple. However, now they can never get close to setting up the cornerstone; they do not have the backing of the international community, but this will gradually change in the future.

Prayer

Father in heaven, I humbly come to you in Yeshua's name, the name above all names, and ask that You would bless the Jewish people in the Land and all around the world. Please continue to regather the Jewish people back to their homeland and bless them immensely in the Land with salvation so that their names are written in the Book of Life. Please help the workers around the world to boldly share the good news message of Yeshua in a way the Jewish people can understand and be saved. Please touch their hearts even now to be ready to receive Yeshua as their Messiah, Lord, and Savior. I pray You will continue to watch over and protect them in the Land against their enemies who are attacking them. Lord, I am praying for the peace of Jerusalem. I know this involves their physical peace from their enemies, but I am also praying for their spiritual peace that is only found in Yeshua HaMeshiach! Please give their leaders great wisdom to deal with these enemies in godly ways. In Yeshua's name I pray, Amen.

Chapter 4

THE EZEKIEL WAR (EZEKIEL 38)

The future invasion of Israel is fully documented in Ezekiel 38–39. A coming confederacy of nations will attack and invade the Promised Land of Israel. The leader of these nations will devise an evil plan to enter into Israel and capture great spoil. Most theologians would agree with this synopsis thus far, but where we part company is *when* this war occurs. Many believe the Ezekiel War is the same Armageddon War that occurs at the end of Jacob's Trouble. Others believe this war takes place during the first half of the Tribulation Period. I believe the Ezekiel War is a different war than these and truly can occur any time in the present. It is also possible that this invasion could occur at a minimum three and a half years before Jacob's Trouble but definitely not inside the seven years of Jacob's Trouble! As we study these two chapters, I will reveal the scriptural clues as to why I believe this.

Gog, Magog and the Confederacy Identified (38:1–6)

> 1 The word of *ADONAI* came to me saying: 2 "Son of man, set your face toward Gog of the land of Magog, chief prince of Meshech and Tubal. Prophesy against him 3 and say, thus says *ADONAI Elohim:* 'Behold, I am against you, Gog, chief prince of Meshech and

Tubal. 4 I will turn you about and put hooks into your jaws. I will bring you out, with all your army, horses and horsemen—all of them splendidly dressed—a vast assembly with breastplate and shield, all of them wielding swords. 5 With them will be Persia, Cush and Put, all of them with shield and helmet, 6 Gomer and all his troops, the house of Togarmah from the extreme north and all his troops—many peoples with you.

In this reading of Scripture we are introduced to a number of nations who are called by their ancient names. Identifying these ancient nations with their modern counterparts has not been without controversy! It certainly is not easy to identify all of these nations with complete assurance that we are correct! However, I will endeavor to do my best.

In verses 1–3, we must remember that it is the Lord who is speaking, and He declared to Ezekiel to bring this message to Gog, Magog, the confederacy, and even to Israel. The Lord is against Gog of the land of Magog. "Gog" is a title for the leader, king, or head prince of the land of Magog. Now "Magog" is an actual person who was the son of Japheth (Genesis 10:2).

In Genesis 10:1-5, we learn some very interesting information concerning some of the nations identified in this section of Ezekiel 38. Noah had three sons with him on the ark: Shem, Ham, and Japheth (verse 1). The ark came to rest at the top of Mount Ararat, which today is found in eastern Turkey, very close to the borders of Armenia and Iran. History tells us that eventually Shem settled to the east, Ham settled to the south, and Japheth settled to the north. If you look at today's world map, you would find the nations of Armenia, Georgia, southwest Russia and even Ukraine are found to the north of Mount Ararat.

Four of Japheth's six sons are mentioned in verse 2: Gomer, Magog, Tubal, and Meshech. In verse 3, Togarmah is introduced as the son of Gomer, Japheth's grandson. From these sons and their families, the coastlands were founded (verse 5). All of these descendants of Japheth settled in lands that bordered the Mediterranean, Black, and Caspian Seas and became pioneers of their own nations. This gives us clues to help us identify who these nations are today.

History also bears witness that Japheth's son Magog settled to the north of Mount Ararat and named the nation "Magog." Today that area would be southwest Russia (or the former Soviet Union). The Lord helps to verify this in Ezekiel 38:15 when He says Gog comes out of the remote parts of the north. On a world map the remote parts of the north from Israel would be southwest Russia. Therefore, Magog is Russia today and Gog would then be Vladimir Putin (or any future Russian president when this war breaks out).

Gog is also considered to be the chief prince of Meshech and Tubal. "Chief" (rosh) actually means "head." It could be used as the head prince like in the Tree of Life Version (TLV) and KJV. However, Rosh is paired with Put, Meshech, and Tubal as one of the distant coastland nations from the Land of Israel (Isaiah 66:19). Meshech and Tubal were sons of Japheth who dwelled in the southeast area of the Black Sea in Asia Minor. However, Jewish sources place Meshech and Tubal among the Scythian tribes to the north. Others believe Meshech and Tubal are Phrygia and Cappadocia located in the neighborhood of Magog which they believed was Asia Minor (Turkey). Tubal was mentioned with Meshech and Rosh as distant coastlands to the north. Tubal was also a trade partner with Tyre (Ezekiel 27:13–14) along with Meshech and Beth-togarmah. All this information indicates that Rosh, Meshech and Tubal are provinces in Russia and/or Turkey today.

Russia has a terrible history of anti-Semitic acts against the Jewish people. In history, anytime an economic turndown occurred, people blamed the Jews. In the late 1800s and early 1900s, Russia killed many Jewish people in what were called "pogroms." These pogroms were organized massacres of

Jewish people simply because they hated the Jews! There were no good reasons for these massacres. Russia continues to have this anti-Semitic attitude today and will once again attack the Jewish people, but this time in the Land. In 2017, Russia (with Iran) established a permanent presence in Syria due to the civil and ISIS war in Syria. Russia has already developed its land entrance route from Russia to Israel! It would be fairly easy for Russian troops to march through Georgia, Armenia, Turkey, and Syria to get to Israel! However, it would be much simpler to fly their troops to their already-established bases in Syria! We do not know exactly how Russia will send their troops; all we know is that they definitely will.

The Lord says He is going to put hooks into their jaws to bring them in to the Land of Israel (verse 4). Ezekiel used this metaphor in 19:4, 9 to show newly-caged slaves being brought to their captive nations. The Lord is going to drag Russia into invading Israel. However, Russia will be a willing participant as we shall see in verses 10–12. It is not going to take much for them to desire Israel's resources. In 2017, Netanyahu and Putin discussed plans for Russia to help Israel develop its vast reserves of oil and natural gas. This could be one of many incentives for Russia to attack Israel.

Russia will like the idea of attacking Israel so much that she will send all of her army. Russia today has almost 3 million in its active and reserve forces. It remains to be seen if all of these forces would enter in an attack against the tiny nation of Israel. However, the point that needs to be made is that hundreds of thousands and even millions of Russian soldiers could easily and quickly attack Israel! But Russia will not be alone.

Verses 5–6 identify the rest of the confederacy of nations that will accompany Russia in this future invasion of Israel. Verse 5 begins with "Persia." Persia today is Iran. Persian territory in its history could also include parts of Pakistan and Afghanistan. So, it is possible that these two nations will join Iran in its attack of Israel. Iran declared in the recent past that its goal is to wipe the nation of Israel off the map! In your wildest imaginations, can you envision that a nation in today's world would have such strong hatred for another nation that they would have as their national goal the desire to completely destroy them? President Barack Obama negotiated a horrendously dangerous nuclear deal with this nation. Iran, as a nation, obviously has no love for the Jewish people and would easily and quickly join Russia in this attack. Russia has a very close relationship with Iran, even helping them to develop their nuclear program. This current close relationship will help to spur both partners to attack Israel in the near future.

Historically, "Cush" has been reported to be Ethiopia. All of our English versions of the Bible state that Cush is Ethiopia. The Septuagint translated Cush as Ethiopia. However, many theologians do not agree with this. I agree with them and believe Cush today is Sudan. In Ezekiel 29:10, the Lord proclaims that He will make the land of Egypt an utter waste and desolation. In this proclamation we find the Lord will cause the desolation of Egypt to occur even to the border of Cush! So, historically, Cush, had a border with Egypt. Today that country is called Sudan. Ethiopia, today, has a border with Sudan on the southeast side, which means that it is possible that some of today's Ethiopia is included in Cush. South Sudan could be included in Cush as well. The rabbis believe Cush today is probably spread out over Sudan, Ethiopia, and Eritrea. In any event, Sudan's national religion is Islam, and its legal system is based on Islamic law (aka sharia law). Sudan is no friend of Israel, either. Relations between Israel and Sudan are hostile at best.

"Put" today is believed to be Libya. Put is associated with Egypt and Cush (Jeremiah 46:8–9; Nahum 3:9). Josephus says Put is Libya and the rabbis believe Put is only a part of Libya.

Libya's first civil war occurred in 2011 when rebels fought against Muammar Gaddafi and his government. The United Nations (UN) helped the rebels overthrow Gaddafi. He was captured and brutally killed by the rebels. Libya's second civil war currently continues between the newly formed government and the newest rebels—the Muslim Brotherhood. ISIS has also joined this war. It seems that Libya under Gaddafi would probably have not joined in a war against Israel. However, Libya under the Muslim Brotherhood or ISIS would gladly unite with others for this war.

Many theologians over the years have believed "Gomer" is currently Germany, linked to the ancient Cimmerians. The Cimmerians were pushed out of the north shore of the Black Sea by the Scythians in the eighth century BC. Today that area is the Ukraine. The Cimmerians eventually settled in Germany. However, Germany is far to the northwest of Israel and would not necessarily be considered to be part of the remote parts of the north. Others associate Gomer as a nation within Asia Minor as one of the coastland nations located to the north. Today that would be Turkey.

As Turkey turned to a more pro-Islamist stance, their relations with Israel deteriorated. A reconciliation agreement in 2016 shed some new light for hopes of a normalized relationship. However, in 2017, President Erdogan gained more political control over the country and turned further toward Islamist policy. Erdogan's rhetoric against Israel is becoming more violent. Turkey is not bound by a peace treaty (like Egypt or Jordan) and could quickly turn on Israel as they have in the past.

"Togarmah" was the son of Gomer, the son of Japheth, who lived to the remote parts of the north of Israel. Togarmah was one of the nations of the north who traded with Tyre (Ezekiel 27:14). Some believe Togarmah is Armenia, although Armenia is not a coastland today. Others say it is another province within Asia Minor (Turkey today). If this is true, then we see Gomer and Togarmah as provinces within Asia Minor (or Turkey) today.

I believe "many peoples with you" does not include any more nations joining the confederacy to battle against Israel.

It could refer to all the soldiers in these countries' combined armies. It could also refer to the peoples (non-soldiers) of their nations joining in the battle or other peoples from neighboring nations joining the armies as they traveled to Israel. In either event, there will be many peoples with Gog in this attack against Israel. I believe we are talking about possibly up to millions of people.

Verses 5–6 identify five specific nations that will attack Israel in this future invasion: Russia, Iran, Sudan, Libya, and Turkey. In the Armageddon War, however, all nations come against Jerusalem to battle. In Zechariah 14:2, the Lord proclaims:

> I will gather *all the nations* against Jerusalem to wage war. The city shall be captured, the houses ransacked and the women ravished. Half of the city will be exiled but the remainder of the people will not be cut off from the city." (emphasis mine)

You don't have to be a Hebrew scholar to know that "all" means *all*. So, every nation under Anti-messiah will send soldiers to annihilate Israel. But in the Ezekiel War, there are only five nations mentioned. This is a major contrast and it helps us to know that these two wars are not one and the same.

In addition, the wars in the first half of Jacob's Trouble involve all nations and all peoples. It looks to be a world without peace, full of chaotic sporadic warring (Matthew 24:6-8; Revelation 6:1–4). Anti-messiah will be the one to bring all of this warring to a close by the middle of the Tribulation Period as he battles three of the ten kingdoms and wins. In any event, these wars within the first half of the Tribulation are much different from the Ezekiel War.

Gog's Invasion of Israel (38:7–9)

> 7 "'Be prepared, prepare yourself, you and all your company gathered around you. Be a guard for them. 8 After many days you will be summoned. In the latter years, you will come against the land that has been brought back from the sword and regathered from many peoples on the mountains of Israel, which had been a continual waste. But they were brought out from the peoples. When all of them are dwelling securely, 9 you will come up, you will come like a storm, you will be like a cloud covering the land—you and all your troops and many peoples with you.'"

The Lord is still speaking here in verse 7. He warns Gog to be a guard for all his armies. Why? Ultimately, the Lord is going to personally judge and wipe them out! So, Gog had better be watching out for his own soldiers.

Verse 8 is loaded with great information. It starts off with the Lord restating that He is the one summoning Gog to come to Israel. The Lord is in charge, and He is the one who turns Russia toward Israel (see also verse 4). Yes, Gog and the other leaders are going to be willing participants, and yes, they will have evil thoughts against Israel and devise an evil plan (verse 10).

The question that comes to mind is, "When is this war going to occur?" The next phrase of verse 8 tells us, "*in the latter years*." This phrase has the very same meaning as the phrase "*in the last days*" (in verse 16). This war will occur in the last days, and are we not living in the last days right now? Of course, we are! Since this war could happen at any time, this helps us to believe it is not the Armageddon War or one of the wars in the first half of Jacob's Trouble.

Verse 8 continues with, "*You will come against the land that has been brought back from the sword*." This is the actual invasion of Gog into the Land of Israel. However, it is a land that was brought back to existence through the sword! I believe this is talking about how Israel was reborn as a nation in 1947 after the sword of World War II. Israel was also "*regathered from many peoples on the mountains of Israel.*" This speaks of the regathering of the Jewish people from around the world, starting in the late 1800s.

However, when this war occurs, the Jewish people will have been already regathered! There are almost 7 million Jewish people in the Land right now. Although not all Jewish people around the world have made *aliyah* to Israel as yet; they have been gathered! Although this regathering prophecy will continue to be fulfilled in the future as more and more Jewish people move back home, the people in general have been gathered and are ready for this next prophecy to be fulfilled. It is not necessary for every single Jewish person on the planet to make *aliyah* to the Land for this Ezekiel War to occur!

Israel had been gathered from all nations to the "*mountains of Israel, which were a continuous waste.*" Israel was a wasteland from the first century until the twentieth century. It was pretty much desert and marshland, and no one really wanted to live there. Even Mark Twain wrote about how desolate and God-forsaken Israel was in his day. God was not blessing the Land because the Jewish people were not living in the Land!

Israel will also be living "*on the mountains*" of the Land. This little phrase helps us to believe that the West Bank will not be given away to the Palestinians because the Jewish people, after they come back to live in Israel, are to live on the mountains of Israel which include the West Bank mountains, as well! It is interesting to note that Prime Minister Ariel Sharon was about to give the West Bank into Yasser Arafat's hands right before he had a stroke in 2006. Obviously, he was unable to fulfill his desire to give the mountains of the West Bank to the Palestinians. Ehud Olmert replaced Sharon but did not give the West Bank away for peace with the Palestinians. It seems to me that the Lord intervened so that the West Bank would not be given away to help fulfill this prophecy.

Not only has Israel been gathered to her Land, but she will also be "dwelling securely" in the Land. "Dwelling securely" (*betach*) means "in trust, full of confidence, feel safe and secure." At the time of the Ezekiel War, Israel needs to be living in full confidence and trust within itself to be able to defend itself against its adversaries. *Betach* does not mean that there cannot be the *intifada* (uprising) from the Palestinians. It simply means that the Jewish people are confidently living in Israel and trust that they will be protected. Israel has the best trained armed forces in the world. Israelis have a lot of confidence in them.

Verse 9 finishes this section by telling us that Gog's troops will cover the Land in this invasion. This tells me that we are looking at perhaps millions of soldiers entering the Land. The soldiers will be covering the valleys and the mountains all over the Land of Israel just like the clouds cover all the sky on a rainy day. This description is much different from what happens in Armageddon and the world war in the first half of the Tribulation. In Armageddon, Anti-messiah's troops will only be deployed throughout the Jezreel and Jordan valleys with spillage flowing down to the Dead Sea and Petra area. It does not say they are stationed all over Israel on the mountains and valleys like in the Ezekiel War. Once again, I believe this supports it being a different war from Armageddon. In the first half of the Tribulation, wars will break out all over the world and this certainly does not match the Ezekiel War at all.

Many "peoples" (*ammim*) will be with Gog. This description could be of the total number of soldiers from these five nations or it could be talking about other neighboring peoples who will join Gog in the invasion. Either way, there will likely be millions of soldiers attacking the Land of Israel. No wonder that no country (including the United States) comes to Israel's defense. Who wants to war against millions?

The Reason for the Invasion (38:10–13)

> 10 Thus says *ADONAI Elohim:* "It will come to pass in that day that things will come into your heart and you will devise an evil plan. 11 You will say, 'I will go up against the land of unwalled villages. I will fall upon the quiet people who live securely, all of them living without walls, having no bars or gates, 12 in order to seize spoil and carry off plunder, to turn your hand against the waste places now inhabited and against the people gathered from the nations, who have been acquiring livestock and property, who live in the center of the world.'
>
> 13 "Sheba, Dedan and the merchants of Tarshish with all its young lions will say to you: 'Have you come to seize spoil? Have you assembled your company to plunder? To carry away silver and gold, to take away livestock and property, to make off with immense spoils?'

Not only is the Lord directing Russia to attack Israel, but Russia will be a willing participant. Gog will have evil thoughts and devise an evil plan to come against Israel (verse 10). Recently, Putin offered to help Israel develop their natural gas and oil fields. Netanyahu has held many meetings with Putin concerning this and other issues. Could Russia's evil plan include becoming friends with Israel and doing business with Israel? Israel is looking for friends since the Obama administration had repeatedly demonstrated its lack of support for Israel and Netanyahu. So, who in the world does Israel turn to for help? How about Russia? However, since Donald Trump won the presidency, he has made the United States to be Israel's big brother once again.

Russia's evil plan includes going against Israel's unwalled villages that have no bars or gates (verse 11). In ancient Israel, all the cities had security walls and gates for safety. Today, cities and towns have no such thing. This is another sign to show Israel is currently ready for this invasion. Verse 12 shares with us the actual reason for the invasion. Russia and the confederacy want to seize the plunder and spoil of Israel. They probably want the oil and natural gas reserves, the Dead Sea minerals with an estimated worth in the thousands of billions, agriculture, technology, gold and silver, and whatever Russia additionally views as valuable. Israel seems to have a lot of plunder that Russia would want.

The Lord restated in verse 12 that Israel was a wasteland, and that the Jewish people were regathered to the Land. These two events have already taken place, and thus the Ezekiel War continues to be imminent. It is fascinating to make a side note, sharing some bad news concerning where we all live. We all tend to believe that, wherever we live in the world, that this is the center of the universe. However, the Lord has made it very clear that Israel is the center (or the navel) of the world! Can you imagine how upset the rest of the world would be if they found out that God says Israel is the center of the world and their nations are not? Oy vey!

Sheba and Dedan (in verse 13) are believed to be from the southern Arabian Peninsula. So, they could be the Saudi Arabians and Yemenites of today. Tarshish was the place where Jonah was sailing to. It is believed to be one of the nations (possibly Spain today) to the far west of the Mediterranean Sea. The "young lions" or young, strong leaders and merchants of these areas are going to ask some very obvious questions like: "Have you come to seize spoil?" Well, isn't it obvious that this is the goal of the invasion?

This question reveals that there is no real concern for Israel and her citizens, but rather concern for the stolen spoil. This is another reason to think this war is different from the Armageddon War and the wars during the first half of Jacob's Trouble. The main purposes of the wars are different. In the Ezekiel War, the enemies want to rob and steal from Israel. In

Armageddon, Anti-messiah sends all nations and soldiers to destroy the Jewish people (Zechariah 14:2). In the first half of Jacob's Trouble, wars break out all over the world between nations with no real purpose. This shows that these wars are different from the Ezekiel War.

God's Intention Revealed (38:14–16)

> 14 "Therefore, son of man, prophesy, say to Gog, thus says *ADONAI Elohim:* 'In that day when My people Israel dwell safely, will you not know? 15 You will come from your place out of the extreme north—you and many peoples with you, all of them riding on horses, a great company and mighty army. 16 You will come up against My people Israel like a cloud covering the land. It will happen in the last days. I will bring you against My land, so that the nations may know Me—when I am sanctified through you, Gog, before their eyes.'"

Why would the Lord allow this horrible war to take place in Israel? Why would He allow such evil to be perpetrated against His chosen ones? Many Jewish people will die and be injured in this invasion. Russia will know that Israel is dwelling "safely." This is the third time the word *betach* is used in Ezekiel 38 for Israel living securely and safely in the Land. The Lord sincerely wants us to know that this attack is a totally unprovoked invasion against an unknowing victim who probably thinks Russia is her new friend.

The age-old question of "Who are God's people?" is answered here in verse 14. Israel, the Jewish people, are God's people! The Lord chose the Jewish people, not because they were the most of all the peoples (because they were the fewest), but He elected the Jewish people because He loved them, and He had made a promise to Abraham (Deuteronomy 7:6–8). Today, the world hardly recognizes the God of Israel. They also hardly recognize whether the God of Israel is watching over and protecting the Jewish people. But sometime in the immediate future they will see this truth!

The Lord is still speaking to Gog in verse 15. He says that Gog will come out of the remotest parts of the north to invade Israel. This is an obvious reference to Russia. In 38:6, we saw the remotest parts of the north connected to Togarmah or Turkey. Is there a contradiction here? No, both Togarmah and Magog were considered the remote parts to the north of Israel. The Lord is simply restating here that a great and mighty army will come from the furthest parts of the north to battle against Israel. That great and mighty army's downfall will help to glorify the Lord's name!

Russia and the confederacy are not only coming up against Israel, God's chosen people, but they are coming up against Israel, God's Land (verse 16). The age-old question of whose land is the Land of Israel is answered here in verse 16. The Lord says the Land of Israel is *His* land! He decided to give it to Abraham, Isaac, Jacob, and their descendants, who are the Jewish people (Genesis 12:7). He did not give the Land to the Palestinians, the Muslims, the Persians, the Russians, the Americans, the Asians, or anyone else for that matter. He gave the Land to the Jewish people!

Russia and the confederacy will be successful in their attack against Israel. They will cover the land like a cloud (verse 16). This is repeated from verse 9. Their soldiers will be on the mountains, the plains, and the valleys. They will be all over the Land! When will this happen? The Lord says it will happen "in the last days." This phrase is similar to the phrase in verse 8, "in the latter years." Both are talking about a general time period before the Messianic Kingdom. We are living in the last days right now! This Ezekiel War could occur at any moment. Finally, the Lord says He will bring Gog into the Land so that He will be sanctified before the nations, and they will know Him!

How is this going to happen? Well, the rest of the chapter tells us. The Lord is going to come to Israel's defense. As we go through the rest of this chapter and chapter 39, you will notice that not one other nation comes to Israel's defense. So, the obvious question arises: "Where is the United States in all of this?" The Scripture is silent and so is America. Under President Obama, the United States had been very obviously and publicly pulling away from supporting Israel. The ideology of this administration was clear. If Israel was attacked by anyone, would Obama be there for her? The obvious answer was no. The political alliance between the United States and Israel under Obama's administration seemed perfect for the Ezekiel War to begin.

However, it truly was not God's timing. Now, we are under Trump's administration and he has dramatically changed U.S. foreign policy toward Israel. The United States is back to being Israel's big brother and it would seem that no nation or confederacy would attack Israel as Trump's United States would defend her. However, the Scripture is clear in its absence that no country, including the United States, will help to defend Israel against this confederacy. So, who is going to be in charge of the United States when this war occurs? Do we actually have a temporary reprisal from the Lord now that Trump is our President? The Lord is in charge, and He can easily push back the prophetic clock a few years as He wishes! Only time will tell.

The Lord could also tell the current president of the United States when the Ezekiel War breaks out not to enter into the war. Why do this? He alone is going to defend Israel and judge those who attack her so that He alone will be glorified and sanctified before the world. We really do not know how this will work out since the Bible gives us no clear information. All I know is that no country comes to Israel's defense—only the Lord Himself fights against Gog, Magog, and the confederacy—and He wins, of course!

The Lord is the sovereign Ruler over the world, and He wants the world to know it! By coming to Israel's defense and destroying her enemies, the world is going to understand that the God of Israel is watching over her and protecting her. He will profoundly and miraculously make this obvious as He destroys the enemies of the Jewish people in this war. He will be "sanctified" or set apart from all the nations' gods, and the world will recognize that He is sovereign. It does not necessarily mean that everyone in the world is going to become believers in Yeshua; however, it does mean they will be taking a step in the right direction toward recognizing and knowing about the one and only Lord God of Israel. No doubt many will turn to Yeshua because of God's intervention, but at a minimum, most of the world will recognize the God of Israel.

Does God really use evil people to set Himself apart from other gods? Yes, He does, and He has in the past. Do you remember the story about the Jewish people living as slaves under Pharaoh? Exodus 14:4 states the Lord hardened Pharaoh's heart to pursue the Jewish people after he had already allowed them to leave Egypt. The Lord hardened an already-hardened heart of Pharaoh (Exodus 8:32) to glorify Himself to the nations.

Later on, we hear Rahab recounting to the two Jewish spies how her people were fearful of them because of what the Lord God of Israel had done to Pharaoh and to the Amorites (Joshua 2:8–11). The Lord's fame had made it all the way to Jericho, and a great effect of fear had fallen upon them as well. I believe the same fear of the Lord is going to happen to the world (at least for a short time period) when they view how God is going to take care of the enemies of the Jewish people in this Ezekiel War.

Gog and Magog Judged (38:17–23)

> 17 Thus says *ADONAI Elohim:* "Are you the one that I spoke about in former times through My servants the prophets of Israel, who prophesied in those days for many years that I would bring you against them? 18 In that day, when Gog comes against the land of Israel"—it is a declaration of *ADONAI*—"My fury will rise up in My nostrils. 19 In My jealousy and the fire of My wrath I have spoken! Surely in that day there will be a great earthquake in the land of Israel. 20 The fish of the sea, the birds of the heavens, the beasts of the field, all creeping things that creep upon the ground and all humans upon the face of the earth will shake at My presence. The mountains will be thrown down. The steep places will fall. Every wall will fall to the ground. 21 I will call for a sword against him throughout all my mountains"—it is a declaration of *ADONAI*—"every man's sword will be against his brother. 22 I will punish him with pestilence and blood. I will pour out rain on him, on his troops and on the many peoples with him, a torrential rain, with hailstones, fire and brimstone. 23 So I will magnify and sanctify Myself. I will make Myself known in the eyes of many nations, and they will know that I am *ADONAI*."

The Lord opens up this section with a rhetorical question to show He is not surprised by Gog's evil behavior. He created the universe and knows the beginning from the end. The obvious answer to the question is "Yes, Gog is the one prophesied to attack Israel, and the Lord is not happy about it." In fact, His furious anger at Gog will be revealed in His nostrils (verse 18)! "Nostrils" (*af*) actually means face, nose, and anger. The idea here is the Lord becoming so angry at Gog that it dramatically shows in His flared nostrils and contorted face. Gog is obviously in a whole lot of trouble with the Lord!

Verse 19 begins the judgment against Gog and his army in the Land. First, a great earthquake will occur in the Land. The context is clear that the earthquake will occur in the Land of Israel and not around the entire world, unlike the great earthquake that is connected to the Armageddon War in Revelation 16:16–18. This earthquake in Ezekiel is not the same earthquake. There certainly will be great damage done to the Land of Israel, but what is fascinating is that the people will shake at His presence in the earthquake (verse 20). The earthquakes in the first half of the Tribulation are located all over the world (Matthew 24:7). This shows they are different earthquakes from the earthquakes that occur during the Ezekiel War.

The second judgment of God against Gog is found in verse 21. Gog's soldiers will fight against themselves. This is not the first time in Israel's history where their enemies become divinely confused and fought against one another. This happened with Gideon versus the Midianites (Judges 7:22) and again with Saul versus the Philistines (1 Samuel 14:20).

The third judgment of the Lord is pestilence and blood (verse 22). "Pestilence" (*dever*) refers to any sudden fatal plague or epidemic. It definitely refers to a quick death. The spilling of blood could be connected to the fourth judgment of an overflowing and abundant rainfall with hailstones, fire, and brimstone. This torrential rainstorm reminds me of the divine plagues of Egypt and God's judgment upon Sodom and Gomorrah. It will be a devastating judgment against Gog and his army. I can imagine fire streams and huge 100-pound hail and brimstones shot by the angels in heaven toward the evil armies in the Land of Israel. Can you imagine the world's response when they see these actions live on the Internet or CNN? The devastation will be of ancient biblical proportions.

The Lord wants it to happen this way so that He will be magnified and sanctified above all other gods (verse 23).

Where are the gods of Russia and Iran to protect their armies and soldiers? They are not found anywhere. The effects of God's intervention in this war will be dramatic. Many nations will now know of the God of Israel. As I stated earlier, they will not necessarily become believers in Yeshua (although they could), but they will definitely know who the God of Israel is. The God of Israel is ADONAI (YHVH), the great "I AM" of Exodus 3:14, where Moses met the "I AM WHO I AM" in the burning bush incident. ADONAI is the one and only God of the universe, and the people of the world will begin to acknowledge this through this devastation in the Land!

God's judgments in the Ezekiel War are quite different from the judgments of Armageddon and the first half of Jacob's Trouble. In Armageddon, Yeshua comes back in His Second Coming and smites the nations with His Word (the sharp sword coming from His mouth in Revelation 19:15). Yeshua will speak the Word and something like an atomic bomb will explode, resulting in a devastating death where blood flows in a three to four feet deep river for about 180 miles (Revelation 14:19–20). Nothing of this devastation is spoken of in the Ezekiel War.

Ezekiel 39 speaks of Israel burying the bodies of the dead. But in Revelation 14, are there any bodies left over to collect and bury? How will they maneuver through all that blood to find any bodies? No. Because of all these differences, I believe they are different wars. In the first half of Jacob's Trouble, the first two seals are broken, with war breaking out all over the world (Revelation 6:1–4). Anti-messiah is also unleashed against the world to conquer it. I believe it is here in the first half of Jacob's Trouble that he will war against the three kings and win. It certainly seems that the Lord will not intervene with any judgments during this time other than allowing Anti-messiah to do his dirty business. This would again show that this war is different from Ezekiel's War.

However, I do recognize there are many similarities among these three wars as well. All involve a great earthquake. Ezekiel's earthquake only affects Israel, but Armageddon's earthquake affects the whole world and Jerusalem is split into three parts (Revelation 16:18), which does not occur in Ezekiel. In the first half of the Tribulation, there are a plurality of earthquakes throughout the world (Matthew 24:7) and there is an earthquake at the end of the seventh seal (Revelation 8:5). Nothing is said of the effects of these earthquakes! Although there is the similarity of an earthquake in all three wars, it certainly seems that there are sufficient major differences regarding the effects of these earthquakes to show that they are different earthquakes.

Two of the three wars also have huge hailstones raining down from heaven (Revelation 16:21). But the Armageddon War does not mention anything about a torrential rainstorm, fire, and brimstones. Any similarities between these wars does not necessitate an equality between the wars. Just because there are similarities in the wars does not mean these wars are all the same. The similarities could easily be explained by the Lord simply using the same judgments in different wars.

Although there are some similarities between these three wars, the many differences in the wars help me to believe that they are all different wars. I believe these three wars are just that—three individual and separate wars. I believe the Scripture shows the Ezekiel War to be imminent. It could occur at any moment. However, at a minimum, it needs to occur at least three and a half years before the beginning of Jacob's Trouble (more on this in the next chapter). The effects of this war could carry into the middle of the Tribulation Period. The world wars in the first half of Jacob's Trouble occur at the beginning of the Tribulation, extending through to the events of the middle of the Tribulation. The Armageddon War happens toward the end of Jacob's Trouble, culminating in Yeshua's Second Coming.

Chapter 5

The Ezekiel War (Ezekiel 39)

In Ezekiel 38, we found out that the confederacy of Russia, Iran, Sudan, Libya, and Turkey will invade Israel sometime in the near future. Although many theologians believe this war is the Armageddon War that ends all wars at the end of Jacob's Trouble or the World War mentioned at the beginning of Revelation, I emphatically do not! I believe Ezekiel's War is a different war than these and that it could occur at any time. These five nations will attack Israel for the main purpose of capturing spoil and seizing plunder from the Jewish people. Although these nations will perform tremendous damage against Israel and the Jewish people, Ezekiel does not tell us their intent is to destroy Israel and wipe them off the face of the earth like the Anti-messiah wants to do in the war of Armageddon. An even bigger issue than this is the fact that no nation (not even the United States) comes to Israel's defense. The Lord defends Israel in dramatic style so that the world, and specifically Israel, realizes that the God of Israel is the Lord and Master of all!

Ezekiel 39 continues this theme of the Ezekiel War and adds some much-needed revelation. Not everyone believes this, though. The rabbis believe Chapter 39 discusses a second war that Israel will have with Gog and Magog. However, the first word of the first verse "*ve-attah*" typically is translated "and you" (although the TLV translates it only as "you"). "And you" suggests a continuation of Chapter 38. It connects the two chapters together, showing this Ezekiel War is simply discussed in both chapters.

God Judges Gog and Magog (39:1–8)

> 1 "You, son of man, prophesy against Gog and say, thus says *ADONAI Elohim:* 'Behold, I am against you, Gog, chief prince of Meshech and Tubal. 2 I will turn you around, drive you along, and lead you up from the extreme north. I will bring you upon the mountains of Israel. 3 Then I will strike your bow from your left hand and make your arrows drop from your right hand. 4 You will fall on the mountains of Israel—you, all your troops and the people that are with you. I will give you as food to all kinds of birds of prey and to the beasts of the field. 5 You will fall on an open field, for I have spoken.'" It is a declaration of *ADONAI*.
> 6 "I will send fire on Magog and on those who live securely in the islands. Then they will know that I am *ADONAI*. 7 So I will make My holy Name known among My people Israel. I will not let My holy Name be profaned anymore. The nations will know that I am *ADONAI*, the Holy One in Israel. 8 Behold, it is coming. It will be done"—it is a declaration of *ADONAI*—"this is the day that I have spoken about.

In verses 1–2, we see a repeated statement that the Lord, although He is against Gog, is going to help them invade Israel. The specific quote is against "the mountains of Israel." I believe the mountains of Israel quoted here include the mountains of the West Bank. How profound is this in light of the development that occurred in 2006? Prime Minister Ariel Sharon was just about to give Yasser Arafat the West Bank when he suddenly suffered a stroke and spent the next eight years in a coma, never to resume his office or his duties. His replacement, Ehud Olmert, did not allow Israel to give up the West Bank to the Palestinians. If the West Bank was given over to Arafat, then the mountains of the West Bank would not be in Israel's ownership and control. But since this did not happen, this scripture passage can be completely fulfilled now.

This is similar to what we learned when the Gaza Strip was given over to the Palestinians in exchange for peace. Once this was done, mortar shells and rockets were shot from the Gaza into Israel, fulfilling prophecy from Psalm 83. Our Lord certainly is in charge of human history! Sometimes we think the world's chaos is gloom and doom, but our Lord is in charge and He is working in all the chaos to bring about His plan!

Once again, we see that the Lord is the only intervenor for Israel in verses 3–5. Where is the United States? The Scripture is silent just as she will be silent. Not too many Bible-believing believers think the Obama administration would have helped Israel in this attack and they were probably right. However, now we are under President Trump, and he is definitely pro-Israel, going so far as to announce that Jerusalem is her capital and willing to move the United States embassy to Jerusalem! Other nations are following suit as well.

So, it seems unconscionable to think President Trump would do nothing to help Israel in this war. So, my current belief is that under the Trump administration, the United States is under God's reprieve. His judgment of the United States may be delayed and the fulfillment of the Ezekiel War may have been pushed back in prophetic time. Why? It is believed that if Russia and the confederacy attack Israel, then the United States under President Trump would act and come to Israel's defense. It might take another ultra-liberal administration to be voted into office in the future for the United States to fail to help Israel. This could possibly mean that Israel will be spared for at least another four to eight years.

Gog's troops and the peoples who are with him will fall on the mountains and open plains of the Land and become food for the birds and beasts of the land. This is definitely a gruesome end to the evil ones, but God is planning on making a point in the darkened hearts of the world! This demise of the evil ones in the Ezekiel War is similar to the end of the evil ones in Armageddon (Revelation 19:17–21). The only difference is that Revelation does not mention the beasts of the field eating the evil ones' flesh. They are absent in the Armageddon War, but not the Ezekiel War. It is possible that these beasts are not mentioned in Armageddon because they do not actually partake in this gross event since they cannot pass through the depth of blood in the valleys (Revelation 14:19–20). The blood is too deep for the beasts of the field to get to the bodies. However, the birds can easily fly there. Once again, just because God has similar judgments in wars does not make the wars the same war! In the wars of the first half of Jacob's Trouble, no flesh-eating animal judgment is mentioned. This shows it is a different war from the Ezekiel War.

Beginning in verse 6, we are told of a new judgment of God. In addition to destroying Gog's armies in the Land of Israel, the Lord will send fire to Magog. One can only imagine how this will occur, but it makes sense to wipe out Russia itself in a similar way to that used to wipe out Russia's army in Israel. "Fire" here could then possibly include fire, hailstones, and brimstones from heaven. This is not out of the question, since the Lord's purpose in this judgment is for them to know who He is—that He is YHVH, the great "I AM," the Lord of all. It would make sense that He would use the same plagues that He has used in the past, so that the nations would not make an error in knowing who has judged them! In any event, Russia is not the only nation to be judged in this way by the Lord.

Verse 6 continues to state that those people who live securely on the "islands" (*iyyim*) will receive God's wrath through the fire as well. This Hebrew word is typically used to mean "coast" and sometimes used for "islands." When *iyyim* is used in a geographic sense as in verse 6, it means coastlands or simply understood as nations that have coasts. I prefer the "coastland" meaning as it is the usual meaning for the word, and it also makes sense that all of the confederacy nations that join with Russia to attack Israel are nations that have coasts. Presumably the "islands" are the nations that corroborated with Russia to attack Israel.

What verse 6 reveals to us is that the Lord will not only send His wrath upon Gog and the confederacy in the Land of Israel, but that He also will destroy the homelands of the nations that attack her (Russia, Iran, Sudan, Libya, and Turkey)! This will be a catastrophic attack upon these nations, and the devastation will be immense. No wonder the world takes notice! Can you imagine what the world is going to be like after this prophetic event? Russia, one of the world leaders of communism, and Iran, the leader of Islamic terrorism around the world, will fall. I believe that this cataclysmic destruction of Russia, Iran, and the rest of the confederacy will help to thrust the revived Roman Empire back to the world stage and begin to move forward with the One-World Order.

What is more devastating to the world is finally figuring out that the God of Israel is much more powerful than Russia's god (they are atheists, so their god is their own power, government, army, etc.), Iran's god is Allah, and Sudan, Libya, and Turkey worship Allah, as well. This has to have a major dramatic effect on the world's viewpoint concerning communism and Islam. The world will have just witnessed the Lord taking out these two religions in a single day! This will drastically affect the rest of the communists and Muslims around the world!

Not only will the nations of the world know who God is, but Israel and the Jewish people will know who the Lord is (verse 7) and they will recognize that He is holy. Through God's intervention, Israel and the world will recognize that the God of Israel is set apart and much more powerful than any other god! Again, this does not necessarily mean that there will be a world-wide revival for Yeshua; however, it could start one! Major catastrophic judgment could have this kind of effect. When the Lord promises judgment upon a nation or people, it shall be done. The only question that remains is "When?" He means what He says, and we can be sure that God's judgment shall happen the way He has described. Why? He is the one and only faithful God who keeps His promises.

Israel Cleanses the Land (39:9–16)

> 9 "The inhabitants of Israel's cities will go out and kindle fires with the weapons—shields and breastplates, bows and arrows, war clubs and spears. They will make fires with them for seven years. 10 They will not take wood out of the field or cut anything from the forests, for they will make fire from the weapons. They will plunder those who plundered them and loot those who looted them." It is a declaration of *ADONAI*.
>
> 11 "On that day, I will give Gog a burial place there in Israel, the valley of the travelers east of the sea. It will block those who travel through, since they will bury Gog and all his multitude there. Then they will call it the valley of Hamon-Gog. 12 The house of Israel will bury them for seven months, in order to cleanse the land. 13 All the people of the land will bury them. It will be memorable for them, a day when I am glorified." It is a declaration of *ADONAI*.
>
> 14 "Men will be continually set apart to travel through the land and bury the travelers remaining on the face of the land, in order to cleanse it. At the end of seven months, they will make their search. 15 When they travel through the land, if any sees a man's bone, he will set up a sign by it, until the buriers have buried it in

the valley of Hamon-gog. 16 Hamonah will also be the name of the city. So they will cleanse the land.

After the Lord defeats the evil ones in the Land by natural means of a torrential rainstorm with hailstones, fire, and brimstone, the Jewish people will begin to cleanse the Land of Israel. Verses 9–10 reveal Israel will begin to collect the weaponry and war implements of the defeated armed forces and use them as firewood instead of regular firewood! What is amazing is that they will have collected enough weaponry to supply the whole nation of Israel to make fires for seven years! This is a whole lot of weapons! That's why I have estimated hundreds of thousands and maybe even millions of soldiers entering the Land! Something like this has happened before in Israel's history. These types of numbers are not improbable. 2 Kings 19:35 and Isaiah 37:36 report that 185,000 soldiers died in one night by the hand of the Angel of the Lord!

The key point of verses 9–10 is that Israel will substitute these collected weapons instead of using regular firewood for their fires for seven years! Seven years is a long time to be burning weapons for firewood. By the way, I have taught this message many times in congregations, and one day a World War II veteran approached me after a service. He told me two truths about Russia that I did not know. He said some of Russia's pistols and rifles are made with very dense wood, and in his opinion, they would make really good firewood! So, this information helps us to understand why Israel would use the weapons for firewood. But he also told me that Russia never collects its dead soldiers from another country in war (we'll see why this is important in verse 11).

Israel will then make personal fires with the weapons for seven years. This is the reason why I believe this war needs to occur at least three and a half years before the beginning of Jacob's Trouble. Why? In the Messianic Millennial Kingdom, Israel will hammer all its enemies' weaponry into plowshares and pruning hooks. It does not say she will use them for fire-wood! Isaiah 2:4 (and Micah 4:3) proclaims:

> He will judge between the nations and decide for many peoples. They will beat their swords into plowshares, and their spears into pruning knives. Nation will not lift up sword against nation, nor will they learn war any more.

Instead of using the weapons used against Israel for fire-wood for seven years, they will hammer these weapons into agricultural implements used for farming. Not only does this difference lead me to believe that these two wars are different, but the seven-year duration does as well.

If the Ezekiel War is Armageddon at the end of Jacob's Trouble, then we are looking at seven years into the Messianic Millennial Kingdom that Israel will be using the weapons for firewood. Isaiah 2:4 says they will be using the weapons as farming implements, not necessarily firewood! This does not make sense.

In addition, I believe the Ezekiel War has to occur at least three and a half years before Jacob's Trouble begins because using the weapons for firewood in the second half of the Tribulation Period makes no sense, either. During the second half, Israel will undergo the most horrific holocaust in their history! The Jewish people are going to be hunted down and killed around the globe by the Anti-messiah! I do not think they are going to be using weapons as firewood in the Land when the Anti-messiah is pursuing them! If they even have those weapons, they will be using them for their own self-defense!

It is possible for Israel to hammer the weapons into farming implements in the first half of the Tribulation Period because they will have some sort of pseudo-peace from the world. So that is why I believe the Ezekiel War has to occur at least three and a half years before the beginning of the Tribulation. Half of the seven years could occur during the first half of Jacob's

Trouble. It is inconceivable and does not fit the Scriptures that Israel would be hammering weapons into farming implements in the second half of Jacob's Trouble!

Verse 10 finishes up with the idea that the Jewish people will also take back from the evil soldiers that which was stolen from them. The very fact that they re-plunder the items plundered from them shows that Gog and Magog were only temporarily victorious in the war. If the Lord had not intervened, then Israel could well have been destroyed and the confederacy escaped with the spoil. Once again, the question remains, "If this is the Armageddon War, then how can Israel wade through three to four feet of 180 miles worth of blood?! And why would they do that just to get weapons to use as firewood?!" And how would they wade through all that blood to find bodies to bury them? It is inconceivable that this would happen and therefore another reason why I believe these wars are separate wars.

After the invading armies and their corresponding countries are wiped out, we find out their dead soldiers are left to rot in Israel (verse 11). Well, no wonder that this is true! First, my World War II veteran friend told us that Russia does not go and collect their dead soldiers from war; it's just their typical practice. Second, who is going to be alive in Russia for them to care enough about going after their dead soldiers? God is going to wipe out their country. This does not necessarily mean that every single Russian person will die. However, it does mean that Russia will be an incapacitated country no longer able to properly function or defend itself! God knows what He's doing, and He knows how to do it! Just look at Pharaoh and Egypt in Exodus 7–14 as an example.

Israel will then be the ones left to bury Gog and all his armies. They will select a place to the east of the sea. Which sea? The Sea of Galilee or the Dead Sea? The rabbis believe the scripture is talking about burying the bodies to the east of the Sea of Galilee. We do not know for sure as the Scripture is silent concerning the answer. However, it is interesting to note that "Hamon-Gog" is the name where they will bury Gog and his multitude of soldiers and "Hamon-Gog" means the "multitude of Gog" (even the city "Hamonah" is named after the multitude in verse 16).

In order to cleanse the Land of Israel, the Jewish people will be collecting and burying the bodies for a total of seven months (verses 12–13). There are so many bodies all over the Land that it takes the Jewish people seven months to cleanse it. This is a very long time. Israel even will assign special people to perform this duty to be sure to cleanse the Land properly (verses 14–15). Every bone must be properly disposed of in the valley of Hamon-Gog. Verse 15 suggests some type of contamination occurred to the enemies of the Jewish people in the Land. This is probable due to the pestilence that was sent by the Lord to judge Gog and Magog in 38:22.

In verse 13, we find an interesting side note that really is not a side note. The Lord wants everyone to see and know that He is the one who glorifies Himself, and He can choose any method He desires to reveal it. Here, He glorifies Himself through the destruction of these five nations and their armies. When the Lord performs this destruction, it will be "memorable." "Memorable" (*leshem*) means "for a name, renowned." So, when God rescues Israel from the clutches of Gog and Magog, He does it in such a way that Israel will become renowned around the world! As I said before, this war will be an earth-shattering event. It will dramatically and cataclysmically affect every person in the world! The world will begin to fear (at least temporarily) the Lord and His chosen people!

Now, if this war was Armageddon at the end of Jacob's Trouble, how does Israel spend seven months cleansing the Land when there are only seventy-five days between the end of Jacob's Trouble and the beginning of the Messianic Kingdom (more on this later)? Israel cannot be cleansing the Land seven months into the Kingdom. The Land has to be cleansed prior to the beginning of the Millennial Kingdom! You cannot begin the Kingdom in a defiled, blood-soaked country! And once again, if there is about 180 miles of blood three to four feet deep throughout Israel, how can the special Jewish people find and set up markers where the bones and bodies are? Again, it is inconceivable, and thus this Ezekiel War is a different war from Armageddon.

God's Sacrifice (39:17–20)

> 17 "You, son of man"—thus says *ADONAI Elohim*—"say to every kind of bird and to every beast of the field: 'Assemble and come! Gather from all around to My sacrificial feast that I have prepared for you, a great sacrifice on the mountains of Israel. You will eat flesh and drink blood. 18 You will eat the flesh of mighty men and drink the blood of the princes of the earth—as rams, lambs, goats, bulls—all of them fatlings of Bashan. 19 So you will eat fat until you are gorged and you will drink blood until you are drunk, from My sacrificial feast that I have prepared for you. 20 You will be filled at My table with horses and horsemen, with mighty men and all the warriors.'" It is a declaration of *ADONAI*.

All kinds of birds and animals of the fields are invited to the Lord's sacrifice (verse 17). Although the TLV calls this sacrifice a "feast," there is no Hebrew word in this verse that indicates this. It is, however, a great "sacrifice" (*zevach*) on the mountains of Israel where the birds and animals will gorge on flesh and blood (verses 17–18). These animals will definitely be feasting! "Sacrifice" (*zevach*) refers to the typical animal sacrifices the Israelites offered up in worship to the Lord in the Mosaic Covenant. How ironic it is that the evil ones have become the sacrifice, and the animals are invited to partake!

Bashan is mentioned in verse 18. This was a broad fertile area just east of the Sea of Galilee. The sheep and cattle of this area were of the finest in the known world. These mighty princes and men are going to make a fine dinner for all these animals (verse 19). All the animals are encouraged to gorge themselves on all the dead soldiers (verse 20). It truly will be a sickening sight. This "Bashan" reference also helps me to link the burial ground of Hamon-gog to the eastern part of the Sea of Galilee where Bashan was once situated. This area includes the Golan Heights today.

The Whole World Will Know (39:21-24)

> 21 "I will put My glory among the nations. All the nations will see My judgment that I will execute and My hand that I will lay on them. 22 The house of Israel will know that I am *ADONAI* their God, from that day onward. 23 The nations will know that the house of Israel went into exile for their iniquity, because they broke faith with Me. So I hid My face from them and gave them into the hand of their enemies. All of them fell by the sword. 24 I dealt with them according to their uncleanness and their transgressions. I hid My face from them."

All the nations will see the Lord's judgment upon those evil ones who come against His people. Hopefully, they will learn the lesson. God is glorified through His actions of delivering the Jewish people (verse 21). Not only does God want the nations to know that He is the God of Israel, but He wants His own chosen people, the Jews, to know that He is Lord (verse 22). Verse 22 adds an important fact that Israel will know and continue to know this in the future! It does not seem that Israel will ever forget this deliverance from the Lord! Praise the Lord for that! Unfortunately, Israel tends to forget a lot about what the Lord has done for her over the millennia.

These events will lead the nations to remember that a long time ago, Israel was exiled to Assyria because of her sin. The

Jewish people had fallen far away from the Lord, so He rightly judged them and sent them to Assyria (verse 23–24). However, this is not the case here. Gog, instead of Israel, is rightly judged, and Israel is rescued. The Lord is not hiding His face from Israel but protecting her from the evil ones!

If this war was the Armageddon War with Israel entering into the Messianic Millennial Kingdom, then these statements would be contradicting what will be spoken of Israel in the Kingdom. Instead of being the country that was banished to Assyria, Israel will be remembered as the nation that the Lord brought out of the north country and around the world. It is the very opposite idea. Jeremiah 23:7–8 boldly proclaims:

> Therefore behold, days are coming," says ADONAI, "when they will no longer say: 'As ADONAI lives, who brought up the children of Israel out of the land of Egypt.' Rather, 'As ADONAI lives, who brought up and led the offspring of the house of Israel out of the north country and from all the lands where He had banished them.' So they will dwell in their own soil.

So once again, these wars are separate wars and should not be seen as the same.

God Restores Israel (39:25–29)

> 25 Therefore thus says *ADONAI Elohim:* "Now I will restore Jacob from exile, when I have compassion on the whole house of Israel. I will be zealous for My holy Name. 26 They will bear their shame and all their disloyalty by which they broke faith with Me, when they were living securely in their land, with no one making them afraid. 27 When I have brought them back from the peoples and have gathered them out of their enemies' lands, I will be sanctified in them in the eyes of many nations.

> 28 Then they will know that I am *ADONAI* their God, since it was I who caused them to go into exile among the nations and I who will gather them back to their own land. I will never again leave them there. 29 I will never again hide My face from them. For I have poured out My *Ruach* upon the house of Israel." It is a declaration of *ADONAI*.

The Lord says He will cause Israel's return to the Land (verse 25). God has already promised many times in Ezekiel He would do this (36:24; 37:21). He will have mercy on her and restore her from her exile. These actions will show the holiness of God's name! Israel will remember her shameful sinful actions against the Lord even when she was living in security (verse 26). When the Lord finally brings Israel back to the Land, He will be sanctified around the world (verse 27). But in verse 28, we see that the Lord will not leave any Jewish people in the diaspora (dispersion), but rather, He will bring all the Jewish people home.

The Lord is now clearly speaking of the Messianic Millennial Kingdom! Verse 29 verifies this, for the Lord will have poured out His Ruach (Spirit) upon all of Israel. This will happen at the end of Jacob's Trouble. Zechariah 12:10 shows a "spirit of grace and supplication" leading the Jewish people to believe and trust in Yeshua as their Messiah. They then receive the Ruach Kodesh (Holy Spirit). The only way for any person, Jew or Gentile, to receive the Ruach is to believe in Yeshua as their Messiah, Lord, and Savior. At the end of Jacob's Trouble, the Lord will save all of Israel and then Israel will call upon Yeshua to physically deliver them from the hands of the Anti-messiah. They will actually look upon Yeshua as He descends to earth in His Second Coming! This sets up Yeshua's Second Coming (more on this later).

The Ezekiel War will be a devastating war against Israel. Russia and the confederacy will win in their initial attack of Israel. They are obviously much too powerful for Israel. However, the Lord comes to Israel's defense. I would imagine that most people around the world think the United States would come to Israel's defense and fight against Russia. But this does not occur in Ezekiel. No country comes to Israel's aid. The war is won by the Lord alone!

The devastation will be catastrophic. It is possible that hundreds of thousands or even millions of soldiers will die at the hand of the Lord! Then the Lord will send fire upon Russia and the confederacy and destroy them as well. We could be seeing many millions of people dying because of this Ezekiel War. The world leaders of communism and Islam will fall. Just as Hitler and the Nazis were not destined for world domination, Russia and Islam will not take over the world, either. The Lord will put a stop to them, as well. A revived Roman Empire is to rule over the world. I believe this Empire will begin to rise to world fame sometime after the Ezekiel War (they may actually begin their rise prior to the war). Wouldn't it be a perfect opportunity for a revived Roman Empire to rise to world power with Russia and the Islamic nations out of the way?

Chart

In looking at the chart, we see three main effects of the Ezekiel War are encircled. These effects are also connected to the results discussed in Chapter 1, "Israel Today." Some of the effects of the Ezekiel War could continue right up to the middle of the Tribulation Period. The Ezekiel War will probably be the culminating event for the Jewish people around the world to greatly desire to be regathered back to the Land. Although this regathering already began in the early 1900s, it will most likely continue to the middle of the Tribulation Period.

The talk of a peace treaty with Israel will dramatically increase after the Ezekiel War. Can you imagine how great the world's fear of the Lord will be after they see how God destroys the enemies of the Jewish people? I am sure many will be wondering if the God of Israel will attack their country next. So, the idea of peace with Israel will come to the forefront and possibly be the impetus for the culmination of a one-world government and a peace treaty between the world and Israel (which begins Jacob's Trouble).

This will also be a great time for Israel to rebuild the Temple. Most of the world would probably then be okay with this rebuilding. They might be thinking that they need to appease the Lord by allowing the Jewish people to build their Temple and worship their God. The actual rebuilding of the Temple could either occur before the Tribulation Period or during the first half of it. The Scripture is not clear as to when. However, we do know for a fact that Anti-messiah will set Himself up as God in the Temple at the middle of the Tribulation Period (Daniel 9:27 with 2 Thessalonians 2:3–4). So, the Temple will be built and used at the very latest during the first half of Jacob's Trouble.

Prayer

Lord, we cannot change your scriptural plan for Israel in the future. So, I pray for Your blessing upon Israel now. Help Israel to continue to deal with their enemies in godly ways to help bring the peace in the Land and the Middle East. I pray for the salvation of the Jewish people and the people of her enemies that will attack her. Please let there be revival in the Land so many can hear the good news message of Yeshua, be saved, and have their names written in the Book of Life. Please help the enemy nations as well to see the light of Yeshua and be saved before these terrible events of Ezekiel occur. Please prepare the hearts of the world to see the truth of Yeshua when the Ezekiel War occurs. Thank you for your mercy, grace, and salvation. I pray in the mighty name of Yeshua, Amen.

Chapter 6

THE ONE-WORLD ORDER

I believe one of the effects of the Ezekiel War on the world will be its desire to have a one-world government and a one-world religion. Talk of the One-World Order has been around for centuries and the powers-that-be have been working behind the scenes to bring it about. In the last ten years of world history, we have drawn closer than ever before to this One-World Order. What better way can they justify keeping the world safe and secure after the catastrophic tragedy in Israel, Russia, and the confederacy? Through the world's reasoning, having a one-world government will be paramount to saving the world! I would think it would be pretty easy to sway all or most nations into believing the one-world government to be necessary for the very survival of the world.

In 605 BC, Daniel and some of the Jewish people were deported to Babylon by King Nebuchadnezzar. God's judgment against Israel was a seventy-year captivity away from the Land of Israel. In Daniel 1, we see Daniel begin his new ministry as prophet of the Lord. In Daniel 2, King Nebuchadnezzar has a troubling dream of a great image. Daniel was the only one who could tell the king the dream and give its interpretation. This dream is the beginning of many dreams reported by Daniel that together forecast the most comprehensive description of world history in the Bible. In Luke 21:24, Yeshua called this world domination by the Gentiles, "the times of the Gentiles." Daniel prophesied that four Gentile kingdoms will rule and reign, not only over the world, but also over Israel. Israel would only see true peace when the Prince of Peace finally returns to His people, destroys the Gentile kingdoms, and sets up the final kingdom, the Messianic Millennial Kingdom.

Daniel's Interpretation (2:36–45)

> 36 "This was the dream. Now we will tell the king its interpretation. 37 You, O king, are the king of kings to whom the God of heaven has given sovereignty, power, might and glory. 38 Wherever mankind, beasts of the field, and fowls of the heaven dwell, He has given them into your hand, and made you ruler over them all. You are the head of gold.
>
> 39 "Now after you another kingdom will arise, one inferior to yours. Next, a third kingdom, one of bronze, will rule over all the earth. 40 Finally, there will be a fourth kingdom, strong as iron—for iron shatters and breaks everything—and just as iron smashes everything, so will it shatter and crush all the others. 41 Just as you saw that the feet and toes were partly potter's clay and partly iron, so this will be a divided kingdom. It will have some of the strength of the iron, for you saw the iron mixed with clay. 42 As the toes of the feet were partly iron and partly clay, so this kingdom will be partly strong and partly brittle. 43 Just as you saw iron mixed with clay, people will mix with one another, but they will not adhere to one another, just as iron does not mix with clay.
>
> 44 "Now in the days of those kings, the God of heaven will set up a kingdom that will never be destroyed, nor will this kingdom be left to another people. It will crush and bring to an end all of these kingdoms. But it will

> endure forever. 45 For just as you saw a stone cut out of a mountain, yet not by hands, crush the iron, bronze, clay, silver and gold, the great God has made known to the king what will happen in the future. Now the dream is certain, and its interpretation is trustworthy."

In Daniel 2, King Nebuchadnezzar had troubling dreams. No one could tell him the dreams or the interpretation of the dreams until Daniel came along. Daniel told the king about his dream of an extraordinary statue. The head was made of gold, the breast and arms were made of silver, the belly and thighs were made of bronze, its legs were made of iron, and its feet were made of iron mixed with clay. Then an uncut stone struck and destroyed the statue, grew into a huge mountain, and then filled the whole earth. The Lord gave this dream to Nebuchadnezzar to reveal to him the four Gentile kingdoms that would successively rule the world until the Messiah's kingdom would come.

In verses 36–38, we are told that King Nebuchadnezzar received his kingdom from the Lord, the one and only God of heaven. The Lord was the one who gave Nebuchadnezzar his dominion, power, and glory, and He caused him to rule over the whole known world. Babylon is the first kingdom of gold with Nebuchadnezzar as its king.

The second kingdom of silver was the Medo-Persian Empire, and the third kingdom of bronze was the Grecian Empire (verse 39). Both of these kingdoms are later identified by name in 5:28, 8:20–21, and 11:2. In this specific interpretation, we are not told very much about these kingdoms. However, the two bronze thighs of the Greek kingdom can be explained. After Greece conquered the world, Alexander the Great died. The world was divided up into four sections, but was predominantly two political divisions: one in the north (Syria) and one in the south (Egypt) (11:5–20). These two divisions would then be considered to be the two bronze thighs. Later history shows the

Roman Empire embraced a wider territory and divided it into east and west rather than north and south.

The fourth kingdom of iron was the Roman Empire (verse 40). Rome is later identified in 9:26 as the "*people of a prince who is to come will destroy the city and the sanctuary*." Titus and the Romans are the ones who came in AD 70 and destroyed not only the Temple, but the entire city of Jerusalem. The Roman Empire was predicted to crush all other kingdoms, and that is exactly what it did.

This Roman kingdom has two iron legs and two feet (verse 41). These probably represent the division of the kingdom into east and west. It was not only divided geographically, but physically (verse 42). It would be a strong kingdom; however, part of it would also be weak and brittle. Then in verse 43, there is a curious statement about how people will be mixed together. The simple understanding here is that the leaders of this kingdom will try to intermarry peoples with other peoples to cause unity in the kingdom, but it will not work.

What is fascinating to note in verses 42–43 is that the number of toes is not discussed. Assuming the statue has the normal number of toes, then the number would be ten. Some of the toes are made out of brittle clay. The brittleness reveals that they are weak. I believe the ten toes represent the ten kings/kingdoms that spring from the one-world government in the future. The Anti-messiah will fight and defeat three of the kings in Daniel 7:23–25 (with Daniel 11:40–44). The rest of the seven kings will then succumb to the Anti-messiah's leadership of the world.

The question that many believers ask is, "How can the Roman Empire live in the future if it has already died?" This is a great question and one that needs to be answered. The Roman Empire officially became a world power in 27 BC. In AD 395, it split into the Western and Eastern Roman Empires. The Western Empire fell in AD 476. The Eastern Empire lasted right up to AD 1453. So, the Roman Empire has definitely fallen, but

I believe the better question to ask is, "Has the Roman Empire completely died?" The answer to this question is a resounding "No!" The life of the Roman Empire continues to touch our everyday lives through culture, religions, politics, languages (Latin and Greek), architecture, philosophy, economics, sciences, law and government, and so forth. Almost every facet of life in the Western world has its roots in the Roman Empire.

In one sense, the Roman Empire continues to live, and I believe that, in the future, the Roman Empire will be revived to its former ferocious self. There is enough biblical evidence in Daniel to show us that this empire will be revived. I believe the ten toes of the statue are the same as the ten horns of the Fourth Beast (which is also the Roman Empire) of Daniel 7. The ten horns are identified as the ten kings that are subdued by the Anti-messiah so that he can rule the world (7:24). That would make the ten toes the same as the ten horns, which are the ten kings who will rule over the world just prior to Anti-messiah dethroning them.

Daniel 2 lays the groundwork for understanding the four Gentile world kingdoms. These kingdoms ruled the world in succession, while the fourth kingdom of Rome still reigns. In the future, the Roman Empire will be revived to take over the world physically once again in the form of the New World Order. I believe this will occur sometime after the Ezekiel War where we see Russia and the confederacy destroyed. It will be the perfect time for the European Union to morph into the revived Roman Empire (probably with the help of the United States, as well). However, this kingdom will not last. The Lord will set up a kingdom that will crush these four kingdoms (verses 44–45). It will be God's kingdom that will last forever!

The bad news was summed up in Daniel 2 in that four kingdoms would rule and reign over the world and Israel. The kingdoms would arise in succession, one after the other, with the fourth kingdom of Rome as the last human kingdom. Verse 44 reveals God's kingdom will be set up in "the days of those kings." This suggests that God's kingdom comes once the fourth kingdom ends. This reveals that the Roman Empire has to be revived since there is not another human kingdom after it. If any nation or potential kingdom tries to assert itself and take over the world, I believe the Lord would stop it since it is not destined for these nations to become world-dominating powers.

For example, Hitler and the Nazis came into power and tried to take over the world. Eventually, the Lord stopped them. Russia and Iran (or any of the Muslim/Persian countries under Islam) have plans to take over the world and dominate it. However, unfortunately they do not know the scriptures where Ezekiel says the Lord will stop them. They just are not ordained to be the next world leaders. The revived Roman Empire is the next world leader and Anti-messiah will spring forth to rule the world from this beast in Jacob's Trouble. Then and only then the true Messiah will come and destroy Anti-messiah's evil kingdom.

This is the good news! The culmination of these four kingdoms will end with the birth of God's kingdom. In verses 44–45, we find God's kingdom will crush all the world's kingdoms. The stone, cut out of a mountain without hands, crushes the statue of gold, silver, bronze, iron and clay. The stone represents Yeshua HaMeshiach—Jesus, the Messiah. When He comes in His Second Coming, He will destroy all the nations and kingdoms that come against Israel to battle. Haggai 2:22 agrees that He will overthrow and destroy all the kingdoms of the world. These kingdoms will be the Gentile nations that try to destroy Israel. Yeshua then will set up His Kingdom, and it will endure forever!

This Kingdom specifically fulfills God's promises given in the Abrahamic and Davidic Covenants. God told Abraham that He would give the Land to him and to his seed forever. God also told David that He would establish his seed to be King forever in His Kingdom. Both promises culminate in Yeshua taking His rightful seat on His kingly throne in His fourth Temple in the Land of Israel as He rules and reigns over all the Earth for 1,000 years! I am definitely looking forward to this Kingdom! How about you?

The Fourth Beast (Daniel 7:23–27)

> 23 "Thus he explained: 'The fourth beast will be a fourth kingdom on earth that will be different from all the other kingdoms. It will devour the whole earth, and trample it and crush it. 24 As for the ten horns, out of this kingdom ten kings will arise. Another will arise after them, but he will be different from the previous ones; he will subdue three kings. 25 He will speak words against the Most High, and will continually harass the *kedoshim* [holy ones] of the Most High, and will try to change the appointed times and law. The *kedoshim* will be handed over to him for a time, times and half a time. 26 But the court will sit and he will be stripped of his power to be destroyed and abolished for all time. 27 Then the kingdom, power, and greatness of the kingdoms under all heaven will be given to the people of the *kedoshim* of the Most High. Their kingdom is an everlasting kingdom, and all dominions will serve and obey him.'

In Chapter 7, Daniel had another vision. He saw four great beasts rising up from the great sea (verses 2–3). The great sea is typically known as the Mediterranean Sea. In Daniel, "the sea" is used as a symbol for the Gentile nations (Rev. 17:1, 15) while "the beautiful land" and "the land" represent the Land of Israel (see Dan. 9:6, 11:16). The fourth beast was terrifying, most dreadful, and crushed the other beasts (verses 7, 8, 19). This extremely strong beast had ten horns, and then another little horn grew up among them. The little horn pulled out three of the first horns by their roots. Daniel's great concern was to know the meaning of the fourth beast, so an angel of the Lord told him in verses 23–27.

The fourth beast is the fourth kingdom that will devour the whole known world. The fourth kingdom is the Roman Empire. One of the differences of this kingdom from the others is that ten kings will arise out of it. Verse 24 explains that the ten horns are actually symbols for these ten kings. I also believe these ten horns are the ten toes of the statue of Daniel 2:42.

The Aramaic word for "out of" (*min*) means "from." The most important idea here that is typically missed by most students of prophecy is that these ten kings come from or out of the revived Roman Empire. These ten kings simultaneously rule the world that is divided into ten kingdoms. There are some scholars who teach these ten kings and kingdoms are the European Union (EU) today. But this makes no sense in light of this section of Scripture. First, the EU has many more members than ten. Second and more importantly, the EU does not comprise the whole world. It is clear from verse 24 that ten kingdoms come from the one-world kingdom that conquers the world! Sometime after the one-world government is set up, then the world will be broken up into ten kingdoms. So, the European Union will comprise one of those kingdoms, but not all ten of them.

The world being divided up into ten kingdoms is not a new idea. It has been around for a while. If you perform an Internet search on "ten kingdoms," you will find many maps (some old ones) that have documented the world already broken up into ten regions or kingdoms. One of these maps is a direct result of a UN commissioned organization that was directed to perform this very act of dividing the world into ten kingdoms! The idea here is to take sovereignty away from nations and transform them into a region/kingdom. It is much easier to control ten kings than it is to control hundreds of nations.

Since the Roman Empire has yet to have ten kings rise from it in the past or present, we can look to the future for this to happen. This helps us to understand that the Roman Empire is to be revived to its former glory. Many global leaders in the past and present have called for a One-World Order where all nations would be governed by a single government. This One-World Order is the revived Roman Empire.

This Roman Empire will be revived sometime in the future. I believe the world will make a tremendous push for this One-World Order after the Ezekiel War. It does make sense that the world will greatly desire peace and want to have a peace treaty with Israel after the God of Israel destroys Russia and the confederacy. Therefore, the One-World Order—the revived Roman Empire will be created after the end of the Ezekiel War. After the One-World Order is around for some time, then its governing board will morph into ten constituent kingdoms. After the ten kings rule for some time, then "another" horn will arise.

This horn in verse 24 is the "small horn" of verse 8 who pulled three horns out of their roots and the "other horn" in verse 20 who caused three horns to fall. This horn also wages war against the *kedoshim* (holy ones) until the Ancient of Days comes and destroys the horn and his kingdom (verse 25). This horn is obviously the Anti-messiah who will arise on the scene after the ten kings take their kingdoms. The Anti-messiah will subdue (shephel) or humble three of these kings (verse 24). It does not necessarily mean these three kings die in these wars. Although Daniel does not mention this, these ten kings will eventually submit their power and authority to the Anti-messiah as the world leader. Anti-messiah will then give these ten kings their kingdoms to rule and reign, but they will be in allegiance to the Anti-messiah (Revelation 17:12–13). They will not receive their kingdoms from the Anti-messiah until he becomes the king of the world and gives them a kingdom to rule.

To summarize, Daniel 7:23–24 reveals that the One-World Order needs to emerge. This will be the revived Roman Empire. From the revived Roman Empire, ten kings will be crowned and will rule over ten kingdoms specified by the One-World Order. After the ten kings, the Anti-messiah arises and humbles three of the kings, takes over as world ruler, and then redistributes ten kingdoms to his newly appointed ten kings.

The Anti-messiah then speaks out against the Lord (verse 25). This will occur at the middle of Jacob's Trouble when he sets himself up as God in the Temple and requires worship from the Jewish and Gentile people of the world (Revelation 13:5–8; 2 Thessalonians 2:3–4). This act is commonly known as the Abomination of Desolation. Actually, the Anti-messiah, who receives his power from HaSatan, speaks arrogant words and blasphemes against God. He also has the authority to fight against the holy ones for forty-two months (three and a half years). He will overcome them and require the world to worship him as God!

The Anti-messiah will also try to change the "appointed times and law" of not only the Jewish people but the Gentiles, too. For the Jewish people, this would involve changing the customs and traditions of Judaism. This includes the Sabbath, feasts, Torah (the Law), and Temple worship. There is nothing new here. This is an age-old anti-Semitic action of the Gentile nations to force the Jews to become Gentiles. Many world and regional rulers have performed this wicked act many times over the millennia against the Jewish people before Anti-messiah will weave his evil web of treachery over the Jewish people.

The holy ones will be handed over to the Anti-messiah for a "time, times, and half a time." Anti-messiah will be allowed to make war with the holy ones for three and a half years. The Aramaic word for "time" (*iddan*) refers to "time or a year." Daniel uses *iddan* to mean years when writing about King Nebuchadnezzar's seven periods of time when he was banished by the Lord as a beast (4:16, 23, 25, 32).

In addition, in Daniel 11:13, the Hebrew word for "times" (*et*) is equated with the Hebrew word for "years" (*shanah*). So, the phrase "time, times, and half a time" equals "a year, two years, and half a year." Totalled up, the phrase equals three and a half years. Three and a half years lines up with the forty-two months of Revelation 13:5 and the Abomination of Desolation occurring at the middle of Jacob's Trouble (which is three and a half years into the Tribulation Period) spoken of by Yeshua in Matthew 24:15 and prophesied in Daniel 9:27.

However, Anti-messiah's reign will be short-lived (verses 26–27). The Lord's court in heaven will judge, and Messiah Yeshua shall return to earth, annihilate and destroy the evil ones, and set up His everlasting kingdom. Yeshua is the stone that crushed and destroyed all four kingdoms (2:34, 44–45). Yeshua's Messianic Kingdom will never be destroyed and will endure forever despite the fact that its duration is for a thousand years (Revelation 20:3). After the thousand years, Yeshua will continue to rule and reign in His Kingdom in the New Jerusalem with His Father for eternity.

Anti-Messiah, the King of the World (Daniel 11:36–45)

> 36 "So the king will do as he pleases, exalting and magnifying himself above every god. He will even speak outrageous things against the God of gods. He will prosper until the time of wrath is completed, for what has been decided will be done. 37 He will show no regard for the gods of his fathers or the one desired by women, nor will he show regard for any god, but will exalt himself above all. 38 Instead of these, he will honor a god of fortresses—a god his fathers did not acknowledge he will honor with gold, silver, precious stones and costly things. 39 He will attack strong fortresses with the help of a foreign god and will greatly honor those who acknowledge him. He will give them authority over many and will parcel out land for a price.
> 40 "Now at the time of the end the king of the south will attack him, and the king of the north will storm out

> against him with chariots, horsemen and many ships. He will invade lands and pass through them like an overflowing river. 41 He will also invade the Beautiful Land. Many will be overthrown, but these will escape from his hand: Edom, Moab, and the chief of the sons of Ammon. 42 He will extend his hand against other countries; the land of Egypt will not escape. 43 He will gain control over the hidden treasures of gold and silver, as well as all of the riches of Egypt. The Libyans and the Cushites will also be under his feet. 44 But reports from the east and north will alarm him, and he will set out in a great rage to destroy and annihilate many. 45 He will pitch his royal tents between the seas and the beautiful holy mountain. Yet he will meet his doom with no one to help him.'

Daniel 11 is a continuation of the vision he received in Chapter 10. The angel continues to prophesy concerning the Persian and Grecian kingdoms. Right up to verse 35, the prophecy has been fulfilled with amazing precision. The king of the north (verse 15) is Antiochus Epiphanes. After the Grecian kingdom was divided into four regions, Antiochus became the king of the northern section which included Syria. He strategically battled against the king of the south (Egypt) a few times in his reign. Verses 15–35 reveal Antiochus' exploits as king of the north, including his very own desecration of Israel's temple carried out in the Abomination of Desolation. Antiochus Epiphanes' act of abomination is the foreshadowing of Anti-messiah's Abomination of Desolation at the middle of Jacob's Trouble.

However, from verse 36 onward, we find no historical fulfillment in King Antiochus Epiphanes. We also know beyond any doubt that the "king" of verses 36–45 has changed identities because of verse 40. What is interesting is that rabbi Rashi believes this new king is the Roman Empire as a whole.

Since there is no historical fulfillment in this scripture reading, I believe it will occur in the future, being fulfilled in the Anti-messiah as the one-world ruler in Jacob's Trouble. As we go through the Scriptures, I will endeavor to prove this.

In verse 36, the king elevates himself above all gods and even speaks blasphemous words against God. He will prosper in his mission for a short time, but in the end, he will be destroyed. Many believers think this king is the Jewish Anti-messiah. The king most certainly is the Anti-messiah; however, the Anti-messiah is not Jewish, but Gentile. He is a ruler who comes out of the revived Roman Empire in Daniel 2:33, 40–43. He is also the little horn of Daniel 7:8, 20–25, who utters great boasts about himself and speaks out against the Most High God.

This king is the beast found in Revelation 13:3-10. He is arrogant and speaks blasphemies against the Lord (verses 5–6). He is allowed to make war against and overcome the holy ones in the Tribulation Period (verse 7). The king is the "one destined to be destroyed" and the "man of lawlessness" of 2 Thessalonians 2:3–4. He even exalts and displays himself as being God in the Temple! In Daniel 9:27, the king is the one who stops the Jewish people's worship of the Lord through the temple system and performs the Abomination of Desolation.

The king, then, shows no regard for three types of beings in verse 37. First, he shows no regard for the "gods of his fathers." This phrase is not without controversy because the KJV translates *elohey* as "God" instead of "gods." *Elohey* is a Hebrew word meaning both God and gods because it is found to be in the plural. So, the context dictates which definition to use. In verse 38, we see the Anti-messiah honors a "god" of fortresses whom his fathers did not know. Since the king shows no regard for any god, but honors a god of fortresses, a god in whom his fathers did not know (verse 38), then *elohey* must be speaking of "gods" and not "God." This shows us the context is discussing "gods" and not "God" and thus in verse 36 *elohey* should be translated "gods." This is important because it dramatically affects our understanding of who the Anti-messiah is!

If we believe *elohey* means "God," then that would make the Anti-messiah Jewish since he had no regard for the God of his fathers. But, if *elohey* means "gods" then the Anti-messiah would then be Gentile. Since *elohey* is correctly translated here as "gods," this tells us that the Anti-messiah is not Jewish but Gentile.

The second type of being that Anti-messiah shows no regard for is "the one desired by women." This phrase is better translated "the desire of women." If the desire of women is speaking only of Jewish women, then the meaning would include the desire to be the mother of the Jewish Messiah! However, if the desire of women speaks of women in general, then it probably means that Anti-messiah has no desire for women to fall in love with him, want to marry, or have children. In either case, the Anti-messiah has no desire to try and fulfill women's desires whatever they be! He only wants them to worship him (and HaSatan), and this makes sense.

The third type of being the Anti-messiah shows no regard for is any other god. Why? His desire is to magnify and glorify himself above all gods so that people will be deceived into thinking he is God. Ultimately, however, the Anti-messiah will honor one god: a god of fortresses (verses 38–39). The god of fortresses is HaSatan (Satan, the adversary) who gives the Anti-messiah his power and authority. HaSatan will give him victories over his enemies, and he will be king over people and land. The Anti-messiah will then give great honor to those who join him in his cause.

In verse 40, the king of the south and the king of the north war against the Anti-messiah king during the "time of the end." This phrase helps us to understand that the time period in question is the seventieth week of Daniel, Jacob's Trouble! This is the end of the ages and the end of the four Gentile kingdoms who dominated the world. In the first half of Jacob's Trouble, we shall see the Anti-messiah rise to power with his army, and here he fights against the king of the south and the king of the north. The king of the south would be the kingdom of Africa including Egypt. The king of the north would be the kingdom including Syria (Assyria is the ancient name).

In verse 40, something very unusual occurs. The exploits of the king of the north are documented in Daniel 11:1–35. He is the main subject matter for the chapter. However, in verse 40 we see the king of the north "will storm out against *him*" (emphasis mine). The question arises, "How does the king of the north war against himself?!" Obviously, he does not. The "him" is no longer the king of the north and has changed identities. The "him" is the Anti-messiah who speaks monstrous words against the God of Israel, exalts and magnifies himself as God, and tries to destroy Israel and the Jewish people! Therefore, the context has changed from historical to prophetic. This attack by the kings of the north and south against the Anti-messiah occur in the first half of Jacob's Trouble. These are two of the three kings that the Anti-messiah battles in Daniel 7 to establish himself as ruler of the world. It is obvious that the Anti-messiah is victorious as he will easy enter into other countries and overtake them.

Anti-messiah does not stop there in that he will also invade the "Beautiful Land" of Israel (verse 41)! His ultimate objective is to wipe Israel off the map and destroy every single Jewish person! He will be victorious in that many countries will fall, except Edom, Moab, and Ammon. Today these three ancient nations make up the western side of Jordan. Jordan signed a peace treaty with Israel in 1994, and I wonder if this escaping the clutches of Anti-messiah is one of God's blessings for Jordan. In any event, this area contains Mount Paran and the city of Petra spoken of by Habakkuk and Isaiah. It is believed that this area is where all the Jewish believers in the middle of Jacob's Trouble will evacuate to (Matthew 24:15). So, it makes sense, then, that this area will be rescued from the Anti-messiah and will be a safe zone for the Jewish people (more on this later).

Many countries will fall into the hands of the Anti-messiah (verse 42). A major conquest will be Egypt. All of its riches will be taken by the Anti-messiah. This will open the door to his conquest of Africa. Libya and Cush (Sudan) willingly submit to his leadership, as well (verse 43). The Anti-messiah then will become alarmed by reports from the north and the east (verse 44). Anti-messiah has fought against the king of the north and the king of the south; now it looks like he will go to war against the king of the east and the king of the north again. The king of the east is the kingdom that would include Mesopotamia (aka Chaldea).

The Anti-messiah will have great wrath against all who battle with him, and he will annihilate many. It seems that during this process of establishing himself as the king of the world, the Anti-messiah will set up his kingly palace (his headquarters) in Israel (verse 45). More specifically, it will be located between the seas and the "beautiful holy mountain." The beautiful holy mountain is Mount Zion, which is a reference to the city of Jerusalem. There are only three major seas in Israel: the Mediterranean Sea, the Dead Sea, and the Sea of Galilee. The valleys between these seas are the Jezreel Valley and the Jordan Valley.

The idea here is that the Anti-messiah will set up his kingly military headquarters somewhere in this valley area, which is between the three seas. The location is certainly large enough to house millions of soldiers, as well. This military camp of the Anti-messiah would be the headquarters and launching spot of the world's attack upon the city of Jerusalem at the end of Jacob's Trouble (Zechariah 14:2). However, in the end we must remember that Yeshua wins (verse 45)! The Anti-messiah will be defeated, come to his end, and no one will be able to help him. The beast (and the false prophet) will be quickly judged by Yeshua and sent to the Lake of Fire (Revelation 19:20).

Chart

As we view the chart, we notice the book of Daniel gives us tremendous insight into the end times and to the order of prophetic events. Four human Gentile kingdoms will rule the world. I believe the fourth kingdom (the Roman Empire), although still ruling the world today in many ways, will be revived after the Ezekiel War. It will lead the way to the One-World Order where ten kingdoms will be set up. After this, the Anti-messiah will rise to political and military power. He will battle three kings of the earth and overpower them in the first half of Jacob's Trouble. He will then appoint ten kings over the ten kingdoms and rule the world. Once he is made king of the world, he will require worship from the world and systemically try to destroy all Jewish people and all believers of Yeshua. The world is currently preparing for this One-World Order. The effects of this transformation will concurrently run through the first half of Jacob's Trouble. It will culminate with the Anti-messiah setting himself up as God in the Temple at the middle of the Tribulation Period. However, prior to Jacob's Trouble, the world will experience one of the most anticipated events in history—the Rapture!

Prayer

Father, we see the developments of the world converging into the One-World Order. Many nations have worked and continue to work to bring it about. Please continue to protect Israel and the Jewish people from the One-World Order that would ultimately try to destroy them. Please help us as believers in Yeshua to continue to use the spiritual gifts that You have given us to Your glory. Help us to share Yeshua with the Jewish people of the world with great boldness, love, and gentleness. I pray that many Jewish people would receive Yeshua as their Messiah, Lord, and Savior during this time of the development of the One-World Order. In Yeshua's name I pray, Amen.

Chapter 7

THE PRE-TRIBULATION RAPTURE: THE JEWISH CONNECTION

Thus far, we have discussed Israel today where hatred of Israel is increasing around the world. Many Middle Eastern nations have attacked Israel and Jewish people all over the earth, and will continue to do so. God is working to protect Israel and also to regather the Jewish people back to the Land. His desire is to judge, save, and then properly restore them back to the Land. Sometime in the near future the next prophetic event will occur.

The Ezekiel War is primed and ready to occur at any moment. Russia and the confederacy will attack Israel with the idea of capturing great spoil. No country (especially the United States) will come to Israel's aid, but the Lord will intervene in such a way that the world will recognize that He is the God of Israel! The Lord will destroy the nations and their armies that attack Israel. With God's victory in hand, the world will probably be ready to engage Israel with a seven-year peace treaty. This peace treaty will begin Jacob's Trouble, Daniel's seventieth week, also known as the seven-year Tribulation Period. However, just prior to Jacob's Trouble is the most anticipated event in the history of the Body of Messiah—the Rapture!

Although the Rapture is a greatly anticipated phenomenon that will greatly affect the world, there is much controversy concerning it within the Body of Messiah. Instead of the great hope Messiah intended it to have, there is great confusion and division. Some believe in a Pre-Tribulation (or Pre-Trib) Rapture, some believe in a Post-Tribulation (Post-Trib) Rapture, while some believe in a Mid-Tribulation (Mid-Trib) Rapture. Others believe in a Rapture that precedes the wrath of God (pre-wrath), and some do not believe in a Rapture at all. Believers tend to get emotionally connected to their view (since only one view can be correct), argue their position, and hence cause division in the body of Yeshua. The purpose of this section on the Rapture is to encourage and comfort believers that our Lord Yeshua is coming back for us! The "us" includes Jewish believers of Yeshua and thus makes the Rapture a prophetic event in Israel's history too! We should praise the Lord, knowing that He loves us so much that He is willing to rapture us to be in heaven with Him!

<u>Titus 2:11–15</u>

> 11 For the grace of God has appeared, bringing salvation to all men, 12 training us to deny ungodliness and worldly desires and to live in a manner that is self-controlled and righteous and godly in the present age. 13 We wait for the blessed hope and appearance of the glory of our great God and Savior, Messiah *Yeshua*. 14 He gave Himself for us so that He might redeem us from every lawless deed and so that He might purify for Himself a chosen people, zealous for good deeds. 15 So communicate these things, and encourage and correct with complete authority. Let no one look down on you.

Verse 11 recaps the good news that by God's grace, Yeshua came to save all people. In verse 12 we are instructed to deny worldly desires and live godly, righteous lives. In this process of growing in godliness, we are to "wait" for the blessed hope of our God and Savior Yeshua HaMeshiach (verse 13)! I believe this means we are to wait for and anticipate the blessed hope of the Rapture. In fact, the Greek word for "wait" (*prosdechomai*) is found to be in the present tense in the Greek grammar. This means that our waiting and expectation for the Rapture should occur on a continuous basis every day!

Now, in this great expectation of the Rapture, we should not only just be waiting on the Lord, but we should be zealous for performing good works out of love and faith (verse 14). Finally, in verse 15 we are exhorted to teach on all these topics and reprove in love with all authority when necessary. So, my goal in writing these chapters on the Rapture is to encourage in the teaching and show why I believe in the Pre-Tribulation Rapture. I have ten great reasons to believe in a Pre-Tribulation Rapture. Although each reason may not be sufficient enough in and of itself to convince you that the Rapture will happen before the Tribulation Period, the culmination of all ten reasons should be strong enough evidence.

The Jewish Connection

The first two great reasons why I believe in a Pre-Trib Rapture involve the Jewish connection. Not too many believers of Yeshua know or understand that the Rapture has a wonderful connection to the Jewish people. The first is the Messianic Jewish prophetic fulfillment and the second involves the prophetic aspects of the ancient Jewish wedding.

The Messianic Jewish Prophetic Fulfillment

The first great reason to believe in a Pre-Tribulation Rapture is the Messianic Jewish prophetic fulfillment of the Feast of

Trumpets (Yom Teruah, aka Rosh Hashanah). The Feast of Trumpets being the Messianic Jewish prophetic fulfillment of the Rapture is rarely discussed in theological circles concerning the Rapture. That's why I've placed this reason as my number one reason—many believers do not know of the Jewish roots of the Feast of Trumpets. If they see the connection between the Feast and the Rapture, then I think many more would believe in a Pre-Trib Rapture. I believe the Pre-Trib Rapture fulfills the prophetic understanding of the Feast of Trumpets.

The Seven Feasts of the Lord

In Leviticus 23, we are introduced to a summary of the seven feasts of the Lord. The Lord gave the Sabbath day and these seven feasts to the Jewish people as appointed times for congregational worship of the Lord during the year. Each feast has a historical and prophetic fulfillment and points to Yeshua being the Jewish Messiah. The first four feasts were all fulfilled in sequential order in the events surrounding Yeshua's First Coming. Pesach (Passover) points to Yeshua as the Passover lamb who shed His blood to become the sacrificial atonement for all of our sins. As our Passover lamb, He redeemed us from death to give us eternal life and have our names written in the Book of Life. Hag HaMatzot (The Feast of Unleavened Bread) reveals that Yeshua was the Lord's bread from heaven to become our sinless sacrifice who was lashed and pierced through. Every time we partake of the Lord's Supper (Seder) we are to remember His body broken, striped, and pierced through for our salvation.

Yom Habikkurim (aka Sfirat HaOmer, The Feast of First Fruits) shows us that Yeshua is the first fruits of the resurrection where all of His believers will join Him in the resurrection. These first three feasts were all fulfilled in Yeshua's death on the tree for our sins and His resurrection on the third day. The fourth feast of Shavuot (Pentecost) was fulfilled in the giving of the Ruach Kodesh (Holy Spirit). In addition, Shavuot is an unusual feast in that it also includes a very important aspect for the current age. Shavuot is the beginning of the age of the Body of Messiah! All believers in Yeshua, whether they are Jewish or Gentile, can enter into the Body of Messiah through faith in Yeshua. Hence, we see the first four feasts all fulfilled in the events surrounding the First Coming of our Lord. I believe we shall see the second set of feasts fulfilled surrounding the events of the Second Coming (which includes the Pre-Trib Rapture).

The fifth feast on the Jewish calendar is Rosh Hashanah. This is the feast that begins the New Year for Israel. Biblically, the feast is called "Yom Teruah," or the Feast of Trumpets. It is a day for blowing the *shofar* (ram's horn) to remind Israel to assemble and prepare for repentance on Yom Kippur (Day of Atonement).

<u>Leviticus 23:23–25</u>

> 23 *ADONAI* spoke to Moses saying: 24 "Speak to *Bnei-Yisrael,* saying: In the seventh month, on the first day of the month, you are to have a *Shabbat* rest, a memorial of blowing (*shofarot*), a holy convocation. 25 You are to do no regular work, and you are to present an offering made by fire to *ADONAI*."

In Leviticus 23:23–25, the Lord spoke to Moses with instructions on how to celebrate the fifth feast, the Feast of Trumpets. In verse 24, He tells Israel to have a worship service on the first day of the seventh month of Tishri. They were to perform animal sacrifices and have a "Shabbat rest." The Hebrew word *shabbaton* means a "day of rest" where the Jewish people were not to perform "regular" or laborious work (verse 25). Most work was forbidden, but they were allowed to prepare and cook food on this day. So, this *shabbaton* was not a "true" *shabbat* (Sabbath day) because they were allowed to do some work on the day, whereas on the weekly *shabbat*, all work was strictly forbidden.

More importantly, they were to blow (*teruah*) the shofar on this day as a memorial or reminder. They were to be reminded that the most important day of the year was coming (Yom Kippur) and that they should congregate in the area of the Tabernacle/Temple and prepare their hearts for repentance. In the Temple, the *shofarot* (ram's horns) were to be blown all day long (Numbers 29:1). They were blown to assemble the congregation to come and worship the Lord and prepare to repent on Yom Kippur. Now with this in mind, let us take a look at some New Covenant verses that discuss the timing of the blowing of the *shofarot* and the Rapture.

1 Thessalonians 4:13–18

> 13 Now we do not want you to be uninformed, brothers and sisters, about those who are asleep, so that you may not grieve like the rest who have no hope. 14 For if we believe that *Yeshua* died and rose again, so with Him God will also bring those who have fallen asleep in *Yeshua*. 15 For this we tell you, by the word of the Lord, that we who are alive and remain until the coming of the Lord shall in no way precede those who are asleep. 16 For the Lord Himself shall come down from heaven with a commanding shout, with the voice of the archangel and with the blast of God's *shofar,* and the dead in Messiah shall rise first. 17 Then we who are alive, who are left behind, will be caught up together with them in the clouds, to meet the Lord in the air—and so we shall always be with the Lord. 18 Therefore encourage one another with these words.

1 Thessalonians 4:13–18 is one of only a few verses in the Bible that specifically document the Rapture. Paul wrote to the

Thessalonians so that they would not grieve for those believers who had already died (verse 13). They should take comfort in the fact that the Lord will rapture all of His family someday in the future, whether they have died or are alive (verse 14). In verse 14, there is a fascinating clue that shows us the Rapture definitely occurs *prior* to the Second Coming of Yeshua! God will bring those who have already died in Yeshua "*with Him*" when He comes! So, what is going here? How can this be? If Yeshua is rapturing everyone from earth to the clouds, then how can there be believers in heaven before His coming? Well, let me explain.

The key is knowing that only those who have died in Yeshua will accompany Him in the Rapture! Those that already died in Yeshua have been separated from their bodies (absence from the body is presence with the Lord!). At their death, their souls and spirits went to be with Yeshua in heaven and their bodies were left on earth. So, when Yeshua comes to rapture believers, He will bring with Him the souls and spirits of those who have died in Him and will reunite them with their bodies. He then will transform the bodies into resurrection bodies. I believe this is the reason why the dead in Messiah rise first before those believers who are still alive at the time of the Rapture. Yeshua needs to complete the dead in Messiah before He translates those who are still alive on earth. This is a most fascinating passage and truly destroys the Post-Trib Rapture viewpoint!

This scripture reading helps us to determine that the Post-Trib Rapture view (that the Rapture occurs while Yeshua descends from heaven in the Second Coming) is incorrect. "Post-tribbers" should have a very difficult time trying to reconcile this point that the dead believers in heaven come back with Yeshua in the Rapture!

To exhort believers further, Yeshua reveals an order to the Rapture. Those who are alive and remain at the time of the Rapture will not go before those who have already died in Messiah (verse 15). However, in verse 16, we find out a few events that have to occur before the dead in Messiah rise. First, the Lord descends from heaven. Second, the voice of the archangel performs the military command to leave heaven. Third, the trumpet of God is blasted. The trumpet of God is the blowing of the *shofar*! Once these three events occur in heaven, then the dead in Messiah will rise first, followed by those believers who are alive on Earth at the time of the Rapture (verse 17). We shall all meet the Lord in the clouds, and thus we shall always be with the Lord. We are to take comfort in knowing this truth, rather than tearing apart and dividing up the Body of Messiah with our differing opinions concerning the timing of the Rapture (verse 18)!

There are a few special points that need to be clarified concerning these verses. First, the word *rapture* is not used in this verse, nor any other Scripture for that matter. Instead "caught up" (*harpazo*) is used to mean "snatching away." The idea here is that the Lord is physically snatching us away from Earth to meet Him in the clouds. We have a great example of Philip who was snatched away in Acts 8:39–40. After Philip baptized the Ethiopian eunuch, the Ruach Kodesh (Holy Spirit) snatched him away so that the eunuch no longer could see Philip. Philip then found himself at Azotus (aka Ashdod), a town about thirty miles away. I believe the Ruach instantaneously delivered Philip from the road leading to Gaza to Ashdod! This instantaneous Rapture is also substantiated by 1 Corinthians 15:52.

The second special point of clarification is found in question form, "Where do we go after we meet the Lord in the air?" Verse 17 gives us the answer. It states, "*and so we shall always be with the Lord.*" So, wherever the Lord goes, the raptured believers will go with Him. Presumably, He returns to heaven to perform the Bema Seat Judgment upon the Body of Messiah since we are not spiritually ready for the Marriage Supper of the Lamb or the Second Coming.

The third clarification concerns the shofar blast of the Rapture. Verse 16 clearly teaches that the shofar is sounded in connection with the Rapture. But this verse does not shed any light on when this shofar blast occurs in prophecy. However, our next scripture passage does!

1 Corinthians 15:50–53

> 50 Now I say this, brothers and sisters, that flesh and blood cannot inherit the kingdom of God, and what decays cannot inherit what does not decay.
> 51 Behold, I tell you a mystery:
> We shall not all sleep,
> but we shall all be changed—
> 52 in a moment, in the twinkling of an eye,
> at the last *shofar.*
> For the *shofar* will sound,
> and the dead will be raised incorruptible,
> and we will be changed.
> 53 For this corruptible must put on incorruptibility,
> and this mortal must put on immortality.

Paul starts this section off by stating that believers cannot inherit our eternal destiny with the Lord in human bodies. Our bodies must absolutely take on a different form for them to survive in the presence of the Lord. Thus, this is another wonderful reason for the Rapture. Our bodies must be transformed into resurrection bodies. These bodies will thus be able to live and thrive in the presence of God's glory! The question therefore is "When will this occur?"

Verse 52 shares with us that the Rapture will occur in the "twinkling of an eye." This phrase assures us that the transformation of our bodies will occur in a very rapid time frame. The twinkling of an eye is actually a whole lot faster than the blinking of an eye. Twinkling can occur in a fraction of a second. Paul's idea here is to show how quickly the Rapture will occur. At one moment, believers shall be on Earth; in the next fraction of a second we shall be flying toward the clouds to meet the Lord Yeshua in the air. It will definitely be an exciting flight!

This Rapture of all believers occurs at the "last shofar" blast. The "last shofar" (*eschatos salpinx*) blast is distinguished from the first shofar blast and thus there is a series of trumpet blasts that are occurring in this verse. Some believe this trumpet blast is the same blast found in Matthew 24:31. However, in Matthew, Yeshua will have already returned to earth in His Second Coming, presumably having performed His attack on Israel's enemies, and now His angels are gathering the elect from around the world at the shofar blast. There is no discussion in Matthew 24:31 of meeting the Lord in the air, nor the transformation of bodies into resurrection bodies.

Besides all this, the gathering here is speaking of only Jewish believers who will make it alive through Jacob's Trouble! It is not talking about all believers since the time of Yeshua's earthly ministry! In addition, this trumpet blast is described as being "great," but is not explained as the "last" trumpet blast. Therefore, Matthew's trumpet blast is not the same shofar blast of Paul's.

Still other believers think this last trumpet blast of 1 Corinthians 15 is connected with the seventh trumpet blast of Revelation 11:15–19. The problem with this understanding is that no Rapture occurs in Revelation! We only read about voices in heaven praising the Lord and announcing Yeshua's eternal kingly reign. There is indication that Yeshua's Second Coming is close, believers' rewards will be given out in the future, and God's enemies will be destroyed. But all of this has not occurred yet in the narrative! In addition, there is no indicator of a Rapture or transformation of bodies. The only connection between these two selections of Scripture is that there is a shofar blast. That is not enough evidence to suggest the Rapture will occur at the seventh trumpet blast some time close to the middle of the Tribulation Period. So, what could the "last trumpet" blast of 1 Corinthians 15 refer to?

Remember that we are discussing Yom Teruah, the Feast of Trumpets. This was the fifth feast of the year where the Jewish people were to blow the shofar (ram's horn) all day long to signal the people to come to worship the Lord and prepare to repent on Yom Kippur. The very last shofar blast of the day is called *tekiah gedolah* (the last longest blast). *Tekiah gedolah* is the longest and loudest blast of the day, signifying the final appeal to call the Jewish people to sincere repentance. Let's remember the "last trumpet" of 1 Corinthians 15 suggests that there must be a series of shofar blasts. I believe Paul was speaking of the *tekiah gedolah*, the longest, loudest, and final blast of the feast.

Therefore, I believe the Rapture is the fulfillment of the fifth feast of the Jewish people, Yom Teruah. What other "last trumpet" blast could this be? I know of no other series of trumpet blasts in Jewish history or culture that is as important or as distinguished as the shofar blasts on Yom Teruah.

<u>John 14:1–3</u>

> 1 "Do not let your heart be troubled. Trust in God; trust also in Me. 2 In My Father's house there are many dwelling places. If it were not so, would I have told you that I am going to prepare a place for you? 3 If I go and prepare a place for you, I will come again and take you to Myself, so that where I am you may also be.

Many believers know of these verses, but many do not understand the significant connection to the Rapture. The context shows Yeshua speaking to His disciples (specifically to Peter). In verse 1, He tells them not to be troubled because of His previous statement in John 13:36–38. There He told them He was leaving them and that they would not be able to follow Him immediately, although later on they would be able to follow. I believe Yeshua was saying that He was going to heaven and that they would not be able to go with Him at that time, but reassured them that when He comes back during the Rapture that they would be able to follow Him. In verse 2, Yeshua speaks of the Father's house in heaven. He is going to heaven to prepare a place for them.

In verse 3, Yeshua makes a promise. If He goes to heaven to prepare a place for them, then He would come back for them. This is the Rapture! In the Rapture, Yeshua is receiving the disciples (and the rest of the Body of Messiah) unto Himself. From that moment onward, wherever Yeshua is, we shall be, too. We shall follow Him wherever He goes. If He goes to heaven, then we go to heaven. If He goes to earth, then we go to earth. The main point here is that Yeshua is preparing a dwelling place in heaven for us to live in! So, the inference is that we shall actually go to heaven with Yeshua.

If the Rapture is "post-trib," then believers do not make it to heaven at all. In typical Post-Trib Rapture belief, believers are raptured while Yeshua is on His way down in the Second Coming. We meet Him in the clouds and then accompany Him to earth. If this is true, then why is Yeshua preparing a dwelling place in heaven for us to live in? If we never make it to heaven in the Rapture, then why is Yeshua wasting His time and effort in preparing dwelling places that no one will live in?

If the Rapture is pre-tribulation, then Yeshua preparing places for us makes much more sense. We shall dwell in heaven for the next seven Earth years while we wait for Jacob's Trouble to begin and end. The inference Yeshua makes here in verse 3 is that, after the Rapture occurs, we all go back to heaven so we can live in our dwelling places. But, where are the dwelling places specifically located in heaven? Many believe the dwelling places are found in the New Jerusalem spoken of in Revelation 21:2. This makes a lot of sense. Hebrews 12:22–23 states the Body of Messiah is already enrolled in the heavenly Jerusalem! This is the New Jerusalem, the city of God, also spoken of in Revelation 21.

"Written in a scroll" (*apographo* from Hebrews 12:23) means "recorded, enrolled, or inscribed in a register." We are officially registered as citizens of the New Jerusalem. The issue is that we have yet to arrive in heaven and claim that citizenship. This will happen at the Rapture. What is also fascinating is that the "spirits of righteous ones made perfect" are there in the New Jerusalem right now as well! These are the Old Covenant believers' spirits that separated from their bodies at death and flew to be in the New Jerusalem in heaven when the Lord set the captives free from Abraham's bosom (Paradise) during His three days in the tomb! So, the Old Covenant believers also take part in the Messianic Millennial Kingdom, as we shall see later in this book.

There is only one other known heavenly structure spoken of in Scripture and that is God's Tabernacle. This is the tabernacle that Moses patterned the earthly Tabernacle after. Neither Tabernacle is structured to house millions (and probably billions) of believers. So, the next-best location we know of is the New Jerusalem that obviously is created to house billions of believers for eternity! It does make sense that this is what Yeshua was talking about in John 14:3.

Revelation 19:5–9

> 5 Then a voice came from the throne, saying:
> "Praise our God,
> all you His servants and
> all who fear Him,
> both the small and the great!"
> 6 Then I heard something like the voice of a great multitude—like the roar of rushing waters or like the rumbling of powerful thunder—saying, "Halleluyah!
> For *ADONAI Elohei-Tzva'ot* [Lord God of Hosts] reigns!
> 7 Let us rejoice and be glad
> and give the glory to Him!

For the wedding of the Lamb has come,
and His bride has made herself ready,
8 She was given fine linen to wear, bright and clean!
For the fine linen is the righteous deeds of the *kedoshim* [holy ones]."
9 Then the angel tells me, "Write: How fortunate are those who have been invited to the wedding banquet of the Lamb!" He also tells me, "These are the true words of God."

This reading focuses on the Marriage Supper of the Lamb and sets up for the Second Coming found in verses 11–21. Verses 5–6 reveal a great multitude of bondservants singing praise to our God. These bondservants are believers in Yeshua and are engaged in the Bema Seat Judgment of the Lord. Verse 7 declares that the bride of Messiah has made herself ready for the marriage of the Lamb. It certainly looks like the wedding of the Lamb with His bride has occurred in heaven before the Second Coming! But first, the Body of Messiah has to prepare for the wedding by putting on their wedding clothes.

Verse 8 tells us that she clothes herself with bright and clean fine linen (robes). The fine linen represents the righteous acts of the believers. This shows us that the Bema Seat Judgment has occurred in heaven with the Body of Messiah; all believers are now wearing their wedding garments of clean linen and are ready for the wedding ceremony! The Bema Seat Judgment is Messiah's judgment of all the good works that believers performed in their earthly lives. Messiah will judge whether these works were performed in love and faith or whether they were accomplished in human fleshly desires. Verse 9 finishes this section to show that all believers who are invited to the Marriage Supper of the Lamb are truly blessed! It looks as though the Marriage Supper is going to occur on earth after the Second Coming (more on the Bema Seat Judgment and the Marriage Supper of the Lamb later).

The main point that needs to be brought home here is that there is a great multitude of believers in heaven who have gone through the Bema Seat Judgment and been married to Messiah, all *before* the Second Coming of Yeshua! "Post-tribbers" should have a very difficult time reconciling this truth with their viewpoint, especially since Yeshua has yet to leave heaven for earth in the Second Coming. The issue is, how does the Body of Messiah get to heaven prior to the Second Coming? Obviously, the Rapture has to happen *before* the Second Coming! In light of these scriptures, the Post-Trib Rapture view is greatly damaged!

I believe the Messianic Jewish fulfillment of the Rapture occurs on the Feast of Trumpets sometime in the future. The blowing of shofarot (ram's horns) all day long on this feast is a compelling argument for the Rapture occurring on the last, longest blast of the day. It is a day of preparation to get ready for repentance on Yom Kippur. I also see it as a day of preparation to get ready for the Second Coming!

The Pre-Tribulation Rapture fulfills the Feast of Trumpets and also ends the age of the Body of Messiah. This age began with the fourth feast of Pentecost (Shavuot) almost 2,000 years ago, and I believe will end with the fifth Feast of Trumpets (aka Rosh Hashanah). Remember, the first four feasts have already been fulfilled in Yeshua in temporal order. The fifth feast, the Feast of Trumpets, is the next feast to be fulfilled in prophetic time. The first great reason to believe in the Pre-Trib Rapture is the wonderful Jewish connection with the feast of Yom Teruah (the Feast of Trumpets).

The Ancient Jewish Wedding and the Rapture

The second great reason to believe in a Pre-Trib Rapture is the wonderful picture of the ancient Jewish wedding. The ancient Jewish wedding was a beautiful depiction of the love between a man and a woman. It is the extension of God's institution of marriage given to all of humankind. Every aspect of the Jewish wedding is a wonderful picture of God's plan of restoration for New Covenant believers in Yeshua. The Lord even calls us the Bride of Messiah. As we shall see in this study, we are the betrothed bride-to-be that is not yet joined to her loving husband. The ancient Jewish wedding process included a number of stages. The first stage is called the *marriage covenant*.

The Marriage Covenant

The first stage of the Jewish wedding process was for the father of the groom to arrange the marriage with the father of the bride. In the ancient world, fathers would often arrange a marriage without their children's consent. Moreover, the children may not have even met one another until the day of the wedding.

This marriage covenant was sealed with the *bride price*. The father of the groom would pay the bride price to the father of the bride, sealing their commitment to the marriage of their children. The newly-formed couple was then betrothed to one another. The betrothal was similar to our modern engagement period before marriage, but with a much greater commitment level. The betrothed couple entered into a covenant relationship as if they were already married. A *ketubah* (marriage contract) was drawn up to document all of the bridegroom's provisions for his bride and to show the legality of the wedding. The couple was considered to be legally married in all respects except for the consummation of the marriage. They would also not live together until after the marriage ceremony. This betrothal period would typically last one year, but in the case of young children, it could be many years.

God the Father has already performed the marriage covenant with the Body of Messiah. The Body of Messiah was betrothed to Yeshua as the bride when the Father paid the bride price with His Son's blood sacrifice. Yeshua is the bridegroom and the bride price at the same time. John 3:16 tells us that the Father gave up His only Son so that all who believed in Him would not perish but have eternal life. Ephesians 5:25-27 states that Yeshua loved the Body of Messiah so much that He gave His life so that she could be cleansed and sanctified. He will eventually present her to Himself as a holy, righteous, and just bride. Acts 20:28 states that Yeshua purchased the Body of Messiah with His own blood. Therefore, Yeshua was the bride price so that the Body of Messiah could enter into a holy, righteous, and just covenant with the Father and the Son.

The Preparation

The second stage of the ancient Jewish wedding process was the preparation. The preparation period was known as the betrothal. During the betrothal, the bride would prepare and ready herself to become a qualified wife for her husband-to-be. The groom, on the other hand, returned to his father's house and prepared the bridal chamber. This bridal chamber would be their home.

The Lord has partially fulfilled this step of the Jewish wedding as well. While the Body of Messiah continues to become a qualified bride here on earth, the groom has returned home to heaven to prepare the bridal chamber. In 2 Corinthians 11:2, Paul states that the Body of Messiah is betrothed to Yeshua and that she is in process of becoming a pure virgin. This process represents the sanctification process the Body of Messiah is currently embarked upon. Our goal in life before the Pre-Trib Rapture occurs is to become just like Yeshua. When we are completely purified, we will be presented to Messiah for the wedding. This purification process concludes with the Bema Seat Judgment in heaven just prior to the wedding ceremony and the Second Coming of Yeshua.

In John 14:2–3, Yeshua makes a promise to His *talmidim* (disciples—representatives for the universal Body of Messiah). He promises that He will ascend to heaven where His Father's house is located to prepare a home for the Body of Messiah. This promise includes that, one day in the future, He will come back to retrieve His bride and bring her to her new home in heaven! This part of the promise has not been fulfilled yet, but will be in the future. Yeshua has yet to come back for His bride since we are not ready to be fetched by our bridegroom. There is much work to be done. We are still being nourished and cherished by the Lord in this sanctification process.

The Fetching of the Bride

The return of the bridegroom was a fascinating event. No one in the community knew when the bridegroom would return for his bride. Neither the bride nor the groom knew. Only the groom's father knew. Once the father determined that the time was right, he would then send the groom to fetch his bride. The groom would then go retrieve his bride and bring her to their new home in a joyous processional. A wonderful example of this type of processional is found in Matthew 25:1–13. In verse 6 of Yeshua's parable, a shout warned the bride's friends that the groom was coming and that they should finalize her preparations. In verses 7–13, the prudent friends who were properly prepared were invited to be a part of the processional and come to the wedding. But the foolish ones who were not ready for the processional were not invited to the wedding.

In 1 Thessalonians 4:13–18, we find the processional order to the Rapture. In verse 16, the Lord descends from heaven with a shout. This is the shout to prepare the bride for her soon-arriving groom. Then the archangel (Michael presumably) reiterates the shout to the commanders of the army and the trumpet of God (the shofar) is blasted, so all the heavenly host know the time of the fetching has come. In verse 17, Yeshua fetches His bride, the Body of Messiah, in the clouds, and thus we shall always be with our groom! Yeshua then brings us home to the bridal chamber He has prepared for His bride in heaven.

The Bride Cleansed

Prior to the wedding ceremony, the bride performs *tevilah*. *Tevilah* is a ceremonial water cleansing (involving a full-body immersion) much like the priests of the Tabernacle and Temple performed before they ministered unto the Lord. It has been performed by Jewish women prior to their wedding ceremonies for millennia. The *tevilah* for the bride is a ceremonial cleansing, symbolizing her physical and spiritual purity as she enters into a new married life.

In 1 Corinthians 3:12–15, we learn of the Bema Seat Judgment of Yeshua. This is the final cleansing stage of the Body of Messiah so that we can live with our holy, righteous, and just God in a covenantal marriage relationship. Although this cleansing is not a specific water cleansing, it is very symbolic of the *tevilah*! In verses 12–13, the Body of Messiah is encouraged to build on the foundation of salvation with good works performed in faith and love. Why? Because all of our good works will be revealed by Yeshua's fire as to whether they truly were good or not. Those works that were good in the eyes of the Lord will remain and we shall have rewards for them. Those works burned up by the fire shall suffer loss. However, even if all of our works are burned up we do not lose our salvation. God's grace secures our salvation in heaven! With Yeshua's judgmental fire of our good works, He finishes the cleansing process of the purification of the bride. Now she is ready for the marriage ceremony!

In Revelation 19:5–8, we find the Body of Messiah already in heaven, singing praises to our Lord and getting ready for the marriage ceremony. In verses 5–6, the bondservants (who are the bride) are praising the Lord with a corporate "Halleluyah."

Verse 7 tells us the bride has made herself ready, for the marriage of the Lamb has come! The bride has already gone through the Bema Seat Judgment. She has been completely purified and has received her rewards. She is now ready for the wedding ceremony itself. Verse 8 shows us that we have been purified since our robes are bright and clean and they represent the righteous acts we performed on Earth. Isn't it obvious that each believer is wearing their robe, signifying how clean and pure they are in the Lord? The sanctification process of the virgin bride is complete and she is now ready to marry her bridegroom!

The Wedding Ceremony

The Jewish wedding ceremony was typically conducted in the home of the groom. Only a few people were invited to this ceremony. Usually the immediate family and two witnesses were the only ones involved.

Revelation 19:7 announces that the marriage of the Lamb to His bride will occur in heaven. Since the bride has made herself ready for the wedding, it is presumed that the actual wedding ceremony will take place in heaven just prior to the Second Coming of Yeshua. It makes sense that the Lord would want His Bride to be complete in the purification process prior to the Second Coming! How can an impure Body of Messiah be of any use in the Messianic Millennial Kingdom? Remember, Yeshua brings His bride with Him wherever He goes! The Greek actually confirms this. The typical word for "bride" (*numphe*) is not used in this verse, but rather the Greek word for "wife" (*gune*) is. This shows the bride of Messiah has officially become the wife of Messiah since she has made herself ready for the wedding ceremony!

The Marriage Feast

The marriage feast would follow the wedding ceremony, and typically many more people were invited to the feast than the few who were invited to the ceremony. The marriage feast could last for up to seven days!

In Revelation 19:9, the marriage feast of the Lamb and His bride is announced after the marriage occurred in verse 7. There is no indication that the marriage feast will occur at this time in heaven. Rather, starting in verse 11, Yeshua and His bride, the Body of Messiah, descend from heaven to earth. It looks as though Yeshua needs to finish destroying the enemy of the Jewish people before He can begin the Messianic Millennial Kingdom. I believe the marriage feast will be served at the beginning of the Kingdom. This makes sense since the world, the people, the bride, and of course the Groom, will all be purified for the Kingdom. This purity is paramount for the Messianic Millennial Kingdom to begin!

In summary, as we can see from the stages of the ancient Jewish wedding, the Body of Messiah is currently found at the preparation stage waiting for the fetching of the bride to come. The Father sealed the marriage covenant relationship between His Son Yeshua and the Body of Messiah with His Son's spilled blood on the tree. When Yeshua shed His blood and died on the tree, He became the bride price for the Body of Messiah. He was the bride price and the bridegroom all wrapped up into one. The Body of Messiah was betrothed to Yeshua, desirous of the future wedding ceremony, but that would have to wait. First, the bride has to become the qualified wife for our husband-to-be. This means that we have to live holy and righteous lives here on Earth. The Lord has encouraged all of us to live in faith and love by the power of the Ruach Kodesh. All along, we are to wait for our bridegroom to return to fetch His bride!

This fetching of the bride perfectly lines up with the Pre-Trib Rapture. It is the next phase of the ancient Jewish wedding process. Once the Lord fetches and brings us to heaven, He will perform His Bema Seat Judgment and finish our cleansing and purification process. After the cleansing process where we become the virgin bride, then we can finally be married to Yeshua in a wonderful ceremony. Then we shall all return to Earth to have the wedding feast and live out our marriage covenant in the Messianic Millennial Kingdom. I don't know how you feel about this, but this will be an awesome sight to see and a great event to participate in. I cannot wait to be there!

Chapter 8

The Pre-Tribulation Rapture: Eight More Great Reasons to Believe

The first two great reasons to believe in the Pre-Trib Rapture involved the Jewish connection. The Messianic Jewish roots are so important to understanding the Bible in general, Israel in prophecy, and the Pre-Trib Rapture, specifically. The Rapture was seen as being fulfilled in the Feast of Yom Teruah. The last shofar blast is the *tekiah gadol,* the last and greatest blast of the feast. The Rapture was also seen as being fulfilled in the ancient Jewish wedding process. Currently, the Body of Messiah is waiting for the groom to fetch her and return to heaven for the wedding ceremony. There are eight more great reasons to believe in the Pre-Trib Rapture.

The Purposes of Jacob's Trouble

The third great reason to believe in the Pre-Trib Rapture concerns the purposes of Jacob's Trouble. These purposes actually conflict with the purpose of the Rapture of the Body of Messiah. One purpose of Jacob's Trouble is for God to execute judgment upon the wicked of the world so that they might repent. The book of Revelation reveals this theme throughout its chapters. Verses discussing the Rapture never talk about judgment of the world or the Body of Messiah. Any verses that connect God's wrath with the Rapture always discuss the Body of Messiah's deliverance *from* God's wrath! This helps to make them different events.

In addition, no scripture is found in Revelation 4–22 that discusses the Body of Messiah. It is mysteriously missing. The only time the Body of Messiah is mentioned is in Revelation 19 which shows the Body already in heaven prior to the Second Coming. If the Body of Messiah is to go through the Tribulation Period, one would think it would be mentioned a number of times in this book, but it is not! Revelation does discuss Israel, Jewish and Gentile people, and especially individual believers of Yeshua, but it never talks about the Body of Messiah going through the Tribulation Period. Therefore, God's purpose for Jacob's Trouble is to judge the world, not to judge the Body of Messiah.

A second purpose for Jacob's Trouble is to prepare Israel (and the world) for Messiah's coming. In Chapter 3 of this book, we examined Ezekiel's prophecy concerning Israel in 36:22–28. In that passage, we find God regathering all the Jewish people from around the world back to the Land of Israel. He will then judge them in the Tribulation Period, save them at the end, and properly restore them back to the Land under the kingship of Yeshua HaMeshiach. So, Jacob's Trouble prepares Israel for Messiah's coming. Many will not like how this preparation works out in their lives, but the end result will be fabulous. There are additional verses that show God preparing Israel during Jacob's Trouble for the coming of Yeshua.

In Daniel 12:1 we see Michael the Archangel who stands guard over Israel. He "will arise" or stand to fight against the evil ones. Why will the great prince Michael have to fight on Israel's behalf? A time of distress like no other will come upon Israel. This "time of distress" will be worse than what the Nazis perpetrated against the Jewish people. This time of distress is obviously Jacob's Trouble. So, no wonder Israel will need help from Michael! Not only is God preparing Israel for the future Tribulation, but He will rescue all Jewish believers found in the Book of Life. That most certainly is preparing Israel for the coming of Messiah!

In Jeremiah 30:3–11 we also see the Lord preparing Israel for Messiah's coming. In verse 3, the Lord promises Israel that He will bring them back to the Land. In verses 5–7, the Lord warns Israel that they will be terrorized in the "time of Jacob's distress." This is the biblical phrase used to help us identify the title "Jacob's Trouble" for the Tribulation Period. It will be a most horrible time for Israel, but the Lord promises Israel will be saved from it (verse 7). But in verses 8–10, we see the Lord telling Israel not to fear because God will take care of the nations so that Israel can once again serve the Lord their God in the Messianic Kingdom. Finally, in verse 11, the Lord encourages Israel to remember that He is with them and will save them. Even though they have to be chastened in the Tribulation Period for their sin, they will not be completely destroyed! The Lord will save them from the hands of the Anti-messiah and deliver them into the Kingdom. What a wonderful promise of the Lord to prepare Israel for her Messiah!

These scriptures show that one purpose of Yeshua's Second Coming is to save and deliver the nation of Israel from Jacob's Trouble. Israel is being prepared throughout the Tribulation for His return! There is no mention of a Rapture connected with these events.

God's Two Economies

The fourth great reason to believe in the Pre-Trib Rapture concerns God's two economies: Israel and the Body of Messiah. God has a special plan and purpose for Israel and a special plan and purpose for the Body of Messiah. It is especially interesting to know that God's timetable for each group is mutually exclusive. He is dealing with each group in different timeframes when it comes to prophecy. Let me explain by exploring Daniel 9:24–27.

Daniel 9:24–27

> 24 "Seventy weeks are decreed concerning your people and your holy city,
> to put an end to transgression
> to bring sin to an end,
> to atone for iniquity,
> to bring in everlasting righteousness,
> to seal up vision and prophecy,
> and to anoint the Holy of Holies.
> 25 So know and understand:
> From the issuing of the decree to restore and to build Jerusalem until the time *Mashiach* [Messiah], the Prince, there shall be seven weeks and 62 weeks. It will be rebuilt, with plaza and moat, but it will be in times of distress.
> 26 Then after the 62 weeks *Mashiach* will be cut off and have nothing. Then the people of a prince who is to come will destroy the city and the sanctuary. But his end will come like a flood. Until the end of the war that is decreed there will be destruction.
> 27 Then he will make a firm covenant with many for one week, but in the middle of the week he will put an end to sacrifice and offering. And on a wing of abominations will come one who destroys, until the decreed annihilation is poured out on the one who destroys.'"

The Lord sends the archangel Gabriel to explain Daniel's vision in Chapter 9. In verse 24, seventy weeks, or 490 years, are decreed for "your people" and "your holy city." Daniel's people are the Jewish people and Daniel's holy city is, of course, the city of Jerusalem! This prophecy is specifically and strictly for the Jewish people alone. No other group of people can be included here. This verse is especially not discussing the Body of Messiah. Gabriel additionally informs us that the Jewish people and Jerusalem need to perform six most important prophetic events within this timeframe of seventy weeks.

Verse 25 tells us that there will be a total of sixty-nine weeks (or 483 years), before the Messiah will present Himself as the Prince (of peace) for Israel. When Yeshua triumphantly entered into Jerusalem just prior to His sacrificial death on the tree, the sixty-nine weeks were fulfilled.

Verse 26 tells us that Messiah will die and have nothing *after* the sixty-nine weeks were over and *before* the seventieth week begins (in verse 27). This verse suggests that there is a mysterious time period between the sixty-ninth and seventieth week that technically should not be there. In verse 27, the Anti-messiah performs the Abomination of Desolation in the middle of the seventieth week and begins his holocaust against the Jewish people.

What I glean from this scripture passage and Ezekiel 36:24–28 is that the Lord is working His plan for the regathering, judgment, salvation, and restoration of Israel within the prophecy of the seventy weeks. Most of this plan will occur during the seventieth week of Daniel, which is Jacob's Trouble. But before He finishes His plan with Israel, He decided to place His plan for the Body of Messiah right between the sixty-ninth week and the seventieth week. This mysterious time period has lasted for almost 2,000 years.

What is the Lord doing here? He put His seventy-week plan for Israel on hold. He set it aside and began His plan for the Body of Messiah whereby any Jewish or Gentile individual person can repent and believe in Yeshua to be saved and become a member of the Body of Messiah. Once the Pre-Trib

Rapture occurs, the age of the Body of Messiah ends, and God re-focuses on His plan for Israel and finishes out the seventieth week of Daniel. We must remember that even though the Lord has set aside His plan for Israel in this age, He is still working to save Jewish people, still working to regather all the Jewish people back to Israel, and still blessing the nation of Israel. So, although His plan for Israel was set aside, He has still been working out some aspects of His plan for Israel over the past 2,000 years.

Jeremiah 31:31–34

> 31 "Behold, days are coming"
> —it is a declaration of *ADONAI*—
> "when I will make a new covenant
> with the house of Israel
> and with the house of Judah—
> 32 not like the covenant
> I made with their fathers
> in the day I took them by the hand
> to bring them out of the land of Egypt.
> For they broke My covenant,
> though I was a husband to them."
> it is a declaration of *ADONAI*.
> 33 "But this is the covenant I will make with the house of Israel after those days"
> —it is a declaration of *ADONAI*—
> "I will put My *Torah* within them.
> Yes, I will write it on their heart.
> I will be their God
> and they will be My people.
> 34 No longer will each teach his neighbor
> or each his brother, saying: 'Know *ADONAI*,'
> for they will all know Me,
> from the least of them to the greatest."

it is a declaration of *ADONAI*.
"For I will forgive their iniquity,
their sin I will remember no more."

Jeremiah 31 helps us to better understand these two economies of the Lord. In verse 31, the Lord predicts He will cut a New Covenant with the house of Israel and the house of Judah. The question is "Who are the house of Israel and the house of Judah?" The house of Israel refers to the northern kingdom, and the house of Judah refers to the southern kingdom. In Old Covenant times, the northern kingdom was called the house of Israel, and the southern kingdom was called the house of Judah (Ezekiel 37:15–22). Ezekiel also confirms that the two kingdoms shall no longer be divided, but united (verse 22).

The issue here in Jeremiah's prophecy is that God will make a covenant with a single nation of Israel, not two kingdoms! In this verse, He is not speaking of cutting a covenant with the United States, Russia, Iran, Sudan, the European Union, or any other nation. Nor is He talking of starting a covenant with the Body of Messiah. The Lord is strictly speaking of a New Covenant for Israel. What is the New Covenant going to be like?

Jeremiah answers this question in verse 32 in the negative, meaning he tells us what the New Covenant is *not* going to be like. The New Covenant is not going to be like the covenant the Lord made with Israel as He brought them out of the land of Egypt. This was the Mosaic Covenant. So, the Lord says the New Covenant is a different covenant from the Mosaic Covenant. Many in the Messianic Jewish movement around the world believe the New Covenant is just an extension of the Mosaic Covenant. However, the Lord is quite clear here in that the New Covenant is not like the Mosaic Covenant. It is most definitely a different covenant! The Lord also wanted Israel to remember that they broke the Old Covenant, even though the Lord was a faithful husband to them. One major difference between these covenants is that the New Covenant is an unconditional covenant that actually cannot be broken! When is this New Covenant going to begin for Israel?

Once again, Jeremiah answers this question in verses 33–34. Suffice to say, the New Covenant for the nation of Israel will begin in the Messianic Millennial Kingdom! The Torah will be written on their hearts, their sin will be forgiven, and they shall all know the Lord (more is written on these verses in Chapter 17). This shall only be fully executed for the nation of Israel in the Kingdom age.

We need to understand the difference now between the nation of Israel and individual Jewish people. God will make the New Covenant with the nation of Israel during the Messianic Millennial Kingdom. So, what happened to the New Covenant beginning almost 2,000 years ago? Well, actually it did begin 2,000 years ago with Yeshua's death and resurrection. However, the nation of Israel did not enter into the New Covenant back then because the Sanhedrin (spiritual leadership of Israel) and most of the Jewish people rejected it by rejecting Yeshua as the Jewish Messiah. It was the only covenant that was rejected by the nation of Israel. So God, in His infinite wisdom, opened up the New Covenant to individual Jewish and Gentile people. Any individual who believes in Yeshua enters into this New Covenant.

Therefore, this section, coupled with Daniel 9, once again shows us a separation of how the Lord is working in His two economies: Israel and the Body of Messiah. God began the New Covenant with the Body of Messiah almost 2,000 years ago, and God will begin the New Covenant with the nation of Israel in the Messianic Millennial Kingdom. The Body of Messiah's time period will end at the Pre-Trib Rapture, while Israel starts their New Covenant at the beginning of the Messianic Millennial Kingdom.

Colossians 1:24–27

> 24 Now I rejoice in my sufferings for you, and in my physical body—for the sake of His body, Messiah's community—I fill up what is lacking in the afflictions of Messiah. 25 I became its servant according to God's commission, given to me for you, in order to declare His message in full—26 the mystery that was hidden for ages and generations, but now has been revealed to His *kedoshim* [holy ones]. 27 God chose to make known to them this glorious mystery regarding the Gentiles—which is Messiah in you, the hope of glory!

The mysterious time period between the sixty-ninth week and seventieth week of Daniel is also found in the New Covenant writings. In Colossians 1:24–25, Paul reveals how he is the called shepherd of the Body of Messiah to preach the word of God. Paul then explains in verse 26 that this mystery was hidden from past ages (i.e., Old Covenant believers) and revealed to the current age (i.e., New Covenant believers). The mystery is the fact that Gentiles are able to be saved by Messiah and are added to the olive tree of Israel (verse 27).

It is interesting to note that, although the Lord loves all people and everyone is equal before His eyes, there still are racial distinctions in the New Covenant. Gentiles are being *added to* the Messianic Jewish Body of Messiah, but the Lord still sees Jewish people and Gentile people as distinctive groups within the Body of Messiah. These scriptures help us to see the mystery of the Body of Messiah during the New Covenant era as opposed to Israel during the Old Covenant. The Lord is dealing with the two groups in two different time periods or ages.

Ephesians 2:11–14

> 11 Therefore, keep in mind that once you—Gentiles in the flesh—were called "uncircumcision" by those called "circumcision" (which is performed on flesh by hand). 12 At that time you were separate from Messiah, excluded from the commonwealth of Israel and strangers to the covenants of promise, having no hope and without God in the world. 13 But now in Messiah *Yeshua,* you who once were far off have been brought near by the blood of the Messiah. 14 For He is our *shalom,* the One who made the two into one and broke down the middle wall of separation.

Ephesians 2:11–14 continues this theme of the mystery of God. In verses 11–12, we read that the Gentiles had no hope because they were separated from Messiah; they were not included in the commonwealth of Israel, and thus were strangers to Israel's covenants. However, Yeshua's death on the tree changed all of that. Instead of being far away from God, Yeshua brought them close to Him through His blood (verse 13).

So, the mystery of God was including the Gentiles with the Jewish people in the Body of Messiah for an unknown period of time once He initiated the New Covenant. This New Covenant includes individual Jewish people, but not the nation of Israel as a whole. Here is where the separation occurs. Before this New Covenant began, the Gentiles were entirely without God in their world and strangers to the promised covenant. But with Yeshua, they have been brought near and have become a part of the New Covenant.

Once again, it is interesting to see the Lord's distinction of the Gentiles and Israel. Even though we are all considered the same children of God in the Body of Messiah, the Lord still uses and sees a distinction between Jewish and Gentile people. Verse 14 shows the Body of Messiah, although made up of individual Jews and Gentiles, were made to be one group through Yeshua's death. How is this so? The enmity between the groups was dealt with on the tree. Yeshua now is our peace (verses 14–15)!

I believe one reason the Lord continues to use these distinctions is to show those who believe in Replacement Theology that they are incorrect. If the Gentiles have *replaced* Israel in God's covenantal promises, then He would not continue to distinguish between them in the New Covenant writings.

Romans 11:25–27

> 25 For I do not want you, brothers and sisters, to be ignorant of this mystery—lest you be wise in your own eyes—that a partial hardening has come upon Israel until the fullness of the Gentiles has come in;
> 26 and in this way all Israel will be saved, as it is written,
> "The Deliverer shall come out of Zion.
> He shall turn away ungodliness from Jacob.
> 27 And this is My covenant with them,
> when I take away their sins."

Romans 11:25–27 is another scripture reading that shows God's two economies at work. God is working with Israel, and God is also working with the Body of Messiah. Once again, Paul writes of a mystery. The mystery is that a *partial* hardening has been placed upon Israel until the fullness of the Gentiles comes in (verse 25). It is most important for the Body of Messiah to see God's truth here in these verses. There is not a complete hardening of Israel, but a partial hardening! This proves beyond any doubt that Jewish people can and do get saved in our current age of grace!

So, why have many believers over the last 2,000 years believed that the Jewish people are reprobate and cannot receive Yeshua as their Messiah? The great reformer, Martin Luther, was one who believed this. He wrote his book, *On Jews and Their Lies*, where he encouraged the world to attack Jewish people and steal their goods. Hitler read this book and acted on it, massacring six million Jewish people in World War II.

Israel's partial hardening will not continue forever. God will lift this hardening when the fullness of the Gentiles comes in. So, when the last Gentile salvation occurs at the end of the Tribulation, then the partial hardening of Israel will be lifted and all Israel will be saved (more on this "fullness" later). In verse 26, we find out that all Israel is saved. After the last Gentile is blessed with salvation in this age and after the Rapture occurs, then Israel will be saved. This salvation comes at the end of the seven years of Jacob's Trouble, the great tribulation upon the Jewish people and Israel, but it does come.

What most believers forget is that the nation of Israel will unfortunately dramatically decrease in number during Jacob's Trouble. Remember, Zechariah 13:8 tells us that during the Tribulation Period, two-thirds of the Jewish population in the Land of Israel will perish from the evil of the Anti-messiah. So, the one-third that make it through the Tribulation will be saved by Yeshua at the end. This one-third that survives the Tribulation is the nation of Israel, the "all Israel" of verse 26.

We know this is true because Romans 11:26–27 continues with the context of the end of Jacob's Trouble. In fact, these verses are an application of Isaiah 59:20–21. The deliverer of the Jewish people will come to save them, remove all ungodliness, and begin the New Covenant. This is obviously talking of Yeshua's Second Coming. When He comes for Israel, He will forgive all of her sins, spiritually and physically save Israel, remove all ungodliness from Israel and the world, and start the New Covenant with the Jewish people in the Messianic Millennial Kingdom! There is no other time period in Israel's history when all four of these events occurred at the same time. It has to be at Yeshua's Second Coming. It is interesting to note that the New Covenant will begin when all of Israel's sins are forgiven. This can only happen when all Israel is saved at the end of Jacob's Trouble.

To summarize, these verses clearly show a prophetic distinction between the Body of Messiah and Israel. The Body of Messiah will end at the time of the Rapture. The timing of the Body of Messiah is the mysterious period between Israel's sixty-ninth and seventieth week of prophecy. The Lord then begins to finish His prophetic plan for Israel shortly after the Rapture in the seventieth week of Daniel.

The Body of Messiah Is Exempt from God's Wrath

The fifth great reason to believe in a Pre-Tribulation Rapture is that the Body of Messiah is exempt from God's wrath. The Lord especially makes this clear in His Word that He will not pour out His wrath against His believers, but against the world.

1 Thessalonians 5:9–11

> 9 For God did not destine us for wrath but for obtaining salvation through our Lord *Yeshua* the Messiah. 10 He died for us so that, whether we may be awake or asleep, we may live together with Him.
> 11 Therefore encourage one another and build each other up—just as you in fact are doing.

The Lord clearly has destined believers to obtain God's salvation rather than His wrath! The question to answer is "What is God's wrath?" The context is revealed as "the Day of the Lord" in 5:2–3. "The Day of the Lord" here is speaking of the entire seven years of Jacob's Trouble. In verse 3, the world is proclaiming peace and safety (presumably because of the signing of the peace treaty with Israel), and then God's destruction suddenly comes upon them. A key point needs to be made that no one in the world escapes God's judgment. His judgment and destruction (verse 3) are connected to His wrath (verse 9).

However, in verse 9, believers are not destined to be under God's wrath! "Destine" (*tithemi*) is used to mean "to put, set, and place." To appoint is the meaning here, and the Greek grammar is clear. This appointment has occurred as a one-time act in the past. So, this appointment occurred because of our salvation in Yeshua. Hence, Yeshua will not pour out His wrath upon His own because we are, in fact, appointed to salvation, but He will pour it out on non-believers because they are being judged for their evil. It is interesting to note that God's "wrath" (*orge*) or anger is used in association with the Lord only in Jacob's Trouble (the Day of the Lord).

In verses 4–8, we see the contrast with believers. Believers in Yeshua will not be overtaken by this Tribulation Period. Therefore, we shall not experience God's wrath in the Day of the Lord! Why? We shall be raptured out of here! However, the fact remains from the book of Revelation that there are definitely believers during Jacob's Trouble. These believers are not a part of today's Body of Messiah. They are a part of a different age: the Tribulation Period. But how do these believers come about in Jacob's Trouble when the Rapture takes all believers out of this world?

First, in Revelation 7:4–8, the 144,000 Jewish men are saved and sealed by the Lord at the beginning of Jacob's Trouble. The Lord knows there is a problem when all believers are raptured and there is no one left to preach the good news. However, He has the solution and miraculously saves these specific Jewish men! The Bible does not tell us exactly how the salvation process occurs, but we do know that the Lord seals them. Second, these 144,000 are the ones who will bring the good news message of Yeshua to the world during the entire seven years of Jacob's Trouble. Multitudes of people around the world will be saved during this period and they will eventually be praising the Lord before His throne in heaven (verses 9–10).

During Jacob's Trouble, there will be plenty of believers to hear the world cry out "peace and safety" and see the Lord's destruction upon them. The Day of the Lord is bad for unbelievers because God's wrath is poured out upon them. But the Day of the Lord is not bad for believers because they are saved and will live together with the Lord wherever He dwells (1 Thessalonians 5:9–10). These Tribulation Period believers should be encouraged by these verses! We, on the other hand, should also be encouraged and build one another up with this knowledge (verse 11). I hope you are lifted up in the Lord by reading this teaching!

1 Thessalonians 1:9–10

> 9 For they themselves bring news about what kind of welcome we had among you, and how you turned to God from idols, to serve the living and true God, 10 and to wait for His Son from heaven, whom He raised from the dead—*Yeshua,* the One delivering us from the coming wrath.

Paul writes to the Thessalonians to encourage them about their godly reputation while he was preaching the good news message in other parts of the world. Paul seemed to be extremely happy over this awesome report. The Thessalonians had turned from worshiping idols to serve the living God, and they were currently waiting for His return. Then Paul mentions Yeshua, "*the One delivering us from the coming wrath.*" "The coming wrath" is obviously the one and only wrath of God coming during Jacob's Trouble. So, believers are "delivered" (*rhuomai*) or rescued and saved from God's wrath during the Tribulation Period. This verse clearly shows the Body of

Messiah is not destined for God's wrath and thus shows a preference for the Pre-Trib Rapture. Believers of the Body of Messiah are raptured prior to God's wrath upon the world.

Revelation 3:10

> Because you have kept My word about patient endurance, I will also keep you from the hour of trial that is coming upon the whole world to test those who dwell on the earth.

The Apostle John wrote to Messiah's Community in Philadelphia, commending their perseverance in following Yeshua's Word. Since they kept His Word, the Lord will keep them from "the hour of trial." The Philadelphian congregation is a microcosm of the Body of Messiah. Therefore, the Body of Messiah will be kept from the "hour of trial."

The Body of Messiah is not just kept from testing but from the "*hour* of trial." The hour of trial is explained to be the time period that the whole world will be tested sometime in the future. This time period is obviously Jacob's Trouble. The testing is God's wrath poured out on the world to see how people react—whether they repent and receive Yeshua or not! Once again, we see a verse that shows believers will not go through God's wrath during the Tribulation Period.

When Is God's Wrath Poured Out?

The controversial question that deserves an answer is "When will God's wrath be poured out in Jacob's Trouble?" There are those that believe God's wrath will be poured out at the middle of the Tribulation Period, and there are those that believe God's wrath will be poured out just after the middle of the Tribulation (this view is called the Pre-Wrath Rapture). Still others believe His wrath comes at the end of Jacob's Trouble.

The answer shows all three of these views are incorrect and that God's wrath will be poured out on the world for all seven years of Jacob's Trouble!

Revelation 6:7–8

> 7 When the Lamb opened the fourth seal, I heard the fourth living creature saying, "Come!" 8 Behold, I saw a horse, pale greenish gray. The name of the one riding on it was Death, and *Sheol* was following with him. Authority was given to them over a fourth of the earth, to kill by sword and by famine and by plague and by the wild beasts of the earth.

Revelation 6:1–17 reveal Yeshua's wrath against the world in six of the seals. These six seals bring about worldwide war, famine, and death. By the fourth seal, at least 25 percent of the world's population will die (verses 7–8)! As a proportion of today's population, that's almost 2 billion people dying by the fourth seal! My friends, this is devastation beyond belief! How can any believer say that this is not God's wrath? This is definitely God's wrath against an evil world. Even the ungodly, evil people of the earth will know that the Father and Yeshua have poured out their wrath on them! In verses 15–17, we find that survivors of the wrath have hidden themselves in caves and are even requesting the mountains to fall on them. What was their great desire? To hide from the presence of God and Yeshua because *their wrath has come*! Even the world will recognize they cannot stand against the Lord's wrath!

Revelation 15:1

> Then I saw another great and wonderful sign in heaven: seven angels who have seven plagues—the last ones, for with them God's wrath is finished.

Revelation 15 begins with identifying the last seven angels who had the last seven plagues of God. These last seven plagues of the total twenty-one judgments are the seven golden bowls filled with God's wrath (15:7). But verse 1 tells us that in these seven golden bowls, the wrath of God "*is finished!*" Through simple biblical logical deduction, this means that the wrath of God was in effect during the first fourteen plagues of the Lord! Therefore, God's wrath is found throughout Jacob's Trouble, and the Pre-Wrath Rapture view falls short.

Revelation 21:9

> 9 Then came one of the seven angels holding the seven bowls full of the seven final plagues, and he spoke with me, saying, "Come, I will show you the bride, the wife of the Lamb."

This verse also alludes to the last set of seven plagues as being the same as the first two sets of plagues which are all God's wrath. The seven bowls were full of the seven *final* plagues! The word *final* connects the last set of seven plagues with the first two sets of plagues. This then reveals that all twenty-one plagues are God's wrath!

I started this section with the understanding that the Body of Messiah would not go through God's wrath. I have been able to show without any doubt that God's wrath occurs throughout Jacob's Trouble, starting with the seven seals. Therefore, it is reasonable to conclude that the Body of Messiah will not go through Jacob's Trouble and will be raptured prior to it!

The Rapture Is Imminent

The sixth great reason to believe in a Pre-Trib Rapture is that the Rapture is imminent. By "imminent," I mean that the

Rapture could occur at any moment. There is no prophetic event *required* by the Bible to occur *before* the Rapture or be connected to the Rapture for the Rapture to occur. However, some prophetic events *could* occur prior to the Rapture or be connected to the Rapture. Although I believe the Pre-Trib Rapture is imminent (as the Scripture will reveal), I also believe there are some prophetic events that will occur before the Rapture occurs (hence the writing of this book).

The following verses indicate that there are no signs or events that must take place prior to the Rapture. In addition, the Scripture actually exhorts believers to wait for the Rapture!

<u>1 Thessalonians 1:10</u>

> 10 and to wait for His Son from heaven, whom He raised from the dead—*Yeshua,* the One delivering us from the coming wrath.

The Thessalonians were commended by Paul on how they had turned from idol worship to serve the living God. They were encouraged to continue waiting for Yeshua who would come from heaven! This is a reference to the Rapture, and the believers were actually encouraged "to wait" (*anameno*). "To wait" is found to be in the present tense, which means the Thessalonians were to continuously wait in the present for the Rapture. If the Rapture is not imminent, then why ask the believers to be consistently and daily waiting for His return? Would this not be a big waste of His children's precious time? This also shows that the Rapture is not "mid-" or "post-trib" since neither of these views believe the Rapture is imminent.

What is additionally fascinating is that there is a reason for consistently waiting on the Rapture. Yeshua delivers us from *the* wrath to come! The wrath to come is God's wrath poured out upon the world for the full seven years of Jacob's Trouble. So Yeshua is "delivering" (*rhuomai*) believers from this time period. "Delivering" means to save or rescue. It is clear that we shall not go through God's wrath in the Tribulation Period but be delivered from it! Interesting, also, is the fact that there is no prophetic sign in this verse associated with the Rapture. There is no prophetic sign that occurs *before* the Rapture, but there is one that occurs *after* it. That is God's wrath upon the world!

Philippians 3:20–21

> 20 For our citizenship is in heaven,
> and from there we eagerly wait for the Savior,
> the Lord *Yeshua* the Messiah.
> 21 He will transform this humble body of ours
> into the likeness of His glorious body,
> through the power that enables Him
> even to put all things in subjection to Himself.

The Philippians are encouraged to continue in Paul's great example of walking with the Lord (3:17). In this walk with the Lord, they were commanded to "eagerly wait" for Yeshua to transform their humble bodies into resurrection bodies. This event is the Rapture (see 1 Corinthians 15:50–54). Once again, believers are told to "eagerly wait" for the Rapture. This Greek word is found to be in the present tense. This means that believers are to continuously wait in the present for the Rapture to come. This most certainly shows that the Rapture could happen at any moment, and we should be ready for it at any moment. In this verse there are no prophetic signs connected to the Rapture whatsoever showing its imminence.

Titus 2:11–13

> 11 For the grace of God has appeared, bringing salvation to all men, 12 training us to deny ungodliness and worldly desires and to live in a manner that is

> self-controlled and righteous and godly in the present age. 13 We wait for the blessed hope and appearance of the glory of our great God and Savior, Messiah *Yeshua*.

Paul instructs all believers to pursue righteousness in our walk with the Lord by waiting for the blessed hope and appearing of Yeshua. I believe the blessed hope and the appearing of Yeshua is talking about the Rapture! We are to continuously be waiting for it. "Wait" (*prosdechomai*) means to expect, be awaiting, and welcome something. Here, it is obvious, we should be looking forward and waiting with high expectation that the Rapture could occur any day.

Romans 8:22–23

> 22 For we know that the whole creation groans together and suffers birth pains until now—23 and not only creation, but even ourselves. We ourselves, who have the firstfruits of the *Ruach,* groan inwardly as we eagerly wait for adoption—the redemption of our body.

Paul tells the Romans that all of creation groans and suffers because of the original sin (verse 22). We believers even groan within ourselves by the leading of the Ruach Kodesh because we are eagerly waiting for the redemption of our bodies (verse 23). The redemption of our bodies is where our immortal bodies will be transformed into resurrection bodies, and this occurs at the Rapture! Since the Greek grammar shows this waiting to occur continuously in the present, we are to eagerly wait in the present for the Rapture to come!

1 Corinthians 16:22

> 22 If anyone does not love the Lord, let him be cursed. *Marana, tha!* Our Lord, come!

Paul proclaims "*marana tha*" at the end of verse 22, which means "our Lord come." Paul is entreating the Lord to come and rapture all the believers out of here! If Yeshua could not come on that day, why did Paul pray for Him to come, knowing He could not come? That would make no sense. If the Rapture is "mid-" or "post-trib," then why would Paul call upon the Lord to come that specific day? It is obvious to me that Paul would not call for Yeshua to come unless He *could* come! This shows the Rapture to be imminent and therefore Pre-Trib.

James 5:7–8

> 7 So be patient, brothers and sisters, until the coming of the Lord. See how the farmer waits for the precious fruit of the earth, being patient for it until it receives the early and late rain. 8 You also be patient. Strengthen your hearts because the coming of the Lord is near.

James is encouraging the brethren to be patient and wait for the coming of the Lord. The coming of the Lord here is the Rapture. They are to wait like the farmer has to wait for his precious crops to grow. The reason given to be patient and strong in the Lord is because the Rapture is near and at hand! This means the Rapture could occur at any moment. It is a stand-alone event requiring no other prior prophetic event; it is imminent!

Now, if the Rapture is imminent, then how can it be the fulfillment of Yom Teruah (the Feast of Trumpets, aka Rosh Hashanah)? This question needs to be answered! The Rapture does *not* need to occur on the exact day of the Feast of Yom Teruah to fulfill it! It can occur on any day of the year, and the feast would then be fulfilled!

Remember, biblically, the feast of Yom Teruah is a mysterious feast. There is no other feast like it! Truly, it is a feast set up for the celebration of the next Feast of Yom Kippur.

According to Torah, on Yom Teruah, Israel was to gather together, worship the Lord, blow the shofar all day long, and get ready to repent on Yom Kippur ten days later. The Feast of Yom Teruah helps the people to get ready for repentance on Yom Kippur.

So, when Yom Teruah is fulfilled, it helps Israel to be set up for her national salvation on Yom Kippur! The Pre-Trib Rapture closes out the age of the Body of Messiah and helps Israel to begin her journey through the Tribulation to finally be saved in the end! This works perfectly with God's two economies (Israel and the Body of Messiah) as well. We have the out-going of the Body of Messiah at the Rapture and the in-coming of Israel into Jacob's Trouble, culminating in her national salvation.

However, it is possible that the Rapture could occur on the actual day of Yom Teruah, although the odds are 360–1 against it. However, the Lord is in charge, and His timing is perfect. We shall see how it all works out in the end!

The Necessity of Time between the Rapture and the Second Coming

The seventh great reason to believe in the Pre-Trib Rapture is the necessity of time needed between the Rapture and the Second Coming.

John 14:1–3

> 1 Do not let your heart be troubled. Trust in God; trust also in Me. 2 In My Father's house there are many dwelling places. If it were not so, would I have told you that I am going to prepare a place for you? 3 If I go and prepare a place for you, I will come again and take you to Myself, so that where I am you may also be.

Yeshua promises His disciples that He's going to heaven to prepare dwelling places for them (verse 2). He then let's them know that He will come once again for them. Wherever Yeshua goes, they will go, too. So, if Yeshua goes back to heaven, then the disciples will go back to heaven. Here we see Yeshua's promise of the Rapture. There is a reason why Yeshua prepares places in heaven for all His believers. When we are raptured to heaven, we shall dwell in these heavenly places for at least seven of Earth's years. Why would Yeshua prepare dwelling places for the Body of Messiah and then not use them? If the Rapture is "post-trib," then there would be no reason for preparing dwelling places when we would not dwell in them. So, this first verse shows the Body of Messiah will spend some time in heaven after the Rapture. This reveals that the Rapture and the Second Coming are two different events that necessitate that there be some amount of time between them.

2 Corinthians 5:10

> For we must all appear before the judgment seat of Messiah, so that each one may receive what is due for the things he did while in the body—whether good or bad.

In 2 Corinthians 5:7–9, Paul encourages all believers to walk by faith and not by sight. We are to be pleasing to the Lord whether we are at home on earth or with the Lord in heaven. Then, in verse 10, we find out that all believers will end up at the Bema Seat Judgment of Messiah. Yeshua will judge our good works whether they were good or bad. An interesting note here worthy of mention is the fact that some of our good works will be judged as being bad, and there will be subsequent adverse effects. I think many believers do not know about this and may reconsider how they perform good works for the Lord. We should perform our good works out of love and faith for the Lord!

The point that needs to be brought out here is that there needs to be time for Yeshua to perform His judgment of our good deeds. There will be billions of believers raptured from the earth, and Yeshua will need some time to judge them all. This eliminates the Post-Trib Rapture view completely.

1 Corinthians 3:10–15

> 10 According to the grace of God which was given to me, like a skilled master builder I laid a foundation, and another builds on it. But let each consider carefully how he builds on it. 11 For no one can lay any other foundation than what is already laid—which is *Yeshua* the Messiah. 12 Now if anyone builds on the foundation with gold, silver, precious stones, wood, hay, straw, 13 each one's work will become clear. For the Day will show it, because it is to be revealed by fire; and the fire itself will test each one's work—what sort it is. 14 If anyone's work built on the foundation survives, he will receive a reward. 15 If anyone's work is burned up, he will suffer loss—he himself will be saved, but as through fire.

These verses are another scripture passage where Paul encourages us to be careful in our performance of good works (verse 10). Each person's good works will be judged by Yeshua's fire (verses 11–13). This is most definitely the Bema Seat Judgment of Yeshua! If the good works survive Yeshua's test of fire, then we shall receive rewards. If the work burns up, we shall lose out on the rewards, but we shall still be saved (verse 15)! So, the condition of our good works has no effect on our salvation; this is a great verse to support eternal security! The idea of the Bema Seat Judgment is that it occurs in heaven *after* the Pre-Trib Rapture. In any event, this judgment once again requires time for Yeshua to judge our good works.

1 Corinthians 4:3–5

> 3 But to me it matters very little to be judged by you or by any human court. In fact, I do not even judge myself. 4 For I know of nothing against myself, yet I am not justified by this. It is the Lord who judges me. 5 Therefore do not judge anything before the time—wait until the Lord comes. He will bring to light the things hidden in darkness and also make clear the motives of the hearts. Then the praise for each one will come from God.

Paul tells the Corinthians that he does not even examine his own good deeds but rather the Lord is the judge (verses 3–4). In verse 5, we are told to stop judging one another before the time of Yeshua's return. This is the Rapture! After He comes back, He will then "bring to light" the hidden things and disclose every believer's motives in their works. Those whose works are still shining brightly after the testing of fire will praise the Lord. So, this verse confirms again that the Bema Seat Judgment occurs *after* the Rapture! And it is essential that there be some time between the Rapture and the Second Coming! The Post-Trib Rapture viewpoint does not allow for this time that is so essential in Yeshua's Bema Seat Judgment.

Revelation 19:8

> She was given fine linen to wear, bright and clean!
> For the fine linen is the righteous deeds of the *kedoshim*."

The Body of Messiah is revealed to be in heaven with Yeshua just prior to the Second Coming. In verse 8, she has received her bright and clean fine linen robes. These wonderful robes are equated to our righteous acts. These are the rewards the Body of Messiah receives from the Bema Seat Judgment.

Now that the bride has made herself ready, she can participate in the marriage ceremony with Yeshua.

Once we reconcile all these Scriptures together, we see a definite order of events and the necessity that time is needed between the Rapture and the Second Coming. Yeshua raptures His body to heaven where we dwell in our prepared places for at least seven Earth years. Yeshua performs the Bema Seat Judgment in heaven on all believers snatched away during the Rapture. He then rewards all of these believers with bright and clean robes that somehow represent our good deeds performed in the Ruach Kodesh by love and faith. Then we shall have the marriage of the Lamb and return with Yeshua in His Second Coming. All of these events require time between the Rapture and the Second Coming. If the Rapture is "post-trib," then there is no time allotted for these events to occur. "Post-tribbers" should have a major problem here!

Revelation 19:5–9

> 5 Then a voice came from the throne, saying:
> "Praise our God,
> all you His servants and
> all who fear Him,
> both the small and the great!"
> 6 Then I heard something like the voice of a great multitude—like the roar of rushing waters or like the rumbling of powerful thunder—saying, "Halleluyah!
> For *ADONAI Elohei-Tzva'ot* [LORD God of Hosts] reigns!
> 7 Let us rejoice and be glad
> and give the glory to Him!
> For the wedding of the Lamb has come,
> and His bride has made herself ready,
> 8 She was given fine linen to wear, bright and clean!
> For the fine linen is the righteous deeds of the *kedoshim*."

> 9 Then the angel tells me, "Write: How fortunate are those who have been invited to the wedding banquet of the Lamb!" He also tells me, "These are the true words of God."

This scripture reading begins with believers commanded to give praise to the Lord in heaven (verse 5). These bond-servants are none other than the raptured Body of Messiah! In verse 6, this great multitude sings halleluyah unto the Lord. This multitude, also called the bride, made herself ready for the marriage of the Lamb! The bride of Messiah is the raptured Body of Messiah. Verse 7 is the only verse in the Bible that shows the Body of Messiah will marry the Lamb in heaven.

Verse 8 shows that she made herself ready by going through the Bema Seat Judgment of Yeshua. She is now bright and clean and ceremonially ready for the wedding. Verse 9 discusses the subsequent marriage feast of the Lamb that looks like it will be celebrated on earth after the Second Coming. Those who are invited to this feast will be greatly blessed by the Lord. Even the birds of the air will be invited to the great feast of the Lord (19:17–18). However, their supper will be the flesh of all the dead people who battle against Yeshua in the Armageddon War.

In any event, these events in heaven require time between the Rapture and the Second Coming. Besides this, believers are coming back *with* Yeshua *from* heaven. This means that this great multitude of believers are already in heaven prior to the Second Coming! Again, "post-tribbers" should have a major difficulty here with their viewpoint. If this group is not the raptured Body of Messiah, then who are they? "Post-tribbers" need to answer these questions.

The Necessity of Believers to Enter the Messianic Millennial Kingdom

The eighth great reason to believe in a Pre-Trib Rapture is the necessity of believers, both Jewish and Gentile, to enter into the Messiah's Kingdom in their human bodies. The Scripture is clear that, not only does Yeshua come back for believers in the Second Coming, and not only does He separate believers from non-believers (and judge them accordingly), but He specifically comes back for Jewish believers located in Israel and elsewhere. They actually call for Yeshua's return! So, these believers are located on Earth when Yeshua comes back.

Matthew 24:31

> 31 He will send out His angels with a great *shofar,* and they will gather together His chosen from the four winds, from one end of heaven to the other.

One event that occurs after the Second Coming of verse 30 is the gathering of Yeshua's chosen from the four winds, from one end of heaven to the other. Yeshua's "chosen" in the context of Matthew 24 is speaking of Jewish believers. This is the prophesied final gathering of Israel in belief of Yeshua found in Isaiah 12:11–12 and 27:12–13. After the Second Coming, Yeshua's angels will gather all the Jewish believers from around the world and bring them all back to the Land of Israel. Why would He do this? He promised Abraham and David that their descendants would live in the Land under the reign of the Jewish Messiah!

At the Rapture, all believers are removed from the earth and brought to heaven to be with the Lord. At the Second Coming there is a large number of Jewish (and Gentile) believers of Yeshua on Earth. If the Post-Trib Rapture view is correct, then how is there a large contingency of Jewish believers on Earth when the Rapture just occurred moments before the Second Coming? With this view, there is no time for all these Jewish believers to come to faith! This view obviously has problems. However, if the Rapture is "pre-trib," then there would be at least seven years available for many Jewish and Gentile people to come to faith in Yeshua—no problem!

Matthew 25:31–46

> 31 "Now when the Son of Man comes in His glory, and all the angels with Him, then He will sit on His glorious throne. 32 All the nations will be gathered before Him, and He will separate them from one another, just as the shepherd separates the sheep from the goats. 33 And He will put the sheep on His right, but the goats on His left. 34 Then the King will say to those on His right, 'Come, you who are blessed by My Father, inherit the kingdom prepared for you from the foundation of the world. 35 For I was hungry and you gave Me something to eat; I was thirsty and you gave Me something to drink; I was a stranger and you invited Me in; 36 I was naked and you clothed Me; I was sick and you visited Me; I was in prison and you came to Me.'
>
> 37 "Then the righteous will answer Him, 'Lord, when did we see You hungry and feed You? Or thirsty and give You something to drink? 38 And when did we see You a stranger and invite You in? Or naked and clothe You? 39 When did we see You sick, or in prison, and come to You?'
>
> 40 "And answering, the King will say to them, 'Amen, I tell you, whatever you did to one of the least of these My brethren, you did it to Me.' 41 Then He will also say to those on the left, 'Go away from Me, you cursed ones, into the everlasting fire which has been prepared for the devil and his angels. 42 For I was hungry and

> you gave Me nothing to eat; I was thirsty and you gave Me nothing to drink; 43 I was a stranger and you did not invite Me in; naked and you did not clothe Me; sick and in prison and you did not visit Me.'
> 44 "Then they too will answer, saying, 'Lord, when did we see You hungry or thirsty or a stranger or naked or sick or in prison, and did not care for You?' 45 Then He will answer them, saying, 'Amen, I tell you, whatever you did not do for one of the least of these, you did not do for Me.' 46 These shall go off to everlasting punishment, but the righteous into everlasting life."

This scripture passage proves beyond any doubt that Jewish and Gentile believers of Yeshua will enter into the Messianic Millennial Kingdom. Yeshua just finished teaching on two kingdom parables: one on the ten virgins and the other on the good and faithful servant. Verse 31 starts to discuss the events surrounding Yeshua's Second Coming and the beginning of the Messianic Kingdom. In verse 32, we find that all living people are gathered before Him. Yeshua separates these people into two groups: the sheep and the goats (verse 33). The sheep are true believers of Yeshua, and they shall inherit the Kingdom (verse 34). Why? Because their actions showed their faith!

In verses 35–36, Yeshua says these believers took care of His needs during Jacob's Trouble! But the righteous believers do not understand (verses 37–39). In verse 40, Yeshua tells them plainly that when they helped "*My brethren*," it was then that they helped Him! Here in verse 40, Yeshua introduces a third group from all the people gathered from around the world. This third group are Yeshua's brothers. So, who is this third group? I believe they are the Jewish believers who make it through Jacob's Trouble alive. These are the "chosen" of Matthew 24:31. So, that makes the sheep group to be Gentile believers. The Jewish believers will enter into the Kingdom right along with the Gentile believers!

On the other hand, the goats are called "accursed" in verse 41 and will be cast into hellfire. Their actions proved their non-belief. Actually, it was their lack of good deeds toward the Jewish people of Jacob's Trouble that reveals their lack of faith in Yeshua (verses 42–45). They did not love the Jewish people and take care of their needs during the Tribulation and hence will face God's judgment. They will be punished for eternity in the Lake of Fire, but the righteous will be blessed with eternal life (verse 46).

What is fascinating here is the fact that the Jewish people are going to be going through the worst holocaust of all history, the second half of Jacob's Trouble, and there are going to be Gentile believers around the world who will help them! This is truly amazing, considering that the Anti-messiah will be attacking the Jewish people and all believers around the world. There will be an all-out war against them, and yet they will still be able to show their love for the Jewish people and help them! This is an awesome display of God's love working in a most tragic time of human history! Praise be to the Lord!

The point of this section is to prove that born-again believers need to be on planet Earth when Yeshua comes back in His Second Coming. The Jewish and Gentile believers are rounded up and then invited to Yeshua's Kingdom! So, if the Post-Trib Rapture view is correct, then how can there be Jewish and Gentile believers found all around the world when all the believers were just moments earlier raptured up to the clouds to be with the Lord? Isn't the earth full of non-believers? There is obviously something amiss here, and it is the Post-Trib Rapture viewpoint. It cannot account for all of these believers that are left on earth. There is definitely a necessity for believers to be on Earth when Yeshua comes back for them! And there absolutely must be a contingent of Jewish believers on Earth that actually call for Yeshua to come back!

Matthew 23:37–39

> 37 "O Jerusalem, Jerusalem who kills the prophets and stones those sent to her! How often I longed to gather your children together, as a hen gathers her chicks under her wings, but you were not willing! 38 Look, your house is left to you desolate! 39 For I tell you, you will never see Me again until you say, '*Baruch ha-ba b'shem ADONAI*. Blessed is He who comes in the name of the Lord!'"

This scripture reading reveals a group of Messianic Jewish people calling upon Yeshua as the Messiah to come back just prior to His Second Coming. They actually have to call upon Yeshua as Messiah to come back *before* He will come back! How is this even possible? Zechariah 13:8–9 and 12:10 show us that at the end of Jacob's Trouble, the one-third of the Jewish people in the Land of Israel who make it through the Tribulation Period will be saved from their sin, will receive the Ruach Kodesh, and will look upon the Lord God who was pierced. All of this will occur towards the end of the Tribulation Period. Then this group of Messianic Jews will call upon Yeshua to come back to Earth to defeat the enemies of Israel.

In Matthew 23, we find Yeshua rebuking the scribes and Pharisees in a scathing report. He calls them hypocrites, serpents, and a brood of vipers. They persecuted and killed the righteous and the prophets and ultimately will receive the judgment of their guilt (verses 29–36). In verses 37–38, Yeshua then proclaims to Jerusalem that He wanted to gather all His children together, but she was not willing. In other words, Yeshua wanted to set up the Kingdom right then, but the Jewish people, led by the Sanhedrin, rejected Him as their Messiah.

In verse 38, He prophesies that their house will become desolate. He is speaking of the Temple and its dynasty. In AD 70, Titus and the Romans destroyed Jerusalem and the Temple in fulfillment of this prophecy. In verse 39, Yeshua makes a profound statement to the Jewish people of Jerusalem that many believers probably miss in their reading of this scripture. Yeshua says the Jewish people of Jerusalem will not see Him again *until* they say, "*Baruch haba b'shem Adonai.*" This means "Blessed is He who comes in the name of the Lord!" So, the Jewish people in Jacob's Trouble have to call upon Yeshua to come back and say, "Blessed is He who comes in the name of the Lord!" This will all take place once these Jewish people get saved in Yeshua's name and then call upon Him to return and destroy the enemies of the Jewish people!

The question is asked once again, "How can this occur if the Post-Trib Rapture is true?" In this view, all believers are raptured from the earth just moments prior to Yeshua's Second Coming. There is no time for Jewish people to get saved and then call upon Yeshua to come back prior to the Second Coming when He is already *en route* in His return!

The Body of Messiah Is Not Found in Jacob's Trouble

The ninth great reason to believe in a Pre-Trib Rapture is that the Body of Messiah is not found in Jacob's Trouble. In the pivotal prophetic chapter of Matthew 24, the Body of Messiah is mysteriously missing from any mention. Instead Yeshua speaks of Israel and the Jewish people. Yes, Yeshua talks about how the world will be at war, and everyone's love will grow cold. But He is speaking to His *talmidim* (disciples) about how the world is going to react to Israel and the Jewish people. Yeshua uses pronouns such as "you," "the one," "he," "those," "the reader," and so forth, all for the Jewish people (in verses 6, 9, 13, 15, 16). He even uses "the chosen" to describe the elect Jewish believers of the Tribulation Period (in verses 22, 24, 31). But He never uses the Greek word *ekklesia* (for the

Body of Messiah) or discusses the Body at all in this chapter. If the Body of Messiah was to go through Jacob's Trouble, then Matthew 24 would be a good place to discuss it in the scriptures. However, it is mysteriously missing from Jacob's Trouble!

In the book of Revelation, the Body of Messiah (*ekklesia*) is mentioned many times in Chapters 2 and 3. But, from Chapter 4 onward, it is missing until 22:16 when Yeshua finishes up the revelation! Again, the question of why the Body of Messiah is not mentioned in the one book of the Bible that summarizes Jacob's Trouble in sequential order needs to be answered! The only time that I see the Body of Messiah mentioned from Chapter 4 onward is in 19:5–9. We have already discussed that this group of believers in heaven just prior to the Second Coming is the raptured Body of Messiah! They come back with Yeshua in verses 12–16!

Matthew 25:31–46, a passage that explains in more detail the worldwide gathering of the elect, makes no mention of the Body of Messiah. It only speaks of Gentile believers (sheep), non-believers (goats), and Jewish believers (My brothers). Again, there is no mention of the Body of Messiah in any of these important sections about Jacob's Trouble. Why is that? I believe because the Body of Messiah is raptured out prior to Jacob's Trouble. If the Body of Messiah is already in heaven during the Tribulation Period, then there would be no need to mention it in the Scriptures concerning the Tribulation Period. Simply put, she is not there! Now, certainly, this ninth reason in and of itself is not sufficient enough to warrant believing in the Pre-Trib Rapture viewpoint. However, coupled with all the other great reasons, it makes a strong argument for the Pre-Trib Rapture!

The Many Distinctions between the Rapture and the Second Coming

The tenth great reason to believe in the Pre-Trib Rapture is the many distinctions between the Rapture and the Second Coming that help us to understand these are two separate events rather than one.

In the Rapture, Yeshua comes for His Body of Messiah and there is encouragement for hope. In the Second Coming, He comes to judge and wage war against His enemies. There is no hope for them at this point. In the Rapture, the holy ones meet the Lord in the air. In the Second Coming, the Lord with His holy ones come to earth from heaven. There is never anything mentioned in the Scriptures about Yeshua stopping during His descent through the clouds to pick up believers on the way down. Judgment is not associated with the Rapture, but is typically a big part of the Second Coming. In the Rapture, Yeshua comes to bless His children, but in the Second Coming, He judges the wicked. In Rapture verses there is no mention of the Messianic Millennial Kingdom. But in the Second Coming, the setting up of the Kingdom is emphasized.

In the Rapture, living and dead believers of Yeshua receive glorified bodies. But in the Second Coming, there is no mention of believers receiving glorified bodies. In 1 Thessalonians 4:14, we already found out that the dead in Messiah will come back *with* Yeshua in the Rapture. The spirits and souls in heaven will come back with Yeshua and receive their bodies in the clouds, as the dead in Messiah will rise first. Those who are alive in Messiah at the Rapture have no need to be reunited with their bodies because they are already in their bodies! Their bodies will be transformed into resurrection bodies as they rise to meet the Lord in the air! At the Second Coming, there is no mention of believers receiving their glorified bodies.

The Rapture is seen as being imminent because it truly could occur at any time. The Second Coming, on the other hand, has numerous signs and events connected to it. The Second Coming occurs just after Jacob's Trouble is over. The Rapture occurs *before* the wrath of God occurs, whereas the Second Coming follows the wrath of God, culminating in Yeshua's wrath. In the Rapture, the Lord presumably returns to heaven since He has created a special place there for each believer to dwell. He then performs the Bema Seat Judgment in heaven. In the Second Coming, there is no time for the Bema Seat Judgment to be performed on all the believers. The Lord descends from heaven to earth, performs the Armageddon judgment, and then sets up the Kingdom. In the Rapture, all believers are removed from the earth to be gathered in the clouds, leaving only non-believers behind. In the Second Coming, all believers and non-believers are gathered after the Armageddon War. Jewish and Gentile believers enter into the Kingdom in their human bodies; non-believers enter into eternal punishment.

Chart

As we look at the prophetic chart, I believe the Pre-Trib Rapture occurs sometime after the Ezekiel War and during the events of the One-World Order. Even though the Rapture is imminent, I believe these two world events will help to set it up. The two arrows leading upwards from "The Body of Messiah Ends" box signify two events. First, the dead bodies in Messiah are raptured, and second, those that are alive in Messiah are raptured too. The cloud shows where the meeting takes place in the clouds as Messiah comes down from heaven to retrieve us and then brings us back to heaven for the Bema Seat Judgment.

Remember, some effects of the Ezekiel War and the One-World Order will continue through Jacob's Trouble. But I believe the Rapture will occur before Jacob's Trouble begins. With the Rapture, the age of the Body of Messiah ends and the age of Jacob's Trouble begins shortly thereafter. The duration of Jacob's Trouble is only seven years. It would be considered small compared to the Body of Messiah's age which has lasted almost 2,000 years. However, it is an extremely important age, when the Lord will bring Israel to her knees so that she can be saved and have their names written in the Book of Life!

There are many compelling reasons to believe in a Pre-Trib Rapture. Most of these reasons taken alone may not completely convince you, but taken as a collective whole, they are a powerful argument for the Pre-Trib Rapture viewpoint.

To summarize, the ten great reasons to believe in the Pre-Trib Rapture are: the Messianic Jewish prophetic fulfillment of the Feast of Trumpets, the ancient Jewish wedding and its prophetic stages, the purposes of Jacob's Trouble, God's two economies for Israel and the Body of Messiah, the Body of Messiah being exempt from God's wrath (which encompasses all seven years of Jacob's Trouble), the imminence of the Rapture, the necessity of time between the Rapture and the Second Coming, the necessity of believers to enter into the Messianic Millennial Kingdom in their human bodies, the Body of Messiah not being found in Jacob's Trouble, and the many distinctions between the Rapture and the Second Coming.

After all of this teaching on the Pre-Trib Rapture, some may be wondering what the connection with Israel is. Simply put, when some of the Jewish people are raptured, Israel will be just as affected as the rest of the world. Some of Israel will just disappear, and they will be looking for answers. In addition, we need to remember that the Pre-Trib Rapture is the fulfillment of the fifth feast of the Lord, the Feast of Trumpets. This fulfillment will be a huge wake-up call for Israel to start the process of national redemption during Jacob's Trouble, and by the end, all Israel will be saved! This salvation of Israel is the prophetic fulfillment of the sixth feast of the Lord, Yom Kippur (Day of Atonement).

In addition, the ancient Jewish wedding customs are a wonderful picture of God's prophetic plan for the Body of Messiah.

Currently, the Body of Messiah, the Bride of Messiah, is eagerly waiting for her groom, the Messiah to come and fetch her. This is the moment of the Pre-Trib Rapture when Yeshua will fetch His bride and bring her in a joyous processional to the wedding chamber located in heaven. Since the Body of Messiah is composed of Jewish and Gentile believers, a part of Israel will be greatly affected when this Rapture occurs.

Prayer

Father in heaven, we thank you for your great love in protecting the Body of Messiah, your bride, from your great wrath of Jacob's Trouble. We look forward to the time we shall all be raptured out of this home and journeying to our new home in heaven. Help us to live our lives down here on Earth with this future heavenly focus in mind. Help us to live in your love, joy, mercy, and grace, being empowered by your Ruach. Let your light shine in our hearts and lives so many others can see the light of Yeshua. And finally, help us to reach many Jewish and Gentile people with the good news message of Yeshua, so that they can be saved and not have to endure Jacob's Trouble. We pray in Yeshua's name. Amen.

Chapter 9

Israel in the First Half of Jacob's Trouble

After the Rapture occurs, we can only imagine the effect that will have on the world! The Rapture will undoubtedly be the greatest mystery the world has ever known. Many will be looking for answers as to how and why so many people disappeared in an instant. Maybe the Anti-messiah will have a wonderful and intriguing reason that most of the world's population will gladly believe. Some people around the world will receive Yeshua as their Lord and Savior only seconds after the Rapture occurs. Unfortunately for them, they will have to live through Jacob's Trouble. Others will be saved during the seven-year period of the Tribulation. Much of the world will receive the delusional spirit of Anti-messiah and will believe in him.

In any event, the Pre-Trib Rapture occurs some time *before* the beginning of Jacob's Trouble. This is why it is called "pre-trib," which means "before the tribulation." The Bible does not tell us how many days or months or years it occurs before Jacob's Trouble; just that it does. Many believers think the Rapture is the beginning of the Tribulation Period. Although this is possible, it is not probable. The actual beginning of the Tribulation Period occurs when the Anti-messiah signs a seven-year peace treaty with Israel. The ending of the Tribulation Period would then be seven years later. I believe the Pre-Trib Rapture will help the Anti-messiah in some way to further negotiate the peace agreement with Israel. It is also possible that the Rapture will help to propel him into the world's spotlight—especially if he seems to have all the answers to the world's problems! Once the document is signed by both parties, then Jacob's Trouble begins!

As we look at the events that surround Israel today, it is easy to see that the world's hatred for Israel and the Jewish people is dramatically increasing. As time moves forward, the world will ultimately have a great desire to wipe out and kill all Jewish people. This desire will gradually increase and result in a future holocaust called Jacob's Trouble and the Tribulation Period. This Tribulation Period is the seventieth week of Daniel (prophesied in Daniel 9:24–27), the last seven-year period for Israel's history in the age of grace. What many believers do not know about the Tribulation Period is that God redirects His focus back upon Israel and the Jewish people. Truly, He never took His attention from them, but in Jacob's Trouble we shall see His plan for Israel develop into its culmination! But before we delve into Israel in the first half of Jacob's Trouble, let's take a look at God's judgment of the world throughout the entire seven years.

God's Judgment of the World

Practically every believer in Yeshua knows about the book of Revelation and how the Lord is going to judge the world for its sin. He judged the world a long time ago with the Flood, and He will once again judge the world with twenty-one plagues in Jacob's Trouble. Jacob's Trouble is typically divided into two segments of three and a half years—the first half and the second half. A typical belief is that the first half of Jacob's Trouble is characterized by world peace, and the second half is distinguished by God's great wrath. As we shall see from this study, this belief is far from the truth! Yes, it is true that people in the Tribulation Period will be saying, "Peace and safety," but does this mean there will actually be peace and safety for the world? I think not!

1 Thessalonians 5:1–3, 9

> 1 Now concerning the times and seasons, brothers and sisters, you have no need for anything to be written to you. 2 For you yourselves know very well that the Day of the Lord comes like a thief in the night. 3 When they are saying, "*Shalom* and safety," sudden destruction comes upon them like a woman having birth pains in the womb—there is no way they will escape.
>
> 9 For God did not destine us for wrath but for obtaining salvation through our Lord *Yeshua* the Messiah.

There actually may be some peace for the world in the Tribulation Period, but it would only last a very short time. Just after the signing of the covenant between the Anti-messiah and Israel, the world will be rejoicing in their "shalom and safety" (verse 3). It is interesting to see how the world is crying out for peace and safety today! We have so many wars, rebellions, and uprisings that it is hard to comprehend—and the Scripture says it will only get worse!

However, our current wars and rumors of wars are not the ones Yeshua spoke about in Matthew 24. Those wars are the Tribulation Period wars, not today's wars. We are not in the Tribulation Period right now. We are in the "end times" or the "last days." That's why I call our wars the "birth pains" of the "birth pains." Our wars and rumors of wars are only the birth pangs of the Tribulation Period wars and rumors of wars! And the world will be getting even worse as time goes on.

Humankind's love will grow colder by the day. So, it makes perfect sense that the world will want peace and safety, but will make the tragic mistake of thinking that the Anti-messiah will be able to supply it!

The phrase "Day of the Lord" here refers to the seven-year Tribulation Period (verse 2). Sudden destruction will come upon the world just like a thief in the night attacks unsuspecting victims. Paul says that none of these non-believers will escape the hand of the Lord (verse 3). They will all come to their destruction. It certainly does not look like peace and safety will last very long in the Tribulation Period. Sudden destruction from the Lord's wrath will come upon them! Verse 9 suggests that there is a connection here between God's wrath and the Day of the Lord. Instead of His wrath, we are destined for His salvation. This time period is then characterized by God's wrath, since today's believers are not destined for God's wrath!

Revelation 6:1–8

> 1 Then I saw when the Lamb opened one of the seven seals, and I heard one of the four living creatures say with a voice like thunder, "Come!" 2 I looked, and behold, there was a white horse. The one riding on it had a bow, and a crown was given to him. He went out as a conqueror so he might conquer.
> 3 When the Lamb opened the second seal, I heard the second living creature saying, "Come!" 4 Then another horse came out, fiery red. The one riding on it was permitted to take peace from the earth, so that people would slaughter one another. He was given a great sword.
> 5 When the Lamb opened the third seal, I heard the third living creature saying, "Come!" And behold, I saw a black horse. The one riding on it held a balance scale in his hand. 6 Then I heard something like a voice in the midst of the four living creatures saying, "A quart

of wheat for a denarius, and three quarts of barley for a denarius—but do no harm to the oil and wine!"
7 When the Lamb opened the fourth seal, I heard the fourth living creature saying, "Come!" 8 Behold, I saw a horse, pale greenish gray. The name of the one riding on it was Death, and *Sheol* was following with him. Authority was given to them over a fourth of the earth, to kill by sword and by famine and by plague and by the wild beasts of the earth.

In Revelation 6, Yeshua, who is described as the Lamb, begins to open the seven seals of God's judgment upon the world. The first seal unlocks the Anti-messiah riding a white horse. Although he may seem to be the "knight in shining armor" with all the answers to the world's problems, he comes out to war against the world in order to conquer it (verse 2). Yeshua breaks the second seal with the horseman riding a red horse (verses 3–4). This horseman was given a great sword to cause great war and take *shalom* away from the world. With the first two seals, we are clearly told that the world will be at war, with the Anti-messiah leading the way. Shalom will be missing from the world. So, why do most believers think there is peace in the first half of Jacob's Trouble?!

In verses 5–6, the third seal is broken, unleashing the third horseman riding a black horse. The pair of scales in his hands symbolizes famine. A day's wages only buys a quart of wheat or three quarts of barley. This is hardly enough food for any family. Famine certainly adds to the problems of the world.

In verses 7–8, the fourth seal is broken. Death is the fourth horseman, with Hades following him around the earth. They have authority over a fourth of the earth. They are allowed to kill with the sword, famine, pestilence, and wild beasts. The point of this fourth seal is the amount of devastation that comes upon the world.

Can you imagine this destruction? At least twenty-five percent of the world's population will die in a very short time within the first part of the Tribulation Period. Devastating also is the way they die, by either war, hunger, disease, or wild animal attacks. This is worldwide devastation that has never been experienced before! So how can anyone believe there is peace on Earth during this first half of Jacob's Trouble? Besides all this, Hades is following the death of these folks, and so these people are all non-believers entering into eternal damnation! Again I ask, how can anyone say there is peace in this world during the first half of the Tribulation Period?

Well, the answer is obvious. The people of the world will not have peace in their personal lives, but they will have a peace treaty with Israel. So, the true peace in the world will be that the world will not attack or have war with Israel. That is, until the Anti-messiah starts the attack in the middle of Jacob's Trouble. At that point, the worst holocaust against the Jewish people will occur. But prior to that time, there will be peace between Israel and the world.

Revelation 6:9–11

> 9 When the Lamb opened the fifth seal, I saw under the altar the souls of those slaughtered for the sake of the word of God and for the witness they had. 10 And they cried out with a loud voice, saying, "O Sovereign Master, holy and true, how long before You judge those who dwell on the earth and avenge our blood?"
> 11 Then a white robe was given to each of them, and they were told to rest a little while longer, until the number of their fellow servants was complete—their brothers and sisters who were to be killed as they had been.

There will not be peace for the people of the world during the first half of Jacob's Trouble. People will be wondering if they are the next ones to die in the judgment. But what about believers in Yeshua? Will they be okay during the first half? Revelation 6:9–11 reveals through the fifth seal that Jewish and Gentile believers are killed for their faith in Yeshua during the first half of Jacob's Trouble! Verse 9 shows the souls of the believers under the altar in heaven. They cry out to the Lord for vengeance for their deaths, and the Lord tells them to wait for the rest of their brethren to be killed in the Tribulation Period (verses 10–11).

In essence, the Lord tells these souls and spirits of believers who were martyred for Yeshua to wait for the rest of the martyrs of Jacob's Trouble. This means they are to wait until the end of the seven-year period before God brings vengeance on their spilled blood. The point of this section is to show that there will not be peace for believers in the first half (or the second half) of the Tribulation Period, since many will be killed for their faith.

Revelation 17:1–6

> 1 Then one of the seven angels holding the seven bowls came and spoke with me, saying, "Come, I will show you the sentencing of the great prostitute, who sits on many waters. 2 The earth's kings committed sexual immorality with her, and those who dwell on the earth got drunk with the wine of her immorality."
> 3 So he carried me away in the *Ruach* [Spirit] into a wilderness, and I saw a woman sitting on a scarlet beast that was full of blasphemous names and had seven heads and ten horns. 4 The woman was clothed in purple and scarlet, and adorned with gold and precious stones and pearls. She was holding a golden cup in her hand full of detestable things and the filth of her immorality, 5 and on her forehead was written a name, a mystery:
> "Babylon the Great, the mother of prostitutes and the detestable things of the earth."

> 6 And I saw the woman drunk with the blood of the *kedoshim* and with the blood of the witnesses of *Yeshua*. When I saw her, I was totally astounded.

Not only does Revelation 6 show first half believers will not have worldly peace, but we must also remember that the woman riding the scarlet beast of Revelation 17:1–6 is drunk with the blood of the believers. This prostitute will have great influence over the ten kings of the earth. They will be carried away with her great immorality (verses 1–3). She will be financially rich, full of abominations and called Babylon the Great. She is the one-world religion that will be totally intolerant of true believers of Yeshua.

This means the one-world religion will be attacking and killing the true believers of Yeshua during Jacob's Trouble, and the world will be in agreement with their treachery (verses 4–6). Now I could argue these believers who die for Yeshua will certainly have peace in Him, but this is not what we are talking about. The idea here is to report that there will not be worldly peace among people (believers and non-believers) in the first half of Jacob's Trouble as many of today's believers might think!

God's Focus on Israel

The Body of Messiah understands that the Tribulation Period is a time destined by the Lord to judge the world for its dramatic sins. What most believers do not understand is that the Lord is additionally focusing His attention on Israel and the Jewish people. He has a plan for Israel, and He is continuously fulfilling that plan. As discussed earlier, Ezekiel 36 and 37 summarize God's plan for Israel. He is currently regathering the Jewish people from around the world to bring them back to the Land of Israel. On the whole, this regathering is in unbelief of Yeshua. The idea here is that the Lord will regather the

Jewish people back to the Land so that He can judge them, save them as a nation at the end of Jacob's Trouble, and then properly restore them back to the Land in belief of Yeshua as their Messiah after the Second Coming.

Daniel 9:24–27

> 24 "Seventy weeks are decreed concerning your people and your holy city,
> to put an end to transgression
> to bring sin to an end,
> to atone for iniquity,
> to bring in everlasting righteousness,
> to seal up vision and prophecy,
> and to anoint the Holy of Holies.
> 25 So know and understand:
> From the issuing of the decree to restore and to build Jerusalem until the time *Mashiach,* the Prince, there shall be seven weeks and 62 weeks. It will be rebuilt, with plaza and moat, but it will be in times of distress.
> 26 Then after the 62 weeks *Mashiach* will be cut off and have nothing. Then the people of a prince who is to come will destroy the city and the sanctuary. But his end will come like a flood. Until the end of the war that is decreed there will be destruction.
> 27 Then he will make a firm covenant with many for one week, but in the middle of the week he will put an end to sacrifice and offering. And on a wing of abominations will come one who destroys, until the decreed annihilation is poured out on the one who destroys.'"

This scripture passage contains the famous seventy weeks of Daniel. It is a prophecy given to Daniel by the angel Gabriel that summarizes Israel's future prophetic history. In verse 24, the prophecy as a whole is presented. In verse 25, the first sixty-nine weeks are described. In verse 26, the mysterious events between the sixty-ninth and seventieth weeks are detailed. In verse 27, the final week, the seventieth week is expounded.

The prophecy begins in verse 24 with seventy weeks decreed for "your people" and "your holy city." Since Gabriel is talking with Daniel, his "people" are the Jewish people, and his "holy city" is obviously the city of Jerusalem. Once again, this prophecy is not talking about any other people group other than the Jewish people. It is not discussing the United States, Russia, China, Japan, Australia, European Union, and so forth. Nor does it talk about the Body of Messiah (however, the mysterious time period between the sixty-ninth and seventieth week does include the Body of Messiah). This prophecy is strictly concerned about Israel!

Seventy "weeks" (shavuim) literally means seventy "sevens." The idea here is that seventy sevens of time have been decreed for Israel. Are these time periods seconds, minutes, hours, days, months, or years? To determine the answer, we look to the context of Daniel 9. In verse 2, Daniel finds out that Israel is to spend seventy years banished from the Land of Israel. This helps us to determine that "weeks" is speaking of years. Also, we have the benefit of looking back in history to see how everything lines up, and *years* is the best answer to the question. Therefore, the seventy weeks of Daniel turns out to be seventy sets of seven years, or a total of 490 years. So what was Israel decreed to do?

I believe the first three deeds of verse 24: to finish the transgression, to make an end of sin, and to make atonement for iniquity were fulfilled in Yeshua's First Coming when He died on the tree and resurrected from the dead. I also believe the second three deeds: to bring in everlasting righteousness, to seal up vision and prophecy, and to anoint the Holy of Holies will be fulfilled in and through Yeshua's Second Coming. When He comes back, He will set up the Messianic Millennial

Kingdom, rule with everlasting righteousness, seal up Daniel's vision, and anoint the Holy of Holies. The Holy of Holies is in the Temple; Yeshua will build and anoint the fourth and final Temple for the Kingdom!

In verse 25, we find two prophecies. One is the issuing of a decree to restore and rebuild Jerusalem. King Artaxerxes of Medo-Persia issued this decree in 445 BC. The first set of "seven weeks," which equals forty-nine years, is the time it took for Jerusalem to be rebuilt with a plaza and moat. It was built even in times of distress.

The second prophecy concerns the coming of the Messiah, the Prince. From the time that Jerusalem was restored until the time when Messiah would come would be "sixty-two weeks," or 434 years. The idea here is that the coming of Messiah would equate with the day Yeshua presented Himself to all Israel as the King of the Jews and Messiah the Prince as He triumphantly entered Jerusalem just prior to His last earthly Passover.

Added together, the seven weeks plus the sixty-two weeks equals sixty-nine weeks or a total of 483 years. Thus, from the time of the kingly decree to rebuild and restore Jerusalem until Messiah Yeshua would present Himself to Israel was sixty-nine weeks or 483 years. So, when Yeshua presented Himself as Messiah to Israel and the world, sixty-nine of the seventy weeks were fulfilled. There is one week, or seven years, of the prophecy left to be fulfilled. When will this occur?

Before the final seventieth week of Daniel can be fulfilled, God in His infinite wisdom, has provided a reprieve (if you will) for the consecutive fulfillment of this timeline. There is a lapse in time, a proverbial bump in the prophetic road, and it is found in verse 26.

In verse 26, the key word *after* suggests there are events occurring after the sixty-ninth week and prior to the seventieth week. The phrase "after the sixty-two weeks" suggests that the events referred to occur, not only after the sixty-two weeks, but also after the seven weeks. So, we see the Messiah will be cut off and have nothing after the total of sixty-nine weeks (or 483 years) have been fulfilled. As of yet in the prophecy, there has not been any mention of the seventieth week of Daniel. That occurs in verse 27. Therefore, as we see events unfolding in the prophecy after the sixty-nine weeks are fulfilled, we are to conclude that there is a mysterious time period occurring between the sixty-ninth and seventieth weeks. What exactly happens during this mysterious time? The rest of the verse helps to answer this question.

First, Messiah will be "cut off" (*karat*). This Hebrew word *karat* means to "cut off, cut down, or exterminate." When it is used with people, it is talking about destroying and exterminating. The idea here is that Messiah will die! In His death He will have "nothing." "Nothing" (ayin) means "nothingness, non-existence and can mean no one." This could mean that no person will help Him in His death. Or it could mean that Messiah did "not" die for Himself but for other people. In either event, the important fact here is that Messiah dies after the sixty-nine week time period is fulfilled!

However, in verse 26, we are given a clue as to when Messiah's death will actually occur! It will happen prior to the time the people and the prince who is to come will destroy the city and the sanctuary. Titus and the Romans destroyed the Temple and the city of Jerusalem in AD 70. Therefore, Messiah was to die prior to AD 70. For those of us who believe Yeshua is the Messiah, this is a wonderful verse to share with our non-believing Jewish brethren concerning the Jewish Messiah! I simply ask them, "What Jewish man claimed he was Messiah and died for the sins of the world prior to AD 70?" The answer is quite obvious! Most Jewish people will answer in question form, "Jesus?" Yes, Jesus!

In verse 27, we see a change in the context of the passage. Now we are talking about the seventieth week of Daniel and the one who will rule the world at that time. The Anti-messiah will make a "firm" (*gavar*) covenant. This means this covenant will be strong and prevailing. It will be made with "many" of the Jewish people, which means the whole nation of Israel. It will last for "one week." This is the seventieth week of Daniel: the last seven-year period for Israel to fulfill Daniel's prophecy. This firm covenant is a covenant that Israel has a great desire to make with the world even today! I met a Jewish Israeli man in Israel years ago and we were discussing a peace treaty for Israel and the world. He proudly declared, "I would sell my soul for a peace treaty in Israel!" Although he was zealous for Israel's peace, he was totally misguided. It saddened my heart, because the only true way to peace is through Yeshua!

After the Anti-messiah signs a peace treaty with Israel on behalf of the world, you would think there would be peace. But unfortunately, there is not! The Anti-messiah will stop the offerings and animal sacrifices at the midpoint of Jacob's Trouble. Beyond any doubt, this scripture reveals that the third Temple will be standing in Jerusalem and will be used for worship of the Lord by the Jewish people! The problem we have is not knowing when the third Temple will be built. It could occur prior to the Tribulation Period because the current Sanhedrin and Temple Mount Faithful groups are calling for the rebuilding of the Temple even as you read this book today! However, it could also be built within the Tribulation Period as a condition of the Anti-messiah's agreement with Israel. Again, we just don't know when the Temple will be built because the Bible does not tell us. However, we do know that it will be standing and in use at the midpoint of Jacob's Trouble!

Not only will the Anti-messiah stop the animal sacrifices in the Temple, but he will perform the most horrifyingly evil act that Jewish people could ever imagine—the Abomination of Desolation! He will set himself up as God in the Temple and require worship from the Jewish people and the world (2 Thessalonians 2:3–4). This very act occurs in the middle of the Tribulation and will begin the second half of the Tribulation Period, which Yeshua calls the Great Tribulation (Matthew

24:21). It will be a time unprecedented in history when the Anti-messiah and his armies will unleash the 666 mark. They will kill all people who do not take the mark and pledge their allegiance to the Anti-messiah. The good news in all of this is the rest of verse 27. No matter how bad it gets during Jacob's Trouble, the one who makes desolate will in the end become desolate himself!

Revelation 7:1–8

> 1 After this, I saw four angels standing at the four corners of the earth, holding back the four winds of the earth so that no wind would blow on the earth or on the sea or against any tree. 2 Then I saw another angel coming up from the east, having the seal of the living God. He cried out with a loud voice to the four angels who were permitted to harm the earth and the sea, 3 saying, "Do no harm to the earth or the sea or the trees, until we have put a seal on the foreheads of the servants of our God."
> 4 Now I heard the number of those marked with the seal: 144,000 from every tribe of *Bnei-Yisrael*—
> 5 12,000 from the tribe of Judah;
> 12,000 from the tribe of Reuben;
> 12,000 from the tribe of Gad;
> 6 12,000 from the tribe of Asher;
> 12,000 from the tribe of Naphtali;
> 12,000 from the tribe of Manasseh;
> 7 12,000 from the tribe of Simeon;
> 12,000 from the tribe of Levi;
> 12,000 from the tribe of Issachar;
> 8 12,000 from the tribe of Zebulun;
> 12,000 from the tribe of Joseph;
> 12,000 from the tribe of Benjamin.

After the sixth seal (Revelation 6:12-17) is opened and the people of the earth proclaim the wrath of God has come, four angels will hold back the wind of the earth so that no wind blows on the earth. The effects of this event will be catastrophic! The earth's temperatures would dramatically be affected. The hot places around the world would get hotter, and the cold places around the world would get colder. Ultimately, if there is no wind long term, everybody might die! No doubt the world will be crying, "Global warming!"

Verse 1 does not tell us for how long the wind won't blow. But in verses 2–3, there are four more angels ready to harm the earth and sea another way. The announcing angel asks these four not to do their job until other angels have sealed the bondservants of the Lord. Who are these bondservants? These bondservants are declared in verse 4 to be 144,000 Jewish people! So, 144,000 Jewish people at the beginning of Jacob's Trouble will be supernaturally saved and sealed for the Lord's service in the Tribulation Period!

Verses 5–8 identify 12,000 Jewish people from each of the twelve tribes. Interestingly, two tribes are not mentioned here: Ephraim and Dan. Although the name of Ephraim is missing, Ephraim is still included in this list. Joseph's tribe is made up of two tribes which are his two sons: Ephraim and Manasseh. Typically, when Joseph is mentioned in the Bible it automatically includes both tribes of Ephraim and Manasseh. However, Manasseh is already mentioned on its own, so it would not be included with Joseph in this list. Joseph would then be comprised of Ephraim's tribe.

Dan, however, is a different story. Many believers think Dan is cursed, and therefore is not mentioned here. However, if this were true, then Dan would not be mentioned in the list for the tribes found in the Messianic Millennial Kingdom in Ezekiel 48, either. A better answer would be that Dan is engulfed by a neighboring tribe like Asher or Naphtali. Therefore, although not specifically mentioned, Dan would then be included in the tribe of Naphtali or Asher.

The question then arises, "Why are 144,000 Jewish people sealed at the beginning of the Tribulation Period?" Presumably they are needed to fill the void of believers on the earth left by the Pre-Trib Rapture! At the moment the Rapture occurs, there will be no believers left on planet Earth. However, people are getting saved every second of every minute around the globe. Can you imagine someone getting saved only one second after the Rapture occurs? They will be saved too late to be snatched up for the Rapture and will have to live in tribulation through Jacob's Trouble. Even though there are some believers saved on earth just after the Rapture, it is not enough to fulfill God's plan for the Jewish people.

The Lord will definitely need people to share the good news message of Yeshua, so He will supernaturally cause 144,000 of the Jewish people to be saved. This makes sense because God is focusing His plan and attention on Israel. Saving 144,000 Jewish people will help bring that plan to fruition. Who better to share Yeshua, the Jewish Messiah, with the Jewish and Gentile people of the world than the chosen Jewish bondservants of the Lord?!

I believe the next scripture reading in Revelation 7 is connected to the 144,000. Verses 9–17 show a heavenly scene of a great multitude of believers arising out of the second half of Jacob's Trouble. They are standing before the Father and the Lamb, praising the Lord through song and waving palm branches. This could very well be a celebration of Yeshua as King of the Jews during the Feast of Tabernacles in heaven! These souls receive some wonderful promises of the Lord, including white robes washed in the blood of the Lamb!

The idea here is that all these people from around the world receive Yeshua as their Lord and Savior through the 144,000 bondservants' preaching of the good news message. The 144,000 are the beginning of the folks saved in the Tribulation

Period, and they help an abundance of people come to the Lord in probably the greatest revival story in the history of the world. To put it simply, the 144,000 are the first fruits of the Tribulation Period!

Revelation 14:1–5

> 1 Then I looked, and behold, the Lamb was standing on Mount Zion, and with Him were 144,000 who had His name and His Father's name written on their foreheads. 2 And I heard a voice from heaven like the roar of rushing waters and the booming of loud thunder. The voice I heard was like harpists playing on their harps. 3 And they are singing a new song before the throne and before the four living creatures and the elders; and no one is able to learn the song except the 144,000 who had been redeemed from the earth.
> 4 These are the ones who have not defiled themselves with women, for they are virgins. These are the ones who follow the Lamb wherever He goes. These have been redeemed from among mankind as firstfruits for God and the Lamb.
> 5 And in their mouth was found no lie—they are blameless.

John sees a special scene in his vision of the 144,000 bond-servants. The 144,000 are standing with Yeshua on Mount Zion, Jerusalem (verse 1). This picture reveals a truth about the 144,000 Messianic Jews—that they will make it through Jacob's Trouble alive and well in the Lord. He will protect them from the evil ones for all seven years. In verses 2–3, they sing a song of praise to the Lamb that only they are allowed to learn. Verses 4–5 reveal character traits of the 144,000. They are Jewish men who are virgins, tell the truth, do the right thing in life, and follow the Lord wherever He goes. These 144,000 are true *talmidim* of Yeshua! Verse 4 also states they are purchased from among men as "first fruits" unto the Lord! What does *first fruits* mean?

This term indicates these 144,000 saved Jewish men are the first of many more people to come who will be saved during Jacob's Trouble. We can actually understand this statement two different ways: the 144,000 are the first fruits of many more Jewish people to be saved in the Tribulation Period, or the 144,000 are the first fruits of many more people in general to be saved in the Tribulation Period. Either way, this group is the first fruits of Jacob's Trouble.

Now a very interesting questions arises, "How can this group be the first fruits of the Tribulation if the Body of Messiah first enters into the Tribulation as the "mid-" and "post-tribbers" believe?" Would the Body of Messiah not be the first fruits of the Tribulation Period since they are the first believers of the Tribulation Period?! If the Rapture is "pre-trib," then we do not have a problem with these 144,000 being the first fruits because the Body of Messiah is in heaven and out of the earthly picture. It does make more sense, and it all lines up better to believe in the Pre-Trib Rapture!

Revelation 11:1–2

> 1 Then a measuring rod like a staff was given to me, saying, "Get up and measure the Temple of God and the altar, and count those worshiping in it. 2 But do not measure the court outside the Temple—leave it out, because it has been given to the nations, and they shall trample the holy city for forty-two months.

Another aspect of Israel in the first half of Jacob's Trouble is the Temple. I have already established that the Temple will be built again and in operation by the middle of the Tribulation Period. This scripture passage verifies this belief. In verse 1,

John is told to measure God's Temple and the altar. The Temple, then, is standing, and the Jewish people are worshiping the Lord in it!

But in verse 2, John is told not to measure the court that is outside the Temple. This court is the court of the Gentiles. There was a short wall that encircled the outside area of the second temple. No Gentile person was allowed to pass by this wall and come any closer to the Lord. If they did, the punishment was death. So, all Gentiles who came to worship the Lord could only come as close as this wall would allow. This is a very symbolic moment for the Gentiles of the world.

Verse 2 continues with the fact that this court will be given over to the Gentiles so that they have control over it! Not only that, but the Gentiles will be allowed to control and have power over the city of Jerusalem as well for a total of forty-two months. These forty-two months are the three and a half years of the Great Tribulation, the second half of Jacob's Trouble.

So, it looks like the Gentiles, led by the Anti-messiah, will assume control over all of Jerusalem for the duration of the Great Tribulation. This makes sense in that Anti-messiah will set Himself up as God in the Temple in Jerusalem in the middle of Jacob's Trouble. He will require worship from both Jews and Gentiles around the world. Anyone who does not worship him, he will kill by cutting off their heads! The point I wish to make here is that the Jewish Temple is standing at the middle of Jacob's Trouble and will be used (unfortunately for evil) throughout the duration of the second half of the Tribulation.

<u>Revelation 11:3–13</u>

> 3 And I will grant authority to My two witnesses and they will prophesy for 1,260 days, dressed in sackcloth." 4 These are the two olive trees and the two *menorot* [menorahs] that are standing before the Lord of the earth. 5 If anyone wishes to harm them, fire comes out

> of their mouths and consumes their enemies. If anyone wants to harm them, he must be killed in this way. 6 These two have the power to shut the heavens, so that no rain may fall during the days of their prophesying. And they have power over the waters to turn them into blood, and to strike the earth with every kind of plague as often as they wish.
> 7 When they have finished their testimony, the beast that rises from the abyss will make war on them, and overcome them and kill them. 8 And their corpses will lie in the open street of the great city that figuratively is called Sodom and Egypt—where also their Lord was crucified. 9 Some from the peoples and tribes and tongues and nations will look at their corpses for three and a half days, not allowing them to be placed into a grave. 10 Those who dwell on the earth will rejoice over them. They will celebrate and send gifts to one another, because these two prophets tormented those who dwell on the earth.
> 11 But after the three and a half days, the breath of life from God entered them, and they stood up on their feet; and great fear fell on those who were watching them. 12 Then they heard a loud voice from heaven saying to them, "Come up here!" And they went up to heaven in a cloud, while their enemies watched them. 13 At that hour there was a great earthquake, and a tenth of the city collapsed. Seven thousand people were killed in the earthquake, and the rest were terrified and gave glory to the God of heaven.

After the Temple and the Gentile court are discussed, we are then introduced to the two witnesses. The greatest question most believers have concerning these two witnesses is probably the least concerning to the Lord. Most believers want to know who they are, but we are not told in the Bible. Therefore, it is obvious to me that the Lord does not want us to know right now! Trying to identify them is pure speculation. Three names usually come up in conversation: Moses, Elijah, and Enoch. I don't believe any of these three are coming back to life on earth in their human bodies to perform more ministry for the Lord. I simply believe the Lord will raise up two special Jewish believers to become His two witnesses during Jacob's Trouble.

Verse 3 states that they will prophesy for twelve hundred and sixty days dressed in sackcloth. Twelve hundred and sixty days is three and a half years according to the biblical Jewish calendar (months are thirty days and so 1,260 days equals forty-two months). This timeframe is the same for the Gentiles trampling the city of Jerusalem underfoot (the forty-two months found in verse 2). The difference is that the trampling of Jerusalem occurs in the second half of Jacob's Trouble, while the two witnesses are found in the first half.

In verse 4, the two witnesses are described as the two olive trees and two *menorot* (plural for *menorah*, meaning lampstand) that stand before the Lord. This is in reference to Zechariah 4:3–14. Zechariah saw a vision of two olive trees and a menorah. The two olive trees represent the two anointed ones of the Lord (verse 14). In Zechariah's time, that would have been Zerubbabel (verses 6–10) and Joshua the *cohen gadol* (high priest) of Israel (referenced in Zechariah 3:8). The menorah represents the Ruach Kodesh (Holy Spirit) and His power. Zerubbabel and Joshua then led Israel by the power of the Ruach in a spiritual revival that culminated in the building of the second Temple.

Zerubbabel and Joshua are the foreshadowing of the future two witnesses of Jacob's Trouble. John, in Revelation 11, then uses both the two olive trees and the two menorahs to represent the two witnesses (John actually adds a menorah to Zechariah's vision to end up with two). The two witnesses are then the two anointed ones from the Lord who will be led by the Ruach as they perform God's will.

The two witnesses perform miracles, signs, and wonders much like the Old Covenant prophets Elijah and Elisha (verses 5–6). If anyone tries to harm them, fire proceeds from their mouths and devours their adversaries! This is quite miraculous! I recall prophets calling fire down from heaven, but never fire coming from within the prophets—talk about Holy Spirit fire! The two witnesses also have the power to stop the rain, turn water into blood, and cause worldwide plagues. No wonder the world throws a party when the two witnesses are killed by the Anti-messiah (verses 7–10)! They were tormented by the two witnesses (but for good reason). Their dead bodies lay in the streets of Jerusalem (which is spiritually called "Sodom and Egypt") for three and a half days.

Calling Jerusalem "Sodom and Egypt" truly shows how spiritually bad the city of Jerusalem will become. This is very unfortunate because Israel will change from rabbinical Judaism to biblical Judaism during Jacob's Trouble. So, even when Israel reinstitutes temple worship, it looks as though God is not pleased with her. Why does the world allow the two witnesses' bodies to lay dead in the street for three and a half days? Maybe because they were tormented for three and a half years and they are celebrating their deaths one day per year of torment. These three and a half days also gives us the clue to determine when the two witnesses prophesied.

I believe the two witnesses prophesy during the first half of Jacob's Trouble. Why? If these events were in the second half, then the three and a half days of viewing the bodies would extend past the end of Jacob's Trouble, and this is highly unlikely. In addition, the timing of the two witnesses occurs prior to the seventh trumpet blast (Revelation 11:14–15). The seventh trumpet blast occurs toward the end of the first half of the Tribulation Period. That makes the events surrounding the two witnesses occur in the first half.

But what happens next is truly amazing! In verses 11–13 we see another miracle of the Lord. The two witnesses are resurrected! They stand on their feet for the whole world to see. As the world is in great fear of the two witnesses, the Lord calls them up to heaven much like He raptured the Body of Messiah up to heaven. The enemies watch the two witnesses fly up to heaven. Shortly thereafter, the earth quakes, one-tenth of the city of Jerusalem falls, and 7,000 people die. The rest are terrified of the Lord and give Him the glory! Will some of the Jewish and Gentile people around the world give their lives to Yeshua when this occurs? Only the Lord knows, but we do know these final events of the two witnesses will occur right around the same time that the Anti-messiah performs the Abomination of Desolation. Maybe it was one last effort on the Lord's part to show His mercy for salvation just prior to the Great Tribulation.

Matthew 24:3–14

> 3 As He was sitting on the Mount of Olives, the disciples came to Him privately, saying, "Tell us, when will these things happen? What will be the sign of Your coming and of the end of the age?"
> 4 *Yeshua* answered them, "Be careful that no one leads you astray! 5 For many will come in My name, saying, 'I am the Messiah,' and will lead many astray. 6 You will hear of wars and rumors of wars. See that you are not alarmed, for this must happen but it is not yet the end. 7 For nation will rise up against nation, and kingdom against kingdom. And there will be famines and earthquakes in various places. 8 But all these things are only the beginning of birth pains.
> 9 "Then they will hand you over to persecution and will kill you. You will be hated by all the nations because of My name. 10 And then many will fall away and will betray one another and hate one other. 11 Many false prophets will arise and lead many astray. 12 Because

> lawlessness will multiply, the love of many will grow cold. 13 But the one who endures to the end will be saved. 14 This Good News of the kingdom shall be proclaimed in the whole world as a testimony to all the nations, and then the end will come.

The *talmidim* (disciples) asked Yeshua three questions (verse 3). When will the Temple be destroyed? What's the sign of your Second Coming? What's the sign of the end of the age? They did not know the last two questions were right around the same time period. They thought Yeshua was coming back much sooner than 2,000 years later! Yeshua then shares in V.4-6 some general characteristics of the age of the Body of Messiah. These characteristics began in the 1st Century and will continue right into Jacob's Trouble. Then in V.7-8, we see the sign of the end of the age predicted. Then in V.9-14, Yeshua shares the characteristics of the First Half of Jacob's Trouble. Yeshua then taught the talmidim what would occur in the Second Half of Jacob's Trouble ending with the sign of His Second Coming in V.15-31.

Yeshua warned all believers for all time not to be misled (verse 4). Many false Messiahs will come and lead people down the road to perdition (verse 5). Believers should also not be afraid of all that befalls the world: wars, rumors of wars, famines, and earthquakes (verses 6–7). Luke 21:11 (a parallel passage to Matthew 24) adds in "epidemics" and "terrors along with great signs from heaven." These "epidemics" are plagues and diseases. This includes all of the old plagues and even new diseases like Covid-19 and any other new variants that come out in the future. The "terrors and great signs" are God's additional judgments flowing from heaven upon the Earth! In V.7, "nation against nation" and "kingdom against kingdom" are Hebraisms meaning World Wars. We have had two World Wars and the experts are predicting a third! Oy vey! These World Wars are the sign of the beginning of the end of the age.

Just like birth pains occur more frequently and intensely as time progresses toward the birth of the child, all these judgments will occur more frequently and intensely as time moves forward to Jacob's Trouble (V.8). If you think the world is a difficult place to live in now, can you imagine what it will be like in the first half of the Tribulation? There will be immense suffering occurring all over the world just through these four judgments, not including everything else already discussed in this book! The devastation will be incredible. Who will the people of the world look to for help and answers?

Also remember that the Anti-messiah will be a part of the worldwide wars and rumors of wars. In Daniel 7:17–28 and 11:36–45 (already discussed in Chapter 6) we determined that the Anti-messiah fought against three kingdoms of the world. I saw a connection with this fact and Daniel 11 where the king of the south and the king of the north fought against him, and rumors of war came from the east. As the Anti-messiah is rising to power in the first half of Jacob's Trouble through war and other means, there will be other regional wars and rumors of wars as well, all around the world. Today, it seems that the world is already engaged in too many regional wars, but Yeshua says it will dramatically increase as time moves forward!

Now in V.9-14, Yeshua specifically speaks about the events in the First Half of Jacob's Trouble. Believers in that time period will also be hated and killed by the world (verse 9). Many will stumble and deliver each other up to the authorities (verse 10). False prophets will take advantage of the world's plight (verse 11). Lawlessness (another name for sin) will overcome societies around the world, causing people's love to grow cold (verse 12). Yeshua's prophecy of the future first half is very bleak. But He ends this section on a good note. Those who endure to the end of Jacob's Trouble will be saved (verse 13).

Is Yeshua saying that believers need to have endurance to be saved? Absolutely not! We are saved by grace through faith in Yeshua and not by works so that no one can boast. So, what is Yeshua saying here? The Greek word for "saved" (*sozo*) does not always mean "saved from sin and hell." It also means "delivered, rescued." In verse 13, Yeshua encourages those believers who endure through the trials and tribulations of Jacob's Trouble. He says they will be delivered in the end!

In verse 14, we also see more good news. The good news is that the message of Yeshua will be preached to the whole world so that everyone has an opportunity to become a believer before the end comes! Once Yeshua comes back, there is no longer any opportunity for salvation. This is God's heart: that even in times of great peril around the world, people will still have the opportunity to turn to Yeshua and be saved. Praise the Lord, many will be!

Revelation 17:12–14

> 12 The ten horns that you saw are ten kings who have not yet received royal power, but receive authority as kings with the beast for one hour. 13 These kings are of one mind, and they give their power and authority to the beast. 14 They will make war against the Lamb, and the Lamb will overcome them—because He is Lord of lords and King of kings, and those with Him are called and chosen and faithful."

This scripture reading confirms the fact that the ten horns of the beast of Anti-messiah are his ten kings. When the Anti-messiah becomes king of the world, he will place his ten kings in charge of the ten kingdoms of the world (verse 12). They will rule in subjection to the Anti-messiah by giving their power and authority over to him (verse 13). They will work in unity to wage the Armageddon War against Yeshua in the Second Coming (verse 14). They will, of course, lose this war and enter into eternal damnation.

Chart

As we look at the chart, we can see the box of "Israel in the First Half" of Jacob's Trouble. Jacob's Trouble begins with the signing of the peace treaty between Israel and the Anti-messiah. This covenant of peace begins some time after the Pre-Trib Rapture occurs. The effects of the Ezekiel War, the One-World Order, the ten kingdoms, Anti-messiah becoming king of the world, and the Rapture will run into the first half of the Tribulation. All of these events, in some way or another, will help the world desire to have a peace treaty with Israel. Not only that, they will also help encourage the Jewish people to regather in the Land of Israel and build a third Temple.

As Israel engages in this peace treaty with the world, the Lord is greatly working within her ranks. He will miraculously save and seal 144,000 Jewish men from among the twelve tribes so that they will be able to preach the good news message of Yeshua to a dying world. They will be great witnesses for Yeshua in preaching, teaching, and living for Him. The world will see the greatest revival of all time during this first half of Jacob's Trouble. Many peoples of all the tribes and nations of the world will be saved. The Lord will also select two Jewish men to be His two witnesses from the city of Jerusalem. These two will preach the good news message as well and will have power like the prophets of old.

While Israel is trying to enjoy its peace treaty with the world, the world will be greatly judged by God. Yeshua predicted that there will be wars, rumors of wars, pestilence, famines, and earthquakes all around the world. Devastation will be vast. By the fourth seal of Revelation 6, more than 25 percent of the people of the world die. That's almost 2 billion people (if there are 8 billion by then). Besides all this, the Anti-messiah will be on his own mission destroying three kingdoms to set up his takeover of the world. By the midpoint of Jacob's Trouble, he will be successful at becoming king of the world.

Prayer

Lord, I cannot imagine how bad it is going to get for the world and for the Jewish people in the first half of Jacob's Trouble. The Scripture is clear, though, that the world will be under Your great judgment, and catastrophic tragedy will prevail. I pray for the peace of Jerusalem and all of Israel and for the good news message of Yeshua to go forth to the Jewish and Gentile people with great boldness in this first half. Help the world to see the light of Yeshua, to be saved, and have their names written in the Book of Life. Please strengthen all the believers who have to live through Jacob's Trouble to follow Yeshua in the power of the Ruach and help bless the Jewish people. In Yeshua's name I pray. Amen.

Chapter 10

Israel in the Middle of Jacob's Trouble

The first half of Jacob's Trouble is no picnic for Israel. She certainly will be greatly excited when they sign the seven-year peace treaty with the Anti-messiah. However, that joy over the "pseudo peace" will turn to sorrow as the world comes under God's wrath for a full seven years. But there is good news! 144,000 Jews will be saved to preach the good news message of Yeshua to a dying world of Jewish and Gentile people. The Lord shall protect them from the evil ones to do His will for the full seven years.

In addition, two Jewish witnesses will preach the good news in the city of Jerusalem for the first half of the Tribulation Period. They will come to tribulation themselves as the Anti-messiah battles against them and finally kills them. However, after a grotesque three and a half days of the world viewing their bodies, the Lord will resurrect them and rapture them to heaven in full view of everyone! It is impossible to put these events in a perfectly correct chronological order because the Bible does not share this order with us. What I do know is that the following events occur during the middle of Jacob's Trouble.

Revelation 13:1–8

> 1 Then I saw a beast rising out of the sea, that had ten horns and seven heads. On his horns were ten royal crowns, and upon his heads were slanderous names. 2 Now the beast that I saw was like a leopard, his feet like a bear's, and his mouth like a lion's. And the dragon gave him his power and his throne and great authority. 3 One of his heads seemed to have been slain, but the fatal wound was healed. The whole earth was amazed and followed the beast. 4 And they worshiped the dragon, because he had given authority to the beast. They also worshiped the beast, chanting, "Who is like the beast, and who can make war against him?"
>
> 5 The beast was given a mouth uttering great boasts and blasphemies. It was given authority to act for forty-two months. 6 Then he opened his mouth with blasphemies against God, to slander His name and His tabernacle—that is, those dwelling in heaven. 7 He was also permitted to make war against the *kedoshim* and overcome them, and he was given authority over every tribe and people and tongue and nation. 8 All who dwell on the earth shall worship him—everyone whose name has not been written from the foundation of the world in the Book of Life of the Lamb who was slain.

Revelation 13 reveals two beasts that will form an unholy triunity with HaSatan (the Satan, our adversary). As we shall see, HaSatan will set up a counterfeit of God's truth every step of the way to his kingly reign. Here, this unholy triunity counterfeits the holy triunity of God (Father, Son, and Holy Spirit).

In verse 1, we are introduced to the beast that rises up out of the sea. The sea represents the Gentile nations (Revelation 17:15). This beast is the revived Roman Empire in all of its own glory. This beast is rearing its ugly head even right now around the world as most of the nations of the world are crying out for a One World Government. Call it what you will: socialism, communism, marxism; it is pure imperialism that desires to take control over the whole world right now. In the end, it will! I have been preaching this message for a long time: the USA cannot survive as a free nation in the One World Government! So folks, get ready because we are fast approaching this One World Government.

By V.3, the Anti-messiah is revealed as the seventh head of the revived Roman Empire Beast! He is labeled as the Beast as well but he is the seventh king of the Roman Empire who will exercise his satanic power over the world as its' newest dictator.

Many believers ask me whether the Anti-messiah is Jewish or Gentile. Most of the time, these believers are hopeful that he is Jewish and thus are desirous for my approval or affirmation. But I cannot affirm peoples' beliefs simply to appease them. My theology has to come from the Scriptures. This verse clearly identifies the Anti-messiah as being Gentile. Coupled with the identification of the Anti-messiah in Daniel 9, he will be a world ruler from the revived Roman Empire. The Scripture identifies Him as a Gentile, not a Jew, from the revived Roman Empire.

The ten horns are ten kings who reign over the ten kingdoms of the world and they ultimately submit themselves to the Anti-messiah. The seven heads are the seven kings that reign over the whole earth in succession from the time of Daniel's vision. Five of those kings have already ruled, one was ruling at the time of John's revelation, and the one-world ruler (Anti-messiah) will be the seventh (Revelation 17:9–10). Each of these seven kings is characterized by their evil hatred of the God of Israel by speaking blasphemously against Him!

In verse 2, we see a description of the beast from the sea having traits like a leopard, a bear, and a lion. This is taken from Daniel 7:12 where the Roman Empire destroyed the first three kingdoms (Daniel 7:1–6). Even though these three kingdoms died, they were granted life for an extended time. They obviously had influence on the Roman Empire as we see John's beast had Greece's leopard body, Medo-Persia's bear claws, and Babylon's lion mouth. The dragon, who is HaSatan, gives the Anti-messiah his power, his throne, and great authority. Again, this is a counterfeit of how God the Father gives His power, throne, and authority to God, the Son!

In verse 3, one of the beasts' heads (I believe the seventh head) is slain. Here, I believe the Anti-messiah will actually die! There are two indications that this is true. The phrase "seemed to have been slain" (*hos sphazo*) actually translates "as having been slain." Unfortunately, there is no "if" in the Greek language and should not be included here as "seemed." This exact phrase is also found in Revelation 5:6.

But here in Revelation, the interpretation concerns Yeshua the Lamb who was slain for the sin of the world. There are no ifs, ands, or buts concerning whether Yeshua was slain or died for the sin of the world! Therefore, we should not have doubts over whether the Anti-messiah can die and be resurrected, either. The same Greek phrase is used for both Yeshua and the Anti-messiah. The idea there is that HaSatan is counterfeiting what the true Messiah has already done—died and resurrected, so the world could believe in Him for salvation! But the Anti-messiah will die and resurrect so that the world will believe in him as their savior from God's wrath during Jacob's Trouble! The question now arises, "How and when does the Anti-messiah die and resurrect?"

It is possible that the Anti-messiah will die from warring against the three kings. He will then resurrect, and with his newfound extra power from HaSatan, attack the two witnesses and kill them. It is also possible that the Anti-messiah will be killed as he kills the two Jewish witnesses. His resurrection would coincide with the witnesses' resurrection, which could help to stifle the amazement over their bodily resurrection and rapture to heaven. However, this is unlikely due to Revelation 11:7–13 (see commentary in this chapter). Sorry to say, I just don't know the exact order here because the Bible doesn't provide us with enough detail. What I do know for sure is that the world will be mesmerized by the beasts' death and resurrection and they will worship him and the dragon (verses 3–4). They will even be amazed over how great a warrior the Anti-messiah is since no one can win battles against him (verse 4). The three kings and the two witnesses lose to him. All nations eventually abdicate to him, as well!

In verse 5, the Anti-messiah's true character is revealed. He will speak blasphemies and arrogant words against the Lord. This is nothing new; Daniel told us a number of times thousands of years ago that he would do this (Daniel 7:8, 11, 20, 25; 11:36). Not only will the Anti-messiah speak horrible things against the God of Israel, he will also have the authority to act as the king of the world for forty-two months! This is the exact duration of the second half of Jacob's Trouble—three and a half years! So, what will the Anti-messiah do in the second half of the Tribulation Period?

In verse 6, he will speak blasphemies against the Lord and the heavenly Tabernacle, including the believers and angels living in heaven with the Lord. He speaks this way concerning the heavenly Tabernacle because Yeshua as the Cohen Gadol (high priest) brought His own blood sacrifice for the sins of the world. He will also speak against the believers and angels in heaven because they are the ones who constantly worship the Lord in holiness. The Anti-messiah will tear down his enemies of truth to build himself up in the eyes of the world. It will work to a certain extent.

In verse 7, we see that the world is given over to him. This verse also shows how evil the Anti-messiah's hatred is for all things set apart for the Lord. Not only will he defile the Temple and try to completely destroy all Jewish people, but he will also make war against the Jewish and Gentile believers around the world. Unfortunately, he will overcome them and have victory.

This certainly shows that there will be some form of battling going on throughout the second half of Jacob's Trouble!

In the end, the Anti-messiah will be very successful in his plan of world domination. By the end of Jacob's Trouble, all who dwell on the earth will eventually worship him—that is, everyone who is not written in Yeshua's Book of Life (verse 8). This means that by the end of the Tribulation, everyone in the world will have made up their minds on whether they will choose to follow Messiah Yeshua or the Anti-messiah.

Revelation 17:12–14

> 12 The ten horns that you saw are ten kings who have not yet received royal power, but receive authority as kings with the beast for one hour. 13 These kings are of one mind, and they give their power and authority to the beast. 14 They will make war against the Lamb, and the Lamb will overcome them—because He is Lord of lords and King of kings, and those with Him are called and chosen and faithful.

The ten horns of the beast are the Anti-messiah's ten kings. During the first half of the Tribulation Period, they will not have received their kingdoms from the Anti-messiah yet. They receive their kingdoms once Anti-messiah is crowned king of the world. This will occur at the middle of Jacob's Trouble. It is possible that these ten kings are different from the original ten kings that received their kingdom from the One-World Order. It is also possible that they are the same ten kings as well. Verse 12 states that they receive their authority as kings from the Anti-messiah for "one hour." This simply means they will rule and reign with Anti-messiah for a short time—specifically, three and a half years. Verse 13 reveals their purpose. They will subject themselves to and perform the Anti-messiah's will.

Ultimately, after Yeshua's Second Coming, they will wage the Armageddon War with Anti-messiah and lose!

Revelation 17:15–18

> 15 Then he tells me, "The waters that you saw, where the prostitute is seated, are peoples and multitudes and nations and tongues. 16 The ten horns that you saw, and the beast—these will hate the prostitute. They will make her desolate and naked, and devour her flesh and burn her up with fire. 17 For God has put it into their hearts to do His will, and to be of one mind, and to give their royal power to the beast until the words of God are fulfilled. 18 And the woman that you saw is the great city exercising kingship over the kings of the earth."

The ten kings have an additional purpose in hating the prostitute. This harlot sits on many waters, which represent the many Gentile nations of the world (verse 15). During the first half of Jacob's Trouble, she entices the world to follow her evil immorality (Revelation 17:1–2). The prostitute is the one-world religion that actually kills true believers in the first half of Jacob's Trouble (Revelation 17:6). When the Anti-messiah and the ten kings come into power, they will destroy the one-world religion as the Anti-messiah sets himself up as God in the Temple. This will occur just prior to, or just after, he is declared to be God. Verse 17 confirms the fact that the God of Israel is in control. He uses their evil intentions for His purpose and glory! God's will shall be done!

Verse 18 refers back to the prostitute again. She is the one-world religion that greatly influences the world, and yet she is called "the great city." The great city is the "Babylon the Great" of verse 5. The real city of Babylon was destroyed a long time ago, but Saddam Hussein of Iraq was trying to rebuild it when President Bush shut him down. Jeremiah 25:12 and

51:29 prophesy that Babylon will become a desolation without inhabitants forever! Today, Babylon is a desolation; however, is the prophecy completely fulfilled? There are two possible answers: one, Babylon will be rebuilt and then destroyed in the future; and two, Babylon has already been desolated and John's Babylon is a different city, possibly a code name for Rome.

Revelation 11:7–13

> 7 When they have finished their testimony, the beast that rises from the abyss will make war on them, and overcome them and kill them. 8 And their corpses will lie in the open street of the great city that figuratively is called Sodom and Egypt—where also their Lord was crucified. 9 Some from the peoples and tribes and tongues and nations will look at their corpses for three and a half days, not allowing them to be placed into a grave. 10 Those who dwell on the earth will rejoice over them. They will celebrate and send gifts to one another, because these two prophets tormented those who dwell on the earth.
>
> 11 But after the three and a half days, the breath of life from God entered them, and they stood up on their feet; and great fear fell on those who were watching them.
>
> 12 Then they heard a loud voice from heaven saying to them, "Come up here!" And they went up to heaven in a cloud, while their enemies watched them.
>
> 13 At that hour there was a great earthquake, and a tenth of the city collapsed. Seven thousand people were killed in the earthquake, and the rest were terrified and gave glory to the God of heaven.

We need to remember that the two witnesses prophesied for 1,260 days or forty-two months (or three and a half years). They prophesied for the full duration of the first half of the

Tribulation. Then the beast, the Anti-messiah, comes out of the abyss to kill them (verse 7) at the midpoint of the Tribulation. How did the Anti-messiah get into the abyss? I believe that this refers to the time that he dies and his evil spirit is cast into the abyss for a short time. The abyss is a special section of hell for HaSatan and his evil demons. Why the Anti-messiah's evil spirit would be cast into the abyss that was made for demons is a mystery.

However, it could be because he is the most evil of all people and possessed by HaSatan himself. This event is the Anti-messiah's counterfeit of Yeshua's spirit having been cast into Paradise (or Abraham's bosom) for a short time before He set the captives there free! So, it makes sense that the death of the Anti-messiah will occur first, his descent into the abyss, then his resurrection, and then his murder of the two witnesses. These events will encourage the world to gratefully worship the Anti-messiah!

As stated earlier, the two witnesses' bodies are not laid in a tomb, but remain in the streets of Jerusalem where they died (verse 8). The people of the world view these bodies for three and a half days, no doubt through the modern technologies of Internet, television, and cell phone video (verse 9). But the sick part of this event is the fact that these evil people rejoice and make merry because the two witnesses die (verse 10).

After the three and a half days, the two witnesses come back to life, causing great fear in the world and in Israel (verse 11)! Then the Lord will call them up to heaven in the sight of all (verse 12). Soon after this, Jerusalem will suffer an earthquake in which the city is damaged, 7,000 people die, and the rest give glory to God (verse 13)! This last phrase suggests there is a mini-revival going on because of all these miraculous events. The Lord certainly knows how to get people's attention for salvation! All these events occur during the middle of Jacob's Trouble and set the stage for the Anti-messiah's holocaust of the Jewish people in the second half of the Tribulation.

Daniel 9:27

> 27 Then he will make a firm covenant with many for one week, but in the middle of the week he will put an end to sacrifice and offering. And on a wing of abominations will come one who destroys, until the decreed annihilation is poured out on the one who destroys.'"

As stated earlier, Daniel prophesied that the Anti-messiah will stop the temple sacrificial system at the midpoint of the Tribulation. He will also set himself up as God in the Temple and require worship from all Jewish and Gentile people of the world. Anyone who does not worship the Anti-messiah and take the 666 mark will die by having their heads cut off. I am reminded of the current practice of ISIS whereby they cut off the heads of their enemies. There has been an influx of Islam streaming into Europe, and so it is possible that the revived Roman Empire will be influenced by Islam and adopt some of their terrorism practices.

The question then remains: "How does the Anti-messiah set himself up as God in the Temple?" The answer is found in two sets of Scripture.

2 Thessalonians 2:3–4

> 3 Let no one deceive you in any way, for the Day will not come unless the rebellion comes first and the man of lawlessness is revealed, the one destined to be destroyed. 4 He opposes and exalts himself above every so-called god or object of worship, so that he sits in the Temple of God, proclaiming himself that he is God.

As we can see from this section of this book, the stage is set for a world leader to take control. World war, tragedy, and death will permeate the globe in the first half of Jacob's Trouble and everyone will be looking for help! The Anti-messiah will be rising in power as the first half races toward the middle of the Tribulation.

In the middle of Jacob's Trouble is when life will dramatically change for Israel. Israel will have signed a peace treaty with the world under the guidance of the Anti-messiah. So, Israel will have what I call "pseudo-peace" under the Anti-messiah. This peace, or should I say, a lack of war with her enemies, will last for three and a half years. However, the Anti-messiah will break this peace treaty with Israel and all hell will break loose when he performs the Abomination of Desolation!

2 Thessalonians 2 gives us more information concerning this treachery against the Jewish people. In verse 3, we see an order of prophetic events established. The rebellion and the man of lawlessness (who is also called the son of destruction or perdition in other Bible versions), are revealed prior to the Day of the Lord. This Day of the Lord is the actual Second Coming of Yeshua. The rebellion is a great falling away from the faith—it truly is apostasy. So-called believers of Yeshua will give up the true gospel of Yeshua for a counterfeit. One could say that this has already occurred in the Body of Messiah around the world. However, I believe that this apostasy spoken of in 2 Thessalonians 2 will be a very dramatic event that will affect the whole world. It looks like the one-world religion will be the impetus to promote this falling away from the Lord Yeshua. This apostasy will occur during the first half of the Tribulation with the one-world religion persecuting true believers from that moment onward.

The man of lawlessness, the son of destruction, will additionally be revealed prior to the Second Coming. This is a description of the Anti-messiah. He will rule as the King of the world with his own set of laws and commandments that will obviously be quite opposite of what the Scriptures promote. But, he will also cause a lot of destruction through his warring against many nations.

Then in verse 4, the Anti-messiah will come against all other gods, exalt himself, and take the Lord's seat in the Temple of God. Obviously, the Anti-messiah will set himself up as God in the Temple, and he then will require worship from all the people of the world. All this takes place at the middle of Jacob's Trouble. The 666 mark will spread throughout the world revealing who his worshipers are. Verse 4 specifically says that the Anti-messiah will take his seat in the Temple of God. However, there are no seats for human beings in the temple! The *cohen gadol* (high priest) does not sit down inside the Temple when he ministers—he only stands. So, what is this talking about?

There is one seat in the Temple, but it is not for humans to sit on. It's the mercy seat! The mercy seat sits atop the Ark of the Covenant where the two golden angels are located. The mercy seat is where the physical manifestation of the Lord rests in the Holy of Holies in the Temple. No human is allowed to enter this location except the *cohen gadol*, and this but once a year on Yom Kippur. When the Anti-messiah performs this Abomination of Desolation, he literally will be taking the place of God in the Temple. I would imagine that with any dramatic event such as this, the Jewish people will be split in their understanding of it. Maybe some will believe the Anti-messiah is the one God and receive his mark, and maybe some will see the truth of his blasphemy. In any event, the rest of the Tribulation Period will be a holocaust for the Jewish people!

2 Thessalonians 2:6-8 is the second set of Scripture that shows how the Anti-messiah will set himself up as God in the Temple.

<u>2 Thessalonians 2:6–8</u>

> 6 And you know what now holds back, for him to be revealed in his own time. 7 For the mystery of lawlessness is already operating; only there is one who holds

> back just now, until he is taken out of the way. 8 Then the lawless one will be revealed. The Lord *Yeshua* will slay him with the breath of His mouth and wipe him out with the appearance of His coming.

For the Anti-messiah to be able to unleash the biggest holocaust against the Jewish people in her history, some dramatic changes must take place in the heavenlies! The restrainer (the one who holds back) must be taken out of the Anti-messiah's way. The age-old question is asked, "Who is the restrainer?" The typical answers we hear are the Body of Messiah or the Ruach Kodesh. For me, neither of these answers is adequate. The purpose of the Body of Messiah is not to restrain evil or even to restrain the Anti-messiah's evil. Even if this was one of our purposes, the body is not doing a good-enough job today because there is so much evil in the world, and it is increasing as time goes on! So why would believers think she can do the job in the future if she can't do the job today? Besides all this, the Body of Messiah will be raptured before Jacob's Trouble begins and is not present at the middle of the Tribulation when these events take place!

I also do not believe that the Ruach Kodesh is the restrainer. Nothing in the Bible tells us the Holy Spirit's job is to restrain evil at any time in history, let alone the Tribulation Period. The Ruach Kodesh has many jobs, but restraining evil is not necessarily one of them.

Paul tells us in verse 6 that the Thessalonians already know the answer of who and what restrains the Anti-messiah and his evil! They knew, but we have a mystery to solve. Verse 6 gives us a clue, though. The restrainer restrains until the Anti-messiah is revealed. When is the Anti-messiah's true identity revealed to the world? I believe at "mid-trib" when he sets himself up as God in the Temple (2 Thessalonians 2:4) and requires worship from the world!

Verse 7 shows us that lawlessness is already at work in the world. This occurs during the first half of Jacob's Trouble. The restrainer is restraining, but it seems that through time, his restraint is becoming looser and looser. By "mid-trib," the restrainer is taken out of the way. This is also the time that Anti-messiah unleashes his biggest assault upon the Jewish people. When the restrainer is taken out of the way, the lawless one, the Anti-messiah, is revealed to the world for who he truly is (verse 8). Messiah Yeshua will then put a stop to him when He comes back in the Second Coming!

So, who is the restrainer? I believe the restrainer is Michael, the archangel. Michael certainly has the power to restrain the Anti-messiah, his evil, and HaSatan's evil angels, too. Daniel additionally shows that Michael and his good angels do battle against the evil angels all around the world (Daniel 10:10-13)! An angel even tells Daniel that he was delayed in responding to Daniel's prayers because he was fighting demonic battles! We definitely know that Michael is the one who stands guard over the Jewish people in Israel (Daniel 12:1). When Jacob's Trouble begins, he will arise, stand up for Israel, and fight against all the evil angels that attack Israel during the first half of the Tribulation. By "mid-trib," the Lord will take Michael and his angels out of the way so that the Anti-messiah, his evil angels, and his evil people will be undeterred in their terror against the Jewish people. This will unleash the worst holocaust against Israel in the history of the world!

Revelation 13:11–18

> 11 Then I saw another beast rising out of the earth. He had two horns like a lamb and spoke like a dragon. 12 He exercises all the authority of the first beast before him, and he makes the earth and all those who dwell in it worship the first beast, whose fatal wound was healed. 13 He performs great signs, even making fire

> come down from heaven in the sight of men. 14 And he deceives those who dwell on the earth through the signs he is permitted to perform, telling those who dwell on the earth to make an image in honor of the beast who has the sword wound yet lived. 15 The second beast was permitted to give life to the image of the first beast, so that the image of the beast could even speak and cause all who would not worship the image of the beast to be killed. 16 He also causes all—the small and the great, the rich and the poor, the free and the slave—to receive a mark on their right hand or upon their forehead. 17 And so no one can buy or sell unless he has the mark—either the name of the beast or the number of his name.
> 18 Here is wisdom: let the one who has understanding calculate the number of the beast, for it is a number of a man, and his number is 666.

Many believers seem to be unable to reconcile this scripture passage with the events of the middle of the Tribulation. However, there are fascinating events found here that have dramatic effects on Israel and the world for the second half of Jacob's Trouble.

We started this chapter by analyzing the first beast of Revelation 13. We saw that the first beast will come up out of the sea. The beast was identified as the revived Roman Empire. The seventh head of this beast was identified as the Anti-messiah, who was called the beast as well. The seventh head is the last king in succession of the Roman Empire history. The second beast of Revelation 13 will come up out of the earth rather than the sea (verse 11). Here, the earth represents the earthly kingdoms as opposed to the heavenly kingdom of verses 6-7. This beast has two horns like a lamb, but speaks like the dragon. Although this beast will try to act like the Lamb of God, he will be quite the opposite. He will speak blasphemous words against the God of Israel. This beast is the False Prophet who will be a spokesman for the Anti-messiah (verse 12). He will receive his authority from the Anti-messiah and make the people of the earth worship him!

It is quite possible the false prophet is Jewish as he imitates the Jewish prophet Elijah by making fire come down out of heaven (verse 13). This event will counterfeit the miracle of Elijah found in 1 Kings 18:16–40. Elijah challenged the false prophets of Baal and the Asherah. Both would perform an animal sacrifice to their corresponding God and the one who was answered by fire would win the challenge. The God of Israel answered Elijah's call by sending fire from heaven to consume the whole sacrifice while the false prophets had no answer (verse 38). So, this false prophet will perform miracles similar to that of Elijah such as making fire come down from heaven, the Jewish people will attest to his authenticity, and this will cause many to worship the Anti-messiah.

However, we know that the false prophet is a deceiver because he is in cahoots with the Anti-messiah. But the world will not know it, and thus the world will be deceived. He even gets the world to build an image of the Anti-messiah who was wounded and came back to life (verse 14). "Image" (*eikon*) refers to the people making an image, form, statue, or likeness of the Anti-messiah. The most likely place for this statue to be set up would be in the Holy of Holies!

After the Anti-messiah performs the Abomination of Desolation, the false prophet will have the world create some sort of image or statue of the Anti-messiah and place it in the Holy of Holies on top of the Ark of the Covenant! This is the full extent of the Abomination of Desolation, and it is another counterfeit! Just as the Lord God lived in heaven while His physical manifestation of Shekinah Glory shone in the Holy of Holies on the Ark, the Anti-messiah will have his "physical manifestation," the statue, revealed on the Ark in the Holy of Holies of the Temple. Once again it will be a horrendous counterfeit!

I am reminded of Daniel 11:31 that predicted a king from the north (11:15) would perform the Abomination of Desolation. This king would be Antiochus Epiphanes who set up a statue of his likeness in the Holy of Holies of the Temple in 168 BC. He also required worship from the Jewish people. Israel revolted against him and started a three-year guerrilla war that ended with the Jewish people's victory and a forever celebration of Chanukah! Antiochus Epiphanes' Abomination of Desolation was a foreshadowing of what the Anti-messiah will do in the middle of the Tribulation Period. He will set himself up as God in the Temple and put his newly-made statue on the Ark of the Covenant and require worship from the world.

In verse 15, we find out that the false prophet will breathe life into the image of the Anti-messiah. This represents another counterfeit of the Lord God breathing life into the first created human, Adam. The image will come to life and requires all Jewish and Gentile people to worship it. Those who will not worship the image will be killed! This event might be the turning point for the Jewish people to wake up and smell the roses. Hopefully they will see the light and recognize that the Anti-messiah is just another "*meshugenah*" Antiochus Epiphanes!

Next, the image will cause all who worship and give their allegiance to the Anti-messiah to have a mark put on their right hand or forehead (verse 16). There will be rewards that come with this mark of membership! Those who take the mark will be able to buy and sell goods. This mark will include the name of the Anti-messiah or the number of his name (verse 17). Those who will not take the mark will not be able to buy or sell. They will also be hunted down and killed.

In verse 18, we are told that the Anti-messiah's number is that of a man, suggesting the Anti-messiah is a man (who is obviously possessed by HaSatan)! His number is 666. This 666 mark is the numerical value of the Anti-messiah's full name in Hebrew. Those believers during Jacob's Trouble who know how to calculate his name into its numerical value will be able to verify who the Anti-messiah is. I would imagine that these folks will be declaring this 666 mark throughout the first half of Jacob's Trouble, trying to warn the people of the earth that the end is coming soon.

When Anti-messiah and HaSatan worshipers receive the mark, it will probably be inscribed in a chip the size of a grain of rice shot into their right hand or forehead. When they desire to buy or sell anything, they will be scanned, and Anti-messiah's name and/or number will appear first: "Member of Anti-messiah's Visa team!" They will then receive all the benefits of being a member of the Anti-messiah's family. Once a person takes the mark, there is no turning back and there is no changing families. This marking is also a counterfeit of the Lord's marking. Remember that 144,000 Jewish men were "sealed" or marked on their foreheads for Messiah and to preach the good news message of Yeshua during Jacob's Trouble (Revelation 7:3). Now, the evil ones will be marked to spread the Anti-messiah's evil message around the world.

Unfortunately, this begins the worst holocaust against the Jewish people in the history of Israel! The Lord will allow the Anti-messiah to unleash his evil vengeance against all the Jewish people, saved and unsaved. Yeshua says that this holocaust will be the worst holocaust ever. It will even be worse than the Nazi regime's killing of 6 million Jews during World War II! The Anti-messiah will also unleash his holocaust against Gentile believers around the world and anyone who refuses to take his mark.

Chart

The beginning of Jacob's Trouble will be a time of great rejoicing for Israel and the Jewish people. Their dreams of having peace in the Land will finally seem to be fulfilled. However, shortly after the signing of the covenant, God's wrath will quickly and dramatically fall upon the world. There will be such devastation on the earth as has never occurred in history! People will actually be calling for mountains to fall upon them so that they can escape from God's wrath.

During this time, the Anti-messiah will be warring against three kings to establish his kingly reign over the world. As we look to the chart, we see these wars will culminate in the events of the middle of Jacob's Trouble. The Anti-messiah will set himself up as God over all the earth and will require worship from all people, both Jews and Gentiles. Here the Anti-messiah will perform the Abomination of Desolation and set up an image or a statue of himself as God on the Ark of the Covenant. If people refuse to worship him and refuse his mark, then they shall be killed. Hopefully, the Jewish people will wake up and recognize that the Gentile Anti-messiah and the false prophet are evil and then believe in the one and only Messiah Yeshua!

The Anti-messiah will also kill the two Jewish witnesses at the midpoint of Jacob's Trouble. Their bodies will be left on the street for three and a half days. The world will rejoice over their deaths, but the Lord will surprise everyone by resurrecting them back to life! He will then rapture them to heaven right in front of the world! After the Anti-messiah claims to be God, the Jewish people will have to endure the worst holocaust ever cast upon Israel. It will occur in the second half of Jacob's Trouble. Yeshua calls this time period, "The Great Tribulation." It will definitely not be a great time for the Jewish people! It is also a great reason to pray for Israel and the Jewish people.

Prayer

Lord God, the events of the middle of Jacob's Trouble will usher in a terrible holocaust against the Jewish people. Please save the Jewish people, helping them to see the light of Yeshua our Messiah. Help them to make it through the Tribulation Period by protecting them from all evil. Evil will be lurking around every corner; please give them wisdom and understanding to live their lives for you. When some of these believers die for Yeshua, please give them miraculous strength and comfort to be great witnesses for You. In addition, please help me today to share the good news message of Yeshua with the Jewish people first. Please open their hearts to Yeshua even now so that they won't have to face the Anti-messiah in the future. And help me also to warn Jewish people of the impending holocaust that is coming their way. Maybe, just maybe, some will see the light, in Yeshua's name, Amen.

Chapter 11

Israel in the Second Half of Jacob's Trouble

In the last chapter, we unpacked the events that will surround Israel in the middle of Jacob's Trouble. The Anti-messiah will have a counterfeit death and resurrection similar to Yeshua's death and resurrection for the world's sin. Once he obtains the favor of the world, he and the ten kings will destroy the one-world religion. The Anti-messiah will then kill the two Jewish witnesses. After this, he will perform the Abomination of Desolation, setting himself up as God in the Temple. The false prophet will then put a statue of the Anti-messiah in God's place within the Holy of Holies on the Ark of the Covenant. This abomination will require the worship of the world. Those who refuse will die by having their heads cut off. This time period is called "The Great Tribulation." This is the second half of Jacob's Trouble that lasts another three and a half years. It will be the worst holocaust ever in Israel's history!

The Jewish people have withstood many holocausts in their history. In 168 BC, Antiochus Epiphanes tried to wipe out the Jewish race. Titus and the Romans destroyed Jerusalem and the Temple in AD 70. The Crusaders of AD 1000–1250 wiped out many Jewish cities in their desire to take back Jerusalem. The Spanish Inquisition killed 100,000 Jewish people, and

300,000 were banished. The Russian pogroms killed 500,000 Jewish people. Hitler's holocaust killed 6 million Jews. Israel is unfortunately used to persecution throughout her history! This persecution continues to be so bad around the world that many Jewish people believe they are the "chosen people," not necessarily called to be God's people, but to be called for persecution! It truly is a sad situation. Since becoming a nation in 1948, Israel has fought eight wars and two intifadas and continues in some armed conflicts. So, why all this persecution against Israel?

We need to step back away from this situation and see a bigger picture. HaSatan is trying to thwart God's plans for Israel. If HaSatan can wipe out the nation of the Jews, then God is not who He says He is. The Lord made promises to the Jewish people and He needs to keep those promises. If HaSatan can stop God from doing this, then he can claim to be like God, just like he did as Lucifer in Isaiah 14:13–14. Since HaSatan's fall, he hates whatever God loves, and God loves the Jewish people. So HaSatan has been trying to destroy the Jewish people since the beginning of their calling!

As discussed earlier, God is presently calling all Jewish people back to the Land of Israel (Ezekiel 36:24–28). He will judge them in Jacob's Trouble, save them at the end of the Tribulation, and then properly restore them back to the Land in the Messianic Millennial Kingdom under Yeshua as King of the Jews! If HaSatan can destroy any aspect of God's plan, then he can again say that he is more powerful than God and try to take his place on God's throne. Now, we know this can never happen, but that doesn't mean HaSatan won't continue to try until his end! He will continue to try to annihilate the Jewish people in the second half of Jacob's Trouble with the worst holocaust ever.

Matthew 24:15–20

> 15 "So when you see 'the abomination of desolation,' which was spoken of through Daniel the prophet, standing in the Holy Place (let the reader understand), 16 then those in Judea must flee to the mountains. 17 The one on the roof must not go down to take what is in his house, 18 and the one in the field must not turn back to get his coat. 19 Woe to those who are pregnant and to those who are nursing babies in those days! 20 Pray that your escape will not happen in winter, or on *Shabbat*.

Matthew 24 is a great summary chapter concerning Jacob's Trouble, much like Leviticus 23 is a great summary chapter on the seven feasts of the Lord. Verses 1–14 discussed the first half of Jacob's Trouble, and verses 15–31 finish out the second half of Jacob's Trouble. Yeshua begins in verse 15 reminding the Jewish people about Daniel's prophecy of the Abomination of Desolation. Although Yeshua is speaking to a large group of Jewish people at this time, the "you" refers to the Jewish group of believers who will actually see with their own eyes the Abomination of Desolation performed in Jerusalem at the middle of Jacob's Trouble! Yeshua refers here to the prophecy in Daniel 9:27 that we already studied. Now the Abomination of Desolation will stand in the holy place. What exactly does this mean, and how can we reconcile this with the abomination "sitting" in the Holy of Holies?

Remember, on top of the Ark is the mercy seat where the physical manifestation of God "sits." Well, the Abomination of Desolation will "sit" on top of the Ark of the Covenant to counterfeit, taking God's place. The statue of the Anti-messiah will "stand" on the mercy seat as well. So, the image of the Anti-messiah will simultaneously sit and stand on the mercy seat of the Ark of the Covenant.

Verse 15 ends with a parenthesis enclosure of the statement "let the reader understand." This indicates that Matthew, as the human writer of the book, inserted a little message for all believers of the Scriptures. Those new believers of the Tribulation Period, who are trying to figure out what has befallen their world, will read Matthew 24 and Daniel 9, will know that they are entering into the second half of Jacob's Trouble and the greatest tribulation ever in the history of the world.

Yeshua then commands these Jewish believers in Judea to flee to the mountains (verse 16). Now, I also believe that there will be Gentile believers leaving along with the Jewish believers, but the directive from Yeshua is to Jewish believers. It makes sense that the Gentile believers are going to want to flee as well because nobody likes tribulation! The Anti-messiah will unleash his hate-filled battle against all believers as we shall soon see. But the idea here is that all these Jewish believers will leave Israel and travel to the mountain range, including the city of Petra (more discussion of this topic later). How do I know they will leave Israel? The term *Judea* is used for Judah, that is, Southern Israel, and for the whole nation of Israel. In either case, the Jewish believers will be leaving Israel to get as far away from the Anti-messiah as possible.

Verses 17–18 tell us that these Jewish believers need to flee very quickly. They will not even have enough time to pack up their household items. Nor will the field workers have enough time to go back to get their coats or outer garments. Yeshua even pronounces a woe on pregnant women and nursing mothers (verse 19). Ladies, you all know how difficult it is just to pack up the family and try to make it on time to congregational services! Can you imagine how terrible it will be for those nursing mothers and pregnant ladies trying to flee from the Anti-messiah's destruction?

In verse 20, Yeshua then tells the Jewish people to pray that these events do not occur in the winter or on a Sabbath day. Why is that? In Israel, the rainy season occurs during the winter months. If there is a good amount of rain, then the rivers will overflow. This will make it even harder to escape from the Land. The Sabbath situation is even scarier for religious Jewish people. It is forbidden for Jewish people to drive or travel in any vehicles on the Sabbath. All public transportation is shut down. Although one can walk, the length of the walking is limited to the next town. In Acts 1:12, we see the limitation the apostles had in walking from the Mount of Olives to Jerusalem. It is called a "sabbath day's journey." The length is only about three-fourths of a mile. So, let me ask you a question? How easy and simple will it be for the Anti-messiah's army to round up Jewish believers who are wholeheartedly following this command? This is why Yeshua says to pray it doesn't fall on the Sabbath.

There is another scripture passage that also documents this mini-exodus of Jewish believers leaving Israel. It supplies us with a wealth of knowledge concerning what will happen to this Jewish group of believers.

Revelation 12:1–6

> 1 A great sign appeared in heaven: a woman clothed with the sun, with the moon under her feet, and on her head a crown of twelve stars. 2 She is pregnant—crying out in birth pains, in agony to give birth.
> 3 Then another sign appeared in heaven: a great fiery red dragon that had seven heads and ten horns, and seven royal crowns on his heads. 4 His tail sweeps away a third of the stars of heaven—it hurled them to the earth. Now the dragon stood before the woman who was about to give birth, so that whenever she gave birth he might devour her child.
> 5 And she gave birth to a son, a male child, who is to rule all the nations with an iron rod. And her child was snatched away to God and to His throne. 6 Then the

> woman fled into the wilderness, where she has a place prepared by God so they might take care of her for 1,260 days.

John writes of two signs in heaven. These two signs are written in metaphors. The first sign is found in verses 1–2. A pregnant woman ready to give birth to her baby is clothed with the sun. Under her feet is found the moon, and she wears a crown of twelve stars. Let's analyze the second sign found in verses 3–6, before we analyze the first sign.

In verse 3, we find a great red dragon who has seven heads and ten horns. On his seven heads, he is wearing seven diadems or crowns. The great red dragon is a symbol for HaSatan (the Satan, our adversary)! In verse 4, his tail swept away a third of the stars of heaven and threw them to earth. This refers to HaSatan leading one-third of God's angels in rebellion against the Lord. They have been judged and are now demons going to and fro on the earth, causing havoc and mayhem. HaSatan stood before the woman so that when she gave birth, he would destroy her child.

In verse 5, the woman gave birth to a son. Who is the son? The son is Yeshua! We know this to be true since verse 5 tells us He will rule all the nations with a rod of iron. This speaks of Yeshua's kingly rule in the Messianic Millennial Kingdom. Yeshua will reign in His Kingdom with an "iron rod." This phrase is repeated in Revelation 2:27 and quoted from Psalm 2:9. In Psalm 2:9, the Son of God, who is Messiah and King in the Psalm, will receive the world as His possession and rule with justice and judgment. This means that, when He returns in His Second Coming, He will harshly judge the world by destroying the evil enemies. And when He sets up the Kingdom, He will judge the world rightly, justly, and swiftly. Sin will not run rampant as it does in this hedonistic lawless world we live in right now! Yeshua will deal with sin and deal with it quickly in the Kingdom.

Verse 5 also tells us that the Son, Yeshua, was "snatched away" to God and His throne in heaven. This refers to Yeshua's ascension after His death and resurrection. "Snatched away" (*harpazo*) is the same word used for the Rapture. Here, Yeshua was "caught up" in His ascension to heaven. Just as Yeshua was "snatched up," we too shall be "caught up" to the clouds when He comes for us in the Rapture! So Yeshua is the Son of this scripture passage. Who is the woman?

Verse 6 helps us to determine who the woman is. The woman fled into the wilderness to a place prepared by God to be nourished for 1,260 days. The woman is Israel! Israel was clothed with the sun and moon showing her dominion as the chosen nation of God (verse 1). The twelve stars of a crown represent the twelve tribes of Israel (verse 1). Israel was pregnant meaning she was the expectant nation to give birth to God's Son, the Messiah (verse 5). And Israel (the Jewish believers of Israel) will leave the nation of Israel when they see the Abomination of Desolation at the middle of Jacob's Trouble! This group of believers is the very same group of believers found in Matthew 24:15!

Believers in Israel will flee the Land of Israel to a place prepared by God. I believe this place includes Petra and other locations around Petra in the Paran Mountain range. Here, she will be nourished by God for 1,260 days. 1,260 days equals three and a half years (according to the biblical Jewish calendar of thirty-day months). This three and a half year period lines up with the second half of Jacob's Trouble where the Jewish believers of Matthew 24:15 flee Israel at the middle of the Tribulation. Not only will the Lord take care of them and nourish them for this three and a half years, He will also miraculously protect them from HaSatan!

Revelation 12:13–17

> 13 Now when the dragon saw that he had been thrown to the earth, he stalked the woman who had given birth to the male child. 14 But the woman was given two wings of the great eagle, so that she might fly away from the presence of the serpent into the wilderness, to the place where she is taken care of—for a time, times, and half a time.
> 15 And from out of his mouth, the serpent spewed water like a river after the woman, in order to sweep her away with a flood. 16 But the earth came to the aid of the woman. The earth opened its mouth and swallowed the river that the dragon had spewed from his mouth. 17 So the dragon became enraged at the woman and went off to make war with the rest of her offspring—those who keep the commandments of God and hold to the testimony of *Yeshua*.

The devil and his demons have been kicked out of heaven by Michael and his angels (verses 7–12). HaSatan is very upset by this defeat and the fact that he only has a short time left until the end. He is therefore allowed to reveal his great wrath against Israel and the world. In verse 13, the dragon persecuted the woman who gave birth to her son. HaSatan has been allowed to persecute Israel from the time that Israel gave birth to her Messiah. This verse emphatically states that for the last 2,000 years Israel has been persecuted by HaSatan! In actuality, Israel has been persecuted by HaSatan from her beginning! But this particular verse speaks specifically of the last 2,000 years.

In verse 14, the woman is given two wings of the great eagle in order that she would fly to God's special place. This is definitely a metaphor! The group of Jewish believers do not actually grow wings to fly away! I have also heard some amazingly fanciful beliefs about these "two wings of the great eagle." Some believe that since the United States has the seal of the eagle, we are the nation who helps Israel fly away. It's a nice thought, and it is certainly true that the United States has been Israel's big brother for a long time. However, the United States is definitely not the answer here.

In this case, scripture answers the scripture question! One needs to know that most of the symbols found in the book of Revelation are explained in the Old Covenant Scriptures! Once a person knows this, one can be confident of finding the answers to the symbolic questions! The answer is found in Exodus 19:4: "*You have seen what I did to the Egyptians, and how I carried you on eagle's wings and brought you to Myself*." Here, the Lord spoke to Moses on Mount Sinai to remind Israel what He did for them. He is the One who brought them out of Egypt (the land of sin) to Mount Sinai, the location of the Lord. "Eagles wings" does not mean they came out quickly since it took them two months to travel to Mount Sinai (Exodus 19:1), and most of the Jewish people were walking through the desert to get to their destination (Exodus 12:37). "Eagles wings" is a metaphor meaning God, through His power and faithfulness, took care and guided the Jewish people to safety (Deuteronomy 32:10–12). In Deuteronomy 32, we see this picture carefully depicted by Moses. The metaphor rings true in Revelation 12:14 as well. The Lord will watch over, guide, and direct the Jewish believers to His place of safety.

Not only will He guide and direct these Jewish believers, He will also bring them to a place that will be able to physically nourish them. A land similar to Israel that will flow with milk and honey! How long will they stay there? Verse 14 states "for a time, times, and half a time." This phrase refers back to Daniel 7:25, 12:7 where both mean "a year, two years and half a year." The total is three and a half years and refers to the duration of the second half of Jacob's Trouble. In verse 14, the Jewish believers will be nourished and cared for in their new location picked by God for three and a half years, the full duration of the second half of the Tribulation Period!

But that's not all—the Jewish believers will also enjoy life in this wilderness "away from the presence of the serpent." This shows us that the Lord will supernaturally protect these Jewish believers from HaSatan. This means that the Anti-messiah will not be able to war against this group, although he will certainly try! In verses 15–16, we have another figure of speech. HaSatan will pursue the group of Jewish believers with his evil army and try to overcome them to destroy them. However, the earth "opened its mouth" and somehow helps this group get to safety. This event is very similar to when Pharaoh tried to pursue and war against the Jewish people who left Egypt in the Exodus. God protected the Jewish people with His fire, and then the Red Sea "opened its mouth" to rescue them away from Pharaoh's army.

This is the reason why many believe Petra and the Paran Mountain range is the mysterious location where the Jewish people will hide away from the Anti-messiah. Petra is basically a big hole in the ground. It is a city well known for its rocky-cliff architecture, militarily defensible position, and fertile land. It is a city that could easily house many people and be a safe and secure location. There are other cities like Petra in this area that could house the many Jewish believers who will leave Jerusalem and Israel at the middle of the Tribulation.

Since HaSatan will be unable to kill this group of Jewish believers that retreat from Israel to a safe location, he will become infuriated at them. He will then, through the Anti-messiah, attack the spiritual children of this group. Obviously, this is talking about other Jewish and Gentile believers around the world. They are keeping God's Word and holding fast to their testimony. This means that they are staying faithful to their Lord and His Word, preaching against HaSatan and the Anti-messiah! HaSatan and Anti-messiah do not like this attack against their world-dominating plan, so they counterattack against all believers around the world. The question remains, "How effective will HaSatan be?"

Matthew 24:21–22

> 21 For then there will be great trouble, such as has not happened since the beginning of the world until now, nor ever will. 22 And unless those days were cut short, no one would be delivered. But for the sake of the chosen, those days will be cut short.

The Anti-messiah will usher in the worst holocaust against the Jewish people that the world has ever seen! It will be so bad that Yeshua even calls it the "Great Tribulation" (NASB). It is even worse than World War II's Nazi holocaust that killed 6 million Jewish people! How can it be worse than that? But that's exactly what Yeshua says in verse 21: "*such as has not happened since the beginning of the world until now, nor ever will.*" The good news is that this Tribulation Period will be the last holocaust allowed by the Lord. HaSatan will try to war against the holy ones after the Messianic Millennial Kingdom, but he will quickly be defeated.

In verse 22, Yeshua also says that if the days of the Tribulation were not cut short, or terminated, then no one would be saved. First of all, Yeshua is definitely not saying that He is decreasing the amount of days in Jacob's Trouble! There are plenty of verses that tell us the second half of Jacob's Trouble is for three and a half years, forty-two months (or 1,260 days)! He simply is stating that if Jacob's Trouble were allowed to continue past the three and a half years, then Anti-messiah would ultimately kill every believer, Jew and Gentile alike!

Second, the word "saved" (*sozo*) does not mean "saved from sin and hell" here. Remember "saved" also means "delivered, rescued." The context here is talking about making it through to the end of the Tribulation Period. If the Anti-messiah were allowed to continue his holocaust on the Jewish and Gentile worlds, then no one would make it out alive, and who would Yeshua ultimately deliver in His Second Coming? This is one of the purposes of Yeshua's Second Coming—to deliver Jewish and Gentile believers from their enemies!

Yeshua will come back to Earth in the nick of time to save the day. He will come back for the very reason that there are still Jewish and Gentile believers alive at the end of the Tribulation! These truly are the chosen ones who make it through Jacob's Trouble! Yeshua will come back to deliver them from the hands of the Anti-messiah.

Jeremiah 30:4–7

> 4 Now these are the words that *ADONAI* spoke to Israel and to Judah. 5 For thus says *ADONAI:*
> "We heard a sound of trembling,
> of dread—there is no *shalom*.
> 6 Ask now, and see
> whether a man can give birth.
> Why do I see every man
> with his hands on his loins, like a woman giving birth?
> Why have all faces turned pale?
> 7 *Oy!* For that day is monumental.
> There will be none like it—
> a time of trouble for Jacob!
> Yet out of it he will be saved.

The "ADONAI" of verse 4 and 5 is really the Hebrew YHVH. ADONAI spoke to Israel to warn them of a time of terror that was coming their way. It would be a time of dread where there would be no shalom (peace) (verse 5). It would be so bad that many men in Israel would be painfully acting like they were giving birth to a child (verse 6). In verse 7, the day is actually called *monumental*. Monumental means "great."

This is why Yeshua calls the second half of Jacob's Trouble the "Great Tribulation." It truly will be a terrible time of trouble in Israel's history. Verse 7 also supplies the name of this period of terror: "Jacob's Trouble"! But the good news is that God will once again deliver Israel from her troubling enemies!

Daniel 12:1–3

> At that time Michael, the great prince who stands guard over the sons of your people, will arise. There will be a time of distress such as has never occurred since the beginning of the nation until then. But at that time your people—everyone who is found written in the book—will be delivered. 2 Multitudes who sleep in the dust of the earth will awake—some to everlasting life, and others to shame and everlasting contempt. 3 Those who are wise will shine like the brightness of the heavenly expanse. And those who turn many to righteousness will be like the stars forever and ever.

Michael, the archangel who stands guard over Israel, will arise at the beginning of Jacob's Trouble. (verse 1). The "time of distress" is Jacob's Trouble, the seven-year Tribulation Period. I believe the reason Michael will arise is to stand and fight against the increased evil forces of wickedness that are rallying against Israel. There will be a tremendous war in the heavenlies between Michael and his good angels, and HaSatan and his evil angels. In the Great Tribulation, the second half of Jacob's Trouble, HaSatan will unleash the greatest demonic assault against the Jewish people in her history. However, I also believe that the Great Tribulation will be the time that Michael and his army will be restrained on Earth so that the Anti-messiah will be able to perform his holocaust against the Jewish people. On Earth, the physical war will break out through Anti-messiah attacking all the Jewish people all around the world. Then, by the end of the Tribulation, all nations will battle against Jerusalem.

Verse 1 also informs us that all of the Jewish people who are written in "the book" (which means the Book of Life) will be rescued from this avalanche of evil. Yeshua will come back in His Second Coming just in time to save the day! Then, His judgment will come.

Verse 2 states that all Jewish people will be resurrected one day. This is the hope of all Jewish people that they will be resurrected by the Lord to enter into the Messianic Kingdom! However, this verse tells us that there are two places one can be resurrected to. The first is to "everlasting life." Everlasting life is located wherever the Lord lives. At first, it will be in the refurbished Land of Israel in the Messianic Millennial Kingdom, and then it will be forever in the New Jerusalem. The second place where Jewish people will be resurrected is to "shame and everlasting contempt." At first, this will be *Sheol* (hell), then it will be the Lake of Fire. This is where the Lord does not live, nor does His presence dwell there, and people will live in abhorrence and terror for eternity. It is not a good place to go; there will not be any partying going on in hell like some non-believers claim. It will be a place of punishment and torture. No one really wants to go there, but people have to realize that Yeshua is the only way to get out of that judgment.

Verse 3 shares more information about the second half of the Tribulation. The Jewish people who are "wise" (meaning having God's wisdom of salvation) will shine bright in a spiritually darkened world. The good news message of Yeshua will go forth throughout the world to Jew and Gentile so that all people will have the opportunity to give their lives to the Lord!

<u>Revelation 16:1–2</u>

> 1 Then I heard a loud voice from the Temple saying to the seven angels, "Go and pour out on the earth the

> seven bowls of God's wrath." 2 So the first angel went and poured out his bowl on the earth, and foul and painful boils came upon the people having the mark of the beast and worshiping his image.

By Revelation 16, the seven seals and seven trumpets will have completed the first half of Jacob's Trouble. God's wrath will have had dramatic effects upon the whole world. But He is not through with His judgment yet. Next up are the seven bowls.

In verse 1, we see God's wrath will continuc to pour judgment out of the seven bowls. Interestingly, in verse 2, the first angel pours out his first bowl upon the earth. In God's judgment, loathsome and malignant boils will grow on people's bodies. However, this judgment is only cast upon those who have the 666 mark of the beast and those who worship the Abomination of Desolation in the Temple. These folks are obviously those who have given their hearts and lives to the Anti-messiah. This judgment should be an interesting wake up call for the world. Only those that align themselves with the Anti-messiah and receive the 666 mark will be affected. A short time after the middle of the Tribulation, we see God's first judgment in the second half of Jacob's Trouble. How bad will the Great Tribulation be for Israel and the Jewish people?

<u>Zechariah 12:1–9</u>

> 1 The burden of the word of *ADONAI* concerning Israel. A declaration of *ADONAI,* who stretched out the heavens, laid the foundation of the earth and formed the spirit of man within him: 2 "Behold, I will make Jerusalem a cup of reeling to all the surrounding peoples when they besiege Jerusalem as well as Judah. 3 Moreover, in that day I will make Jerusalem a massive stone for all the people. All who try to lift it will be cut to pieces. Nevertheless, all the nations of the earth will

> be gathered together against her. 4 In that day"—it is a declaration of *ADONAI*—"I will strike every horse with confusion and its rider with madness. I will keep My eyes on the house of Judah but will blind every horse of the peoples. 5 Then the leaders of Judah will say in their heart, 'The inhabitants of Jerusalem are my strength through *ADONAI-Tzva'ot* their God."
> 6 "In that day I will make the leaders of Judah like a firepot in a woodpile, like a burning torch among sheaves. They will devour on the right and on the left all the surrounding peoples, yet Jerusalem will remain in her place, in Jerusalem. 7 *ADONAI* also will save the tents of Judah first, so that the honor of the house of David and the honor of the inhabitants of Jerusalem will not exceed that of Judah. 8 In that day *ADONAI* will defend the inhabitants of Jerusalem so that the weakest among them that day will be like David and the house of David will be like God—like the angel of *ADONAI* before them. 9 It will happen in that day that I will seek to destroy all the nations that come against Jerusalem.

There is no doubt that it will be very bad for Israel. However, at least we see in this section that Israel will fight back against the Anti-messiah and his forces! It certainly looks like she will have some success against her foes. We must also remember that the Lord is speaking throughout Zechariah 12–14. The words in these three chapters are directly from the mouth of the Lord! The Lord begins this scripture reading declaring that He was the One who created the universe and everyone in it (verse 1). If this is true, then don't you think we can trust Him to take care of Israel in her most strenuous time? I believe that's the point the Lord is making. If He is so powerful as to create the heavens and the earth, then He should not have any problem taking care of the enemies of the Jewish people when they attack Israel.

In verse 2, the Lord declares that He is going to make Jerusalem a cup that causes reeling to the world. This means that all the nations who come up against Jerusalem will be staggering from the Lord's blows against them! Although these nations think they have the upper hand on Israel, the Lord, in the end, will come to her rescue and cause the nations to reel in agony! We are also informed that when these nations rise against Jerusalem to battle, they will battle against Judah, as well. Judah is the southern half of Israel.

Jerusalem will not only be a cup of reeling, but she will also be a heavy stone that causes injury to all who try to lift her (verse 3). The Lord's point is to show that any nation or people who come against Jerusalem and Israel to do her harm shall ultimately be destroyed.

But isn't this the case for Jerusalem in the present? It certainly seems so. The Muslim nations of the world greatly desire to take the Land of Israel and the city of Jerusalem by force. Many world dictators today desire to wipe Israel off the map. The Palestinians even claim eastern Jerusalem to be their capital. The capital of what? There is no Palestinian state or nation at the time of this writing. However, the world through the United Nations is trying to change this fact and pressure Israel into submission! They want almost half of the Land of Israel and half the city of Jerusalem to secure peace in the Land. A treaty that gives land for peace will not work with the Palestinians who desire much more than land. Remember, the Scripture says they want to wipe away all the Jewish people off the face of the earth. Appeasing them with land for peace will never work with a people who truly do not want peace!

In January 2018, President Trump declared Jerusalem to be the capital of Israel. He even moved the US Embassy to Jerusalem in May 2018. This set a firestorm among the Muslim nations around the world. In retaliation, Abbas has proclaimed Jerusalem to be the capital of Palestine. He has additionally tried to gain support from the European Union for statehood, but he has been running into problems with that. So, there has been a whole lot of reeling over Jerusalem in our time and it will continue. However, it will be much worse during Jacob's Trouble!

In verse 4, we find the phrase "in that day." This is a reference to the "Day of the Lord." This is speaking of the seven-year Tribulation Period. I believe this scripture reading is specifically talking about the second half, when Israel will defend herself against the attack of the Anti-messiah's army. In this battle over Jerusalem, which will occur toward the end of the Great Tribulation (Zechariah 14:2), the Lord will cause great confusion upon the Anti-messiah's entire army, and their horses will be blinded as well. This is not the first time the Lord has performed this in Israel's history. In Judges 7:19–22, the enemies of Gideon were very confused and even battled each other. In 1 Samuel 14:20, the enemies of Saul did the very same thing and battled each other. In Ezekiel 38:21, during the Ezekiel War, Israel's enemies will fight against each other as well.

The peoples of Judah will see the Jewish people of Jerusalem fighting against the Anti-messiah's armies (verse 5). They will be greatly encouraged by these victories and rise up to help in the battles over Jerusalem and Judah (verse 6). Then the Lord will declare that He will save Judah first before He saves Jerusalem (verse 7). I believe He is speaking about saving Judah first and then Jerusalem in the Second Coming of Yeshua! This is one of the reasons why I believe Yeshua does not land on the Mount of Olives in His Second Coming (more on this later). The Lord's reason to save Judah first is to let Israel know that the Jewish people who live in Jerusalem are not thought of as better than all the other Jewish people who live in Judah. All Jewish people are to be thought of as equals—there are no second class citizens!

Verse 8 shows us that the battle over Jerusalem is going to be ferocious. The people who are thought to be feeble will turn out to be great warriors like David. And those of the house of David will war like the Angel of the Lord battled against the evil ones in the olden days. The idea here is that even the feeblest of soldiers will become a great warrior in battle and do great damage against the Anti-messiah's armies. God will have to perform this miracle because the number differential between the Anti-messiah's army and that of Israel's will be great. The Anti-messiah will have millions, maybe even up to hundreds of millions of soldiers, compared to Israel's active military possibly numbering in the hundreds of thousands at that time (however, presently Israel does have about 3 million male and female people fit for battle).

Can you imagine the odds against Israel? Can you imagine hundreds of millions of soldiers versus 3 million in battle? Who should easily win? If the Lord were not helping Israel, she would easily and quickly be wiped out! The Lord even says His will is to destroy all the nations that come up against Jerusalem to battle (verse 9). His will be done! But before we get to the end of the Tribulation Period, let us take a look at how effective HaSatan will be in his holocaust against the Jewish people.

<u>Zechariah 13:7–9</u>

> 7 Awake, O sword, against My shepherd,
> against the man who is My companion!
> It is a declaration of *ADONAI-Tzva'ot*.
> Strike the shepherd
> and the sheep will be scattered!
> I will turn My hand against the little ones.
> 8 Then it will happen
> —it is a declaration of *ADONAI*—
> that in the entire land
> two-thirds will be cut off and die,
> but a third will be left in it.

9 This third I will bring through the fire.
I will refine them as silver is refined,
and will test them as gold is tested.
They will call on My Name
and I will answer them.
I will say, 'They are My people,'
and they will answer, '*ADONAI* is my God.'

This prophecy of Zechariah 13 is fascinating because it encompasses both the First and Second Comings of Messiah! Verse 7 shows that when the Shepherd would be struck, the sheep would disperse. When Yeshua was arrested in the garden of Gethsemane, His talmidim (disciples) scattered. On the night in which Yeshua was betrayed, He prophesied that His disciples would fall away and scatter because of His arrest. Yeshua quoted Zechariah 13:7 in Matthew 26:31, and it was fulfilled that very night!

Then verse 8 changes direction, prophesying about the Second Coming of Yeshua. This is similar to the famous verses of Isaiah 61:1–2 that speak of both Comings as well. In verse 1, Isaiah tells us that Messiah will bring good news to the afflicted and proclaim freedom to the prisoners. In verse 2, we find two lines of a poem. The first line states the Messiah will proclaim the favorable year of the Lord. Yeshua fulfilled all of these prophecies in His First Coming. But in the last line of verse 2, the Messiah will proclaim the Lord's day of vengeance! This did not occur during Yeshua's First Coming, but it will happen during His Second Coming! This is when God's judgment will be poured out upon the whole world in Jacob's Trouble.

The point to focus on is that the First Coming and the Second Coming are both mentioned in the first two verses of Isaiah 61. In fact, verse 2 has both appearances in the one verse. In the middle of the verse is when the context changes from the First Coming to the Second Coming. This is difficult to discern (especially if you do not have the New Covenant writings). No wonder the rabbis were confused and believe two Messiahs will come at different times rather than one Messiah coming twice! They could not reconcile these two appearances within one verse!

The Lord profoundly declares in Zechariah 13:8 that two-thirds of the Jewish people will be cut off and perish in the Land of Israel during Jacob's Trouble! Did you read this correctly? Two-thirds of the Jewish people in the Land of Israel during the Tribulation Period will die! This is how effective HaSatan will be against the Jewish people. "Cut off" (*karat*) means to destroy, consume and cut off. "Die" (*gava*) means to perish and to die. Both of these words when used with humans mean extermination! It is beyond any doubt that many Jewish people are going to die during the second half of the Tribulation Period, and there is nothing we can do to change this!

However, what we can do right now is pray for the Jewish people and share the good news message of Yeshua with them so that many unsaved Jewish people will know about the truth of Yeshua before entering into the Tribulation. Maybe, just maybe, some will be saved prior to Jacob's Trouble and never have to enter into it! We just have to do our part—Amen?! Yeshua said this holocaust would be the worst one ever, and I believe Him. However, there is some good news coming out of this devastating time.

The last line of verse 8 tells us this good news. One-third of the Jewish people in the Land will be left in the Land alive! How will one-third of the Jewish people escape the evil hands of the Anti-messiah? The only possible answer is *the Lord*! Verse 9 shows us that the Lord brings the remnant of the Jewish people through the fire—that is the "tribulation fire." He will refine and test them just like gold and silver are refined and tested. When these metals are heated up, the dross rises to the top of the kiln and is scooped away. The remaining metal is much more pure, shiny, and ready for use.

Just like refining metal, the Jewish people will be tested in the tribulation fire. The ones who do not believe in Yeshua and do not make it through the Tribulation are tossed away like dross. The ones who make it through with God's help are like the finished metal, looking shiny and purified. These who are purified "call on My name" and have their names written in the Book of Life! They call on the name of the Lord and are saved. The Lord says, "They are My people" and the Jewish believers say, "Adonai is my God!"

Finally, the Lord's promise will come true after about 3,500 years! The Lord has been waiting for the nation of Israel to come to Him through His Son, Messiah since the prophecy was spoken! In Exodus 6:7, the Lord promised Moses that "I will take you to Myself as a people, and I will be your God." Finally, the Jewish people as a nation will become God's people. They will open up a personal relationship with the eternal God of Israel through Messiah Yeshua! Now how do I know this for sure? Zechariah has the answer.

Zechariah 12:10

> Then I will pour out on the house of David and the inhabitants of Jerusalem a spirit of grace and supplication, when they will look toward Me whom they pierced. They will mourn for him as one mourns for an only son and grieve bitterly for him, as one grieves for a firstborn.

Remember, the Lord is still speaking in this verse. He profoundly states that He will pour out a "spirit" (ruach) of grace and supplication on the inhabitants of Jerusalem and the house of David. It is important to note that most English Bibles translate *ruach* as "the Spirit" (meaning the Holy Spirit). However, there is no "ha" in the Hebrew, suggesting we add "the" to "spirit." However, it is not always necessary to have the Hebrew word "ha" to translate "the Spirit." The context helps to translate and here the context does not demand this "spirit" to be "the Spirit." So, it seems to me this translation of "a spirit" is the correct one.

Toward the end of Jacob's Trouble, God will let loose a spirit or angel of grace upon the inhabitants of Jerusalem, and they will then recognize Yeshua as their Messiah, repent, and believe in Him. It seems that the salvation of Jerusalem is the impetus for the rest of the nation to follow suit. At about the same time, this is when the one-third of Israel will receive Yeshua as their Messiah, get saved, and then receive the gift of the Ruach Kodesh. Romans 11:26 forecasts this salvation at the end of the Tribulation when it states, "*all Israel will be saved*." The only way to be saved in this age is by believing and receiving Yeshua as Lord and Savior. This is exactly what the one-third of Israel will do just prior to the end of Jacob's Trouble.

There are actually two fulfillments of this Scripture: one historical and one prophetic. The historical application occurs when Yeshua was placed on the tree and the Jewish people looked "on Me whom they have pierced" and mourned for Him. John 19:37 quotes from a section of Zechariah 12:10. It states, "*And again another Scripture says, 'They shall look on Him whom they pierced.*'" This quote is an application of Zechariah 12:10 where Yeshua had just died on the tree, was pierced in His side, and the Jewish people were looking on! Some of those who were watching were mourning, but not all of them! Some were happy that Yeshua was finally put to death. To me, Zechariah 12:10 surely shows the whole city of Jerusalem in mourning. So, I see a partial fulfillment in Yeshua's death on the tree in this historical application of Zechariah 12:10.

The complete prophetic fulfillment will occur when Yeshua comes back in His Second Coming. Revelation 1:7 states:

> Look, He is coming with the clouds, and every eye shall see Him, even those who pierced Him. And all the tribes of the earth shall mourn because of Him. Yes, amen!

Revelation 1:7 actually combines two Old Covenant prophecies into one declaration. Daniel 7:13 is combined with Zechariah 12:10 to show John is definitely speaking of Yeshua's Second Coming! Daniel 7:13 revealed that the Son of Man would receive His Kingdom from the Ancient of Days and return to Earth in the clouds! John then says that every eye on earth will see His return, even the Jewish people who pierced Him! These Jewish believers who see Yeshua come back will then mourn. I wondered why they would mourn over Yeshua after receiving Him as their Messiah just a short time before. One would think they would be super joyous over having their names written in the Book of Life and that Messiah was coming back to deliver them from the evil one!

Then the Lord reminded me that they are not mourning for themselves, but for all the Jewish people who had just died in the Great Tribulation—all those Jewish mothers and fathers, grandparents, and other family members who just recently died in Jacob's Trouble. If only they could have made it to the end so that they, too, could be saved and see Messiah come back! All that carnage and death will come back to their hearts and minds when they see Yeshua descending to Earth! They might think, "Oh my, why couldn't they have been saved just like us?" I am sure these Jewish believers will be feeling, not only sadness for their lost family members and friends, but they might also be feeling guilty that they made it and their family members did not! Oy vey, I cannot imagine how sad this mourning will be!

After the remaining one-third of the Jewish people receive the Ruach, then they shall "*look toward Me whom they have pierced.*" Notice the order of occurrence. First, the Jewish people get saved by receiving Yeshua. Second, they see Yeshua return in His Second Coming. First, they get saved; then Yeshua returns! There is a definite connection here between the nation of Israel's salvation and the Second Coming of Yeshua. It will be explored more closely later in the book.

Zechariah 14:1–3

> 1 Behold, a day of *ADONAI* is coming when your plunder will be divided in your midst. 2 I will gather all the nations against Jerusalem to wage war. The city shall be captured, the houses ransacked and the women ravished. Half of the city will be exiled but the remainder of the people will not be cut off from the city. 3 Then *ADONAI* will go forth and fight against those nations as He fights in a day of battle.

You might be wondering why so many Jewish people end up in the city of Jerusalem? Well, Zechariah 14:1–3 somewhat answers the question. In verse 1, the Lord promises the Jewish people that He will return all of their possessions that will be stolen when their enemies come into Israel to battle against them. This occurs during the Tribulation Period, and I believe it occurs right at the end. Why? Verse 2 shows that the Lord is the one who will gather all the nations to battle against Jerusalem. This is similar to the time the Lord brought Gog and Magog and the confederacy against Israel in the Ezekiel War. Remember in Ezekiel 38:4, the Lord put hooks into their mouths and led them up to Israel! Gog and Magog were certainly happy participants in that war, just like the Anti-messiah and his army of mega-millions will be thrilled to attack Jerusalem.

These enemy soldiers are going to perform horrific acts against the Jewish people of Jerusalem when they capture the city in battle. They will steal all their goods, the women will be obscenely violated, and half the city will be exiled. The good news is that the other half of the city will be allowed to stay. Certain destruction is in the balance over Jerusalem in this final battle of Jacob's Trouble. There is no doubt that Jerusalem will soon completely fall into the Anti-messiah's hands. When all hope is believed to be lost, this is when the Lord will perform His miracles!

The great news follows in verse 3. The Lord Yeshua will come to Israel's (and Jerusalem's) defense and return to the Earth in His Second Coming! This is why I believe the battle over Jerusalem is the final battle over Israel and occurs at the end of Jacob's Trouble. While the city is still reeling over her defeat at the hands of the Anti-messiah, the Lord returns at just the right time to defend the Jewish people against her enemies! This battle over Jerusalem begins the final battle of the Armageddon War.

Revelation 16:12-16

> 12 The sixth angel poured out his bowl over the great river Euphrates; and its water was dried up, to prepare the way for the kings from the east. 13 Then I saw—coming from the dragon's mouth and from the beast's mouth and from the false prophet's mouth—three unclean spirits like frogs. 14 For they are demonic spirits performing miraculous signs, who go out to the kings of the whole world—to gather them for battle on the great Day of *Elohei Tzva'ot* [God of Hosts].
> 15 "Behold, I am coming like a thief! How fortunate is the one who stays alert and keeps his clothes on, lest he walk around naked and they see his shamefulness."
> 16 Then the spirits gathered the kings to the place called in Hebrew *Har-Megiddo*.

As we move quickly toward the end of Jacob's Trouble, HaSatan will gather the world's armies for the final battle over Jerusalem. Ultimately, this battle will progress into a war against Yeshua and His holy ones! In verse 12, the sixth angel will pour out his bowl and the Euphrates River will dry up! This miracle has to have some effect on those around the world who have yet to make up their minds whether they are for Yeshua or HaSatan. The kings of the East will then be able to easily travel by land to Israel.

Many believers think the "kings of the east" automatically refers to China, but this is not necessarily true. The east in the Bible always refers to Mesopotamia, which includes Assyria and Babylon. Today, the region east of the Euphrates includes eastern Turkey, northeastern Syria, northeastern Iraq, and Iran. Remember, during the Tribulation Period the world will be divided into ten kingdoms. This identified eastern area could have more than one king reigning over it. And it is possible for China to be one of the nations of the eastern kingdom so that they might be included in this attack upon Israel.

Verse 13 reveals a very profound spiritual truth found especially in Jacob's Trouble. Demons (evil angels) are alive and well and living on planet Earth! Believers live in spiritual warfare against these demons every day of our lives. In Jacob's Trouble, demons will physically manifest on Earth in great numbers. Demons will fly out of the mouths of the unholy triunity (HaSatan, the Anti-messiah, and the false prophet) and gather the kings of the whole world (verse 14). They will gather to Israel for what they think will be an easy victory. What they don't know is that this war is the great day of Almighty God! Although the evil ones will have some initial victory over Jerusalem, when Yeshua comes back, He will usher in the Great Day of God! In verse 15, we are reminded that Yeshua's Second Coming will be like the thief that comes in the night. All believers at any moment are to keep alert, be ready, and stay faithful to the Lord.

HaSatan's world armies are then gathered to the place in Israel called "Har-Megiddo" (verse 16). Har-Megiddo means "the mountain of Megiddo" and is more commonly known as Armageddon. If you have traveled to Israel on a tour of the Land, then you know about the mountain of Megiddo. This is a famous stop to show where the final battle over Jerusalem will emanate from. Remember, the world's armies will be gathered to the Anti-messiah's kingly headquarters that is stationed between the three seas of Israel (Daniel 11:45). This valley area includes the Jezreel and Jordan valleys and can house literally hundreds of millions of soldiers! I believe this is exactly what we shall all see—hundreds of millions of soldiers barreling down on Jerusalem for the final battle of Armageddon.

Romans 11:25–27

> 25 For I do not want you, brothers and sisters, to be ignorant of this mystery—lest you be wise in your own eyes—that a partial hardening has come upon Israel until the fullness of the Gentiles has come in;
> 26 and in this way all Israel will be saved, as it is written,
> "The Deliverer shall come out of Zion.
> He shall turn away ungodliness from Jacob.
> 27 And this is My covenant with them,
> when I take away their sins."

Prior to the war of Armageddon and prior to Yeshua's Second Coming, the Lord will perform one of the most blessed, kindest acts for Israel. Sometime right before the end of Jacob's Trouble, all Israel will be saved! This will be the greatest day in Israel's history when she, as a nation, finally believes that Yeshua is her Messiah. And this is the day that all of us believers who share the good news with Jewish people around the world have dreamed of! We are hoping and praying for this day to come, and we are overjoyed to have any kind of effect on it as well (more on this later)!

Paul identifies another mystery in verse 25. The mystery is that a partial hardening has fallen on Israel until the fullness of the Gentiles comes in. Some Jewish people will be saved in this age of grace as the good news message of Yeshua traverses around the world, saving a set number of Gentiles. Paul is very clear that a partial hardening has happened to Israel in this age, not a complete hardening! This means that some Jewish people will believe in Yeshua and become the saved remnant.

Verse 25 is an extension of Romans 11:5–7 where Paul explains the remnant theology of Israel. He states that some Jewish people were chosen to become the remnant of believers from Israel while the other Jewish people were hardened. Therefore, some Jewish people will be saved in this present age and some hearts will be hardened! So verse 25 continues the argument that there is a partial hardening of Israel and not a complete hardening of Jewish hearts. Some will be saved, and some will not be saved. However, at the end of Jacob's Trouble, God's promise that all Israel will be saved will be fulfilled. This national salvation of Israel will not occur until the fullness of the Gentiles is fulfilled in the Tribulation Period. What is the "fullness of the Gentiles?"

There is much speculation concerning the "fullness of the Gentiles." The word "until" (*achris*) is a key word in this verse. "Until" is a time-sensitive word meaning that the partial hardening that has happened to Israel in the present will be lifted only when the fullness of the Gentiles comes in. "Fullness" (*pleroma*) can have a few different meanings like "that which fills, that which makes something complete, or a full number." Some believe the "fullness" refers to God's blessings upon the Gentiles, which includes salvation. Others think the "fullness" refers to Gentile salvations during the Tribulation Period. Since "fullness" can mean a full number and the context of the verse and the chapter are discussing Jewish salvation, I believe the "fullness" is talking about the full number of Gentile salvations during Jacob's Trouble.

Therefore, when the final Gentile somewhere around the world believes in Yeshua, the partial hardening of Israel will be lifted by the Lord, and the remaining nation will then be saved! Then the fulfillment of verse 23 will occur with the re-grafting of Israel into the olive tree of God's blessings! So, it is very important for the Body of Messiah to not only share the good news of Yeshua with the Jewish people first (which is God's expressed directive in Romans 1:16) but to fulfill Yeshua's command to preach the good news to all the world. Once this is accomplished by the Tribulation believers and the final Gentile receives salvation toward the end of the Tribulation Period, then all Israel can and will be saved (verse 26).

It is important to know that the mystery is not that all Israel will be saved, but that Israel's national salvation comes after the last Gentile receives Yeshua during Jacob's Trouble. I know this is true because of verse 26. Paul declares that all Israel will be saved just as it is written. Well, it was written that all Israel would be saved a long time ago in the prophets of the Tenach (Old Covenant writings). So, the mystery is the timing of when Israel will be saved and the connection it has to the end of Gentile salvation in Jacob's Trouble.

If this is all true (and it is!), then why do more than 50 percent of Bible-believing believers around the world think the Body of Messiah has replaced Israel in God's covenantal promises? This belief is called Replacement Theology. Replacement Theology asserts that the Jewish people, Israel, are no longer God's chosen people because of her national sin of rejecting Yeshua as Messiah. God then rejected Israel and replaced her with the universal Body of Messiah. All God's covenants and promises were then given to the Body of Messiah. This belief is obviously not true as this whole book sheds light upon this dark teaching. However, this question needs to be answered, "Why do more than 50 percent of Bible-believing believers around the world think they have replaced Israel in God's covenantal promises?"

In verses 26–27, Paul quotes from Isaiah 59:20–21. Whenever a New Covenant writer quotes from the Tenach, one should investigate the context of the passage. Isaiah 59:16–21 is a Messianic passage where the Lord will bring wrath to the adversaries and save the Jewish people. The Lord will then invoke His covenant upon Israel, and the Ruach will be upon them. This most certainly reveals Yeshua's Second Coming where He destroys the enemies of the Jewish people and saves the nation of Israel. He then will set up the Messianic Kingdom and begin the New Covenant with the nation of Israel! The Ruach will clearly be upon the people in the Kingdom. This is exactly what Paul is writing about! At the end of Jacob's Trouble, all Israel will be saved; then Yeshua will come back to Earth, destroy the enemies, and deliver the Jewish people. He will then begin the New Covenant with Israel in the Messianic Kingdom. What is interesting is that all of this prophecy was already established in Isaiah. What we did not know was the mystery identified that Israel would be partially hardened until the last Gentile gets saved during the Tribulation, and then all that's left of Israel will be saved!

Chart

As we view the chart, we can see that the Jewish people are in for major trouble. Jacob's Trouble will last for seven years; it is the seventieth week of Daniel. However, the worst holocaust against Israel in her history will occur in the Great Tribulation. It is the second half of Jacob's Trouble when the Anti-messiah attacks the Jewish people in Israel and throughout the world. The bad news is that the Anti-messiah will be successful in that two-thirds of the Jewish people will die in this holocaust!

But the good news is that one-third will make it through and be saved. This one-third will be the Jewish remnant that is saved toward the end of Jacob's Trouble and this will usher in the most sought-after event in history—the Second Coming of Yeshua! We do not know exactly how much time will pass between the day that all of Israel is saved and the end of the Tribulation Period.

Hence, you see the question marks on the graph at the end of the Tribulation and the two dotted arrowed lines pointing from the "All Israel Is Saved" box to the ending timetable of

Jacob's Trouble. It is possible that all Israel gets saved towards the last days of the end of Jacob's Trouble or it could land on the very last day of the Tribulation! We just don't know for sure since the Scripture does not specifically tell us. Nor do we know if there is an actual event that ends the Tribulation Period. What we do know is that the end of Jacob's Trouble occurs exactly seven years after the signing of the peace covenant between the Anti-messiah and Israel. For example, if they sign the document before dusk on the eve of Yom Kippur, then seven years later, Jacob's Trouble will end before dusk on the eve of Yom Kippur.

Prayer

Father in heaven, I once again pray for today's Jewish people around the world. Please encourage believers the world over to share the good news message of Yeshua with the Jewish people so that some may be saved today and not have to go through Jacob's Trouble! Please help the universal Body of Messiah to scripturally see that this is a great need for the Jewish people. Romans 1:16 declares, "For I am not ashamed of the Good News, for it is the power of God for salvation to everyone who trusts—to the Jew first and also to the Greek."

Please also call more believers to stand firm with the good news to work the harvest that will come. Lord, I pray for the Jewish people in Jacob's Trouble. I pray that You will glorify Your name in mighty ways in their lives. Please save many Jews and Gentiles in the Tribulation. Let there be a great revival all around the world! Once again, I pray for the peace of Jerusalem. Let Your *shalom* prosper in the Land. In Yeshua's name I pray, Amen.

Chapter 12

THE JEWISH ROOTS OF THE SECOND COMING OF YESHUA

The end of Jacob's Trouble will usher in the Second Coming of Yeshua. Before He can come, though, the worst holocaust to ever strike Israel must occur. The Anti-messiah and his evil ones will do great damage to the Jewish people. Two-thirds of the Jewish people in Israel will die. If Yeshua had not come back in the nick of time, then all the Jewish people would have been killed by Anti-messiah. But the good news is that the one-third of the Jewish people that survive will accept Yeshua at the end of Jacob's Trouble. Once "all Israel is saved," then Yeshua returns in His Second Coming. It is amazing that every person on Earth will see Yeshua return when the time comes! How can this be?

Revelation 1:7

> Look, He is coming with the clouds, and every eye shall see Him, even those who pierced Him. And all the tribes of the earth shall mourn because of Him. Yes, amen!

John proclaims that Yeshua will return in His Second Coming with the clouds, and every person on Earth will see it. When Yeshua comes back, He comes with the clouds. The clouds are made up of His body of believers (those that were raptured) and His angels. So Yeshua comes back with a large multitude of believers and angels. This is something we need to remember.

Just as important is the fact that every eye on Earth will see Yeshua come back, even those who pierced Him! "Every eye" refers to all people—Jewish and Gentile. However, then John specifically calls out a specific group of people: "*even those who pierced Him!*" What people group is he talking about? Even though the Roman guards specifically put Yeshua on the tree, John is calling out the Jewish people here! They are the ones who specifically tried Yeshua and turned Him over to the Romans to be pierced and crucified! Yeshua is already coming back to save the Jewish people from complete annihilation, so it makes sense that John refers to them especially as seeing Yeshua return (more on this later)!

Now a problem can and has arisen because of this analysis of this verse. Believers of the past recognized here that the Jewish people put Yeshua on that tree. But the problem is that they carried this thinking way too far. Instead of believing what the Scripture says that every human being (including Jewish people) on Earth for all time put Yeshua on that tree and that we should be grateful He willingly and joyfully went, they blamed the Jewish people for Yeshua's death, called them "Christ killers," and persecuted them.

The ignorance of this type of persecution is astounding! Instead of being grateful that Yeshua was killed on our behalf so that we all could be saved, they persecuted the Jewish people for killing who they deemed as their Christ! It seems to me that this was just another avenue of HaSatan to persecute and kill Jewish people. Remember, his plan is to try and wipe out the Jewish people so that he can try to take control of the universe away from God. If he could actually destroy God's plan for Israel, then he could say that he is more powerful than God and take His place. Well, that will never happen. However, that doesn't mean HaSatan won't continue to try.

Verse 7 ends with the idea that all the people of the Earth will mourn over Yeshua's Second Coming. In Zechariah 12:10 we found out that the recently saved Jewish believers will mourn, probably because they are remembering all the Jewish people who will have just recently died not believing in Yeshua during the last seven years of Jacob's Trouble. But why does the rest of the world mourn? I believe these evil folks are mourning because they know their end is coming soon, and they are mourning over their eternal judgment! Although they will try to fight Yeshua to the death, they ultimately know their demise is at hand and so they mourn over that! Think about it; how would you like to battle against the Messiah who just flew in from heaven with His army of billions, making the grandest of all glorious entrances?

Matthew 24:29–31

> 29 "But immediately after the trouble of those days,
> 'the sun will be darkened,
> and the moon will not give its light
> and the stars will fall from heaven
> and the powers of the heavens will be shaken.'
> 30 Then the sign of the Son of Man will appear in heaven, and then all the tribes of the land will mourn, and they will see 'the Son of Man coming on the clouds of heaven' with power and great glory.
> 31 He will send out His angels with a great *shofar,* and they will gather together His chosen from the four winds, from one end of heaven to the other."

I have yet to answer the question, "How does every person on earth see Yeshua return?" This scripture reading tells us. But first, verse 29 reports a most important fact about the Second

Coming that few acknowledge! The Second Coming of Yeshua comes *after* the tribulation of those days. The "trouble of those days" is the Tribulation Period—so Yeshua's Second Coming comes after Jacob's Trouble ends. "After" (*meta*) means "after in time or after in sequence of time." Either way "after" is related to time! Again, Yeshua's Second Coming comes after the end of Jacob's Trouble! This is a major find in the sequencing of end-time Jewish events.

However, the first event that will happen immediately after the Tribulation Period ends (and before the Second Coming occurs) is the shaking of the powers of heaven (verse 29)! God moves in His power to darken the sun and the moon and cause stars to fall from the sky! This powerful move of the Lord reminds me of what He did to the Egyptians when Pharaoh would not let His people go! In Exodus 10:21–23, the Lord brought a thick darkness over the land so that each Egyptian could even feel it! No one could see the sun, the moon, the stars, or each other, for that matter, for three whole days. I wonder if the darkness after Jacob's Trouble will last three days as well (Matthew 24 does not tell us exactly how long this darkness lasts).

We must remember that the last event in our chronology will be the capturing of Jerusalem by the Anti-messiah. He and his evil ones will ravage the Jewish people and the city, but half of the city will not be exiled. Yeshua comes back at the right time (as always) and saves the day. But it seems to me that during this continued battle over Jerusalem and its aftermath is the time of the darkened skies. It seems this darkening of the skies around the world also will give the people of the earth a reprieve in a sense. It is like the Lord is granting a time out to the world before the arrival of Yeshua. It is a grandiose heavenly introductory warning that Yeshua is coming back real soon! He is almost saying, "You can have your little ceasefire right now during My blackout, but watch out and get ready, for My Son Yeshua will come in great power and great glory!"

It is amazing to know that Matthew quotes from a number of prophetic sources in the Tenach (Isaiah 13:9–11, 24:21–23; Joel 2:1–11, 3:9–15; Amos 5:18–20, Zephaniah 1:14–18). Each of these scriptures connects the darkening of the sky with the Lord's judgment in the end times.

However, Joel 2:30–32 (NASB) is specifically significant to our study of Matthew 24:29. In verse 30, the Lord declares that blood, fire, and smoke will billow throughout the earth. Typically, this judgment would be brought on by war occurring all over the world. The heavenly wonders include the sun and moon not sharing their light (verse 31). Although Joel does not mention the stars losing their brightness here in verse 31, he documents it in 2:10 and 3:15 (as do the other prophets, as well). However, it seems from this verse that the amount and intensity of fire and smoke will cause the sun, moon, and stars to be darkened. For the heavenly creation to be darkened or even to turn a blood-red color, there needs to be a whole lot of smoke to cover them up!

The key to verse 31 is that the darkening of the sky occurs *before* the great and awesome Day of the Lord comes! The Hebrew word "before" (*panim*) when combined with a prefix "le" literally means "facing" and is interpreted "before or in front of." The meaning here is clear: the darkening of the sky will literally occur before the Lord comes back in His Second Coming! This is the reason why the chart has the Second Coming of Yeshua occurring after the end of Jacob's Trouble. Verse 32 is important because it shows Yeshua delivering the Jewish believers of Jerusalem who have escaped the clutches of the Anti-messiah in His last battle over Jerusalem! Yeshua comes back to save these and other believers as well.

Thus far in Matthew 24:29 we have learned that the darkening of the sky will occur after the end of Jacob's Trouble. God's power from heaven will be shaken. Matthew quoted from a few Old Covenant sources including Joel 2:30–32 that additionally confirm that God's great judgment through Yeshua's Second Coming comes after the Tribulation Period ends.

What's fascinating is that Matthew claims, not that the stars will lose their brightness, but that they "fall from heaven." "Fall" (*pipto*) means "to fall, fall down, fail." Although it is possible Matthew is referring to the failing of the stars, which shows their inability to shine their light; it is more probable he is using the primary meaning of "fall" whereby the stars actually fall from the sky. This sign would greatly reveal God's power from heaven, which is His goal!

Now, in verse 30, Matthew declares that the sign of Yeshua will appear in the sky just prior to His descent! When the sign of Yeshua appears, all the tribes of the "land" will mourn. The Greek word for "land" (*ge*) means "land or earth."

There is an interesting dilemma concerning which meaning is indicated. Is Matthew discussing all the tribes of the Land of Israel mourning or all the peoples of the world mourning? The Lord definitely wants the whole earth to see Yeshua's glorious return and not just the Jewish people in the Land! Revelation 1:7 reveals "land" as all the earth since there is a contrast between all the peoples of the earth versus the Jewish people. However, Matthew's context is concerned with how the Jewish people are affected in Jacob's Trouble. Zechariah 12:10 tells us that all the Jewish people of Jerusalem will see Yeshua return in His Second Coming and mourn for Him! I believe Matthew is speaking about the Jewish people in verse 30, and therefore "all the tribes of the land" will mourn.

Another controversial issue in verse 30 is knowing what the sign of Yeshua is. Some believe the world will see a gigantic cross in the sky. This understanding is highly suspect because Yeshua's Second Coming is not focused on repentance but judgment of the evil ones. Actually, the answer is revealed in the same verse. The world will see Yeshua coming on the clouds of the sky with power and great glory! In Revelation 19:14, the "clouds" are Yeshua's armies in heaven coming back with Him. The context dictates the armies include believers who have made it through the Bema Seat Judgment.

Matthew 24:31 additionally tells us that immediately following the Second Coming, Yeshua will send forth His angels around the world to collect His believers. So, God's angels obviously come back with Yeshua and are a part of the "clouds." I believe the "clouds" that come back with Yeshua include both the Jewish and Gentile raptured believers and Yeshua's angels!

If you can imagine this scene, I believe the world will be looking at billions upon billions of believers and angels all throughout the sky! From Earth's vantage point, it will look like the entire sky around the earth will be filled with these beings! To the evil ones, it will be a terrifying scene; to believers, it will be glorious!

We must remember that the world is going to be a very dark place. Not only will the wars knock out power for lighting, but the Lord will darken the sky! Then the world will see Yeshua and His bride come back in power and great glory! I believe His "power" is revealed not only in the sheer numbers of Yeshua's contingent, but that there will also probably be some sort of great noise accompanying His return. Do you remember what happened in Exodus 19:16–20 when the Lord physically descended upon Mount Sinai to reveal Himself to the Jewish people? There was thunder, lightning, thick clouds, a very loud trumpet blast, smoke, fire, and a violent earthquake! Obviously, the Lord wanted Israel to know and fear His presence! I think the Lord wants to show the world His presence through Yeshua's coming in the same way. In verse 31, we also see a great trumpet blast in the collection of the "chosen," revealing this great power.

The "great glory" in Matthew 24:30 is the *Shekinah Glory* of God. The Shekinah Glory is the visible powerful presence of God usually revealed as a great light. Yeshua will be wearing this Shekinah Glory in His Second Coming (Ezekiel 43:1–5) for all the world to see! This glory is also spoken about in

Daniel 7:13–14, which is the verse that Matthew was quoting here. Yeshua's glory will be so bright that it will encompass all the believers and angels who return with Him, so the sky all around the earth will be one gigantic lamp, shining brighter than the sun!

Yeshua quoted Daniel 7:13 with Psalm 110:1 when He proclaimed to the Sanhedrin council to be the Son of Man who will come with the clouds of heaven (in Mark 14:62). They knew exactly what He was claiming and thought it to be blasphemy. In 7:13–14, Daniel describes a night vision where he saw the Son of Man, the Messiah, coming with the clouds of heaven. The Son of Man was presented before the Ancient of Days, the Father, to receive His dominion, glory, and an everlasting kingdom. Yeshua will receive this dominion, glory, and kingdom just prior to His Second Coming! He receives the authority, honor, and glory from the Father to come to Earth and set up His everlasting kingdom. The glory here, once again, is the Shekinah Glory of God. This is where we get our understanding that "Yeshua is the light of the world!" This Shekinah Glory is the brilliance and light of God, and Yeshua will come back to Earth wearing it!

In Matthew 24:31, we find Yeshua's angels are sent out to collect all the surviving Tribulation Period believers from around the world after the Second Coming. Yeshua's angels are sent out with a great trumpet blast that I believe is a shofar blast! Notice that this great trumpet blast occurs *after* the Second Coming. The shofar blast would also occur after the Armageddon War is over. It is the rallying cry for the collection of all the Tribulation believers who made it alive to the end of the war.

Once again, Matthew quotes from the Tenach. He combines Isaiah 11:12, 27:13, and Deuteronomy 30:4 (and others) to establish this bold prophecy that the Lord will finally regather Israel from around the world to the Land of Israel! These verses show the gathering of God's people will occur at a great trumpet blast! God's "chosen" are the "elected ones" who are the Jewish believers who make it alive to the end of the Armageddon War. But don't worry, the Lord is not forgetting about the Gentile believers. They will be gathered, too! Matthew, however, is responding to the prophets who prophesied about Israel's final regathering! The phrases "four winds" and "one end of heaven to the other" are Hebraisms that mean the whole earth (Nehemiah 1:9, Daniel 7:2, and Zechariah 2:6 use similar phrases)!

Although Matthew leaves out some information concerning the Second Coming, such as the collection of the Gentile believers and the Armageddon War, he does provide us with an important understanding of the order of events. After Jacob's Trouble is over, the powers of the heavens will be shaken. The Lord will darken the sun and moon, and the stars will begin to fall from the sky. Then the sign of Yeshua will occur in the heaven, all the Earth will mourn, and He will come back in great power and glory! After the events of the actual return of Yeshua, the regathering of the believing remnant of Israel from all over the world will occur. Yeshua most certainly collects the Gentile believers in this gathering, Matthew just does not document this fact in his account.

Zechariah 14:3–15

> 3 Then *ADONAI* will go forth and fight against those nations as He fights in a day of battle. 4 In that day His feet will stand on the Mount of Olives which lies to the east of Jerusalem, and the Mount of Olives will be split in two from east to west, forming a huge valley. Half of the mountain will move toward the north and half of it toward the south. 5 Then you will flee through My mountain valley because the mountain valley will reach to Azel. Yes, you will flee like you fled from the earthquake in the days of King Uzziah of

Judah. Then *ADONAI* my God will come and all the *kedoshim* with Him.
6 In that day there will be no light, cold or frost. 7 It will be a day known only to *ADONAI,* neither day nor night—even in the evening time there will be light. 8 Moreover, in that day living waters will flow from Jerusalem, half toward the eastern sea and half toward the western sea, both in the summer and in the winter. 9 *ADONAI* will then be King over all the earth. In that day *ADONAI* will be *Echad* [One] and His Name *Echad.*
10 The whole land, from Geba to Rimmon south of Jerusalem, will become like the Arabah. Jerusalem will be raised up and occupy her place, from the Benjamin Gate to the place of the First Gate, to the Corner Gate, and from the Tower of Hananel to the king's winepresses. 11 People will dwell in her, and no longer will there be a ban of destruction—Jerusalem will live in security.
12 Now this is the plague with which *ADONAI* will strike all the peoples that wage war against Jerusalem: their flesh will rot while they are standing on their feet; their eyes will rot in their sockets; and their tongues will rot in their mouths. 13 It will happen in that day that a great panic from *ADONAI* will be among them. Each person will seize the hand of his neighbor and they will attack each other. 14 Even Judah will fight at Jerusalem. The wealth of all the surrounding peoples will be gathered together—an abundance of gold, silver and apparel. 15 A similar plague will strike the horse, the mule, the camel, the donkey and all the animals in that camp.

Before the Second Coming of Yeshua, Zechariah discusses the final battle over Jerusalem in verse 2. The Anti-messiah with his many millions of soldiers will attack Jerusalem in this last battle over Israel. In his narrative, it seems the battling over the city is still current. Jerusalem has been captured, but only half of the city was exiled. Then ADONAI goes forth and battles against the evil ones. But, before Yeshua can do this, He must first come back in His Second Coming (verse 3)!

Verse 4 is the famous verse concerning the Lord's feet standing on the Mount of Olives. I believe this is the Lord's ascent to the top of the Mount of Olives after He has already destroyed the enemies from Petra all the way back to Haifa. As will be discussed in more detail later, He ascends to the Mount of Olives to declare to Jerusalem that He is the Messiah who has saved and rescued the Jewish people! As Yeshua stands on the Mount of Olives, He causes an earthquake and splits the mountain down the middle, east to west.

This action creates a very large valley so that the Jewish people who are left in the city of Jerusalem can flee to safety (verse 5). Why do they need to flee to safety? The Anti-messiah and his army are still battling over Jerusalem. The after-effects of the battle are still occurring, and Yeshua is coming to save the city, so there will be one last battle over Jerusalem between Yeshua and the Anti-messiah. Yeshua comes with His holy ones—these are the raptured believers and the angels. We come with Yeshua, but we are not fighting along with Him. This He does alone!

Verse 6 proclaims that in that day, there will be no light. Remember, Matthew 24:29 showed us that the sun and moon will not shine their light, and the stars will fall from the sky. There will be mayhem in the dark day when the Lord returns to Earth! In verse 7, this day is declared as being unique. It will not be like any other day or night, but at evening time there will be light. This light is the Shekinah Glory resting on Yeshua! His light will shine brightly through all the darkness because He is the light of the world! Verse 8 reveals that later in the Messianic Millennial Kingdom, living waters will flow from the newly-built Temple in Jerusalem. These living waters will flow eastward to the Dead Sea (making it alive) and westward toward the Mediterranean Sea. These are the same living waters spoken of in Ezekiel 47:1–12.

Verses 9–11 share the results of Yeshua's Second Coming. In verse 9, He will be the one and only King of the world. He will rule and reign from His throne in His Temple in the Land of Israel! This certainly shows Yeshua ruling from earth and not from heaven! He is the King over all the earth! Many believers today think Yeshua is not going to be King over the earth for a thousand-year Messianic Kingdom. However, verse 9 is very clear that this is the case!

Verse 10 reveals that Israel will undergo some geographical changes. Jerusalem will physically rise up, and the land around it will become a plain. Jerusalem will be the focus of all the believers of the Messianic Millennial Kingdom in that they will have to go up to Jerusalem to worship the Lord. Verse 11 resoundingly confirms God's promises to Abraham and David that the Jewish people will finally live in the city of Jerusalem (and in the Land of Israel) under the rule of Messiah! And verse 11 says that they will live there in security. This is what the Jewish people have always wanted, and finally their desire will become reality!

Verses 12–15 take us back to the war of Armageddon. The Lord's judgment against all the people who battled against Jerusalem is proclaimed in verse 12. The Lord's plague will cause their tongues to rot in their mouths, their eyes will rot in their sockets, and their flesh will rot while they are standing! This judgment results in the catastrophic river of blood flowing through the Land of Israel. His plague is the very same "sharp sword" that comes from Yeshua's mouth in Revelation 19:15. This sword is also spoken of in Isaiah 11:4 as the rod of His mouth. This is His spoken Word of judgment against all the evil ones. The Word that proceeds from His mouth will be an instantaneous attack of plague on the mega millions of soldiers. This judgment will destroy them! The damage will be catastrophic, but the cleanup will be immense!

When Yeshua speaks, it is like the detonation of an atomic bomb. Their flesh, eyes, and tongues will rot while they are standing and fighting against Yeshua! This is substantiated by Haggai 2:22 where the Lord Himself will overthrow and destroy all the kingdoms of the nations of the earth. Specifically, these kingdoms are Gentile kingdoms that are trying to destroy the Jewish people of Israel. This is also in fulfillment of Daniel 2:44 where the Lord says He will crush all the Gentile kingdoms and set up His Kingdom that cannot be destroyed!

Before the plague is cast upon the enemies of the Jewish people, the Lord causes a great panic to fall upon the Anti-messiah's soldiers (verse 13). Instead of continuing to fight against the Jewish people, they will battle one another. Zechariah 12:4 documents this event as well. It says the soldiers will be struck with madness and their horses with blindness and bewilderment. This is not the first time this has happened in Israel's history (see Judges 7:19–22; 1 Samuel 14:20; Ezekiel 38:21).

Verse 14 takes us back to the end of Jacob's Trouble. Judah will fight against the Anti-messiah as he and all the nations attack Jerusalem. This is also stated in Zechariah 12:5–6 where the clans of Judah see the Jewish people's resistance in Jerusalem. This resistance against the Anti-messiah will be a great encouragement to them. Verse 14 also shows a result of Yeshua's victory over the evil ones. As the Jewish people are regathered to Israel from around the world, the wealth of the nations will be brought to Israel as well. Some of this wealth will most likely be used to rebuild the Temple. Verse 15 then refers back to the plague. This plague will be so devastating to the enemies of the Jewish people that even all their animals will be affected. The Lord obviously sees these animals as being defiled and does not want the Jewish people to plunder them afterward.

In summary, Zechariah 14 is a powerful passage proclaiming the Lord's Second Coming. Yeshua will save Judah prior to delivering Jerusalem. He will stand on the Mount of Olives just prior to entering Jerusalem for the final battle against the Anti-messiah. He will have already destroyed the Anti-messiah's army located from the Petra area to Haifa. The Armageddon War is a complete plague that flows throughout the enemies' stronghold and wipes them all out. Their blood will flow for about 180 miles, most of which will occur in the Land of Israel. Yeshua will take His rightful position as King of the Jews and King of the world and begin the Messianic Millennial Kingdom. Jerusalem will live in safety and security under the righteous watchful eye of the Lord.

Revelation 19:11–21

> 11 Then I saw heaven opened, and behold, a white horse! The One riding on it is called Faithful and True, and He judges and makes war in righteousness. 12 His eyes are like a flame of fire, and many royal crowns are on His head. He has a name written that no one knows except Himself. 13 He is clothed in a robe dipped in blood, and the name by which He is called is "the Word of God."
> 14 And the armies of heaven, clothed in fine linen, white and clean, were following Him on white horses.
> 15 From His mouth comes a sharp sword—so that with it He may strike down the nations—and He shall rule them with an iron rod, and He treads the winepress of the furious wrath of *Elohei-Tzva'ot* [God of Hosts]. 16 On His robe and on His thigh He has a name written, "King of kings, and Lord of lords."
> 17 Then I saw a single angel standing in the sun, and with a loud voice he cried out to all the birds flying high in the sky, "Come, gather for the great banquet of God—18 to eat the flesh of kings and the flesh of generals and the flesh of mighty men, the flesh of horses and those riding on them, the flesh of all men, both free and slave, both small and great!"

> 19 Also I saw the beast and the kings of the earth and their armies gathered together to make war against the One who sat on the horse and against His army. 20 Then the beast was captured, and along with him the false prophet who had performed the signs before him by which he deceived those who had received the mark of the beast, as well as those who had worshiped his image. These two were thrown alive into the lake of fire burning with brimstone. 21 The rest were killed with the sword coming out of the mouth of the One riding on the horse. And all the birds gorged themselves with their flesh.

Revelation 19:5–9 reveals the preparatory work necessary before the Second Coming. In this scripture passage, we already found out that the Body of Messiah was in heaven, preparing for the wedding of the Lord. We received our bright and clean robes which somehow miraculously reveal our righteous acts performed in our lives on Earth. The marriage of the Lamb occurs in heaven, but it seems that the Marriage Supper will occur on Earth. In any event, those who are invited to the wedding reception will be very blessed! After the prep work is finished, then we see the only passage of the Bible that specifically and minutely details the Second Coming of Yeshua!

The word *then* (kai, also means *and*) that begins verse 11 helps us to understand that the narrative continues in consecutive order. The Second Coming comes *after* the Bema Seat Judgment and the wedding of the Lamb. Verse 11 begins by identifying a rider on a white horse in heaven. He is given the titles of "Faithful" and "True" and is characterized as being righteous in His judgment of wrath. This is the One and only Yeshua HaMeshiach (Jesus the Messiah)!

In verses 12–13, Yeshua is then described as the conquering King. His eyes are blazing like fire and His robe is dipped in blood. This obviously symbolizes the results of His return: the blood of the evil ones will be spilled on the earth. He is wearing many "royal crowns" (diadems) revealing His Kingship. Although He has an unknown name written on His body, He is additionally known by the title "The Word of God." This is in reference to John 1:1 where Yeshua is called the *logos* or "the Word of God." Yeshua, the Son of God, is the human manifestation of the wondrous content, fullness, and divine nature of God's Word.

In verse 14 we find out who comes with Yeshua in His return. The "armies" are described as wearing beautiful white and pure robes. I believe Yeshua's army is the very same group of believers described earlier in 19:6–8—the raptured Body of Messiah that has already gone through the Bema Seat Judgment. Their robes are white and pure because they have been purified by the Lord through the judgment seat process. Their robes reveal their good works performed in faith and love in their earthly ministries.

The fun part about returning with Yeshua in His Second Coming is that we will be riding on white horses! These horses are obviously spiritual, heavenly horses. However, each New Covenant believer will have their own horse. When I teach this message in congregations, I receive many concerns from folks who don't know how to ride horses. I tell them not to worry because the Lord will either instantaneously cause us to be able to ride or He will have His angels teach us. This promise of God is such a great blessing to all believers and their children. Believing parents no longer have to feel bad when they say "no" to their children who want horses for their birthdays! Now you can tell them they will receive their horses in heaven at the Second Coming!

Verse 15 then reveals one of the themes of the Second Coming—the judgment of God. In one quick mention, Yeshua judges the nations through His sharp sword. The "sharp sword" is a metaphor for His Word. Like we saw in Zechariah 14, the damage will be apocalyptic! After He treads the proverbial winepress of the wrath of God, He will set up the Messianic Millennial Kingdom. In this Kingdom, the King will rule with a rod of iron. This means He will rule the world according to His Word, the righteous standard of God. Sin will not be allowed to run rampant like it does in our current world system. Yeshua will judge the world's sin quickly and decisively. Life in the Kingdom will have peace, love, joy, righteousness, and justice with most of the curse lifted. People will be required to conform to His righteous standard of living or face the rod of His judgment.

In verse 16, we see the fourth time in this scripture section that Yeshua is identified with a name. He is called Faithful and True (verse 11), the Word of God (verse 13), and an unknown name that only He knows (verse 12). The fourth name is "King of kings and Lord of lords." This name is written on His thigh, and it surely proclaims Yeshua is Messiah and God! In light of this result, it is a wonder that folks around the world are not currently flocking to be saved by Yeshua!

In verses 17–18, an angel found standing in the sun invites all the birds to join the great supper of God on earth! This supper will be great in God's eyes but bad in the world's eyes. Why? It involves the Armageddon War and their complete and utter destruction. The birds of the air will eat the flesh of all the dead army of the Anti-messiah. It will be a gruesome sight.

However, before the Armageddon War begins, both sides prepare their armies for the battle (verse 19). The beast (Anti-messiah), the kings of the earth that were earlier summoned to Israel, and their armies will congregate at Anti-messiah's headquarters in the Jezreel and Jordan Valleys. A portion of their army attacks Jerusalem, the final frontier of Israel that needs to be conquered by Anti-messiah. This assembling of the world's armies involves God's wrath upon the nations of the world found in Zephaniah 3:8. The Lord says in Zephaniah that He gathered and assembled these nations against Israel so that He could pour out His anger and wrath upon them! This is when all the earth will be devoured.

Once this attack upon Jerusalem takes place, then and only then does Yeshua return to Earth with His army. Verse 19 tells us that the Anti-messiah and his army are gathered specifically to make war against Yeshua and His army. Maybe in their own warped thinking, they believe if they attack Jerusalem, Yeshua will come back, and they will finally battle against Him and win!

Verse 20 tells us otherwise. The beast and the false prophet are somehow captured by Yeshua. They were quickly judged for their evil and cast into the Lake of Fire. They are the first visitors to the Lake of Fire that burns with brimstone forever. After the Anti-messiah and the false prophet are taken, the rest of their army is killed by Yeshua's sword (verse 21). This sword that comes out of His mouth is the same one found in verse 15. This sword is also known as the plague found in Zechariah 14:12–15. He will strike the Earth and slay the wicked with the breath of His lips! The decimation of the enemies of the Jewish people will be tremendous! How bad will it be?

Revelation 14:17–20

> 17 Then another angel came out of the Temple in heaven, and he also had a sharp sickle. 18 Then another angel—the one who has authority over fire—came out from the altar; and he called out with a loud voice to the one holding the sharp sickle, saying, "Put in your sickle and gather the grape clusters from the vineyard of the earth, because her grapes are ripe." 19 So the angel swung his sickle over the earth and gathered the clusters from the vineyard of the earth and threw them into the great winepress of the wrath of God. 20 And the winepress was stomped on outside the city, and blood

flowed from the winepress as high as a horse's bridle for 1,600 stadia.

The devastation that will occur in the Armageddon War will be beyond belief! It just goes to show us how truly evil the world will have become for the Lord to judge it in such a way. In verses 17–18, we are introduced to two angels. One angel will come forth from the heavenly Temple with a sharp sickle in his hand. The sickle is a short, curved, metal-bladed tool specifically used in Israel to cut grapes from the vine. The second angel will come from the heavenly altar and instruct the first angel to use his sickle on the earth. The grapes will be ready for harvesting.

In verse 19, the angel complies with the request. He swings his sickle, gathers the grape clusters, and throws them into the winepress. But, as we read the last part of the verse we find out John is speaking in a metaphor. The winepress represents God's wrath. So, the idea here is that the pressing of grapes into wine represents God's wrath against the Anti-messiah's army gathered in Israel and their blood being spilled in His attack against them! As we saw in Zechariah 14:12–15, this plague will be devastating.

Verse 20 shows us the judgment will occur outside the city. The city spoken of here is the city of Jerusalem, and the area outside it is the Jezreel and Jordan valleys. The blood of the evil ones is going to flow because of Yeshua's spoken word. This plague, which sounds like an atomic bomb exploding, will cause the blood to flow for a distance of 1,600 stadia or about 180 miles! We need to remember that Israel is only about 263 miles long and 71 miles at its widest width. So, if this tremendous river of blood flows through only Israel (it is possible for the blood to flow into the Dead Sea area and even into Jordan; more on this later) then much of the Land will be covered by this river of blood! This devastation will be incomprehensible to the human mind!

In addition, verse 20 tells us the depth of this river of blood will be up to the horses' bridle. Depending on the height of the horse, this depth could be from 3–4 feet deep! The number of soldiers required to die and spill their blood to fulfill this prophecy is immense. We are talking about mega-millions of soldiers here! These soldiers will be located exactly where they are supposed to be—in the Jezreel and Jordan valleys (Daniel 11:45)!

Chart

So, the scene of the Armageddon War is set. After Israel is devastated by the Anti-messiah and his evil army in Jacob's Trouble, all Israel will be saved at the end. After receiving the Ruach Kodesh, Israel then cries out to the Lord for help, and Yeshua returns with His army to battle the evil ones of Anti-messiah. Yeshua's return occurs *after* Jacob's Trouble has ended. This is depicted in the chart with a long, dotted arrow protruding from the cloud entitled, "Second Coming and Armageddon." The dotted arrow lines up after the darkened line of the box titled "Israel in the Second Half" of the Tribulation. The dotted arrow ends up at the question mark indicating that we do not know the day or the hour of the Second Coming, nor do we know how many days it occurs after the Tribulation Period is completed. This truly is God's mystery!

Yeshua returns to a very spiritually and physically dark world, wearing the Shekinah Glory of God! Yeshua is the light of the darkened world. The bloodshed will be immense in the Armageddon War, but the judgment of God is even greater! Jeremiah 25:30–33 emphatically declares God's judgment will also be worldwide! So, the catastrophe will not only occur in Israel, but around the world as well. At the end of the war, the Anti-messiah and the false prophet will be thrown into the Lake of Fire. Their judgment will be a forever judgment! After the War is over, the Lord's angels will then perform a world-wide gathering of all believers and non-believers who make it through Jacob's Trouble alive.

Prayer

Father in heaven, I know the devastation will be immense around the world and especially in Israel when Yeshua returns to Earth in His Second Coming. There is nothing I can say or do to change this prophecy. Your Word is Your truth! Just as Yeshua said in the garden of Gethsemane just prior to His death, "Not My will, but Your will be done." So, let Your will be done with this world and with the Jewish people!

However, I can help the Jewish and Gentile people of my world know what's coming in their future and warn them. Help me to warn as many folks as possible of the coming holocaust to the Jewish people and to share the good news of Yeshua with them, too. Yes, there is good news for Israel in that Yeshua saves the day in His Second Coming, but a lot of people are going to be terrorized by Anti-messiah. Help many Jewish and Gentile people in this time of trouble to receive Yeshua. Let your mercy and grace be upon them as they live for You throughout the rest of the Tribulation Period. In Yeshua's Name I pray, Amen.

Chapter 13

THE SECOND COMING AND THE JEWISH PEOPLE

Most believers think Yeshua is only coming back to judge the world of its evil. This is far from the truth! The Second Coming most definitely involves the judgment of the world. Just read the book of Revelation, and one can surmise this. However, this is not the *only* reason why Yeshua returns. Did you know there is an amazing connection between Yeshua's Second Coming and the nation of Israel? Did you know that the Second Coming could never happen unless two specific actions of the Jewish people take place first? Let us delve into this Israeli connection to Yeshua's Second Coming and also learn how we can personally affect this future glorious occasion!

Hosea 5:13–15

> 13 When Ephraim saw his sickness
> and Judah his wound,
> Ephraim went to Assyria
> and sent envoys to a warring king.
> But he cannot heal you
> nor will he cure your wound.

14 For I will be like a lion to Ephraim,
and like a young lion to the house of Judah.
I, even I, will tear and go away.
I will carry off, and nobody will rescue.
15 I will go and return to My place
until they admit their guilt.
Then they will seek My face.
In their distress they will seek Me earnestly.

The first event that needs to occur before the Second Coming is the salvation of the nation of Israel! This requires the nation of Israel to repent and confess her sin. In Hosea, God deals with Israel's sin by pouring out His wrath. Israel looks to other nations to help her in the onslaught from Assyria (verse 13). Unfortunately, she does not look to the Lord for help. In verse 14, the Lord even says He will continue to judge an unrepentant Israel.

In verse 15, the Lord states He will go away from Israel and return to His place in heaven. It is obvious that the Lord is on earth when He makes this statement and will depart to go back to heaven! Here, I see the Lord Yeshua claiming He will die for Israel's sin, resurrect, and ascend back to heaven where He came from. He will stay in heaven *until* Israel recognizes their guilt and seeks His face! *Until* is a time-sensitive word and shows Yeshua will not come back until Israel confesses her sin of rejecting Him. Finally, after they go through much affliction in Jacob's Trouble, they will seek after Yeshua and be saved! Hosea encourages Israel to repent and return to the Lord (in 6:1–3). God has judged but He will restore as well. Once Israel repents, she is exhorted to stay in personal fellowship with Him.

Jeremiah 3:11–18

11 Then *ADONAI* said to me, "Backsliding Israel has proved herself more righteous than unfaithful Judah. 12 Go! Proclaim these words toward the north, saying:
"Return backsliding Israel," says *ADONAI*.
"I will no longer frown on you,
for I am merciful," says *ADONAI*.
"I will not keep a grudge forever.
13 Only acknowledge your iniquity.
For you sinned against *ADONAI* your God
and scattered your favors to foreign gods
under every green tree.
You have not obeyed My voice."
It is a declaration of *ADONAI*.
14 "Return, O backsliding children," declares *ADONAI*.
"For I am your Husband.
I will choose you—one from a city
and two from a clan—
and will bring you to Zion.
15 I will give you shepherds
after My own heart
who will feed you knowledge
and understanding.
16 It will be in those days
when you multiply
and become fruitful in the land."
It is a declaration of *ADONAI*.
"They will no longer talk about the ark of the covenant of *ADONAI*, nor will it come to mind or be remembered. Neither will it be missed or another one made again. 17 At that time they will call Jerusalem the throne of *ADONAI* and all the nations will gather into it, to Jerusalem, in the Name of *ADONAI*. No longer will they walk according to the stubbornness of their evil

heart. 18 In those days the house of Judah will walk with the house of Israel. They will come together out of the land of the north to the land that I gave your fathers as an inheritance."

Jeremiah was told by the Lord to go and preach repentance to the northern kingdom of Israel (verses 11–12). Even though she is faithless, she is more righteous compared to Judah (the southern kingdom). The Lord says He is gracious and just wants Israel to confess her iniquity (verse 13). "Iniquity" is in the singular. This fact and verses 15-18 help us to understand the context of the passage is the Messianic Millennial Kingdom and what the nation of Israel has to do to enter into the Kingdom. They have to acknowledge one sin. That one sin is not believing in Yeshua as the Jewish Messiah in His First Coming! His promise is to take those who repent back to Jerusalem (verse 14). This certainly sounds like the regathering of the believing remnant after the Second Coming!

Verses 15–18 make the connection to the end times and the Messianic Millennial Kingdom. The Lord then promises that He will provide shepherds that will lead and guide Israel into true knowledge and understanding. This can only occur in the Messianic Millennial Kingdom with Yeshua as King! Verse 16 profoundly announces that the Ark of the Covenant will not be remembered nor missed. When the Kingdom begins, it will be so awesome and beautiful that the Israelites will not even think of the old Ark of the Covenant. Who could blame them? Yeshua, in all His splendor, will be there! What more could anyone want? The timing of verse 16 could only occur in the Kingdom. Today, the Ark of the Covenant is discussed all the time in Christian and Jewish circles. People wonder where the Ark is located right now and have elaborate theories as to its location. So, Jeremiah's prophecy cannot be talking about his day or even today. It must be speaking of the future during the Messianic Millennial Kingdom. Then, no one will wonder where the Ark is!

In verse 17 we find out that Jerusalem will be called, "The throne of *ADONAI*." All nations will be gathered to Jerusalem, and they will not be walking after their evil hearts like we find in the present age. This most certainly describes life in the Messianic Millennial Kingdom! Finally, verse 18 reiterates God's promise of regathering the northern kingdom of Israel and the southern kingdom of Judah to live together as one in the Land of Israel. This promise will be fulfilled in the Kingdom as well! But before this can happen, first Israel must confess her national sin of rejecting Yeshua as Messiah.

<u>Hosea 3:4–5</u>

> 4 For *Bnei-Yisrael* [Children of Israel] will remain for many days without king, without prince, without sacrifice, without sacred pillar, and without ephod or teraphim. 5 Afterwards, *Bnei-Yisrael* will return, and they will seek *ADONAI* their God and David their king. Then they will turn in awe to *ADONAI* and to His goodness in the last days.

In Chapter 3, Hosea makes a bold prediction concerning Israel. The Jewish people will be without the temple worship system for "many days." Many days have turned into almost 2,000 years! Although this is the bad news for Israel, verse 5 declares the good news. After the "many days," Israel will return to the Lord in repentance and seek His face and David their King! So, Israel will be saved as a nation then seek after the Lord and His Messiah (I believe this reference to "David their King" is Messianic). When will this occur? Verse 5 finishes with the declaration that Israel will seek after the Lord in the last days. This is a reference to the end times, which includes Jacob's Trouble. Israel will come trembling before the

Lord because the Anti-messiah and the world will attack her, and they fear the end is near. So why not turn to the Lord? He will definitely help the Jewish people!

It needs to be clarified that this salvation for the Jewish people has to be national. This is not talking about *some* Jewish people getting saved or even a great revival occurring. God's promise to Israel is that "*all Israel will be saved*" (Romans 11:26)! This means that at the end of Jacob's Trouble, all the Jewish people who make it through the Tribulation Period alive will be saved! It does not take a rocket scientist to understand that "all" means *all*! So, this is talking about salvation for the nation of Israel.

Matthew 23:37–39

> 37 "O Jerusalem, Jerusalem who kills the prophets and stones those sent to her! How often I longed to gather your children together, as a hen gathers her chicks under her wings, but you were not willing! 38 Look, your house is left to you desolate! 39 For I tell you, you will never see Me again until you say, '*Baruch ha-ba b'shem ADONAI*. Blessed is He who comes in the name of the Lord!'"

The second event that needs to occur in Israel prior to the Second Coming is the recently saved nation of Jewish people must call on Yeshua to return. Not too many believers know that Yeshua cannot return in His Second Coming until Israel calls Him back. In verse 37, Yeshua laments over Jerusalem just prior to His passion week. First, He recalls history, how the religious leaders of Jerusalem killed the prophets who were sent by God to preach repentance to the people. They did not listen to the prophets, so why would they listen to Yeshua? He knows they will kill Him, too. However, His heart is still for Jerusalem and the Jewish people. He states how often He felt like gathering His children into His Kingdom, but they were unwilling to believe in Him as the Messiah.

Verse 38 makes a connection between the Jewish people's unwillingness to repent and believe in Him and God's desolation of the Temple and the city. This destruction occurred in AD 70. Yeshua also prophesied this connection in Luke 19:41-44. Can you image this? The Lord God allowed Jerusalem and the Temple to be destroyed because the nation of Israel rejected Yeshua as Messiah!

In verse 39, Yeshua then makes a most provocative statement. He says Jerusalem will not see Him again until they make a very profound statement concerning Yeshua in the future! In the Messianic Jewish Movement, we have a Hebrew song that we sing in worship of the Lord. The words are "*Baruch haba b'shem Adonai*." They mean, "Blessed is He who comes in the name of the Lord!" This is the phrase that the Jewish people of Jerusalem must proclaim *before* Yeshua will return to conquer the enemies of Israel and set up His Kingdom. Yeshua says they will not see Him again until they say these words. This occurs after all of Israel is saved and before Yeshua comes back in His Second Coming!

Shortly before speaking these words in Matthew 23, the Jewish people proclaimed Yeshua as their Messiah in His triumphal entry into Jerusalem! The multitudes in Matthew 21:9 shouted out loud:

> *Hoshia-na* [Hosanna] to *Ben-David* [Son of David]!
> *Baruch ha-ba b'shem ADONAI*!
> Blessed is He who comes in the name of the Lord!
> *Hoshia-na* in the highest!

It was the correct theology to call Yeshua the Son of David and the Messiah and that He was coming in the name of the Lord! Most certainly this was true, but it was not the right timing. He was not coming to Jerusalem to become their King Messiah but to die on the tree as the Suffering Servant Messiah!

If you have not noticed as yet, the city of Jerusalem takes a prevalent position in our study of Israel in prophecy. By far, it is the most important city when the topic of prophecy is discussed. Jerusalem is the cup of reeling for the world. It is the final destination and battle of Armageddon. It is the destiny of where all Israel will be saved in the future. Finally, it is the destination of the call of Israel to Yeshua to come back and deliver them (more on this later)!

2 Peter 3:10–13

> But the day of the Lord will come like a thief. On that day the heavens will pass away with a roar, and the elements will melt and disintegrate, and the earth and everything done on it shall be exposed. 11 Since all these things are to be destroyed in this way, what kind of people should you be? Live your lives in holiness and godliness, 12 looking for and hastening the coming of the day of God. In that day the heavens will be dissolved by fire, and the elements will melt in the intense heat. 13 But in keeping with His promise, we look for new heavens and a new earth, where righteousness dwells.

If I were to tell you that believers in Yeshua could actually have an effect on when Yeshua comes back in His Second Coming, you would probably think I was "*meshugenah*." However, this is exactly what I am saying, and I'm not crazy or mad! Verse 10 gives us the context of the Day of the Lord. Although many believers may think this phrase *only* speaks of the actual day Yeshua comes back in His Second Coming, they would be wrong! This phrase actually can include a number of prophetic events determined by the context of the verse.

The Day of the Lord can represent the actual day of the Second Coming, the timeframe of the First Coming through to the Second Coming, the seven-year Tribulation Period, or the timeframe between the Second Coming and the creation of the new heavens and earth of Revelation 21:1. Here in 2 Peter, the Day of the Lord is connected to the timeframe including the Second Coming, the destruction of the old heavens and earth, and the creation of the new heavens and earth!

Verse 10 reveals this connection in a straightforward way. The Day of the Lord comes like a thief in the night. This represents the Second Coming of Yeshua. Then the Day of the Lord is connected to the destruction of the old universe (verse 10) and the creation of the new one (verse 13). The old universe will be burned up and dissolved by intense fire (probably at a nuclear level). The new universe will be created by the Lord Yeshua after the Messianic Millennial Kingdom. So, this time period of the Day of the Lord lasts from the Second Coming of Yeshua to the creation of the new universe. This time period is over 1,000 years!

Peter then encourages his readership to live holy and godly lives since these future events are going to happen (verse 11). Everything is going to be burned up by fire, so why get so attached to our worldly possessions? We are to live righteous lives and focus our attention on the Lord. While we are living godly lives, we are to be "looking for" and "hastening" the Day of the Lord (verse 12)!

"Looking for" (*prosdokao*) means to "wait for, look for, anticipate, and expect." So, Peter begins verse 12 by revealing that all believers in Yeshua should be actively anticipating and waiting for the Day of the Lord. "Hasten" (*speudo*) actually means to speed up or accelerate. It also means to eagerly await. Since we are already encouraged to wait for the Day of the Lord through *prosdokao*, I believe *speudo* is used to mean to speed up the Day of the Lord. It would be redundant to encourage us to wait for the day twice!

Speudo is found to be in the present tense and active voice of the Greek grammar. The present tense reveals the speeding up is to be continuous in the present time. The active voice shows the doer of the action of speeding up is placed upon us! Thus, the phrase "hasten the Day of the Lord" can be rewritten as "you ought to hasten the Day of the Lord on a continuous basis in the present time." The Greek grammar definitely shows that we can have a dramatic effect on the timing of the Day of the Lord! So, the question that needs to be answered is, "What can believers do to hasten the Second Coming of Yeshua?"

This idea of hastening the Second Coming is reminiscent of the rabbinical belief that if all the Jews of the world would keep Torah for one day, then the Messiah would come and set up the Kingdom! This is one reason why the orthodox are so set in their desire to keep Torah. They want the Messiah to come!

Part of the answer to the question lies in the context of 2 Peter 3. The context says to be holy and godly. But this is something we should always try to obtain. In Matthew 28, Yeshua encouraged the apostles to go and make disciples of all the nations. This certainly requires the apostles to go and preach the good news message of Yeshua to a dying world. All believers were encouraged to get active in this Great Commission. However, there is a specific group of people that needs to hear the good news message *before* Yeshua can return!

Acts 3:17–21

> 17 "Now brothers, I know that you acted in ignorance, just as your leaders did. 18 But what God foretold through the mouth of all His prophets—that His Messiah was to suffer—so He has fulfilled. 19 Repent, therefore, and return—so your sins might be blotted out, 20 so times of relief might come from the presence of *ADONAI* and He might send *Yeshua,* the Messiah appointed for you. 21 Heaven must receive Him, until the time of the

restoration of all the things that God spoke about long ago through the mouth of His holy prophets.

In Acts 3, Peter preaches his second recorded sermon to the Jewish multitude at the Temple. This Jewish crowd rejected Yeshua as their Messiah and delivered Him up to Pontius Pilate. In verse 17, Peter acknowledges that they and the Jewish leaders acted in ignorance. They truly did not know that they were delivering up their Jewish Messiah! Even though they acted in ignorance, Peter states that all of the events of Messiah's suffering were prophesied by the prophets of old (verse 18). What were the Jewish people to do? Peter tells them to repent and return to God so that their sins would be forgiven (verse 19). Peter adds that if they were to repent then the "times of relief" of the presence of the Lord would occur (verse 20). This is talking about when Messiah comes back to set up His Kingdom! It will be a time of refreshing for Israel. Peter's proclamation indicates a strong connection between the Jewish people's salvation and the Lord's Second Coming!

In verse 20, Peter makes this connection even stronger. If Israel were to repent, then the Father would send the appointed Messiah for them! So, Israel must repent and be saved before Yeshua can return in His Second Coming! This falls in line with what I've been teaching in this book. Then Peter clarifies in verse 21 that heaven must receive Yeshua (in His ascension) until the "time of the restoration." Yeshua will not return to Earth until the time of the restoration of all things. The word "until" (*achri*) is a time-sensitive word that connects the two events. The beginning of the restoration of all things specifically occurs when all the nation of Israel repents and receives Yeshua as their Messiah. Once all of Israel is saved, then Yeshua is allowed to come back and set up the Kingdom!

Chart

The chart documents one of the two Jewish events that have to occur prior to Yeshua's Second Coming. The first is when all of Israel is saved. This occurs sometime toward the end of Jacob's Trouble. We do not know for sure exactly when this event occurs and hence the question marks under the dotted lines that protrude from the box, "All Israel Is Saved!". Israel will recognize that the end is near when the Anti-messiah with millions of his soldiers attacks Jerusalem from the Jezreel and Jordan valleys in the final battle over Israel. God will somehow cause them to realize that Yeshua has always been their Messiah and they will be saved with their names written in the Lord's Book of Life.

The second Jewish event that has to occur prior to the Second Coming is for these newly-saved Jewish people to call upon Yeshua to return. They will proclaim His Messiahship and ask Him to come and deliver them by stating, "*Baruch haba b'shem Adonai*" (Blessed is He who comes in the name of the Lord). As Yeshua stated, the Son cannot come until His newly born-again Jewish brothers cry out to the Lord for the Messiah. Then the Father sends the Son to come back to earth to deliver the Jewish people from their enemies through the Armageddon War.

Prayer

Lord, I pray for the peace of Jerusalem that Israel would receive Your *shalom!* Truly, the only way to do this is to receive Yeshua as their Messiah. So, I pray the good news of Yeshua be shared with all the Jewish people today so that all would have the opportunity to believe in Yeshua and not have to go through the terror of the Tribulation Period. Thank you, Lord, for allowing believers in Yeshua to have an effect on the timing of the Second Coming. Help us to live godly and righteous lives, sharing the good news message of Yeshua with all people, and fulfilling your Great Commission. However, help us especially reach the Jewish people first with the wonderful news that Yeshua is their Messiah and let many Jewish names be written in the Book of Life through our efforts. Thank you; in the mighty name of Yeshua I pray, Amen.

Chapter 14

Where Does Yeshua Land in the Second Coming?

Before Yeshua can return in His Second Coming, all of Israel needs to be saved and then call on Him to come back. This all happens at the end of Jacob's Trouble. The Tribulation Period ends, and then Yeshua returns to Earth in His glorious Second Coming. The Second Coming will not be like His First Coming where He came as Mr. Nice Guy, saying, "Go ahead and put me up on the tree so I can die for the sin of the world." No! In the Second Coming, He is coming back as the conquering King Messiah to destroy and completely will wipe out the enemies of the Jewish people! But the question arises, "Where will Yeshua land in the Second Coming?" Many believers think He will land on the Mount of Olives because of Zechariah 14:4. However, does this verse actually say that this is where He lands in His Second Coming? I beg to differ, and believe the typical teaching about Yeshua's landing area is very suspect. Let us first take a look at this typical teaching.

Acts 1:9–11

> 9 After saying all this—while they were watching—He was taken up, and a cloud received Him out of their

> sight. 10 While they were staring into heaven as He went up, suddenly two men stood with them in white clothing. 11 They said, "Men of Galilee, why do you keep standing here staring into heaven? This *Yeshua,* who was taken up from you into heaven, will come in the same way as you saw Him go into heaven."

Acts 1 speaks of Yeshua's ascension into heaven. Verse 9 tells us that Yeshua was taken up into a cloud in heaven. Two angels then appeared next to the disciples and asked them why they were gazing up into heaven (verses 10–11). This same Yeshua would come back in the "same way" (*hos tropos*) as He left! These Greek words mean in "like manner." Yeshua coming back in like manner does not necessarily mean He is coming back to the *same location* of His ascension, which is what most believers are taught from the pulpit! In the same way, or in the same manner, speaks of His actual ascension into the clouds in heaven, not the location of His exit. He left this earth in the clouds, and He will return to this earth in the clouds! We have already studied Matthew 24:30 that showed us His return would be in the clouds of heaven! Here is Zechariah's version:

Zechariah 14:4–5

> 4 In that day His feet will stand on the Mount of Olives which lies to the east of Jerusalem, and the Mount of Olives will be split in two from east to west, forming a huge valley. Half of the mountain will move toward the north and half of it toward the south.
> 5 Then you will flee through My mountain valley because the mountain valley will reach to Azel. Yes, you will flee like you fled from the earthquake in the days of King Uzziah of Judah. Then *ADONAI* my God will come and all the *kedoshim* with Him.

Earlier we studied Zechariah 14:1–3 and found that the Anti-messiah and his huge army will attack the last stronghold of Israel at the city of Jerusalem. They will be victorious and will actually still be involved in the aftermath of the battle when Yeshua comes back at just the right time to fight against them. Verse 4 begins with the phrase, "In that day," which describes the Second Coming and the timeframe of the Armageddon battle between Yeshua and the Anti-messiah. Yeshua comes back to fight against the Anti-messiah and his army. Then the Scripture says that "His feet will stand on the Mount of Olives."

When Yeshua stands on the Mount of Olives, an earthquake will occur and split the mountain in half. If and when you are able to visit Israel on a tour, your guide will tell you that the Mount of Olives has an earthquake fault lying right down the middle of the mountain! It is already set up and waiting for Yeshua's return. Now the question to ask is, "Does Yeshua need an earthquake fault to cause an earthquake?" The answer is a resounding "No!" However, it is nice to know the Lord has precisely set up the Mount of Olives to geographically fall in line with His will when Yeshua does return!

The Mount of Olives will then become a big valley stretching all the way westward to the city of Jerusalem! Why does Yeshua create this valley area just east of Jerusalem? This is so the Jewish believers of Jerusalem can flee from the treachery of the Anti-messiah into Messiah's newly created safety zone (verse 5). Verse 5 says then the Lord God will come with all His *kedoshim* (holy ones). Well, think of this, the Lord God has already returned in His Second Coming to Earth and now is standing on top of the Mount of Olives. He creates an earthquake so that the Jewish people can flee Jerusalem to safety. Then the Lord God goes to Jerusalem to finish the battle, destroy the enemies, and lock up Anti-messiah and the false prophet in the Lake of Fire. The holy ones are going with Him. The holy ones are the believers of the Rapture and Yeshua's angels. We do not fight with Yeshua, but we certainly tag along with Him to do whatever His bidding for us is.

The real issue in this section is whether the phrase, "In that day His feet will stand on the Mount of Olives," means that Yeshua will land on the Mount of Olives in His Second Coming? This phrase does not say that Yeshua will *land* on the Mount of Olives in His Second Coming! What it does say is that "His feet will *stand*" on the Mount of Olives. If this phrase does not mean what most believers think it means, then what does it really signify? The Jewish roots understanding will explain what "His feet will stand" actually means! There are two other places in the Tenach where a man's feet are talked about on top of a mountain.

<u>Nahum 1:15</u>

> 15 Behold, on the mountains the feet of him who brings good news,
> Who announces peace!
> Celebrate your feasts, O Judah;
> Pay your vows.
> For never again will the wicked one pass through you;
> He is cut off completely. (NASB)

In Nahum 1:15, the Lord is comforting a hurting Israel under the grips of the king of Assyria. In His prophecy, the Lord speaks of a future time when Messiah will rule and all the wicked will be completely cut off. This, of course, is the Messianic Millennial Kingdom. When Messiah comes for His people, "*the feet of him*" will stand on the mountains of Israel and proclaim to His people the good news that He has returned, will set up the Kingdom, and finally will bring *shalom* to His people! The idea here is very clear that the Messiah Himself will be standing (*the feet of him*) on a mountain, proclaiming good news and peace to Israel! This is a prophecy of Yeshua *standing* on the top of the Mount of Olives, not necessarily Yeshua *landing* on the Mount of Olives in the Second Coming!

Isaiah 52:7–10

7 How beautiful on the mountains are
the feet of him who brings good news,
who announces *shalom,*
who brings good news of happiness,
who announces salvation,
who says to Zion, "Your God reigns!"
8 The voice of your watchmen—they will lift up their voices.
Together they are shouting for joy!
For they will see eye to eye
when *ADONAI* returns to Zion.
9 Break forth in joy, sing together,
you ruins of Jerusalem,
for *ADONAI* has comforted His people.
He has redeemed Jerusalem.
10 *ADONAI* has bared His holy arm
before the eyes of all the nations.
All the ends of the earth will see
the salvation of our God.

Here again we see a Messianic passage that declares how lovely it is that a man's feet will stand on the mountains, bringing good news and peace to Israel (verse 7). This man is none other than the Messiah Himself. This is clearly speaking of the Second Coming of Yeshua and His Kingdom reign when the Lord restores Zion and redeems Jerusalem, and the world sees the salvation of Israel (verses 8–10). When Yeshua returns, "*the feet of him*" will stand on the mountains, declare good news of salvation, happiness, and shalom (verse 7). Finally, He will announce to Jerusalem (Zion) that, "Your God reigns!"

Yeshua will announce from the Mount of Olives to the Jewish people in the city of Jerusalem that He has returned, destroyed the enemies of the Jewish people in Armageddon, and will now reign as King of the Jews. I believe this declaration happens towards the end of the war of Armageddon and before He enters Jerusalem to finish the job. Remember, Zechariah 14:2–4 tells us that Yeshua comes back just in time to save Jerusalem from utter destruction. Only half the city will be exiled by the Anti-messiah, but the other half will still be dwelling in the city.

In summary, the feet of Him who stands on the Mount of Olives is Yeshua standing in victory over the enemies of the Jewish people. After the victory in the Jezreel and Jordan valleys, He will ascend to the Mount of Olives and declare He is the God of Israel and He is ready to rule and reign in His Kingdom of peace and happiness for 1,000 years! Then He will go into Jerusalem and finish the battle against the evil ones who have captured the city. Also, remember the Lord will save Judah first before He saves Jerusalem (Zechariah 12:7)—so Armageddon occurs before His ascension to the Mount of Olives.

In no way do any of these three sets of Scriptures reveal the landing place of Yeshua when He returns to Earth. They simply state that the feet of Him who brings good news to Israel will stand on the mountain. It never says the feet of Him that touches down in His descent. Yeshua could have just as easily hiked up the mountain to have His feet stand on top! I believe this is what will happen. So, if Yeshua does not land on the Mount of Olives in His Second Coming, then where does He land?

Where Does Yeshua Actually Land?

Before I can answer this question, we need to remember some of the details of Jacob's Trouble and the Second Coming. Revelation 12:16 describes the earth helping the woman by opening up its mouth and drinking the dragon's water. This is a metaphor for the people of the world helping Jewish people from the persecution of HaSatan (and the Anti-messiah) in Jacob's Trouble. This help could be partially fulfilled in the city of Petra. This is where I believe the Lord will protect and hide a Messianic Community from the clutches of the Anti-messiah. This is true because Petra is essentially a hole in the ground (Petra is like the earth opening its mouth drinking up the river of the dragon in Revelation 12:16)! Daniel 11:40–45 tells us the southwestern area of Jordan is rescued from Anti-messiah's hand during the first half of the Tribulation Period. Southwestern Jordan is where Petra and the Paran Mountain range are located. This is also where the Messianic Jewish group who left Judea at "mid-trib" possibly dwells in safety for the second half of Jacob's Trouble (Matthew 24:15–16).

In Zechariah 12:2–7, the Lord will save the tents of Judah before He saves the tents of Jerusalem in His Second Coming. Some of the "tents" of Judah will have been living in Petra and the Paran Mountain range for the last half of the Tribulation Period. Zechariah 14:5 says Yeshua will attack the Anti-messiah and his evil ones in Jerusalem at the end of the Armageddon War. This occurs after Yeshua stands on the Mount of Olives in His Messianic victory pose. So, I believe the probability that Lord will land at Petra in His Second Coming is much greater than His landing on the Mount of Olives! He will save the Messianic Community in Petra before He saves those in Jerusalem! Now, let's take a look at four sets of Scripture that are not typically analyzed for teaching on Yeshua's Second Coming! These Scriptures will help us to understand that Yeshua lands in the area of Petra in His Second Coming.

Isaiah 34:1–10

1 Draw near, O nations, to hear,
and listen, O peoples!
Let the earth hear, and all it contains,

the world, and all its offspring!
2 For *ADONAI* is enraged at all the nations,
and furious at all their armies.
He will utterly destroy them.
He will give them over to slaughter.
3 So their slain will be thrown out,
and the stench of their corpses will rise,
and the hills will be drenched with their blood.
4 Then all the host of heaven will dissolve,
and the skies will be rolled up like a scroll—
so all their array will wither away,
like a leaf drooping from a vine,
like a fig shriveling from a fig tree.
5 For My sword has drunk its fill in the heavens.
See, it will come down upon Edom,
upon the people I have devoted to judgment.
6 The sword of *ADONAI* is filled with blood,
gorged with fat—
the blood of lambs and goats,
the fat of kidneys of rams.
For *ADONAI* has a sacrifice in Bozrah,
a great slaughter in the land of Edom.
7 Wild oxen will go down with them,
bull calves with mighty steers.
So their land will be soaked with blood
and their dust greasy with fat.
8 For *ADONAI* has a day of vengeance,
a year of recompense for the hostility against Zion.
9 Its streams will be turned into pitch,
its dust into brimstone,
and its land will become burning tar.
10 It will not be quenched night or day.
Its smoke will go up forever.
From generation to generation it will lay waste—forever
and ever none will pass through it.

In verses 1–2, the Lord warns the earth and all the nations in it. His wrath and indignation is against them and their armies. He will utterly destroy them. The mountains will be drenched with their blood (verse 3). Verse 4 tells us the sky will be rolled up like a scroll. The old sky will be rolled up and destroyed just before the new heaven and new earth are created after the Messianic Millennial Kingdom. This indicates that the timeframe is the Day of the Lord. At that time, the Lord will call out Edom specifically by name and declare His sword and judgment is against her (verse 5)! Edom is destined for God's destruction! The question I have is, "If the Lord is warning the world's armies about His destruction, why does He only call out Edom?"

In verse 6, the Lord continues the warning that His sword will be filled with blood. He then makes an astonishing announcement! Using His personal name of YHVH, He proclaims there will be a sacrifice in Bozrah and a great slaughter in Edom. Who or what is Bozrah? Bozrah was the ancient capital of Edom. Today, it is a ruin and is next to the modern city of Bouseira. In this verse, Bozrah is equated with the nation of Edom. How so? Synonymous parallelism is a Hebrew poetic device that includes the repetition of an idea in successive lines of Scripture. The first line of a verse will make a statement while the second line will essentially convey the same message by using different words. In this verse, because of synonymous parallelism, Bozrah is considered to be the same as Edom.

In verse 7, Isaiah tells us Edom will be a land soaked with blood! Unfortunately, this is a gruesome description. But it has yet to occur in Edom's history. Verse 8 reveals the Lord's judgment is a day of vengeance. I believe this is again speaking of the Day of the Lord! More specifically, it is speaking of Yeshua's Second Coming and the battle of Armageddon. Verses 9–10 tell of Edom's devastation. The land will be uninhabitable, its fire will not be quenched, and its smoke shall never go out. Edom will become a desolation, and no one will ever walk through it again!

Edom has never been destroyed in the manner that this scripture passage describes. If Edom had not been destroyed in the past, nor the present, then when will she be destroyed? In the future! It clearly will be destroyed by Yeshua in His Second Coming, and its land will be a desolation of fire and smoke never to be occupied again. Back to the question at hand, "If the Lord warns the world's nations, why does He only call out Edom?"

I believe Edom was spared during Jacob's Trouble because the Lord was supernaturally protecting the Messianic Jewish believers who fled Judea at the middle of the Tribulation Period. This group lived in Petra and the Paran Mountain range for the second half of Jacob's Trouble. I also believe Yeshua will come back in His Second Coming and land in Petra to rescue this Messianic Jewish group! They will have been there for three and a half years, protected by the Lord, but the Anti-messiah will continue to try to attack this group even though they were protected.

Yeshua will land in Petra, deliver the Messianic Community, and then begin the devastating judgment against all the nations' armies that are stationed throughout the region from Petra and Edom area all the way back to Jerusalem and the Jezreel and Jordan valleys. Remember there are multiple millions of soldiers in Anti-messiah's army, and they are stationed from Petra area all the way back to Haifa. The blood is going to flow for about 180 miles!

This battle, starting at Petra, is the Lord's sacrifice at Bozrah and the great slaughter of Edom (verse 6). He only calls out Edom because all the nations armies will be located there and Edom will be the beginning point of the massacre. An interesting note needs to be revealed. Petra is about 180 miles away from Haifa as the crow flies. This mileage is the same as how far the blood will flow in God's wrath versus the world's armies in Revelation 14:20. Most English Bibles use the phrase "200 miles" but the Greek phrase is "1,600 stadia." A "stade" (singular for stadia) denotes a unit of measure known also as a "furlong." The classical Greek definition equates it to be about 1/8 of a Roman mile which works out to be about 600 feet.

1,600 stadia times 600 feet equals 960,000 feet. Divide this number by 5,280 feet/mile and the number of miles the blood will flow is 181.81—about 180 miles! Although this number is not exact (since we are dealing with "abouts"), it definitely lines up with scripture. I believe when Yeshua comes back He will start His devastation against all the nations' armies in Edom and fight against them all the way back through the Jezreel and Jordan valleys and end it in the Haifa area. This is what causes the about 180 miles of blood three to four feet deep! It will be the worst battle in the history of the world! What is amazing is that Yeshua will simply speak the Word, and this devastation will occur. Exactly how it will go down is not known, but Zechariah 14 tells us it will be Yeshua's sword that proceeds out of His mouth (Isaiah calls it His rod and His breath in 11:4)! It is fascinating to see this connection with Isaiah 34 where the Lord's sword will be satiated with all the nation's blood in Edom!

Isaiah 63:1–6

> 1 "Who is this coming from Edom,
> in crimsoned garments from Bozrah?
> This One splendid in His apparel,
> pressing forward in His great might?"
> "It is I who speak in righteousness,
> mighty to save."
> 2 "Why is Your apparel so red,
> and Your garments like one who treads in a wine press?"
> 3 "I have trodden the winepress alone—
> from the peoples, no man was with Me.

I trod them in My anger,
and trampled them in My wrath.
Their lifeblood spattered My garments,
so I stained all My robes.
4 For a day of vengeance was in My heart,
and My year of redemption has come.
5 I looked, but there was no one to help.
I was amazed, but no one was assisting.
So My own arm won victory for Me,
and My wrath upheld Me.
6 So I trod down the peoples in My anger,
and made them drunk in My wrath,
and I poured out their lifeblood on the earth."

This second scripture reading discussing the Second Coming and Edom's involvement is a question-and-answer session between Isaiah and the Lord. In verse 1, Isaiah asks who is the One who comes from Edom? This certainly is an unusual question that concerns the prophet. He seems to be somewhat shocked by the One who is wearing "crimsoned" (*chamuts*) garments from Bozrah. Chamuts actually means "becoming red or to be made red." This lines up contextually with verse 2 as well. The One wearing clothes that were made red was marching in the greatness of His strength. At the end of verse 1, the Lord proclaims that, "It is I!" He is the righteous One ready to save His people!

Although the Lord has a great desire to save, He has an additional purpose to perform here. Isaiah asks Him why His garments are red in color or like the one who works in the wine press (verse 2). The Lord answers in verse 3 that He is the one who trampled the peoples in His wrath and anger. Their blood was sprinkled all over His garments. This is how His garments become red! No man of the peoples will be fighting along with Yeshua; He will war against the enemies by Himself. This does not invalidate the idea that human believers could be among

His flank. Just because the humans are not fighting along with Yeshua does not mean they cannot be right at His side. We already know the Body of Messiah and His angels are with Him—we come back with Him in His Second Coming, and wherever Yeshua is, we are, too!

Why are the people's blood being spilled in the first place? Verse 4 tells us it is the day of vengeance. This same phrase is also used in Isaiah 34:8. It is the Day of the Lord; specifically, it is the war of Armageddon occurring after Yeshua's Second Coming commencing at Edom (specifically Bozrah)! In Jeremiah 49:13, the Lord specifically calls out Bozrah by name and says it will become a horror, a curse, and a perpetual ruin! This will occur in the Armageddon War. Although Bozrah is equated with Edom in Jeremiah 49, Bozrah is definitely included in the Lord's complete destruction of Edom.

In verses 5–6, the Lord proclaimed He poured out the people's blood on the earth in His wrath. This scripture passage is quite clear in that the war of Armageddon starts in Edom where it just so happens that Anti-messiah's soldiers are stationed. So, how does the Lord get to Edom? I believe this is the place He lands in His Second Coming!

<u>Habakkuk 3:2–7, 12–13</u>

> 2 *ADONAI,* I have heard the report about You
> and I have come to fear.
> *ADONAI,* revive Your work throughout the years,
> throughout the years make it known,
> In wrath remember compassion.
> 3 God comes from Teman,
> and the Holy One from Mount Paran. *Selah*
> His majesty covers the heavens,
> and His praise fills the earth.
> 4 With brilliance like light,
> rays emanate from His hand.

There His power was hidden.
5 Pestilence goes before Him,
a fiery bolt goes forth at His feet.
6 He stood, and the earth shook.
He looked, and startled nations.
Ancient mountains were shattered,
hills of antiquity sank down.
His ways are everlasting.
7 I saw tents of Cushan under calamity.
The curtains of the land of Midian are trembling.
12 With indignation You pace the land.
With anger You thresh nations.
13 You went out for the salvation of Your people—for the deliverance of Your anointed one.
You shatter the head of the house of the wicked—to lay it bare from foundation up to the top. *Selah*

The third scripture passage that connects Edom with the Second Coming of Yeshua is found in Habakkuk 3. In his prayer to the Lord, Habakkuk begins in verse 2 by asking the Lord to have mercy in His wrath. In verse 3, He declares that God comes from Teman and Mount Paran. Teman was a region in Edom and it was also a town about fifteen miles away from Petra. Mount Paran is in the vicinity of Petra and is a part of the same mountain range as Mount Seir (which is in Edom). Deuteronomy 33:2 also connects Mount Paran with the Sinai and with Seir. So, it is believed that the Paran Mountain range included southern Israel, Edom, and the northeastern part of the Sinai.

In His wrath, the Lord will come from Edom while His splendor covers the heavens and His radiance shines like the sun. The Lord has flashing rays protruding from His hands where His power hides (verse 4). I am reminded of the Lord Yeshua's description in Revelation 1:16. Here, He is described as having seven stars shining in His right hand, His mouth has a sharp two-edged sword, and His face was shining like the sun. Habakkuk most definitely describes the Lord in His wrath during the Second Coming. Once again, we see Him coming from the land of Edom. I believe this is where He lands in His Second Coming.

In His Second Coming, Messiah will startle the nations (verses 5–6). The mountains and the hills will bow down to the Lord. Pestilence will go before Him, and plague comes after. This is the sword and the rod that comes out of His mouth. His breath is the pestilence and plague that causes the about 180 miles of the enemies' blood in the Armageddon War. Cushan and Midian will tremble because the Lord comes from Teman (verse 7). Cushan is believed to a poetic term for Cush, which today is Sudan, and Midian is northwest Saudi Arabia. In any event, these two nations neighboring Israel will view the disaster that starts in Edom and will greatly fear the Lord!

Verses 12–13 tell us the Lord is going to march in His anger through the earth against all the nations. He will strike down the leader of the evil ones—that's the Anti-messiah. This day of vengeance is for the salvation of His anointed ones, the Jewish people! These dramatic statements connect the Second Coming of Yeshua with His landing in Edom to fight against the enemies of the Jewish people all the way back to the Jezreel and Jordan Valley area! How clearer can the Lord say it?

Zechariah 9:11–17

> 11 As for you also,
> by the blood of your covenant,
> I will release your prisoners
> from the waterless Pit.
> 12 Return to the stronghold,
> you prisoners of hope!
> Today I declare that I will restore
> twice as much to you.

13 I will bend Judah as my bow
and fill it with Ephraim.
I will rouse your sons, O Zion
against your sons, O Greece.
I will wield you like a warrior's sword.
14 Then *ADONAI* will be seen over them
as His arrow flashes like lightning.
ADONAI Elohim will blow the shofar
and march in whirlwinds of the south.
15 *ADONAI-Tzva'ot* will defend them.
They will consume and conquer
with sling stones.
They will drink and roar as with wine
and be filled like a bowl,
like the corners of the altar.
16 *ADONAI* their God will save them on that day
as the flock of His people.
They will be like gems of a crown
sparkling over His land.
17 How good and beautiful it will be!
Grain will make the young men thrive
and new wine the virgin women."

This fourth scripture passage connects Yeshua's Second Coming with Edom and Petra once again. Although these places are not specifically mentioned here, we do see Yeshua coming to Jerusalem from the south in His Second Coming! The Lord declares He is restoring the Jewish people back to the Land because of His blood covenant (verses 11–12). You see, the Lord is a faithful God to His promises given to Abraham, Isaac, Jacob, and the Jewish people. This will finally be fulfilled in the Messianic Millennial Kingdom.

Judah, Ephraim and Jerusalem (Zion) are mentioned in verse 13. Israel will battle against the Greeks (or the Gentiles) in the end. This is substantiated by Zechariah 12. ADONAI will appear over them in the Second Coming, blow the shofar, and swiftly attack the enemies of the Jewish people marching in the storm winds of the south (verse 14)! This certainly falls in line with what I have been teaching about the Jewish roots of Yeshua's Second Coming! Yeshua will blow the shofar in heaven right before He appears in the Second Coming. He will land in the Petra area, pick up the group of Messianic Jewish believers and then march to Judah from the south!

In verse 15, the Lord defends the Jewish people and devours the enemy. The Lord even saves them "on that day" (verse 16). This is a reference to the end of Jacob's Trouble with Yeshua's return! Afterward, Israel and the Jewish people will sparkle and shine like gemstones on a crown. Israel is declared to be beautiful and the blessings will flow for the people (verse 17). Coupled with the other Scriptures in this section, it certainly looks very clear that Yeshua will land in the Petra area in all His glory and attack the enemy from the south, completely destroying them.

Chart

When we add in these four passages (Isaiah 34 and 63, Habakkuk 3, and Zechariah 9) to our study, we see an awesome connection between the Lord's Second Coming and Israel. He will come back for the Jewish people just in time because a moment too late and the evil ones will have destroyed Jerusalem and the Jewish people. We need to remember that one of the purposes of Yeshua's Second Coming is to save and deliver the Jewish people from HaSatan's harm!

In His Second Coming, the Lord will land somewhere in Edom (probably in Petra) and deliver the Messianic Jewish Community that's been living there for the last three and a half years from the clutches of the Anti-messiah's armies. Yeshua will supernaturally protect them for all that time, but the Anti-messiah will still keep trying to war against them. That's why their armies are close by. Yeshua will then begin His attack against the evil ones in Petra and fight them all the way back to the Jezreel and Jordan valleys and even up to Haifa. Along the way, pestilence and plague will destroy the enemies, spilling their blood all over the place. The enemy's blood flows for about 180 miles three to four feet deep. That's a whole lot of blood, and that's a whole lot of soldiers dying to produce that blood. We are talking about mega (probably 100s of) millions of soldiers littered all throughout the Land!

The chart simply shows Yeshua descending from heaven in His Second Coming. The arrow pointing downward reveals this descent to Earth. Remember, the Second Coming will occur after the seven years of Jacob's Trouble has ended. He will destroy the enemies in dramatic fashion so that the world will forever remember the power and authority of the Lord. After the enemies are destroyed in Judah and Armageddon, Yeshua will then ascend to the Mount of Olives. Armageddon is not yet complete, but He will take His victory stand on the Mount of Olives, declaring to the Jewish people of Jerusalem that He is Adonai and the Jewish Messiah who is saving them from the clutches of the Anti-messiah. He causes the earthquake to roar, creating a new valley so that the Messianic Jews in Jerusalem can escape. He then will enter into Jerusalem to finish the war, save the Jews, and capture the Anti-messiah and False Prophet. He then will set up the Messianic Millennial Kingdom. But wait! Is the setting up of the Kingdom the very next event after the end of the Armageddon War?

Prayer

Avinu (our Father), who art in heaven, holy is your name! In your wrath, there is definitely mercy and the idea that you are declaring your holiness to an evil world. Please help the Jewish and Gentile people of the world to see that Yeshua is the Jewish Messiah who died for the world's sin and resurrected on the third day to give eternal life to all who would repent and believe in Him. Also, please help all those people who turn to Yeshua in the Tribulation to live their lives for You and supernaturally be able to give up their lives for Yeshua when needed. Let thy Kingdom come and thy will be done on Earth as it is already done in heaven.

I pray for all those who have read this chapter—that you would touch their hearts to know and understand and believe the Jewish roots of Jacob's Trouble and the Second Coming. Sometimes it is hard to receive new information in light of doctrines believed for most of our lives. Help us all to have open hearts to the Ruach's leading with this material. Help all of today's believers to be bold in sharing these Jewish roots and the good news of Yeshua. Please help us to warn the Jewish people of the eventual holocaust that is coming in the Tribulation, but also remind them of the ultimate deliverance at the hands of Yeshua! In Yeshua's name, I pray, Amen.

Chapter 15

THE SEVENTY-FIVE-DAY INTERVAL

After Yeshua comes back in the Second Coming, wipes out the enemies of the Jewish people in the Armageddon War, and saves and delivers the Jewish people from certain destruction from the Anti-messiah, He then will begin his reign in the Millennial Kingdom. Right? Well, not exactly. There seems to be a problem with most believers' understanding of this transition from the end of Jacob's Trouble to the Second Coming and then to the beginning of the Messianic Millennial Kingdom. Most do not know of the mysterious seventy-five-day interval! This is the time period between the end of Jacob's Trouble and the beginning of the Messianic Millennial Kingdom.

Daniel 12:5–12

> 5 Then I, Daniel, looked and behold, two others stood there, one on this bank of the river and the one on the other bank of the river. 6 One said to the man clothed in linen, who was above the waters of the river, "How long until the end of the wondrous things?"
> 7 Then I heard the man clothed in linen, who was above the waters of the river, as he raised both his right and left hands toward heaven and swore an oath by Him who lives forever, saying, "It is for a time, times, and a half.

> Then when the breaking of the power of the holy people comes to an end, all these things will be finished."
> 8 Now I heard, but I did not understand. So I said, 'My Lord, what will be the outcome of these things?'
> 9 Then he said: "Go your way, Daniel. For the words are closed up and sealed until the time of the end. 10 Many will be purified, made spotless and refined, but the wicked will act wickedly. None of the wicked will understand, but the wise will understand.
> 11 "From the time that the daily burnt offering is taken away, and abomination of desolation is set up, there will be 1,290 days. 12 Happy is the one who keeps waiting, and reaches the 1,335 days.

This scripture reading is the only place found in the Bible that actually quantifies the time period between the end of Jacob's Trouble and the beginning of the Messianic Millennial Kingdom. Verses 5–6 document a discussion between two angels in Daniel's vision. The question one angel asks the other is, "How long until the end of the wondrous things?" Another way to rephrase this question is, "How long will it take for the second half of Jacob's Trouble to end?"

In verse 7 the angel answers the question. The time it will take to get to the end of the second half of Jacob's Trouble is "a time, times, and a half." A "time" (*moed*) has a number of definitions: meeting place, meeting time, assembly, or a feast of the Lord. Here, it refers to a period of time or one year. Daniel used three different words (*iddan, et, moed*) in his prophetic book to mean a period of one year! A better English rendition of the phrase would then be "an appointed time, times, and a half." In any event, it would take three and a half years for all of the events of Jacob's Trouble to be completed.

Therefore, three and one half "times" equals to three and one-half years. This is no different to our understanding of how long each half of Jacob's Trouble lasts. The answer is and always will be three and a half years. However, verse 7 adds some rather interesting information concerning the second half of the Tribulation Period. All the events will be completed in the three and a half years when "the breaking of the power of the holy people" is completed. In other words, the evil ones of the world will try to destroy the Jewish people for the three and a half years of the second half. This directly reveals one of the purposes of the evil ones in the world during the Tribulation Period—to annihilate the Jewish people!

In verses 8–9, Daniel relates that he is somewhat confused by the angels' statements, and the angel then tells him to seal up the vision until the end time. In verse 10, the angel tells Daniel that the evil ones will act wickedly, not understanding the real truth behind their actions. But many will have wisdom and be purified through the persecution process of the Great Tribulation.

Verses 11–12 are the key to understanding the seventy-five-day interval. Verse 11 marks two events that both begin at "mid-trib." Anti-messiah abolishes the regular sacrifice in the Temple and sets up the Abomination of Desolation at "mid-trib" (Daniel 9:27). Verse 11 tells us that from the time of "mid-trib," there will be 1,290 days. There is a problem here because 1,290 days is thirty days too long! The second half of the Tribulation Period only lasts for 1,260 days. So, what is going on here? It is believed the Abomination of Desolation will be allowed by the Lord to last thirty days past the end of the Tribulation Period. Why wait to destroy this abomination thirty days after Jacob's Trouble is over? I have no idea! But the fact remains that there are thirty extra days past the end of the Tribulation Period!

Verse 12 reveals that the person who actually makes it alive till the 1,335th day will be happy or blessed. The 1,335th day would then be seventy-five days after Jacob's Trouble ends. Hence, we have the seventy-five-day interval. So, what's going on here? It seems that those believers who make it through

Jacob's Trouble alive and who make it alive to the seventy-fifth day after Jacob's Trouble ends will be blessed. What is the blessing? I believe those who make it till the 1,335th day will be blessed with entering into the Lord's Messianic Millennial Kingdom and receive His great promises and the blessings of the Kingdom! I also believe that they will live in the beautiful Kingdom for 1,000 years (more on this later).

The real question that needs to be answered is, "Why is there a total of seventy-five days between the end of Jacob's Trouble and the beginning of the Messianic Millennial Kingdom?" This is the time period the Lord has given for Messiah Yeshua to perform all His good works that need to be completed *before* the Kingdom can begin! He just cannot immediately set up the Kingdom. He needs some time to perform these deeds that absolutely need to be performed before the Kingdom begins.

To summarize, Daniel is the only place in Scripture that gives a timeline between the end of Jacob's Trouble and the beginning of the Messianic Millennial Kingdom. First, Daniel reveals the Abomination of Desolation lasts for thirty days beyond Jacob's Trouble. We are not told how or why this occurs, but it seems evident that this is the case. Daniel then reveals that those Jewish and Gentile believers who make it alive to the 1,335th day will be blessed. This is the seventy-fifth day after the end of the Tribulation Period. I believe the reason the believers are blessed is because the Messianic Millennial Kingdom begins seventy-five days after the end of the Tribulation Period. The Messianic Millennial Kingdom is not only going to be blessed for all believers, but it will be blessed for the nation of Israel. This Messianic Kingdom is exactly what most of today's Jewish people are looking forward to! The unfortunate problem is that most of the Jewish people do not know how to truly enter into this Kingdom. Most are trying to enter in through their good works instead of repenting and then believing and trusting in Yeshua HaMeshiach!

What's Yeshua Doing in the Seventy-Five-Day Interval?

There are a whole lot of tasks the Lord must perform prior to the beginning of the Kingdom. First things, first! If the Abomination of Desolation lasts thirty days beyond the 1,260 days of the Great Tribulation, then there must be an ending date of the Abomination of Desolation (Daniel 12:11). Yeshua has to dispose of this abomination; it cannot enter into the Kingdom. It was the epitome of evil during Jacob's Trouble and the people of the Kingdom need to know that Messiah Yeshua is the Lord God in charge. Maybe this is why the abomination is allowed to "live" past the end of the Tribulation Period for thirty days. Messiah demonstrates to His captive audience of believers exactly how God deals with evil by destroying the Abomination of Desolation!

In Revelation 19:19–20, after the Anti-messiah and the false prophet are captured in the war of Armageddon, Yeshua judges and sends them to the Lake of Fire. Yeshua not only judges the Anti-messiah and the false prophet, but HaSatan (Satan) himself (Revelation 20:1–3). One of Yeshua's angels binds HaSatan and seals Him away in the abyss for the 1,000 years of the Messianic Millennial Kingdom. I believe this moment is the fulfillment of Isaiah 14:15–17 when the people of the earth will gaze at him and wonder how he made the world tremble.

In Matthew 24:31, Yeshua sends out His angels to gather all the Jewish believers from around the world. This occurs after the Second Coming and Armageddon War and prior to the beginning of the Kingdom. In Matthew 25:31–46, we see the gathering of the nations after the Second Coming. Presumably this is done at the same time that the Jewish believers are gathered. This scripture section is the famous sheep versus goats passage. The sheep (Gentile believers) inherit the Kingdom while the goats (Gentile non-believers) inherit eternal punishment. However, many believers forget about the third group that Yeshua identifies as "these My brethren" (verse 40). These are the Messianic Jews who make it alive through Jacob's Trouble. They, too, will inherit the Kingdom and eternal life. Not only will the gathering of believers and non-believers take some time, but the judgments that come down on these three groups will take some time, as well.

Yeshua needs to perform the first resurrection in order to finish the gathering of all His believers who will enter into the Kingdom. The resurrection is discussed in general in Isaiah 26:19-21. Verse 19 states the dead will live, and their bodies will rise. Those who lie in the dust will awake and shout for joy! At the end of the verse, it even says these righteous ones will join with their spirits! The context in verse 21 reveals ADONAI coming from heaven and punishing the whole earth for their sin. This describes the Second Coming and the Armageddon War. After the war, we will see the resurrection of the joyous ones!

Daniel 12:1–2 reveals what will happen to the Old Covenant believers. In verse 1, Daniel details how bad it will get for Israel in Jacob's Trouble. Michael, the archangel who guards over Israel, will have to rise up and fight against all the wicked angels. At the end of the Tribulation Period, all righteous people who are found written in the Book of Life will be rescued. They are rescued from the Anti-messiah and his evil ones for the purpose of entering into the Messianic Millennial Kingdom. This is the context of the passage.

Then in verse 2, we are told that the righteous believers who are dead and buried will awake to everlasting life. The evil ones who are dead and buried will awake to everlasting contempt. Here, the bodies of the Old Covenant (OC) believers will rise and forge a union with their spirits that are already in heaven with the Lord. In Hebrews 12:22–23, the ultimate glory is to come to the New Jerusalem, which is in heaven. The "assembly of the first-born" who are already enrolled there is referring to the New Covenant believers. The "spirits of righteous ones made perfect" are referring to the Old Covenant believers. But this phrase is not referring to their bodies but only their spirits! This proves beyond any doubt that Old Covenant believers' spirits are currently in heaven with the Lord! But, where are their bodies? Most of them are buried in the ground as their dust has turned to dust. Daniel 12:2 and Isaiah 26:19 imply that their bodies will rise and unite with their spirits in the resurrection that occurs within the seventy-five-day interval!

New Covenant believers will be resurrected in the Pre-Trib Rapture. Old Covenant believers will be resurrected in the seventy-five-day interval between Jacob's Trouble and the Messianic Millennial Kingdom. What group of God's believers are we forgetting about? The Tribulation Period believers! When do they resurrect? Revelation 20:4–5 gives us the answer. After an angel throws HaSatan into the abyss and locks him up for a thousand years, the souls of the Tribulation believers who died for Yeshua and those believers who did not take the mark of the beast all "come to life!" What does this mean? I think it means both groups receive their resurrection bodies for eternity. Verse 5 compares these two groups with the rest of the dead. So, these two groups died for their faith in Yeshua during Jacob's Trouble. The rest of the dead will not come to life until the Great White Throne Judgment. This is the first resurrection, and it seems to take place in three parts.

First, New Covenant believers are raptured "pre-trib" and receive their eternal resurrection bodies. Second, the souls of believers who were beheaded for Yeshua receive their resurrection bodies in the seventy-five-day interval. Other believers who died during Jacob's Trouble because they did not worship the Anti-messiah or his Abomination of Desolation and did not take the mark of the beast receive their resurrection bodies in the seventy-five-day interval. Third, Old Covenant believers receive their resurrection bodies during the seventy-five-day interval as well. Therefore, all groups of believers from the beginning of time have been bodily resurrected prior to the time of the beginning of the Messianic Millennial Kingdom.

All believers are accounted for and will enter into the Kingdom, fulfilling God's promises to Abraham and King David.

What else does Yeshua need to perform before the Kingdom begins? Zechariah 13:2 tells us He will rid the Land of Israel of all the idols, false prophets, and the unclean spirit. The idols will be destroyed, the false prophets will be judged, and the evil unclean spirit will be cast out of the Land. These events help to cleanse the Land for the Messianic Millennial Kingdom. It is absolutely necessary for the Land to be completely cleansed of all evil and anything unclean so as to begin the Kingdom with a spiritually clean slate.

We found out earlier, in Revelation 14:19–20, that Yeshua causes the blood to flow through the Land for about 180 miles at about three to four feet deep. The birds of the skies are invited to the carnage of the great supper of God to eat the flesh and blood of all the dead bodies (Revelation 19:17–18, 21). However, all these birds and any other animals that help will not be able to fully cleanse the Land. And who could blame them? That is going to be a huge clean-up job! I used to joke that while the Body of Messiah comes back with Yeshua in His Second Coming riding on our horses, we would not only have our swords with us but each of us would need to bring a mop, too! The issue comes down to this: someone has to clean up the mess, and I do not think humankind can do the job perfectly, which is absolutely necessary. This is most certainly a God-sized problem, and it therefore needs a God-sized answer. Isaiah 4:3–4 may just have that answer.

The context here is the Day of the Lord and the aftermath of the Armageddon War. Verse 3 declares that all believers who are left in Israel and Jerusalem after the war will be called holy! They will be called holy in the Messianic Millennial Kingdom. Verse 4 says the Lord will then wash away the filth of the daughters of Zion. He will also purge (*duach*) the bloodshed of Jerusalem from her midst! "Purge" here means to "cleanse by washing." It can be used metaphorically or physically. I believe it is to be taken literally here. This certainly suggests that the Lord is the One who will perform the cleanup of the bloodshed in Israel. It does make sense that, because the Lord caused the bloodshed, He should be the One to clean it up! Seriously, I believe He is the only one who can clean it up properly! How is He going to do this? Verse 4 answers with the spirit of judgment and the spirit of burning. It looks like the daughters of Zion's filth will be washed away in judgment and the bloodshed of Jerusalem; the river of blood that is left over from Yeshua's decimation will be burned!

Zechariah 14:9–10 also reveal a great work that Messiah needs to accomplish before the Kingdom can start. Verse 9 shows the context is the Day of the Lord, and Yeshua will be king over all the Earth! Verse 10 tells us Israel will undergo some geographical changes. The idea here is when all the world in the Messianic Millennial Kingdom travels to Israel to worship the Lord, they must "go up" to the mountain of the Lord. The greatest God of all will live on the highest mountain of the earth. The Lord will cause the city of Jerusalem to rise up on the highest mountain, and a good portion of Israel will be a plain. Isaiah 2:2–3 and Micah 4:1–2 help to confirm this. Both prophets say the mountain of the house of the Lord will be the chief of the mountains. The house of the Lord is the Temple, and the mountain is Moriah that Jerusalem sits on. Jerusalem will be raised above the hills as well. The idea here is that all the people of the world will have to "go up" to the mountain of the Lord to worship Him! This is exactly what the people of the world during the Kingdom are quoted as declaring.

The final accomplishment Yeshua must perform in the seventy-five-day interval is the building of the Millennial Kingdom Temple. 1 Chronicles 17:10–14 is a Messianic passage documenting a part of the Davidic Covenant. The prophet Nathan was directed by God to tell King David a message. In verse 10, the Lord declares He will build a Temple for David. In verse 11, the Lord will set up a descendant or seed (*zera*).

Zera is found in the singular and is thus only talking about one of David's descendants. Verse 12 helps us to know who. It states that this seed shall build the Temple for the Lord, and the Lord will establish his throne forever. Forever is for a long time! There is only one person who will rule and reign on His throne forever, and that is Yeshua HaMeshiach! The culmination of this promise to David is for Yeshua to take His throne in the Messianic Millennial Kingdom and the New Jerusalem. He will rule and reign forever.

Zechariah 6:12–13 is another Messianic passage that shows Messiah will build the Temple. Verse 12 tells us the "Branch" will build the Temple of the Lord. The "Branch" is a reference to the Messiah. After Messiah comes in His Second Coming, He will build the Millennial Kingdom Temple. How do we know this is a Messianic verse? Verse 13 shows the Branch will then sit on His throne and unite the two offices of priest and king together. Only the Messiah will be able to do this! Actually, Yeshua unites a total of three offices together: priest, king, and prophet.

Daniel 9:24 shares about the last event that will occur before the beginning of the 1,000 year reign. Seventy sevens have been decreed for the Jewish people and the city of Jerusalem to "anoint the Holy of Holies." The Holy of Holies is most certainly the Temple of God. Yeshua's last act in the seventy-five-day interval after building the Temple will be to anoint the Temple! Why anoint the Temple? For service unto the Lord! So, the Jewish and Gentile believers of the Messianic Kingdom can properly worship the Lord! The idea here is that the Kingdom will be a Messianic Jewish Kingdom, so believers of today had better start learning about this Messianic Jewish Kingdom now so they will have a greater part in it in the future (more on this in the next chapter).

Chart

The chart simply shows that the seventy-five-day interval will begin right when Jacob's Trouble ends and concludes with the beginning of the Messianic Kingdom. The Second Coming and Armageddon will also occur during this timeframe. In fact, the Second Coming occurs after the end of Jacob's Trouble. But the Bible clearly shows there is a seventy-five-day interval and a great need for it! There is a lot of work that needs to be completed before we all can enter into and enjoy the Kingdom. Israel needs to be cleansed of all the evil that had befallen it for the last many years. This cleansing will be both spiritual and physical. The regathering of the Jewish people from around the world will also take some time to accomplish. But let's not forget the Gentiles, either. Yeshua will only allow Jewish and Gentile believers into the Kingdom. The rest will be harshly judged. Finally, the Lord will build and anoint His Temple where He will rule and reign for 1,000 years in His Messianic Kingdom as the Lord promised to Abraham and David.

Prayer

O Lord God, thank you for the understanding about your Word when it comes to this seventy-five-day interval. It is a time for you to clean up the Land of Israel from its defilement and get it properly restored and prepared for clean living in the Messianic Millennial Kingdom. This is a time that all believers should be looking forward to. You care so much about the Jewish people and your Land of Israel that you are desirous to clean up the mess that the Anti-messiah and his evil ones will perpetrate against Israel. Thank you for your love, mercy, and grace shining great in a time of great distress for the world and for Israel. In Yeshua's name I pray, Amen.

Chapter 16

THE MILLENNIAL KINGDOM

Preterism is a viewpoint that believes all the prophecies of the Bible were fulfilled by the first century. Preterists are amillennial, which means they do not believe in a future 1,000-year Kingdom reign of Messiah Yeshua. They believe that Yeshua has been reigning in His Kingdom from heaven since the ascension. Preterists typically believe that Israel has found its fulfillment in the Body of Messiah. In other words, many of the preterists believe the Body of Messiah has replaced Israel in God's covenantal promises. This belief is called Replacement Theology (and has already been dealt with in this book). Preterists use the metaphorical technique (spiritualizing the text) of Bible interpretation as their primary tool of understanding biblical prophecy.

Unfortunately, preterism is becoming more and more popular and accepted within the believers' world. In this book, I have taken a more literal interpretation to God's Word. We have studied the Bible at its face value, meaning we shall take the Scriptures literally when they are presented literally and metaphorically when they are presented metaphorically. We see Yeshua is prophesied to be King over Israel and the world for 1,000 years in the Millennial Kingdom. It most certainly is true that Yeshua is sitting with the Father on His throne in heaven right now (Psalm 110:1), but He is not ruling over His promised Kingdom at this same time! That needs to occur on Earth! Yeshua will rule over the whole world in peace, righteousness, justice, and faithfulness. He will reign over the earth when most of the curse of Genesis 3 is lifted. And additionally, He will rule in a Messianic Jewish style (more on this later).

General Kingdom Characteristics

Revelation 20 is a pivotal chapter on determining how long the Millennial Kingdom will last. It is also controversial because the preterists view the timeframe mentioned here as a metaphor and spiritualize the text. Since the book of Revelation has many metaphors, preterists automatically include the 1,000 years as an allegory to mean something other than 1,000 years. Let's take a look at this chapter and decide for ourselves.

Revelation 20:1–9

> 1 Then I saw an angel coming down from heaven, holding in his hand the key to the abyss and a great chain. 2 He seized the dragon—the ancient serpent, who is the devil and satan—and bound him for a thousand years. 3 He also threw him into the abyss and locked and sealed it over him, so that he would not deceive the nations any longer, until the thousand years were completed. After these things, he must be released for a short while.
> 4 Then I saw thrones, and people sat upon them—those to whom authority to judge was given. And I saw the souls of those who had been beheaded because of their testimony for *Yeshua* and because of the word of God. They had not worshiped the beast or his image, nor had they received his mark on their forehead or on their hand. And they came to life and reigned with the Messiah for a thousand years.

> 5 The rest of the dead did not come to life until the thousand years were completed. This is the first resurrection. 6 How fortunate and holy is the one who has a share in the first resurrection! Over such the second death has no authority, but they shall be *kohanim* [priests] of God and the Messiah, and they shall reign with Him for a thousand years.
> 7 When the thousand years has ended, satan shall be released from his prison, 8 and he shall come out to deceive the nations at the four corners of the earth, Gog and Magog, to gather them for the battle. Their number is like the sand of the sea. 9 And they came up on the broad plain of the earth and surrounded the camp of the *kedoshim* [holy ones] and the beloved city—but fire fell from heaven and consumed them.

In verses 1–3, an angel from heaven comes to Earth, then binds and casts HaSatan into the abyss for 1,000 years. Afterward, he will be released for a short time. One of the reasons why HaSatan is bound in the abyss for 1,000 years is so he cannot deceive the nations anymore. Since the Kingdom lasts for 1,000 years, HaSatan should be bound for 1,000 years! Now, that would make sense since Yeshua will be ruling and reigning in peace, righteousness, justice, and faithfulness for 1,000 years. Humankind actually will greatly benefit without HaSatan's involvement in the world! It also makes sense that he would not be allowed in the Kingdom when most of the curse is lifted—especially since he was the one who helped the curse to be levied against humankind in the first place!

Verse 4 shows the believers who were beheaded and died for their faith in Jacob's Trouble will receive their resurrection bodies and reign with Yeshua for 1,000 years. They actually receive thrones where they shall sit and judge with Yeshua. These positions will be prominent in the Kingdom. Verse 5 shares that this is the first resurrection, and the rest of the dead will not live until after this 1,000 years is over. Clearly, the believers of Jacob's Trouble are greatly rewarded by Yeshua in the Kingdom for their willingness to die for Him. If this is all a metaphor, then is the first resurrection a metaphor, too? If it is, then we are not guaranteed the promises that God promised all believers! In that case, all of God's promises could just as easily be metaphors. We would then be in a whole lot of trouble with the Lord!

Verse 4 specifically speaks about Tribulation Period believers. But verse 6 now includes all New Covenant believers who were raptured. The promise for us is that we shall be priests and kings with Yeshua for 1,000 years. The second death has no power over anyone who is resurrected in the first resurrection. The promise here is slightly different from the promise given to the Tribulation believers. They have thrones to sit and judge from with Yeshua. We shall be priests and kings and rule and shepherd the people all over the newly refurbished world. Verses 7–8 then profoundly state that HaSatan will be let out of the abyss after the 1,000 years is ended so that he can deceive the nations one more time. He will go forth and gather evil ones from around the world for one last battle against Yeshua (verse 9). However, this battle truly is not a battle. No weapon shall be fired, but only a complete and utter destruction of the evil ones will occur.

Now, as we read through this scripture passage, there is no indication in the Greek grammar that shows us that we should be analyzing it as a metaphor! This means there is nothing in the Greek grammar that tells us we should be spiritualizing the text to mean something other than what it says. In fact, there is a lot of Greek grammar that teaches us we should be accepting the text as straightforward statements and not metaphors! Actually there are many verbal phrases found in these nine verses that are in the indicative mood. This means that these phrases are positive and clear-cut statements, and that they are to be taken literally just as the Scripture intended. Why would anyone want to change the understanding of the Scripture? Obviously, so it would fit their own theology. This is called *eisegesis*; when people read into the Scripture rather than perform *exegesis* when the interpretation is pulled out of the Word using proper grammatical guidelines! The Lord is definitely not happy about anyone who performs eisegesis on His Word!

There are many verbal phrases in this section of Revelation that are found to be in the indicative mood. This means the text is written in positive and clear-cut statements to be taken literally. In fact, there are six phrases mentioning 1,000 years in Revelation 20:1–9, and each of them is found to be in the indicative mood! This indicates that each time the 1,000 years is mentioned, it is to be taken as a literal 1,000 years of time! When the text discusses the Millennial Kingdom lasting for a thousand years it means just that—the Kingdom will last for 1,000 years! There are no ifs, ands, or buts—just the plain and straightforward truth that the Messianic Millennial Kingdom will last for 1,000 years.

Jeremiah 23:5–8

> 5 "Behold, days are coming"
> —it is a declaration of *ADONAI*—
> "when I will raise up for David
> a righteous Branch,
> and He will reign as king wisely,
> and execute justice and righteousness in the land.
> 6 In His days Judah will be saved,
> and Israel will dwell in safely;
> and this is His Name by which He will be called: *ADONAI* our righteousness.
> 7 "Therefore behold, days are coming," says *ADONAI*, "when they will no longer say: 'As *ADONAI* lives, who brought up the children of Israel out of the land of Egypt.' 8 Rather, 'As *ADONAI* lives, who brought

> up and led the offspring of the house of Israel out of the north country and from all the lands where He had banished them.' So they will dwell in their own soil.

In verse 5, the Lord recalls His covenant with David that through his seed, a King would reign forever. This is the primary promise of the Davidic Covenant—that one of David's descendants would become King of Israel and rule forever! However, this King is called the righteous Branch (*tsemach*) who would rule with wisdom, justice, and righteousness. Tsemach physically refers to a sprout, shoot, plant, new growth, or branch. Metaphorically, the branch is used of the righteous branch of David—the Messiah! This Branch is the same Branch found in Zechariah 6:12 (discussed earlier). So where will Yeshua, the Branch, rule and reign from?

The Scripture at the end of verse 5 says, "*in the land.*" (emphasis mine) This means in the Land of Israel! It does not say Yeshua is ruling and reigning from heaven, although He certainly is currently ruling right now—just not on His Davidic throne! But remember, this reigning as King is in the Land of Israel, and it is connected with the Davidic Covenantal promise! Those who believe Yeshua is ruling in heaven on His Davidic throne are just plain wrong, and this verse is one proof text.

During Yeshua's reign as King over Israel, Judah will be saved (verse 6). I believe the word *saved* here has a two-fold understanding. One, the Jewish people who are living as humans (as opposed to the resurrected believers) in the Kingdom will all be saved from their sin and given eternal life (Jeremiah 31:33–34). Judah will also be completely delivered from all her enemies throughout history and will finally be living in the Land in shalom and safety! Verse 6 also calls the righteous Branch Yeshua, *ADONAI tsidkenu*. This title refers to God as our righteousness. The righteous Branch is our Lord God who is our righteousness, too!

In the Kingdom, the Jewish people will not refer to God as their Lord who brought them out of the land of Egypt (verse 7). Which is what they said for thousands of years! Why? There will be a more current description of another exodus the Lord will have performed for the Jewish people. In the past, the Lord cast ten plagues on Egypt so that the chosen ones would be let go. This was the first exodus. This verse proclaims that there will be another exodus.

This second exodus will flow from the north country and all the nations from around the world (verse 8). This second exodus is caused by the Lord's Armageddon War where He destroys the enemies of the Jewish people in the worst bloodbath ever! I believe because of the context here that this is the worldwide gathering of the saved Jewish people after the Armageddon War. This is another great miracle just like the first exodus. The wonderful result here is that the Jewish people will finally dwell in their own Land of Israel in shalom, and Yeshua will finally rule and reign as King over Israel! Now this is God's promise to Abraham, Isaac and Jacob, finally fulfilled in the Messianic Millennial Kingdom!

Isaiah 24:21–23

21 It will come about in that day,
ADONAI will punish the host of heaven on high,
and the kings of the earth on the earth.
22 They will be gathered together,
like prisoners in the Pit,
and will be shut up in the prison,
and after many days be punished.
23 Then the moon will be abashed
and the sun ashamed,
for *ADONAI-Tzva'ot* will reign
on Mount Zion and in Jerusalem,
and before His elders, gloriously.

Isaiah 24 speaks of a time when the Lord will judge the whole earth. In verse 21, the Lord will punish the kings of the earth. They will be gathered together and confined to an area like they are in a prison (verse 22). This is describing the end of Jacob's Trouble when the kings of the earth are summoned by the demons of the Anti-messiah to finally come to the Jezreel and Jordan valleys to attack and destroy Jerusalem. Their ultimate goal will be to war against Yeshua in His return. They will be punished many days after the time they congregate together to attack Jerusalem.

Verse 23 reveals that at the same time, the moon will be abashed and sun ashamed. This means they will lose their light. This occurs just prior to the Second Coming of Yeshua. Then, the Lord of hosts will reign in His glory on Mount Zion and Jerusalem! This is very clear that the Lord of hosts, who is Yeshua, will reign in His glorious Kingdom from Mount Zion and Jerusalem. Mount Zion is another name used for Jerusalem. The Scripture here does not say He will reign in His Kingdom from heaven, but on Earth, and specifically in Jerusalem where He will build and anoint His fourth Temple. The following passage is similar to the one in Matthew 24:29–31.

Zechariah 2:10–12

> 10 Sing for joy and be glad, O daughter of Zion; for behold I am coming and I will dwell in your midst," declares the Lord. 11 "Many nations will join themselves to the Lord in that day and will become My people. Then I will dwell in your midst, and you will know that the Lord of hosts has sent Me to you. 12 The Lord will possess Judah as His portion in the Holy Land, and will again choose Jerusalem. (NASB)

Zechariah 2:10–12 shows beyond any doubt that Yeshua will come and dwell in the holy Land of Israel with the Jewish people in the Messianic Millennial Kingdom! In 2:3–5, Zechariah describes the miraculous way in which the Lord will manifest Himself in the Messianic Millennial Kingdom. After the Lord encourages Israel to flee from Babylon (verses 6–7), He declares the evil nations judged because they touched the "apple of His eye" (verses 8–9).

An interesting side note in verses 8–11 show two "LORD of Hosts" (*ADONAI-Tzva'ot*)! The Lord Himself says two times that "*the LORD of Hosts has sent Me*." The issue here is that the LORD of Hosts is speaking, and He says the LORD of Hosts sent Him! There is no doubt that there are two "LORD of Hosts!" This certainly falls in line with the understanding that the Lord God is a triunity: Father, Son, and Holy Spirit.

In verse 10, ADONAI declares that He is coming to Israel and will dwell in their midst. This is talking about Yeshua's Second Coming and the fact that He will dwell among the Jewish people in the Messianic Millennial Kingdom. In that day, many nations will join themselves to the Lord and become His people (verse 11). This shows that the Gentile believers of the Lord are welcomed into the Kingdom right along with the Jewish people. When this happens, Israel will know that the "*ADONAI-Tzva'ot (the LORD of Hosts) has sent me to you*." When Jews and Gentiles live together as one in the Kingdom, then the Jewish people will know without a doubt that Yeshua, the "*me*" in this verse, was sent to the Jewish people to fight their enemies, protect them, and be their King. Finally, in verse 12, the Lord reiterates that He will possess or inherit Judah, and the city of Jerusalem will be the place where He will dwell. How clearer does the Scripture need to be for those who do not believe Yeshua will reign on Earth for 1,000 years?!

<u>Isaiah 9:6–7</u>

> 6 For a child will be born to us, a son will be given to us;
> And the government will rest on His shoulders;

And His name will be called Wonderful Counselor, Mighty God, Eternal Father, Prince of Peace.
7 There will be no end to the increase of *His* government or of peace,
On the throne of David and over his kingdom,
To establish it and to uphold it with justice and righteousness
From then on and forevermore.
The zeal of the LORD of hosts will accomplish this. (NASB)

Isaiah declares in this short passage that a son shall be born to Israel, and He will be the Jewish Messiah, the King and the Prince of Peace (verse 6). He will reign over His government and be identified as the Mighty God and Everlasting Father. Even though He is a man, He is also God. This most certainly identifies Yeshua as the God/man!

Verse 7 speaks of His Kingdom that will have no end on the earth, and His kingship is once again connected to the throne of David! This brings us back again to the Davidic Covenant. The Lord is fulfilling His promises to David through Yeshua HaMeshiach! He will zealously establish His Kingdom in peace, justice, and righteousness. These will be the general characteristics of life in the Millennial Kingdom. The Kingdom age will be completely different from our current age of grace where sin runs rampant, mostly unchecked around the world! Yeshua will rule the Kingdom with a rod of iron from the Land of Israel!

Isaiah 11:6–13, 16

6 The wolf will dwell with the lamb,
the leopard will lie down with the kid,
the calf and the young lion
and the yearling together,

and a little child will lead them.
7 The cow and the bear will graze,
their young ones lie down together,
and the lion will eat straw like an ox.
8 A nursing child will play by a cobra's hole,
and a weaned child will put his hand into a viper's den.
9 They will not hurt or destroy
in all My holy mountain,
for the earth will be full
of the knowledge of *ADONAI*,
as the waters cover the sea.
10 It will also come about in that day
that the root of Jesse will stand
as a banner for the peoples.
The nations will seek for Him,
and His resting place will be glorious.
11 It will also come about in that day
that my Lord will again redeem—
a second time with His hand—
the remnant of His people who remain
from Assyria, from Egypt, from Pathros,
from Cush, Elam, Shinar, Hamath,
and from the islands of the sea.
12 He will lift up a banner for the nations,
and assemble the dispersed of Israel,
and gather the scattered of Judah
from the four corners of the earth.
13 Ephraim's envy will end,
those hostile to Judah will be cut off.
Ephraim will not be jealous of Judah,
and Judah will not harass Ephraim.
16 So there will be a highway for the remnant of His people who remain, from Assyria,
as there was for Israel in the day
they came up out of the land of Egypt.

Not only is shalom brought to the Jewish people in the Kingdom, but there will be peace in the animal kingdom as well. Verses 6–7 state that predator will not feed on prey, but rather, they shall dwell together as friends. Lions will eat straw like the ox, and young children will play with all the animals that normally would eat them! Verses 8–9 proclaim the young children and babes will play with the previous deadly venomous snakes in their dens, and none of the animals will hurt or cause destruction in the Holy Land! Why? The earth is full of the knowledge of the Lord. This means the curse of Genesis 3:14–19 is finally lifted from the ground and the animal kingdom!

In that day of the Kingdom, the nations will finally worship the Messiah because He is the standard and the signal for life, and He is eternal life for all the peoples (verse 10). The Kingdom and especially the Temple Mount area will be glorious! Verses 11–12 discuss the regathering of all the Jewish believers of Yeshua from around the world. This occurs after the Armageddon War (Matthew 24:31). Israel will then become the standard for living in the Kingdom for all the nations to see and emulate. The Lord will provide the way back home for all the Jewish people (verse 16). In the Kingdom, the jealousy that occurred in history between the northern kingdom and the southern kingdom of Israel will be no more (verse 13). Jealousy will not be allowed, but rather unity will reign in Israel.

Isaiah 12:1–6

1 In that day you will say:
"I will give You thanks, *ADONAI,*
for though You were angry with me,
Your anger is turned away,
and You comfort me.
2 Behold, God is my salvation!
I will trust and will not be afraid.

For the Lord *ADONAI* is my strength
and my song.
He also has become my salvation."
3 With joy you will draw water
from the wells of salvation.
4 In that day you will say:
"Give thanks to *ADONAI*.
Proclaim His Name!
Declare His works to the peoples,
so they remember His exalted Name.
5 Sing to *ADONAI*, for He has done gloriously.
Let this be known in all the earth.
6 Cry out and shout, inhabitant of Zion!
For great in your midst
is the Holy One of Israel."

The timing of this scripture reading is "in that day" (verse 1). This is the Day of the Lord and specifically is talking about when the Jewish people as a nation are saved and then are living in the Land for the Kingdom. In verses 1–2, the Jewish people will give thanks unto God for their salvation. They shall draw water out of the wells of salvation (verse 3). This is the verse the rabbis use to symbolize the Ruach Kodesh pouring out salvation on the nation of Israel in the Feast of Sukkot (Tabernacles)! In verse 4, the Jewish people will call upon and exalt His name. They will tell the whole earth of the great deeds of the Lord (verse 5). Finally, the Holy One of Israel will live in the midst of the Jewish people in the Land of Israel (verse 6). This is just another verse that confirms the fact that the Lord will reign over the Jewish people while dwelling in the Land of Israel!

Zechariah 14:8–11, 16–18

> 8 Moreover, in that day living waters will flow from Jerusalem, half toward the eastern sea and half toward the western sea, both in the summer and in the winter. 9 *ADONAI* will then be King over all the earth. In that day *ADONAI* will be *Echad* [One] and His Name *Echad*.
> 10 The whole land, from Geba to Rimmon south of Jerusalem, will become like the Arabah. Jerusalem will be raised up and occupy her place, from the Benjamin Gate to the place of the First Gate, to the Corner Gate, and from the Tower of Hananel to the king's winepresses.
> 11 People will dwell in her, and no longer will there be a ban of destruction—Jerusalem will live in security.
> 16 Then all the survivors from all the nations that attacked Jerusalem will go up from year to year to worship the King, *ADONAI-Tzva'ot,* and to celebrate *Sukkot* [feast of Tabernacles].17 Furthermore, if any of the nations on earth do not go up to Jerusalem to worship the King, *ADONAI-Tzva'ot,* they will have no rain. 18 If the Egyptians do not go up and celebrate, they will have no rain. Instead, there will be the plague that *ADONAI* will inflict on the nations that do not go up to celebrate *Sukkot*.

In the Kingdom, we shall see some very interesting changes not only to the whole earth, but more specifically to the Land of Israel. In verse 8, living waters will flow from the city of Jerusalem. The waters will flow to the eastern sea and the western sea. The eastern sea is the Dead Sea, and the western sea is the Mediterranean Sea. These waters will flow year-round from the city of Jerusalem, but more specifically from the Temple. Verse 9 boldly proclaims that in this Kingdom, the Lord shall be King over all the earth! He is the one and only God to rule and reign over the Jewish people in Israel. Once again, the Scriptures clearly proclaim that Yeshua will be King of the world, and more specifically, King of the Jews in the Land of Israel. The Land of Israel itself shall go through some major geological changes. The Land shall be leveled off like the desert of the Arabah (verse 10).

However, Jerusalem will be lifted up and become the highest mountain in the world. The Jewish people will dwell safely in it, and there shall be no more curse (verse 11). God's promise that the curse of humankind (that occurred in Genesis 3) would be lifted in the Messianic Millennial Kingdom is finally fulfilled here. However, there is one aspect of the curse that will not be lifted. What is that? The sin nature found in all of humankind will not be lifted from the human body during the Kingdom. Humans born in the Kingdom age will still be born with the sin nature and have the same need to repent and believe in Yeshua for salvation.

Humankind's three greatest adversaries are the world, the sin nature, and the devil. In the Messianic Millennial Kingdom, the world is dramatically changed from evil to holy. So no one will be able to blame the temptations of the world for their personal evil. The world will also be without HaSatan and his demons since they are judged and sentenced to the abyss for 1,000 years. So, Satan is taken out of the picture, and no one will be able to make the excuse for their sin: "Satan made me do it." The world and HaSatan will be subdued. But the sin nature will not undergo any transformation. Humans born in the Kingdom will still have to deal with their sinful nature. This will help them understand their need for Messiah Yeshua for salvation.

Finally in verse 16, we see the wonderful grace of God in action. The believers of those nations that attacked Jerusalem at the end of Jacob's Trouble shall go up to Jerusalem to worship the Lord Yeshua every single year of the Messianic Millennial Kingdom. Specifically, all believers from around the world will be required to come up to Jerusalem during the

Feast of Sukkot (Tabernacles) to worship King Yeshua! One of the themes of Sukkot is, "God is with us." The Jewish people recognized that God was with them and taking care of their needs while Israel was wandering in the desert for forty years after the exodus of Egypt. He gave them the rock, providing water, and the manna, providing food. Building and living in a *sukkah* (temporary shelter) during the Feast of Sukkot memorializes this theme. So, when Yeshua is King over Israel in the Messianic Millennial Kingdom, He will be in charge of taking care of Israel's needs. He will, of course, be "God is with us."

How ironic it is that the people of the world will be required to worship the King during this Feast of Sukkot! Those of the people who voluntarily and lovingly worship the Lord will continue to be blessed with Yeshua's provisions of water and food. Those who decide not to worship the Lord and King Yeshua will have no rain fall in their lands (verse 17). No rain in their land means drought and eventually no food. This is the plague that the Lord will smite all the nations who do not come up to Jerusalem and worship Him (verse 18). So, those who do not commemorate and worship Yeshua as Lord and King (as "God with us") will not receive the life provisions of water and food, the very provisions this Feast of Sukkot memorializes in our God!

Ezekiel 47:1–12

> 1 Then he brought me back to the door of the House. Behold, water was flowing out from under the threshold of the House eastward—for the front of the House faced east. The water was flowing down from under the right side of the House, south of the altar. 2 He brought me out by way of the north gate and led me around outside by the way of the outer gate, the way of the gate looking east. Behold, water was trickling out from the right side.

3 When the man went out eastward with a line in his hand, he measured a 1,000 cubits. Then he led me into the water—water to the ankles. 4 Again he measured a 1,000, and led me into the water—water to the knees. Again he measured a 1,000, and he led me into the water—water up to the waist. 5 Again he measured a 1,000, and now it was a river that I could not pass through, for the water had risen, water to swim in—a river that could not be crossed. 6 He said to me, "Have you seen this, son of man?"
Then he brought me back to the bank of the river. 7 When I had returned, behold, there were very many trees on one side and on the other, along the bank of the river. 8 Then he said to me, "These waters go out toward the eastern region. They go down to the Arabah and enter the sea. When they arrive at the sea, the waters of the sea will flow and will become fresh. 9 It will be that every living creature that swarms will live wherever the rivers go. There will be a very great multitude of fish, because this water goes there and makes the salt water fresh. So everything will be healed and live wherever the river goes. 10 Fishermen will stand by it; from En-gedi to En-eglaim, it will be a place for spreading of nets. Their fish will be of many different kinds—like the fish of the Great Sea, a huge quantity. 11 Its swamps and marshes will not become fresh; they will be set aside for salt. 12 On the river, on its bank, on this side and that side, will grow every kind of tree for food. Its leaf will not wither; its fruit will not fail; it will bear new fruit every month, because its water flows out from the Sanctuary. Its fruit will be for food and its leaf will be for healing."

Ezekiel adds some much-needed details to the truth of Zechariah's declaration of the living waters. The living waters don't just flow from Jerusalem, but from the threshold of the

Temple (verse 1). Ezekiel only discusses the living waters that flow to the east and actually does not talk about the location of their ending. Since the Temple faces east, the living waters will flow straight from the Temple to the east. Verses 2–5 reveal the angel showing Ezekiel the gradual increase in depth of the river the further it runs away from the Temple. So the water starts out as a trickling and ends up as a gushing river into the Dead Sea where people could swim in it without touching the bottom.

The angel then introduces Ezekiel to the banks of the river where trees line up on both sides (verses 6–7). The living waters flow through the Arabah (southern area of the Dead Sea) into the Dead Sea and actually make the Dead Sea alive (verse 8)! Creatures will thrive with life wherever the river runs, and fish will be plentiful (verse 9). The fisherman of the sea from En Gedi to En Eglaim will be blessed with an abundance of fish (verse 10). En Gedi is an oasis just west of the Dead Sea and near to the Qumran caves and Masada. En Eglaim's location is unknown. The idea here is that the location along the river where fishermen will be able to fish will be plentiful and sufficient to fulfill their needs.

However, not every place will come alive around the river and the sea. The marshes around the newly reborn Dead Sea will remain marshes so that they can provide the Jewish people with salt (verse 11). This area has always been a haven for the Jewish people to harvest salt, which is a staple of life in Israel. It will continue to be the place for the Jewish people to collect their salt for the Kingdom. In verse 12, we read that the trees on both sides of the river will never fail to grow fruit every month for food and leaves for healing. It certainly seems like the Land of Israel in the Kingdom will be tremendously blessed with enough trees for food and leaves for good health. Many of the needs of the people will be met in this almost utopian type society.

Ezekiel 47:13–14

> 13 Thus says *ADONAI Elohim,* "This will be the border, by which you will divide the land for inheritance according to the twelve tribes of Israel, Joseph receiving two portions. 14 You will inherit it, each one like another, as I lifted My hand to give to your fathers. So this land will fall to you as an inheritance.

In the Messianic Millennial Kingdom, the Land is finally given by God to Israel in fulfillment of the Abrahamic Covenant (beginning with Genesis 12:1–3). Actually, in verse 13, the Lord God Himself declares that the twelve tribes of Israel shall divide and inherit the Land. Joseph shall have two portions because he had two sons: Ephraim and Manasseh. In verse 14, the Lord promises that He will give the Land to them. Can God ever break His promises? God forbid! I wrote this earlier in this book, but it needs to be stated again. If God could break His promises to the nation of Israel, then what would stop Him from breaking His promises to the Body of Messiah? So the Lord has to give the Land of Israel to the nation of Israel to fulfill His promise to Abraham.

Some folks think this scripture was fulfilled in 1948 with the rebirth of Israel in the Land. However, the rest of Ezekiel 47 clearly reveals the giving of the Land in 1948 was not the fulfillment. In 1948, the Land of Israel was not divided up into the twelve tribes prescribed by this scripture passage.

In verses 15–23, the Lord goes on to spell out exactly where the new borders are located for the Land of Israel in the Kingdom. The borders will span from the Euphrates River all the way down to the brook of Egypt. The nation of Israel has never lived in this amount of territory. King Solomon ruled over most of this territory, but Israel under his kingship never lived in its entirety.

In Ezekiel 48, the Lord provides the order and the portions of each plot of land for each tribe. There are a number of changes from the original instructions given to Moses! The order of the tribes from north to south is quite different from the original order. The size and location of each plot of land for the tribes is quite different as well. In the Kingdom, Judah is located in the northern section of Israel (as opposed to the southern section in Mosaic Covenant times), and the city of Jerusalem is not located within it!

Chart

As you look to the chart, the box marked "Messianic Millennial Kingdom" reveals Yeshua as the Jewish Messiah will be King of the Jews for 1,000 years. The Jewish people on a whole are looking forward to this coming Messianic Kingdom. Unfortunately, most of them do not believe that this Kingdom will be ruled by Messiah Yeshua! Amillennialists are definitely not looking forward to the Messianic Millennial Kingdom because they believe we are currently already living in it. If this current world is the Kingdom spoken about in the Scriptures, then they can certainly have it! I don't want to live in this kind of sinful world for 1,000 years! The future Kingdom is definitely coming as this section of this book clearly proclaims! Yeshua, the Messiah, first has to come back and defeat the enemies of the Jewish people. After that, the seventy-five-day interval of preparation work for the Kingdom will occur; then finally the Messianic Millennial Kingdom begins!

Revelation 20 clearly reveals through the Greek grammar that the 1,000 years should not be seen as a metaphor but a literal, positive and clear-cut statement. There are many verbal phrases throughout the first nine verses that reveal the entire passage should be taken from a literal perspective. Yes, there are still some metaphorical words used in this section like "dragon" and "serpent of old." However, just because there are a few words used as metaphors does not make the whole passage a metaphor!

At the start of the Messianic Millennial Kingdom, HaSatan is bound in the abyss for 1,000 years, which is the same amount of time that the Kingdom will last. The Lord and King Messiah, Yeshua, will reign over the whole world from His throne in His Temple from the Land of Israel in fulfillment of the Abrahamic and Davidic Covenants. He will reign for 1,000 years in shalom, justice, righteousness and faithfulness. Living waters will flow through a much-changed landscape of Israel. These living waters will flow down from the exulted Temple Mount area to the eastern and western seas.

The Jewish people will live in safety and security in the Land without God's curse! Even the Lord's curse of Genesis 3 will be lifted from the world, and the animal kingdom will also be greatly affected. The only aspect that is not lifted from humankind is the sin nature. They will have to deal with the sin nature for 1,000 years, and unfortunately, many will succumb to it to their eternal detriment (more on this later)! The Lord Yeshua will be King over all the earth and begin to greatly take care of the needs of His people. How will the Jewish people respond? With wonderful worship of the Lord Yeshua! The Jewish people will finally be God's people, and He will finally be their God!

Prayer

Lord, thank you that you are the King of kings, Lord of lords, and God of all gods! Thank you for your Word which clearly shows that Messiah's Kingdom to come will last for 1,000 years and that you will fulfill your promise to Abraham, Isaac, Jacob, and the Jewish people to gather the nation of Israel to live in the Land of Israel! Thank you that you are a faithful, loving, and merciful God—the one and only God of the universe! I bless you and praise you and look forward to participating in this wonderful Kingdom as a priest and king, ruling and reigning along with Yeshua! In Yeshua's name I pray, Amen.

Chapter 17

THE MESSIANIC MILLENNIAL KINGDOM

Many believers know that Yeshua will reign for 1,000 years in the Messianic Millennial Kingdom. He will rule and reign over the whole world in peace, righteousness, justice, and faithfulness. Our prayers for the peace of Jerusalem will finally be answered. Yeshua will also rule over the earth with most of the curse of Genesis 3 lifted! But how many believers realize that Yeshua will be reigning from His Davidic throne in a Jewish way? He will be living in His Jewish Temple, sitting on His Jewish throne on the Jewish Temple Mount in the Jewish country of Israel. And there will be a Jewish style of worship with what I call the "new and improved" Jewish Torah. This Kingdom Torah will have new rules and regulations for Jewish living in the Jewish Kingdom. I guess you can figure out by now that the Millennial Kingdom will be a Messianic Jewish Kingdom!

Jewish Characteristics of the Millennial Kingdom

Hosea 2:16–20

16 "It will come about in that day," declares the Lord,

"That you will call Me Ishi
And will no longer call Me Baali.
17 "For I will remove the names of the Baals from her mouth,
So that they will be mentioned by their names no more.
18 "In that day I will also make a covenant for them
With the beasts of the field,
The birds of the sky
And the creeping things of the ground.
And I will abolish the bow, the sword and war from the land,
And will make them lie down in safety.
19 "I will betroth you to Me forever;
Yes, I will betroth you to Me in righteousness and in justice,
In lovingkindness and in compassion,
20 And I will betroth you to Me in faithfulness.
Then you will know the Lord. (NASB)

First and foremost, Israel is the betrothed wife of the Lord! Even though she has broken God's covenant and even though He temporarily divorced her, Israel is God's betrothed wife and will always be. Verse 16 shows us that this will occur in the Messianic Millennial Kingdom as it is proclaimed to take place "in that day." Israel will also call the Lord *ishi*, meaning "my husband." In the Kingdom, the Baals (and all other gods) will be removed from the Land, and no one will mention their names again (verse 17). God then will make a covenant with Israel (verse 18). In this new covenant, war will be abolished, and the Jewish people will live in safety. This can only occur in the Messianic Millennial Kingdom. Then the Lord affirms that Israel is betrothed to Him forever (verse 19). She is betrothed to the Lord in righteousness, justice, lovingkindness, compassion, and faithfulness. These are all characteristics of the Kingdom. Then and only then, during the Messianic Millennial

Kingdom, Israel as a nation will have a personal knowledge and relationship with the Lord (verse 20). This all will happen because the Lord is a faithful and loving God who does not go back on His promises. The fact that the Jewish people, Israel, are the focal point of God's love in the Kingdom shows that it will be a Jewish Kingdom!

Isaiah 2:2–5

> 2 It will come to pass in the last days
> that the mountain of *ADONAI*'s House
> will stand firm as head of the mountains
> and will be exalted above the hills.
> So all nations will flow to it.
> 3 Then many peoples will go and say:
> "Come, let us go up to the mountain of *ADONAI*,
> to the House of the God of Jacob!
> Then He will teach us His ways,
> and we will walk in His paths."
> For *Torah* will go forth from Zion
> and the word of *ADONAI* from Jerusalem.
> 4 He will judge between the nations
> and decide for many peoples.
> They will beat their swords into plowshares,
> and their spears into pruning knives.
> Nation will not lift up sword against nation,
> nor will they learn war any more.
> 5 Come house of Jacob,
> let us walk in the light of *ADONAI*.

The Messianic Millennial Kingdom Temple will be built on Mount Moriah (verse 2). This mount will become the top of the mountains of the world. It will be lifted up and become the highest mountain in the world (Zechariah 14:10). Yeshua will cause this to happen in the seventy-five-day interval between

Jacob's Trouble and the Messianic Millennial Kingdom. The idea here is that the world will have to go up to Jerusalem to worship the Lord! What will the Lord be doing on that mountain in His Temple?

Verse 3 tells us. He will teach the many peoples of the world of His ways! These ways are the new and improved Torah for the Kingdom. I say "new and improved" because there are many new rules and regulations discussed in Ezekiel 40–48 that are quite different from the commandments in Moses' Torah! To me, Torah is a progressive understanding of God's commands through the dispensations and the covenants. The definition of Torah cannot be confined to only God's instruction given in the first five books! The dispensation in question here is the Messianic Millennial Kingdom dispensation.

The believers of the Kingdom will walk in this new path that the Lord Yeshua is teaching. His new Torah will go forth from Zion and His Word (*davar*) will go forth from Jerusalem (verse 3). In the Hebrew here, His Torah is equal to His Word! What else is the Lord doing in the Kingdom?

He will judge between nations and make judgments for the peoples in the Kingdom (verse 4). This suggests there will be nations in the Kingdom, and there will still be issues and problems between these nations. This only proves my point that *most* of the curse is lifted in the Kingdom. The only aspect of the curse that will not be lifted is the sin nature in human beings. Humans in the Kingdom will still have the sin nature and have to deal with their sin. Both Jewish and Gentile people will have to believe on the Lord Yeshua for salvation and live by faith in the Ruach to live above their sins. They will still have to fight the war between their flesh and the Ruach that entangles us every single moment of every single day of our lives!

Another aspect under Yeshua's reign will be shalom (verse 4). Actually this aspect of peace in the world is the lack of war. All the world's implements used for war, such as swords and spears, will be turned into farming equipment like plows and vineyard pruning hooks. The world will never again learn about how to war against one another. The world will be enjoying the shalom of the Lord. In verse 5, Isaiah encouraged the Jewish people of this time to walk in the light of the Lord because the future of Israel is bright! I believe the New Covenant writings encourage all believers to be Messianic Millennial Kingdom-minded as well. We are to live our lives in the present for the Lord because of His glorious future promises!

Isaiah 60:10–18

> 10 Foreigners will build up your walls,
> and their kings will minister to you.
> For in My fury I struck you,
> but in My favor I will show you mercy.
> 11 Your gates will be open continually.
> They will not be shut day or night,
> so that men may bring to you the wealth of the nations,
> with their kings led in procession.
> 12 For the nation and the kingdom which will not serve you will perish—
> those nations will be utterly ruined.
> 13 The glory of Lebanon will come to you
> —cypress, elm and pine together—
> to beautify the place of My Sanctuary.
> I will give to the place of My feet glory.
> 14 The sons of those who afflicted you will come bowing to you,
> and all those who despised you will fall at the soles of your feet.
> They will call you the city of *ADONAI*,
> Zion of the Holy One of Israel.
> 15 Instead of deserted and hated,
> no one passing through,
> I will make you an eternal pride,

joy from generation to generation.
16 You will also suck the milk of nations
and nurse at the breast of kings.
Then you will know that I, *ADONAI*,
am your Savior and your Redeemer,
the Mighty One of Jacob.
17 "Instead of bronze I will bring gold,
instead of iron I will bring silver,
instead of wood, bronze,
and instead of stones, iron.
I will make *shalom* your overseer,
and righteousness your taskmasters.
18 No more will violence be heard in your land,
devastation nor destruction within your borders.
But you will call your walls Salvation
and your gates Praise.

Isaiah 60 summarizes some more Jewish characteristics of the Kingdom. Verses 10–11 tell us that although the Lord's wrath struck Israel in Jacob's Trouble, His favorable compassion would be upon them in the Messianic Millennial Kingdom. The Gentiles will help build the walls of the city of Jerusalem. The kings of the earth shall lead the processions of the peoples, bringing the world's wealth to Jerusalem! Any nation that does not serve Israel in the Kingdom will perish (verse 12). Lebanon, famous for its forests, will bring their trees to build the Sanctuary of the Temple (verse 13). The family members of those evil ones who despised and attacked the Jewish people will change their tune and actually bow down before Israel (verse 14). In the end, they will call Jerusalem "The city of ADONAI, the Zion of the Holy One of Israel." This is an obvious reference to Yeshua HaMeshiach, the Holy One of Israel, who had just destroyed the nations with their evil ones and set up the Kingdom!

In the Kingdom, Jerusalem will be the pride and joy of the Jewish people and not hated and forsaken of the nations like in the past (verse 15). The blessings of the nations will be brought to Jerusalem for the Jewish people's needs (verses 16–17). Once all these predictions come true, the Jewish people will recognize the Lord God as their Savior, Redeemer, and Mighty One! Peace and righteousness will oversee the Kingdom. Violence and destruction will be a thing of the past (verse 18). Jerusalem will be filled with praise and salvation. It will certainly be the greatest city of the Kingdom!

<u>Isaiah 65:17–25</u>

17 For behold, I create new heavens
and a new earth.
The former things will not be remembered
or come to mind.
18 But be glad and rejoice forever
in what I am creating.
For behold, I am creating Jerusalem
for rejoicing, and her people for joy.
19 Then I will rejoice in Jerusalem,
and be glad in My people.
No longer will the voice of weeping
or the voice of crying be heard in her.
20 No longer will there be in it an infant
who lives but a few days,
or an old man who does not fill out his days.
For the youth will die at a hundred years,
But one who misses the mark of a hundred
must be accursed.
21 They will build houses and inhabit them.
They will plant vineyards and eat their fruit.
22 They will not build and another inhabit,
nor plant and another eat.

For like the days of a tree,
so will be the days of My people,
and My chosen ones will long enjoy
the work of their hands.
23 They will not labor in vain
nor bear children for calamity.
For they are the offspring
of those blessed by *ADONAI,*
as well as descendants with them.
24 And it will come to pass
that before they call, I will answer,
and while they are still speaking,
I will hear.
25 The wolf and the lamb will feed together.
The lion will eat straw like the ox,
but dust will be the serpent's food.
They will not hurt or destroy
in all My holy mountain," says *ADONAI*.

Isaiah begins this scripture passage in a fascinating way. Verse 17 states God will create a new heavens and a new earth. When "create" (*bara*) is paired with the Lord, it speaks of His creation and specifically His creation that comes from nothing. A great example is found in Genesis 1:1 where God originally created the heavens and the earth. He obviously created all the heavens and the earth from nothing. It is interesting to see the connection from the beginning where the Lord created the heavens and the earth to the ending of human history where the Lord will again create the heavens and the earth for the Eternal Kingdom. This new creation occurs after the Messianic Millennial Kingdom is over.

So, here in Isaiah 65, the promise of God is that the old heavens and earth will disappear and not even be remembered or come to mind while we all live in this wonderful new creation of God. Is it possible that this phrase "the former things will not be remembered" includes the understanding that believers will not even have a vague thought about our past lives? Yes, it is possible, and who could blame the Lord for doing this? In eternity, everyone who makes it will be in eternal peace, happiness, and joy! We shall be with the Lord, so why would we want to remember anything from our past? However, this probably refers to only the old heaven and earth not being remembered. I would imagine we should be able to remember all of the Lord's past wonderful workings in our lives!

In verse 18, the word *but* shows a transition from the future eternity of God's new creation to Isaiah's present time. He says the Jewish people should rejoice over the present Jerusalem right now because God is going to create a new heaven and earth in the future! I have preached this concept many times in sermons before. Our forward focus on God's promises for eternity should help us in our present walk with Him right now! It helps to take the pressure off of us, knowing the Lord is going to greatly bless us in the future!

Then the Lord proclaims He will rejoice in the city of Jerusalem and be happy with the Jewish people (verse 19)! When exactly will this be? At a time when there will be no weeping and crying in the city. When has Jerusalem never wept or cried in its history for any length of time? This can only be in the Messianic Millennial Kingdom when Messiah Yeshua will reign from His throne!

Verse 20 then boldly proclaims the Jewish people will live much longer lives in this time period. How long? How about the whole length of the Messianic Millennial Kingdom? Yes, one-thousand years! I believe those godly believers who are blessed by making it to the beginning of the Kingdom could live and not die in those 1,000 years. So, we could see some Kingdom folks who live to be over 1,000 years old! How is this possible? Well, for one, the curse of the earth is mostly lifted, and hence the earth is going to be remodeled. In this remodeled state, life will be greatly enhanced. Second, verse 20 tells us the Kingdom will be characterized by longevity. Babies will not die at a few days old, and old people will be able to live out their days. Youth who die at the age of 100 will be thought to be accursed by God. Anyone who dies at the young age of 100 will be considered a sinner and one judged by God to Sheol! Obviously if 100 years old is considered young, then folks are going to live throughout the whole Kingdom!

Verses 21–22 verify that the Jewish people will live in peace in the Land. There will no longer be any Gentile nations taking control of the Land and forcing Israel to submit to their wishes. The timing here will most definitely be in the Kingdom. Then verse 22 ends with a curious phrase. The days of God's chosen people will last as long as the lifetime of a tree. I would imagine the Lord is not speaking of a normal tree that lasts anywhere from fifteen to thirty years or so, but of the redwoods, such as those in California that can live up to 2,000 years old! Can you imagine living for 1,000 years and trying to continuously be fruitful in your personal life and work? No wonder this verse says the Jewish people will wear out and enjoy their work!

The Lord has promised tremendous blessings and not curses in the Kingdom (verse 23). The Jewish people of the Kingdom will not labor in vain nor bear children for calamity. These children are the seed of those blessed by the Lord. These are the Jewish believers who begin the Kingdom with Yeshua! The blessings are not only physical in nature. Before the Jewish people pray, the Lord will have already answered their prayers (verse 24). In verse 25, the Lord confirms that the curse will be lifted from the animal kingdom. The predator and the prey will have peace between them, and there will be no harm or evil in all the Kingdom. However, there is another aspect of the curse that is not lifted! The snake still has to eat the dust of the earth as its curse. And how appropriate is this! Everyone will rejoice in the Lord that HaSatan and his evil ones are in the pit for 1,000 years every time they see a serpent crawling around the earth, tasting the dust!

Zechariah 8:18–23

> 18 Again the word of *ADONAI-Tzva'ot* [LORD of Hosts] came saying: 19 "Thus says *ADONAI-Tzva'ot,* "The fast of the fourth, the fast of the fifth, the fast of the seventh and the fast of the tenth month will become joy, gladness and cheerful *moadim* [appointed times]. Therefore, love truth and *shalom!*' 20 Thus says *ADONAI-Tzva'ot,* "Peoples and the inhabitants of many cities will again come. 21 The inhabitants of one city will go to another saying 'Let us go to entreat the favor of *ADONAI* and to seek *ADONAI-Tzva'ot*. I also am going.' 22 Indeed, many peoples and powerful nations will come to seek *ADONAI-Tzva'ot* in Jerusalem, and to entreat the favor of *ADONAI*." 23 Thus says *ADONAI-Tzva'ot,* "In those days it will come to pass that ten men from every language of the nations will grasp the corner of the garment of a Jew saying, 'Let us go with you, for we have heard that God is with you.'"

In Zechariah 8, the Lord says He will return to Zion and dwell in the city of Jerusalem (verse 3). At this time, the city will be called the "city of truth" and the mountain of the Lord will be called the "holy mountain." This time period is obviously the Messianic Millennial Kingdom where the Lord Yeshua will reign as King of the Jews. In verses 7–8 we find the Lord confirming the regathering of the remnant from the east and the west (of the world). The remnant will be God's people and the Lord will be their God! This is the fulfillment of God's promise to Moses (Exodus 6:7). There will be so much peace and blessing in the Land (verse 12) that Israel will be a blessing to the rest of the world as well (verse 13)!

In the Messianic Millennial Kingdom, Jewish life will be different in the Kingdom. The fast days of Judaism will be changed into joyful feasts for the Jewish people (verses 18–19).

The Lord says the peoples of the world will greatly desire and seek the Lord in Jerusalem (verses 20–22). In verse 23, we see that ten men from the nations will grab the corner of the garment (where the tzitzit hangs from the tallit [tassel hangs from the prayer shawl]) of a Jewish person. These ten men will ask the Jewish person if they can accompany them on their trip to Jerusalem to see the Lord for they had heard that "God is with you." It is fascinating that this phrase in the Hebrew is *Immanuel.* This is the same Hebrew word used to describe the Lord's sign given to the Jewish people that God had become a human being through a miraculous virgin birth (Isaiah 7:14). Yeshua's name would be called Immanuel, meaning "God is with us!" And now in the Messianic Millennial Kingdom, God who is with us is actually going to be right there in Jerusalem! We shall be able to see Him face to face.

In Zechariah 8, we find the Jewish people are actually held in high esteem. Since when in the history of humankind have the Jewish people been held in high esteem all around the world? It is possible it occurred under David or Solomon. However, the true answer is in the Messianic Millennial Kingdom! The Jewish people will enjoy this newfound status throughout the whole world in the Kingdom.

<u>Jeremiah 31:31–34</u>

> 31 "Behold, days are coming"
> —it is a declaration of *ADONAI*—
> "when I will make a new covenant
> with the house of Israel
> and with the house of Judah—
> 32 not like the covenant
> I made with their fathers
> in the day I took them by the hand
> to bring them out of the land of Egypt.
> For they broke My covenant,

though I was a husband to them."
it is a declaration of *ADONAI*.
33 "But this is the covenant I will make with the house
of Israel after those days"
—it is a declaration of *ADONAI*—
"I will put My *Torah* within them.
Yes, I will write it on their heart.
I will be their God
and they will be My people.
34 No longer will each teach his neighbor
or each his brother, saying: 'Know *ADONAI*,'
for they will all know Me,
from the least of them to the greatest."
it is a declaration of *ADONAI*.
"For I will forgive their iniquity,
their sin I will remember no more."

Jeremiah prophesied before and during Babylon's three sieges of Judah (605 BC, 597 BC, and 586 BC). The northern kingdom of Israel had long been taken by Assyria in 722 BC. So now Jeremiah is trying to encourage the southern kingdom of Judah and the northern kingdom of Israel with God's wonderful message of forgiveness in a future New Covenant. Although the current times were difficult and bleak, the future was bright and filled with God's forgiveness.

In verse 31, the Lord boldly proclaims that He will cut a New Covenant with the house of Israel and the house of Judah. This covenant would not be like the covenant the Lord made with Moses and the Jewish people while they lived as slaves in the land of Egypt (verse 32). The Lord viewed the Mosaic Covenant like a marriage covenant with the typical *ketubah* (Jewish marriage contract) signed by both parties. The Lord was a faithful husband to Israel, took her by the hand in the bridal processional out of the land of Egypt, and brought her to the bridal chamber of the Promised Land of Israel! However, the whole nation of Israel (except for a few godly ones) played the harlot and sinned against the Lord by worshiping other gods. Unfortunately, that's how they got into this *mishegas* (craziness) of sieges and captivities! God was judging their sin of idolatry. You cannot worship other gods and expect the Lord to bless you!

Here, I have to stress two points. The first is that the New Covenant is made with the nation of Jewish people and not with any other nation or group of people (for example, the Body of Messiah, the United States, Russia, China, etc). The Hebrew word *Israel* always means the Jewish people or the nation of Jewish people. It never is used in the Bible for any other people groups and especially not Gentiles! The second important point that needs to be stressed is the New Covenant is not like the Mosaic Covenant. This means it is a different covenant, an entirely new covenant that is not similar to the Mosaic Covenant and cannot be grafted together with the other covenants of the Bible to make one covenant of grace! It is its own separate covenant just like all the other seven covenants. The New Covenant has its own separate commandments (although some are the same commands as the Mosaic Covenant), rules, regulations, and rewards for compliance.

In verse 33, the Lord declares this New Covenant will be cut "after those days." What is the Lord talking about here? In verses 27–28 the Lord gives us the answer. He will start a New Covenant after the days of destruction He is going to bring on Israel in the future. I believe this is talking about the horrible disasters that will come upon Israel during Jacob's Trouble! After those days, the Lord will make this New Covenant with the whole nation of Israel—that is, what is left of the nation. Remember, only one-third of the Jewish people survive Anti-messiah's onslaught of terror.

In this New Covenant, the Torah (this is the new Messianic Millennial Kingdom Torah) will be written on the hearts of the Jewish believers. This is fascinating to me since it does not say (like in Ezekiel) the Ruach will indwell them. It seems that the Lord is not focusing on that truth here. Instead, he wants the nation of Israel to know that in the Kingdom, his Torah will be in their hearts, and they will lovingly and willingly fulfill it in the power of the Ruach. In the New Covenant during the Messianic Millennial Kingdom, they will not break the agreement like they broke it in the Mosaic Covenant! The Lord is making this very clear, and He will finally be the Jewish people's God and the Jewish people will finally be His people!

This New Covenant is the ultimate fulfillment of God's promises to Moses and the Jewish people when He took them by the hand out of the land of Egypt. In Exodus 6:6–8, the Lord spoke a total of five promises to the enslaved Jewish people:

1. I will bring you out from under the burdens of the Egyptians.
2. I will deliver you from their bondage.
3. I will also redeem you with an outstretched arm and with great judgments.
4. I will take you for My people, and I will be your God. Here is where Jeremiah repeats the promise and reveals the ultimate prophetic conclusion is found in the Messianic Millennial Kingdom. Why? Because then the Jewish people will finally *know* and have an intimate personal relationship with the Lord!
5. I will bring you to the land that I swore to give to Abraham, Isaac, and Jacob, and I will give it to you for a possession; I am the Lord. Finally, then the redeemed nation of Israel starting the New Covenant with the Lord in the Messianic Millennial Kingdom will live in the Land of Israel and fulfill the Abrahamic and Davidic promises as well.

Jeremiah 31:34 then tells us that in the Messianic Millennial Kingdom, the Jewish people will not have to teach one another that they must *know* the Lord. "Know" (*yada*) here refers to an intimate personal experiential knowledge of the Lord. So the Jewish people will not have to teach one another to know the Lord intimately because they all will already have this personal relationship! Either they will all be born with this knowledge and have automatic salvation, or each Jewish person will come to a saving grace of Yeshua at a very young age within the confines of their own household or community. The Lord's point here is that every single Jewish person in the Messianic Millennial Kingdom will be saved and have their names written in the Book of Life!

How does this all come about? In the New Covenant, the Jewish people's sins will be forgiven and forgotten! The Lord boldly proclaims that He will forgive their sins and remember them no more. This is an awesome spiritual place for the Jewish people to be. My only wish is that more Jewish people would join their future saved brethren right now! Then Isaiah's prophecy will be fulfilled in 60:21: *"Then your people will all be righteous. They will possess the land forever—the branch of His planting, the work of My hands—that I may be glorified."*

When the peoples' sins are forgiven and forgotten, they become righteous before God's eyes. But Isaiah says, "all" the people will be righteous! That means that all of the Jewish people in the Messianic Millennial Kingdom will be saved! They will then live in the Land of Israel forever, and the Lord will be glorified! We all must remember the ultimate reason for God's fulfillment of His promises to Israel is not necessarily for Israel's sake but to truly glorify Himself! All the glory be to the Lord!

The question that needs to be answered is, "When does this New Covenant for the Jewish nation of Israel begin?" The context dictates that the Lord cuts the covenant with Israel at the beginning of the Messianic Millennial Kingdom. So, how do we reconcile this fact with the actual beginning of the New Covenant era at the time of Yeshua's death and resurrection?

Herein lies the problem. In Luke 22:17–20, at His last Passover Seder, Yeshua said He was instituting the New Covenant with His body and blood. Jeremiah 31 tells us the New Covenant would begin with the Messianic Millennial Kingdom. So, do we have a contradiction? God forbid! Jeremiah 31 proclaims that a New Covenant will be cut *with the nation of Israel*. This is the key to understanding this problem.

Yeshua did not begin the New Covenant at His death and resurrection with the nation of Israel. The nation actually rejected Yeshua's claim that He was their Messiah even though He biblically proved it through His teaching, miracles, signs, and wonders. The Sanhedrin (both Pharisees and Sadducees), as Israel's spiritual leadership, rejected Yeshua as Messiah going as far as claiming His miracles were performed by Beelzebub (Matthew 12:24). Even though the Sanhedrin performed the unpardonable sin, they also influenced much of the nation to believe this abomination as well. They actually helped to cause this specific generation to be judged by the Lord in AD 70 with the destruction of Jerusalem and the Temple (Luke 19:41–44).

Therefore, the nation led by the Sanhedrin did not enter into the New Covenant. In fact, they rejected it since they rejected Yeshua. This was the first covenant from the Lord that the nation of Israel rejected! Since the nation did not enter into the New Covenant, the Lord invited any and all individual Jewish and Gentile people who would believe in Yeshua to enter. This is the New Covenant for individual believers from the death and resurrection of Yeshua to the end of Jacob's Trouble. Then the New Covenant for the nation of Israel will begin with the Messianic Millennial Kingdom!

Ezekiel 45:21–24

> 21 "In the first month, on the fourteenth day of the month, you will have the Passover, a feast of seven days when *matzah* [unleavened bread] will be eaten. 22 On

> that day the prince will prepare a bull as a sin offering for himself and for all the people of the land. 23 He will prepare a burnt offering to *ADONAI* for the seven days of the feast—seven bulls and seven rams without blemish daily for seven days and a male goat daily for a sin offering. 24 He will prepare as a grain offering, an ephah for a bull, an ephah for a ram and a hin of oil for each ephah.

In this reading the Lord leaves instruction for the nation of Israel to celebrate the feast of Passover in the Messianic Millennial Kingdom. Actually, the nation of Israel will celebrate all the feasts and even the *shabbat*. Ezekiel 44:24 states, "*In a lawsuit, they will stand to judge, and judge in accordance with My ordinances. They will keep My laws and My statutes in all My moadim and keep My Shabbatot holy*." Israel will actually be required to keep all the feasts (*moadim*), the sabbaths (*shabbatot*) and the new and improved commandments (*Torah*) of the Messianic Millennial Kingdom!

In verse 21, the Lord proclaims the Passover as a seven-day feast! Biblically, Passover is actually only a one-day feast. However, the seven-day Feast of Unleavened Bread begins the first night of Passover when the Seder is celebrated, so the two feasts have always been seen as a week-long combined feast (although it would be a total of eight days!). Even the New Covenant writings combine the two feasts as one (Luke 22:1).

In verse 22, the prince of the people then provides a sin offering for himself and the people. He offers up sacrifices and the appropriate grain offerings for each day of the feast (verses 23–24). In fact, he will provide sacrifices for sin for the people on the Feast of Sukkot (Tabernacles), as well (verse 25).

It is especially fascinating to note a few particulars of these verses. First, the temple sacrifices for the Feast of Passover in the Messianic Millennial Kingdom are completely different from the temple sacrifices of the feast in the Mosaic Covenant!

For each day of the feast in the Messianic Millennial Kingdom, the burnt offering to the Lord is seven bulls and seven rams, and the sin offering is one male goat. In Numbers 28:16–25, we find the Lord's instruction to Moses on how to sacrifice in the Tabernacle/Temple on the Feast of Passover. For each day of the feast, the burnt offering was two bulls, one ram, and seven one-year-old male lambs, and the sin offering was one male goat. Although the sin offering for each day of the feast stays the same, the burnt offerings are quite different for the two timeframes! This is just one of many differences between the two Torahs. This proves beyond any doubt that the Torah given to Moses will not be used in the Messianic Millennial Kingdom! The Kingdom has its own "new and improved" Torah that is quite different from the Mosaic Covenant Torah!

The second interesting fact of the Messianic Millennial Kingdom is the new position of intercessor taken by the prince! In the Mosaic Covenant, there is Aaron, the high priest and his sons, the priests. But there is never mentioned in Torah about an intercessor prince! But there is a prince who intercedes on behalf of the people in the Messianic Millennial Kingdom! Who is the prince of the Kingdom? Some believe the prince is Yeshua the Messiah. Others believe he is the resurrected King David. The Lord proclaims that His servant David is the prince (34:24). The Lord even says that David His servant will be the Jewish people's prince forever (37:25)! This obviously reveals the resurrected King David will be the prince of Israel for the Messianic Millennial Kingdom and beyond. However, before we can be completely convinced that David is the prince, there are some issues that need to be worked out.

The prince will eat bread before the Lord in the Temple compound (44:3), he will own land in the Kingdom (45:7), and he has the power and authority to give part of his land to his sons or servants (46:16–18). Obviously, the prince cannot be the Messiah if he eats bread before the Lord in the compound! Another issue is that the prince has fathered sons during the Kingdom to be able to give them land! This prince certainly cannot be Yeshua! But how could the prince then be the resurrected David? Will the resurrected David be allowed to marry and have children? I guess the better question would be, "How can the resurrected David have children in the Messianic Millennial Kingdom when Messiah Yeshua said in Luke 20:34–36 the resurrected righteous would not marry or be given in marriage in the Kingdom? Also remember, in Ezekiel 45:22, the prince offers a Passover sacrifice for his own sins and that of the people. This prince definitely cannot be Yeshua or the resurrected David. Yeshua, who is God, can never sin, and David in his resurrection body cannot sin either! So, maybe there are two princes: (1) a human Jewish man from the Kingdom age; and (2) the resurrected David.

Ezekiel 45:17, 46:9–12

> 17 It will be the prince's role to give the burnt offerings, grain offerings and drink offerings at the feasts, New Moons and *Shabbatot,* in all the *moadim* of the house of Israel. He will prepare the sin offering, the meal offering, the burnt offering and the fellowship offerings, to make atonement for the house of Israel." (Ezekiel 45:17)
> 9 When the people of the land come before *ADONAI* at the *moadim,* whoever enters by way of the north gate to worship will exit by way of the south gate. Whoever enters by way of the south gate must exit by way of north gate. He should not return by the way of the gate where he came in, since he must exit straight ahead. 10 When they enter, the prince will come in among them. When they go out, they will go out together.
> 11 "At the feasts and the *moadim,* the grain offering will be an ephah for a bull and an ephah for a ram, and for the lambs a gift of his hand and a hin of oil for an ephah.
> 12 Now if the prince prepares a freewill offering, burnt

> offering or fellowship offerings as a freewill offering to *ADONAI,* the gate for him facing east must be opened for him. Then he will prepare his burnt offering and his fellowship offerings as he does on *Yom Shabbat* [Day of the Sabbath]. Then he will go out. After he exits, the gate should be shut. (Ezekiel 46:9-12)

In the Messianic Millennial Kingdom, the prince is the intercessor between the Lord and the people. In 45:17, he will provide the animal sacrifices for the people's atonement for all the feasts, new moons, and Sabbaths. He will specifically provide the sin offerings for the house of Israel. In 46:9–12, the Lord additionally provides specific instructions for the prince and the people on how to enter the Temple compound when they come to worship and sacrifice. Did we read that right? Are there going to be animal sacrifices for sin to make atonement for the Jewish people in the Messianic Millennial Kingdom? Yes, absolutely! The question many believers ask me is, "How can there be animal sacrifices for sin in the Kingdom when Yeshua was the one and only sacrifice for sin?" Great question, but many believers don't like the biblical answer I will share!

First, there is a misconception as to the reason for animal sacrifices. Most believers think the animal sacrifices helped the Jewish people to be saved. However, salvation in the Mosaic Covenant is the same as it is for the New Covenant. One must repent and have faith in the Lord God to be saved. Then, why the animal sacrifices? They helped the Jewish people's sanctification. When a Jewish person sinned, they were required to bring their animal sacrifice to the temple, lay hands on the head of the animal, confess their sin, and give the animal over to the priests for sacrifice. This process helped the Jewish people atone for their sins and keep their fellowship with the Lord. There was no salvation ever given for any animal sacrifice.

Second, the animal sacrifices for sin and guilt in the Mosaic Covenant were a memorial to Yeshua's once-for-all sacrifice.

When the Jewish people were engaged in these animal sacrifices, the very act of sacrifice was looking forward to Yeshua's sacrifice for sin. So when the Jewish people perform animal sacrifices in the Messianic Millennial Kingdom, it will be a memorial, looking *backward* to Messiah's sacrifice!

Third, the animal sacrifices will be efficacious for the sanctification process of the Kingdom believers. The believers in the Messianic Millennial Kingdom will be required to confess their sin and perform animal sacrifices for the Lord to forgive their sin in their sanctification process. This new process will be completely effective in returning the erring believer to fellowship with the Lord. In one sense, the Mosaic Covenant system will be combined with the New Covenant system to produce a new and improved Torah system in the Messianic Millennial Kingdom!

In the Mosaic Covenant, the *cohen gadol* (high priest), priests, and the Levites were the intercessors for the people. However, in the Messianic Millennial Kingdom, the prince is introduced as the newest member of the priestly team. He also seems to be the leader of the people and their intercessor. The only other difference in the Messianic Millennial Kingdom is the position of the *cohen gadol*. Yeshua will combine all three offices of King, prophet, and priest into one. What most believers do not know is that the priestly position Yeshua holds is the *cohen gadol* (Hebrews 2:17, 3:1, and others). He is the perfect sinless High Priest that sacrificed Himself as the perfect sinless blood sacrifice for the sin of the world for all time. His perfect sacrifice fulfilled the feast of Passover as the perfect Passover Lamb so that Jewish and Gentile people could apply His blood to the doorposts of their hearts so that their names could be written in the Lamb's Book of Life!

The characteristics of the Messianic Millennial Kingdom are quite Jewish as this chapter proclaims. The lifestyle of the Kingdom will be Jewish. If believers of today do not like engaging in their Jewish roots now, how are they going to enjoy them in the Kingdom? Actually, I encourage today's believers to embrace their shared Jewish roots. Once a Gentile believer receives Yeshua as their Lord, Savior, and Messiah, they are spiritually grafted into Israel and connected to the Jewish Messiah and His culture! The Jewish roots of the faith are all of ours to embrace and explore! I believe the more you know about your Jewish roots today, the more blessings and rewards you shall receive in the Kingdom.

Malachi 3:1–5

> 1 Behold, I am sending My messenger,
> and he will clear the way before Me.
> Suddenly He will come to His Temple
> —the Lord whom you seek—
> and the Messenger of the covenant
> —the One whom you desire—
> behold, He is coming,"
> says *ADONAI-Tzva'ot*.
> 2 But who can endure the day of His coming?
> Or who can stand when He appears?
> For He will be like a refiner's fire,
> and like soap for cleaning raw wool.
> 3 And He will sit as a smelter
> or a purifier of silver,
> and He will cleanse the sons of Levi,
> and purify them like gold or silver.
> Then they will become for *ADONAI*
> those who present an offering in righteousness.
> 4 Then the offering of Judah and Jerusalem will be pleasing to *ADONAI*,
> as in days of antiquity and years of old.
> 5 "Then I will draw near to you in judgment,
> and I will be a swift witness against
> sorcerers, adulterers, perjurers

those who extort a worker's wage,
or oppress the widow or an orphan,
those who mislead a stranger.
They do not fear Me,"
says *ADONAI-Tzva'ot.*

Malachi 3 is another Messianic passage that actually combines the First and Second Comings of Yeshua. In verse 1, the Lord proclaims that He will suddenly come to His Temple. This was fulfilled in Yeshua's First Coming. Then the context changes to the Second Coming.

In verses 2–3, the Lord is compared to the refiner's fire and the laundryman's soap. No one will be able to stand when He appears. This will be obvious when He completely destroys the enemies of the Jewish people. However, the refiner's fire and the laundryman's soap refer to purification. The Lord will purify the Levites so that they can offer the animal sacrificial system to the Lord in righteousness! This most certainly did not occur during Yeshua's First Coming, so it must be performed in His Second. The Levites will become righteous only by repenting and trusting in Yeshua as their Messiah. This will occur during the events of the Second Coming (although some Levites will be born again at the beginning of Jacob's Trouble, too).

When the Levites are purified, then their offerings will be pleasing unto the Lord (verse 4). The Lord will also purge the evil from the Land to start the Kingdom (verse 5). So, it is clear that the Lord will set up His "new and improved" Torah system, with the Levites helping the people to perform animal sacrifices in worship of the Lord. This perfectly falls in line with the Messianic Jewish aspects of the Kingdom presented thus far in this chapter.

Miraculous in the Messianic Millennial Kingdom

Not only is life and culture in the Kingdom going to be Jewish, but life will also be characterized by the miraculous. And why should it not be that way since the Lord Yeshua Himself will be ruling and reigning from His throne in His Temple in His Land of Israel. Therefore, we should expect God's miracles to abide with us!

Isaiah 4:4–6

> 4 After *ADONAI* has washed away the filth of the Daughters of Zion and has purged the blood of Jerusalem from her midst by the spirit of judgment and by the spirit of burning, 5 then *ADONAI* will create over the whole area of Mount Zion and over her convocations, a cloud by day, and smoke and shining of a flaming fire by night. For over all, glory will be a canopy. 6 Then there will be a *sukkah* [temporary booth] for shade by day from the heat, and for refuge and for shelter from storm and from rain.

After the Lord judges the evil of the Jewish people and cleans up the bloodshed of Jerusalem, He will create a new Temple Mount area (verses 4–5). Obviously, the Lord will build a new Temple for the Messianic Millennial Kingdom after the Armageddon War is cleaned up! But the Lord will miraculously cover this new Temple Mount compound with some type of canopy. This canopy will be like a cloud cover by day and a flaming fire cover by night! The idea here is to give the Jewish and Gentile people who live on or visit the Temple Mount shade from the heat of the day, shelter from the storms (verse 6), and light at night. God will provide the miraculous every day of the Kingdom!

This reminds me about how the Lord provided for the Jewish people in the desert for forty years. Exodus 13:21–22 states:

> ADONAI went before them in a pillar of cloud by day to lead the way and in a pillar of fire by night to give them light. So they could travel both day and night. The pillar of cloud by day and the pillar of fire by night never departed from the people.

It certainly seems like the Lord is creating the same type of cloud by day and fire by night over the whole assembly of the Temple Mount!

The only difference will be that this newly-created cloud covering will be a whole lot larger, and it is called a "canopy" in verse 5. The Hebrew word for "canopy" (*chuppah*) means "a covering or canopy." In Judaism, the *chuppah* is a covering for the bride and groom to stand under when they get married. The *chuppah* is typically adorned with beautiful flowers and decorations with a *tallit* (prayer shawl) as the covering on top. The *chuppah* acts as a wonderful symbol of the Lord who watches over and protects His people—especially when they engage in His covenantal institution of marriage! Isn't it interesting that the Lord chose to use the chuppah as our covering for the Temple Mount area? It will be the most beautiful *chuppah* ever created, and it will symbolize the Lord's covering over His newly wed, betrothed bride and wife!

We need to remember how big this newly created Temple Mount area is to truly grasp the greatness of this miracle! Ezekiel 48:20 speaks of the future Messianic Millennial Kingdom Temple Mount area: "*The whole allotment will be 25,000 by 25,000, square; you will set apart the holy allotment with the property of the city.*" It is interesting to note that there is no measurement standard in this verse. In actuality, we do not know the size of the allotment!

However, it has to be either cubits or reeds. Most scholars choose cubits since a cubit is believed to be approximately eighteen inches long and a reed is about ten feet long. If reed was intended, the Temple Mount area would be way too large for all the other Messianic Millennial Kingdom measurements found to be in cubits! So, the physical and textual context dictates this measurement is cubits. Calculating it out, the Temple Mount area would be about seven miles long by seven miles wide! Therefore, the chuppah has to cover the entire area of the Temple Mount area which equals forty-nine square miles. That is one humongous chuppah, Temple Mount area, and mountain as well! It will be *the* mountain of mountains in the world and the only mountain that the people of the world will go up to worship the Lord!

Zechariah 2:3–5

> 3 And behold, the angel who was speaking with me was going out, and another angel was coming out to meet him, 4 and said to him, "Run, speak to that young man, saying, 'Jerusalem will be inhabited without walls because of the multitude of men and cattle within it. 5 For I,' declares the Lord, 'will be a wall of fire around her, and I will be the glory in her midst.'"

Not only will there be a cloud and fire chuppah covering the Temple Mount area of forty-nine square miles, the Lord will manifest Himself in other ways as well. In verses 3–4, one angel orders another angel to tell Zechariah about the Messianic Millennial Kingdom in Jerusalem. The Jewish people will live in unwalled villages like the ancient Jewish people did. Why? The Lord's blessings of cattle and people will be so abundant that there will be no room for walls! Verse 5 reveals the Lord's declaration. He proclaims that He will be a wall of fire around the city of Jerusalem and the glory found in her midst! Although Yeshua will be sitting on His throne in His Temple in the middle of the priestly allotment (the Temple will not be located in the city of Jerusalem!), the Father will still create a miraculous physical manifestation on earth around and in Jerusalem.

A wall of fire will encircle the city of Jerusalem probably on a constant basis and the Lord's Shekinah Glory will radiate from the Temple! Now, the Shekinah Glory will be upon Yeshua as He enters the newly-built Messianic Millennial Kingdom Temple (see Ezekiel 43:1–5). The Shekinah Glory will fill the whole house of the Lord! As the glory fills the house, the Lord will also manifest His physical presence in the wall of fire around the city of Jerusalem. Can you picture in your mind a wall of fire around the city of Jerusalem?! How awesome would that be? What is its purpose? Well, for one, it reveals the miraculous power of the Lord. Two, there is a possibility this wall of fire will serve as a protective wall since it looks like there will not be any defensive fortification walls built around cities like in biblical times. How many evil folks will brave trying to go through this fiery wall, thinking they are going to attack or do any evil within the city? That would certainly be a foolish plan!

By the way, yes, there will be evil people in the Kingdom. This will be an unfortunate truth. It is hard to imagine the Lord manifesting Himself in miraculous ways with Yeshua sitting right there on His throne accessible to all people *and* there will be non-believers in the Kingdom! However, salvation has always been about repentance and faith. In Revelation 20:7–10, HaSatan, the devil, will be released from the pit after the 1,000 years of his judgment is up. He will then deceive the peoples of the nations to turn against the Lord Yeshua and muster up one final war against Him! These peoples are definitely evil non-believers living in the Kingdom, and they shall be harshly judged.

Chart

During the seventy-five-day interval, Yeshua will have plenty of time to prepare the world, the Land of Israel, and all the Jewish and Gentile believers for the Messianic Millennial Kingdom. This includes building and anointing the Temple for service. Many believers know that Yeshua, our Messiah, will rule and reign as King of the Jews over all the world for 1,000 literal years. He will rule in righteousness, peace, love, faithfulness, and justice. However, what many do not know is that He will reign in a Messianic Jewish way from His Davidic throne in the fourth Jewish Temple in the Jewish Messianic Millennial Kingdom.

If you haven't understood it yet, life in the Messianic Millennial Kingdom is going to be very Jewish! Kingdom worship will revolve around the Lord in His Temple. The Torah will go forth from Zion in the Kingdom. However, I believe it will be a "new and improved" Torah. Believers of the Kingdom will keep the shabbat, the feasts, and even the animal sacrifices. Confession of sin and animal sacrifices will be the norm for all the peoples of the earth. This will be a requirement for keeping fellowship with Yeshua. Jewish people and Jewish lifestyle will be held in high esteem during the Kingdom era. All the Jewish people will have salvation and it will certainly be miraculous! A miraculous chuppah will also cover the Temple Mount while a wall of fire will surround the city of Jerusalem. Living waters will flow from the Temple to the Dead and Mediterranean Seas. All life closest to this water will be greatly blessed. Yes, life on earth in the Kingdom will be awesome!

Prayer

Thank you, Lord, for your Word, which is your truth! The truth is, you will bless all believers with your future Messianic Millennial Kingdom. What a wonderful time this will be for the world and especially all believers who have resurrection bodies. I look forward to this glorious time of being in perfect harmony and fellowship with you and fulfilling your calling upon me to be a priest and king with you. Thank you so much for these great rewards, all for believing and trusting in Yeshua HaMeshiach! It is in His name I pray, Amen.

Chapter 18

THE ETERNAL KINGDOM

After the Lord completes His promises in the Abrahamic and Davidic Covenants through the 1,000 year Messianic Millennial Kingdom, will the end then come? Actually, the end of the Messianic Millennial Kingdom ushers in the Eternal Kingdom. However, there are still a few prophetic events in our history that need to occur before the end comes. One of them is entitled, "Gog and Magog II."

Gog and Magog II

After the Messianic Millennial Kingdom has ended, there is a mysterious amount of time afforded to HaSatan for one last roundup of the evil ones for one last war on Earth.

Revelation 20:7–10

> 7 When the thousand years has ended, satan shall be released from his prison, 8 and he shall come out to deceive the nations at the four corners of the earth, Gog and Magog, to gather them for the battle. Their number is like the sand of the sea. 9 And they came up on the broad plain of the earth and surrounded the camp of

the *kedoshim* and the beloved city—but fire fell from heaven and consumed them.
10 And the devil who deceived them was thrown into the lake of fire and brimstone, where the beast and the false prophet are too, and they shall be tortured day and night forever and ever.

This scripture reading starts off declaring that the 1,000 years of the Messianic Millennial Kingdom are completed (verse 7)! If the 1,000 year reign of Yeshua was a metaphor of time, then it would not have an actual completion date. Besides this, HaSatan is then released from the pit he was imprisoned in for 1,000 years, why would he be allowed to be released? The simplest answer would be that he did his time. The sentence for his crimes was exactly 1,000 years, the same amount of time allotted for Yeshua to rule His Kingdom. I believe the Lord wanted HaSatan and his evil ones out of the way for the full duration of the Kingdom age. Nobody during the Kingdom could then say that the devil made them do their evil! Once a prisoner does his time for his crime, he is set free. So HaSatan is set free after the 1,000 years has been served.

In addition, in verse 8, HaSatan will be allowed to do what he does best, which is deceive the nations to fight against Messiah Yeshua! The nations here refer to the Gentiles of the world. There will be no Jewish people fighting against Yeshua and Jerusalem since they will all become believers of Yeshua!

The "four corners of the earth" is a metaphor, meaning all over the earth (see Isaiah 11:12 as an example). Wherever there are evil people around the world, HaSatan will find them and gather them together for the war. The four corners of the earth are also called "Gog and Magog." Many believers get confused with this phrase since it is used for the first war of Gog and Magog! This first war, however, is the Ezekiel War where Russia and the confederacy attack Israel. If you look at the chart, I have the timing of Gog and Magog I occurring as the next prophetic event in Israel's history and prior to the Pre-Trib Rapture. This second Gog and Magog war is not the same war as the first one. This one includes peoples from all nations and occurs after the Messianic Millennial Kingdom. There is over 1,000 years that separate the two wars.

At the end of verse 8 we find out how successful HaSatan is with the world. He is able to gather together many evil people from the Kingdom. Their number is like the sands of the seashore! This means we are looking at millions or maybe billions of evil ones joining HaSatan in the final war of Jewish history. Is this possible to even have billions of people in the world? Yes, under optimal conditions starting out, it will be easy in the Messianic Millennial Kingdom, with millions of Jewish and Gentile people, to fulfill the Lord's original command to humankind to "*Be fruitful and multiply, and fill the land*" (Genesis 1:28).

What is really horrifying is that millions or billions of folks will once again be deceived by HaSatan. It truly amazes me that this many people will fall into the clutches of HaSatan once more. Just think about this, for 1,000 years Yeshua will sit as King of the world. Miracles, signs, and wonders are performed throughout the duration, and the world and its systems are completely transformed into godliness. Yet there will still be people that do not believe in Yeshua! The sin nature is very strong, and this is why I stated earlier that most of God's original curse is lifted in the Kingdom. The sin nature is the only piece of the curse that is left over from the earlier age (Body of Messiah and Tribulation Period ages). However, it seems to be a most powerful adversary to humankind!

In verse 9, we find out why the Lord uses the term "Gog and Magog" to describe this uprising against Yeshua and His holy ones. It is so similar to the first Gog and Magog war. Anti-Semitism is at the root of it. HaSatan hates Yeshua and the Jewish and Gentile believers so much that he recruits his army from around the world for one last war. Well, it's really not a war; it's more like a massacre! He is able to surround the camp of the holy ones and the city of Jerusalem. The camp here would be considered the whole Temple Mount area. This tells us he has a whole lot of evil ones with Him—to be able to surround forty-nine square miles of land! But the war is over even before it starts—fire comes down from the Lord in heaven and devours all the enemies! All of the verbal phrases in verse 9 are found to be in the indicative mood. This means, once again, that these assertions are positive and clear-cut statements meant to be taken literally and not figuratively. In the Lord's words, these events will literally take place in the future!

HaSatan's demise is not completed just because he loses this war (verse 10). He is then thrown into the Lake of Fire where his protégés, the beast and false prophet, are already living. They will be tormented all the time forever and ever. Sometimes I don't think we believers quite understand this point. People are going to be tortured for their sins in the Lake of Fire forever! They will experience complete anguish all the time without a break! This should spur us on to share the good news message of Yeshua with as many people as we can, for their destiny is a fiery tormented hell. This is God's perfect judgment for sin!

Chart

As we look at the chart, we can see question marks for the amount of time between the end of the Messianic Millennial Kingdom and the Gog and Magog II War. The Scripture does not give us any timeframe here. It simply says HaSatan is released from prison, deceives the nations, and gathers them for the war. This could take days, weeks, months, or even years. We just don't know. But until HaSatan is finally defeated, judged, and sentenced to the Lake of Fire, the Great White Throne Judgment will just have to wait.

The Great White Throne Judgment

Next on our prophetic calendar after HaSatan is defeated in the Gog and Magog II War and sent to the Lake of Fire for the rest of eternity, the Lord performs the Great White Throne Judgment.

Revelation 20:11–15

> 11 Then I saw a great white throne, and the One seated on it. The earth and heaven fled from His presence, but no place was found for them. 12 And I saw the dead—the great and the small—standing before the throne. The books were opened, and another book was opened—the Book of Life. And the dead were judged according to what was written in the books, according to their deeds. 13 The sea gave up the dead that were in it, and death and *Sheol* gave up the dead in them. Then they were each judged, each one of them, according to their deeds. 14 Then death and *Sheol* were thrown into the lake of fire. This is the second death—the lake of fire. 15 And if anyone was not found written in the Book of Life, he was thrown into the lake of fire.

The next scene we see in John's vision is of the Lord sitting on His Great White Throne (verse 11). This must have been a wonderful, awesome sight for John to behold! Only a few chosen have ever seen the beauty of the Lord and lived to tell about it! After HaSatan is judged, now the time will come for the Lord to judge everyone else from all time. White is symbolic for the Lord's purity and holiness. It also reveals the glory and majesty of the Lord. One day, all believers will truly be in awe of the Lord when we finally see Him!

Earth and heaven then fled away from the Lord's presence. I believe this refers to the burning up of the old earth and heaven written about in 2 Peter 3:10. Every physical object ever created will be burned up and destroyed with intense heat. This action reminds me of the splitting of atoms and how intense the heat and atomic blast can be. Everything in the billions of universes (there are literally billions of universes out there!) will be atomically split right up by the Lord! But we shall be set apart and protected in the area where the Lord's Great White Throne is located.

I wonder why the Lord would destroy His creation that originally He called "very good" in Genesis 1:31. Possibly it is because the earth and heaven have been defiled with sin. Humankind and the demonic forces of wickedness have certainly had their hands in this defilement. And even heaven has been defiled with HaSatan's presence as he has been allowed to go back and forth between heaven and earth and stand right before the Lord in heaven. So I guess the question to ask is "Why wouldn't the Lord want to start over with a new creation of heaven and earth that will never ever be defiled by sin again?" 2 Peter 3:13 seems to support this view. Righteousness will dwell in the newly created heaven and earth. This suggests that the prior heaven and earth did not have this complete righteousness but was somewhat defiled.

In verse 12, we see the judgment come down on all the evil ones. However, the Lord calls them "the dead." Scrolls are opened with one scroll being the Book of Life. This book has all the names of the believers of the Lord for all time written in it. This is the famous book that all Jewish people want their names written in during the feast of Yom Kippur!

Perplexing is the idea that the Lord will judge the dead by their deeds and not by their lack of faith! Certainly anyone's name that is not written in the Book of Life will be judged and sentenced to the Lake of Fire (verse 15). So why does the Lord judge their works instead at the Bema Seat? I believe it's to show these evil ones that their deeds are truly evil in His sight! I think many folks around the world do not know that what they do is truly evil—they are deceived by HaSatan and do what is good in their own sight like the Israelites did in the Tenach. Here at the Judgment Seat, they will truly understand what true holiness, righteousness, and justice is. I also believe the Lord is revealing the number and gravity of their sins to determine the degree of punishment. Remember, there are differing degrees of punishment in the Lake of Fire. Those who perform great evil will have great punishment thrust upon them. HaSatan will have the highest degree of punishment.

Daniel had a similar vision of the Lord to John's. In Daniel 7:9–10, he actually saw the physical manifestation of the Father in this vision and he called Him "the Ancient of Days." He is seated at His throne in heaven. His robe and hair are pure white in color and His throne is surrounded by fire. Actually, there was a river of fire flowing from before Him! Millions of angels were ministering to Him. In verse 10, we see the full picture of the Lord sitting on His throne in His heavenly courtroom, judging the billions of people at the Great White Throne Judgment. The scrolls that contained the evil deeds of the evil ones were opened! Judgment is imminent.

Verse 13 (of Revelation 20) clarifies that all the dead people throughout all time will come before the Judgment Seat. No one will be able to slip away and not be judged. Those who have died at sea and those who are found in Sheol (hell) will be judged according to their evil deeds. It is fascinating to see that no one needs to worry about the bodies of those who drowned at sea, are buried, or are cremated. The Lord knows how to put them all back together again. He created humans from the earth, so it should not be an issue for Him to piece us together again at the appropriate time. We can have peace about the piecing-together issue!

Death and Sheol will be thrown into the Lake of Fire (verse 14). This means that there will be no more death in God's Eternal Kingdom, and there will no longer be people sent to hell. The Lake of Fire is the second death for all people and is the final judgment of humankind. There will be no more judgments after this! If anyone's name is not found in the Book of Life, then they will be judged by the Lord and sentenced to eternity in the Lake of Fire (verse 15)!

Most people of the world, including the Jewish people, think they are good enough to make it to heaven. They believe they have performed enough good deeds to outweigh their bad sins, and God will forgive them because they are good folks. Well, this is not how the Lord is going to judge! His judgments are perfect, holy, righteous, and just. He expects perfection from His people. When we are not perfect and we sin against Him and His commandments, then He says He will judge those sins. The judgment is a harsh judgment of separation in the Lake of Fire forever! However, there is good news!

This is the very reason why Yeshua, God's Son, was sent 2,000 years ago. He took the penalty and judgment for our sins upon Himself as our blood sacrifice so that the Father could forgive us of all of our sins and give us eternal life with Him. Yeshua also resurrected from the dead to show all "the dead" people of the world that He is God and He has the power to resurrect from the dead. He will execute that power at the Rapture and during the seventy-five-day interval upon all His believers! So that's the key, one must repent from their sinful lifestyle, believe and trust in Yeshua as their Lord, Savior, and Messiah so that their names can be written in the Book of Life and have eternal life with the Lord in the New Jerusalem! If you are not a believer in Yeshua at this moment, then I exhort you to accept and receive Yeshua immediately, before it's too late! Once we die, there are no second chances. Hebrews 9:27 tells us that it is appointed for humankind to die once and then the judgment.

The Introduction of the New Jerusalem

After the Lord summarizes the major events of Messiah's 1,000-year reign and the Great White Throne Judgment, He introduces the holy city, the New Jerusalem. Many believers think heaven is their future eternal home, but this would be wrong! Heaven is not our eternal home, although I'm sure we shall be able to visit heaven. Our eternal home will be in the New Jerusalem on the newly-created Earth!

Revelation 21:1–8

> 1 Then I saw a new heaven and a new earth; for the first heaven and the first earth had passed away, and the sea was no more.
> 2 I also saw the holy city—the New Jerusalem—coming down out of heaven from God, prepared as a bride adorned for her husband. 3 I also heard a loud voice from the throne, saying,
> "Behold, the dwelling of God is among men,
> and He shall tabernacle among them.
> They shall be His people,
> and God Himself shall be among them
> and be their God.
> 4 He shall wipe away every tear from their eyes,
> and death shall be no more.
> Nor shall there be mourning or crying
> or pain any longer,
> for the former things
> have passed away."
> 5 And the One seated upon the throne said, "Behold, I am making all things new!" Then He said, "Write, for these words are trustworthy and true."
> 6 Then He said to me, "It is done! I am the Alpha and the Omega, the Beginning and the End. To the thirsty

> I will freely give from the spring of the water of life. 7 The one who overcomes shall inherit these things, and I will be his God and he shall be My son. 8 But for the cowardly and faithless and detestable and murderers and sexually immoral and sorcerers and idolaters and all liars—their lot is in the lake that burns with fire and brimstone, which is the second death."

In verse 1, John reports that he saw a new heaven and new earth. John does not say this new heaven and earth were created. However, I believe he does infer this because the first heaven and first earth "passed away." "Passed away" (*parerchomai*) translates to things coming to an end or perishing. Combined with Isaiah 65:17, we know these new heavens and new earth are created holy, righteous, and specifically just for eternity! Peter also spoke of this new creation (2 Peter 3:13). So the old passes away and perishes while the new is created and lives forever.

Fascinating is the fact that there will be no more sea on the new earth (verse 1). This would suggest that there will be no need for oceans, seas, lakes, rain, or even clouds. It seems that the current worldwide weather system will be absent in eternity. Why? The Lord will have the River of Life flowing from His throne down the middle of the New Jerusalem (Revelation 22:1–2). This will be the only water necessary in the Eternal Kingdom.

The holy city, the New Jerusalem, comes down from heaven after the Lord creates the new heavens and earth (verse 2). The New Jerusalem is holy as opposed to the Jerusalem of Jacob's Trouble. In Revelation 11:8, that Jerusalem is called "Sodom." This reveals how spiritually bad the city is going to get!

Abraham was looking for this city of God, the New Jerusalem. Hebrews 11:10 states, "*For he was waiting for the city that has foundations, whose architect and builder is God.*" Hebrews 12:22–24 also shows us who will be living in the New Jerusalem. God's angels, New Covenant believers, Mosaic Covenant believers, Yeshua, and the Father Himself will all live in this city of God!

The New Jerusalem was made beautiful like a bride ready for her groom (verse 2). I believe this refers to Yeshua's promise in John 14:3 that He would return to heaven to prepare a place for the talmidim (disciples). I think He was speaking of His work on the New Jerusalem where the raptured Body of Messiah would live during Jacob's Trouble and all believers of all time would live in the Eternal Kingdom.

The reason for the New Jerusalem coming down to the newly created Earth from heaven is answered in verse 3. The New Jerusalem is the Lord's Tabernacle (home), and He is going to dwell among us! "Dwell" (*skenoo*) means to live or tabernacle. The Lord will tabernacle among His people, and He Himself will live with us! It is clear that the Father Himself will live with His people, and we shall see Him face to face. What is interesting to note is that the Father only descends from heaven to the New Jerusalem after all evil is judged at the Great White Throne. There will not be any sin in the Eternal Kingdom on Earth! This Kingdom will be characterized by holiness, righteousness, purity, justice, faithfulness, and sinlessness—a perfect place for the Father Himself to tabernacle!

Verse 4 tells us that the Lord's curse of Genesis 3 will now be completely lifted. There will be no more pain, mourning, or death. God's chosen will not even cry! Life will be filled with God's peace, love, and grace. So by the time of the Eternal Kingdom, the sin nature in humankind will be completely eradicated! Humankind will never be able to sin again. God's promise is to make eternal life on earth completely new (verse 5). The Lord proclaims this is a done deal and that His words are faithful and true.

How do we know for sure this will happen? He is the Alpha and the Omega, the beginning and the end. He is the One who is in control of the whole creation and does as He wants with it! And He wants to give the free Water of Life to all His thirsty children (verse 6). All who overcome the trials and tribulations of life will inherit these wonderful promises of God as great rewards in eternity (verse 7). Overcomers are believers who live by their faith in Yeshua (1 John 5:4). Then the Lord reiterates His promise given to Moses and the Jewish people from long ago. He proclaims to Jewish and Gentile overcomers that He will finally be their God, and they shall finally be His people (verse 7)! This section ends with a resounding judgment against all non-believers in Yeshua (verse 8). These evil ones will be tormented for their evil for eternity in the lake of fire and brimstone.

The Description of the New Jerusalem

The New Jerusalem is unequivocally the greatest, biggest, most beautiful city ever created by God! In this section, we shall see an angel's description of the holy city.

Revelation 21:9–21

> 9 Then came one of the seven angels holding the seven bowls full of the seven final plagues, and he spoke with me, saying, "Come, I will show you the bride, the wife of the Lamb."
> 10 Then he carried me away in the *Ruach* to a great and high mountain, and he showed me the holy city, Jerusalem, coming down out of heaven from God, 11 having the glory of God—her radiance like a most precious stone, like a jasper, sparkling like crystal. 12 She had a great, high wall, with twelve gates, and above the gates twelve angels. On the gates were inscribed the names of the twelve tribes of *Bnei-Yisrael*—13 three gates on the east, three gates on the north, three gates on the south, and three gates on the west. 14 And the

wall of the city had twelve foundations, and on them the twelve names of the twelve emissaries of the Lamb. 15 The angel speaking with me had a gold measuring rod to measure the city and its gates and walls. 16 The city is laid out as a square—its length the same as its width. He measured the city with the rod—12,000 stadia. Its length and width and height are equal. 17 He also measured its wall—144 cubits by human measurement, which is also an angel's measurement. 18 The material of the city's wall was jasper, while the city was pure gold, clear as glass. 19 The foundations of the city wall were decorated with every kind of precious stone—the first foundation was jasper; the second, sapphire; the third, chalcedony; the fourth, emerald; 20 the fifth, sardonyx; the sixth, carnelian; the seventh, yellow topaz; the eighth; beryl; the ninth, topaz; the tenth, chrysoprase; the eleventh, jacinth; the twelfth, amethyst. 21 And the twelve gates were twelve pearls—each of the gates was from a single pearl. And the street of the city was pure gold, transparent as glass.

One of the seven angels who poured out his bowl in Jacob's Trouble is now the one speaking with John (verse 9). The New Jerusalem is described as the bride and wife of the Lamb! This is an obvious metaphor as the bride and wife of the Lamb are believers found in the Body of Messiah from the time of the death and resurrection of Yeshua until the Rapture. In the Bible, cities were often identified by their inhabitants (i.e., Yeshua in Matthew 23:37–39). I believe this is what this angel is doing here in verse 9.

This is the second time in Revelation that the bride of Messiah is called the "wife" of Messiah. Although it sounds peculiar, it is not! By this time, the bride of Messiah has become the wife of Messiah! Actually, the bride became the wife at the wedding ceremony in heaven after the Rapture and just prior to the Second Coming (Revelation 19:7). To conclude this verse, the bride of Messiah (the Body of Messiah) will live in the bride of Messiah (the New Jerusalem)!

Next, the angel carries John to a great and high mountain where the New Jerusalem will land as it descends from heaven (verse 10). This Temple Mount will be the highest mountain on Earth as the believers of the world will always have to "go up" the mountain of the Lord to worship Him! The New Jerusalem will be distinguished by the Shekinah Glory of the Lord (verse 11). The New Jerusalem reflects all the luminosity of the Lord—His light will shine bright! The Shekinah Glory will illuminate the Temple in the Messianic Millennial Kingdom (Ezekiel 45:1–5), and the Shekinah Glory will illuminate the New Jerusalem in eternity.

The New Jerusalem is characterized with tall walls that include a total of twelve gates (verse 12). The gates will be used for entering and exiting the city. Each gate is named after one of the original twelve tribes of the sons of Israel. Each of the sons of Jacob will have a great honor from the Lord for eternity! Twelve angels will be guards over the twelve gates.

Each wall (north, south, east, and west) of the city will have three gates (verse 13). This shows the city is laid out as a square. The wall of the city not only has twelve gates but twelve foundation stones as well (verse 14). Typically, only one foundation stone is laid when building the Temple, but here we see twelve foundation stones for the walls. Why do we see twelve? The Lord also wants to honor the twelve apostles of Yeshua for eternity! Foundation stones emphasize strength and permanence. The strength of the Body of Messiah was laid with, first of all, the Messiah, and then the twelve apostles. The Lord's New Jerusalem will obviously be a strong and permanent city—it will last for a long time!

The angel had a gold measuring rod to measure all aspects of the city (verse 15). This "rod" (*kalamos*) in the ancient world was typically a reed grown in water and used as a common measuring tool about ten feet long. The New Jerusalem is laid out as a "square" (*tetragonos*), much like many of today's cities around the world (verse 16). Tetragonos actually means "four squares, four corners or angles." The idea here is that the base of the city is laid out as a square with four corners!

Some believe the city is a sphere or pyramid. However, the Greek construction of the verse reveals it is a cube. First, the length and width are equal, and they have four corners. Second, the height of the city is added at the end of the verse, and it is equal with the length and width. This suggests the height of the city is taken from all four corners. This confirms the city of Jerusalem is cube-shaped.

The length, width, and height of the city is 12,000 stadia. In many English Bibles the phrase "fifteen hundred miles" is used. A "stadia" is about 600 feet long. So the total comes out to be about 1,363.63 miles (the translators of English Bibles probably used an English furlong equaling 660 feet, which would then equal 1,500 miles). In verse 17, the height of the outside wall of the city is declared to be "144 cubits." If the cubit is eighteen inches, then 144 cubits equals seventy-two yards. That's one tall wall! It is interesting to know that man's measurements are the same as angelic measurements. Despite all the differences in measurements, I believe the idea the Lord wants to bring across to all of us believers is that the New Jerusalem is going to be humongous! If anyone was worried about how the Lord would fit all of us into the city, these measurements should put you at ease!

Not only is our eternal home huge, but it is absolutely beautiful! Verse 18 begins the stunningly gorgeous description. The wall of the city is made out of jasper, a green-colored stone. The city is made out of pure gold that is somehow see-through like glass. Can you imagine a whole cubed city 1,363 miles long being totally made of pure see-through gold? In verses 19–20, we are told the twelve foundation stones of the city wall are made out of twelve precious stones. Interestingly, the twelve apostles have different stones (some of the stones are the same) than the twelve tribes' stones used for the *cohen gadol's* (high priest) breastplate (Exodus 28:17–20). Jasper is green, sapphire is blue, chalcedony is a greenish color, emerald is green, sardonyx is red and white, carnelian is a fiery red, yellow topaz is a golden yellow, beryl is aqua green, topaz is a greenish yellow, chrysoprase is a golden green, jacinth is violet, and amethyst is purple, too. From what we know about these ancient stones, there is going to be a lot of greenish colors in eternity!

Since the wall of the city is seventy-two yards high, it would make sense that the pearly gates were seventy-two yards high as well. The fascinating idea here is that each gate is not made out of a plurality of pearls but actually only one pearl (verse 21). It is a gigantic pearl! The street of the city is made out of transparent gold just like the city. It is amazing that there is only one street that we know of since the Greek word here is found in the singular. That will certainly be one long street!

Revelation 21:22–27

> 22 I saw no temple in her, for its Temple is *ADONAI Elohei-Tzva'ot* and the Lamb. 23 And the city has no need for the sun or the moon to shine on it, for the glory of God lights it up, and its lamp is the Lamb. 24 The nations shall walk by its light, and the kings of the earth bring their glory into it. 25 Its gates shall never be shut by day, for there shall be no night there! 26 And they shall bring into it the glory and honor of the nations. 27 And nothing unholy shall ever enter it, nor anyone doing what is detestable or false, but only those written in the Book of Life.

In this passage, we see the Eternal Kingdom has no Temple, sun or moon. There is truly no need for them. Verse 22 tells us there is no Temple in the New Jerusalem. Why? The Lord God and the Lamb are the Temple! As the Father and Son sit on their throne ruling and reigning forever, there is no need for them to be enclosed in a temple. It's funny to think that after all this Jewish history where the Lord had Israel build the Tabernacle and four temples for Him to dwell in, there will be no temple in eternity. The Lord truly could never be restricted to a building structure! This, then, makes sense that the Lord does not want to be confined inside a temple as He rules and reigns for eternity because truly He is the Temple!

In verse 23, we find an unusual situation for the new creation. There is no need for the sun and moon to shine on the New Jerusalem. It actually does not say there is no sun or moon but that there is no need for their light. It is assumed, however, that the sun and moon are not re-created in the new heavens and earth since there is no need for them! This, too, is unusual since in the beginning of creation there was a sun and moon. However, in the beginning creation, the sun and moon were not created until the fourth day and yet there was light already in existence (see Genesis 1:3; 1:14). The light created here before the sun and moon was of course the Shekinah Glory!

Why is there no need for the sun and moon in the Eternal Kingdom? The glory of God will be all the light that the new earth will need. The glory of God is the Shekinah Glory that will radiate from Yeshua, the lamp and Lamb of God! Yeshua came the first time to reveal the light of the Father, and of course, was the light of the world. In eternity, He will physically be wearing the Shekinah Glory and shine the glory of God forever!

The Shekinah Glory will be the only light around the world that believers will need to see (verse 24). What is interesting is that the world will be divided up into nations with kings as their leaders. These kings will bring the glory and honor of their nations to the New Jerusalem (verses 24–26). Presumably, this would occur on the Feasts of the Lord, when the nations would travel to the New Jerusalem to worship the Lord! It is interesting to note that the mention of the nations or Gentiles shows the distinction between Jew and Gentile will be forever, and yet we know there is no functional difference between the two groups in the Eternal Kingdom. We are all equal before the Lord and equally loved by the Lord!

The New Jerusalem will also not have any nighttime, just daytime. This makes sense since the Shekinah Glory will always shine. There will be no need for night. The gates of the city will always be open, too. Verse 27 tells us that nothing unclean and no evil people will defile it or even enter the New Jerusalem! It is actually impossible for evil people to enter it since they have all been judged and sentenced to the Lake of Fire. The point here is to show that no person nor any sin will defile the New Jerusalem; it will surely be a perfect, pure Kingdom forever! Only believers who are found in the Lamb's Book of Life are allowed to enter the New Jerusalem! The Lamb's Book of Life has to be the same as the Father's Book of Life discussed by Moses in Exodus 32:32–33. It has to be the same since all believers for all time will be allowed into the New Jerusalem. This means all the names of believers from the Old Covenant and New Covenant are found in the Lamb's Book of Life!

Revelation 22:1–5

> 1 Then the angel showed me a river of the water of life—bright as crystal, flowing from the throne of God and of the Lamb 2 down the middle of the city's street. On either side of the river was a tree of life, bearing twelve kinds of fruit, yielding its fruit each month; and the leaves of the tree were for the healing of the nations. 3 No longer will there be any curse. The throne of God and of the Lamb shall be in the city, and His servants shall serve Him. 4 They shall see His face, and His

> name shall be on their foreheads. 5 Night shall be no more, and people will have no need for lamplight or sunlight—for *ADONAI Elohim* will shine on them. And they shall reign forever and ever!

Besides the New Jerusalem being adorned in beautiful gold and jewels, it will have the River of Life flowing from the Lord's throne (verse 1). This river will be the most purest, clearest, and brightest water that the Lord has ever created. It is probably very similar to the River of Life in the Messianic Millennial Kingdom. The River of Life flows from the throne of God, presumably throughout the whole city area. It is important to remember that Yeshua is still on the throne in the Eternal Kingdom despite giving the Messianic Millennial Kingdom back to the Father. Since "throne" is in the singular, the Father and the Son are going to rule from one throne together. This shows that the Father and Son are co-equal as God and King of the Eternal Kingdom!

In verse 2, the River of Life that is clear as crystal will run down the middle of the New Jerusalem's street. How far the street goes is unknown. What we do know is that the Tree of Life grows on either side of the river. It is possible that this tree is the original Tree of Life. However, it is more probable that this is a new Tree of Life for the New Jerusalem. The Tree of Life is found to be a singular noun, and yet it is located on both sides of the river. Either there are multiple trees on both sides of the river or one large tree with its trunk extending to both sides of the river while the river flows through it.

The singular suggests one large Tree of Life. I believe the Tree of Life is very large because the New Jerusalem is very large! And the Tree of Life will be supplying fruit and leaves for the billions of believers living in the New Jerusalem—it needs to be humongous! I would imagine the Tree of Life will be enormous, the largest, biggest tree in the Kingdom. It will probably be many hundreds of miles tall. If the city of Jerusalem is 1,363 miles high, then a Tree of Life only hundreds of miles tall would be considered small!

As you can see, verse 2 is packed full of valuable information about the Eternal Kingdom. And there is more. The Tree of Life will bear twelve kinds of fruit each month in the Kingdom. First, "months" are mentioned, so this reveals there will be some sort of system of time. We've already established that there will probably not be any sun or moon needed for light. However, there is time! Maybe the one purpose for having a sun and moon would be solely for telling time! However, it's more probable that there will be no sun or moon, and the Lord will create a new system of telling time.

Second, believers will be eating the fruit of the Tree of Life. But why? In Genesis 3:22, we find out that if Adam and Eve were to eat of the tree of life then they would have lived forever. So it seems that, although we have eternal life in Yeshua, the fruit of the Tree of Life will somehow help sustain that eternal life forever! Besides, I believe this will be the very best-tasting fruit ever, and we shall desire to eat of the fruit that God provides!

Third, the Tree of Life will also supply leaves for the healing of nations. If we as believers already have eternal life, then why do we need leaves for healing? What are we going to need healing from? "Healing" (*therapeian*) actually means healing and health. Since there is no longer any sickness or death, it seems the leaves will be used to somehow help keep believers healthy for eternity. Believers having to somehow eat fruit and consume leaves for eternal health and maintenance is certainly mysterious, especially in view of verse 3!

God's curse placed upon all of humankind because of Adam and Eve's sin is finally and completely lifted (verse 3). Remember, in the Messianic Millennial Kingdom, the curse was mostly lifted except for the sin nature from humankind. In the Eternal Kingdom, there is no more sin nature, no more sin, no more death and no more curse!

Even though there is no temple in the Eternal Kingdom because the Lord is the temple, there will be a throne (verse 3). This is the second time we see God's throne found in the singular (see 22:1). Both God the Father and the Lamb, God the Son, will sit on their one throne and rule in the New Jerusalem for all eternity!

Many believers ask me the question, "What are we going to be doing for eternity?" Verse 3 partly answers the question. We and all the believers from history will be serving the Lord! Daniel 7:14 verifies that all the peoples of the earth from all time who make it to the Eternal Kingdom shall serve the Lord forever. Exactly how we shall serve the Lord for eternity is not mentioned here, but we shall serve Him and get to see Him face to face (verse 4)! Now that will be exciting! To be able to see the Lord face to face, we would have to have our resurrection bodies. Otherwise, we would instantly die (Exodus 33:20). The Lord will also put His name on our foreheads. Whether the name is YHVH or Yeshua, we don't know for sure. Maybe it will be both! In either event, the Lord shall mark us as His own bond-servants forever, much like the 144,000 Jewish believers of Yeshua were sealed or marked on their foreheads for the seven years of Jacob's Trouble (Revelation 7:3–4).

What else will we be doing in the Eternal Kingdom? Verse 5 says we shall be reigning with God and the Lamb forever and ever! Reigning over who or what, we are not told. It is possible we shall be reigning over nations since it is mentioned in verse 2. There must be some sort of organizational system concerning the whole world, and believers will be reigning in it. I cannot tell you how excited I am about our future. All believers are going to be serving the Lord and reigning with the Lord for eternity. To be face to face with God is going to be an awesome time that truly cannot be described in this world.

The Eternal Kingdom will also be filled with the light of the Lord (verse 5). There will be no need for a lamp or a sun and there will be no darkness or night. There will only be light. The Shekinah Glory shall shine throughout the New Jerusalem and presumably the entire new creation of the heavens too. Wherever we are allowed to travel to, that's where the Lord's light will shine as well. And isn't this poetic justice, once HaSatan and his darkness are judged to the Lake of Fire, God's light will shine everywhere! We can rest assured that we shall be worshiping the Lord, loving the Lord, and basking in His Shekinah Glory for all eternity!

Chart

In looking at the chart, I believe the Eternal Kingdom technically begins after the Great White Throne Judgment and right when the new heavens and earth are created. It makes sense that this is true since the Eternal Kingdom can never be defiled with sin. Therefore, sin has to be dealt with at the Great White Throne Judgment before the new creation. The only place in the new creation where sin and evil will ravage will be in the Lake of Fire. But it will definitely be confined there.

After the Messianic Millennial Kingdom is finished, HaSatan will be allowed out of his prison for a short time. He will scavenge the Earth looking for evil people to participate in one last plot against Yeshua and the believers. Before they can war against the city of Jerusalem, the Lord in heaven rains down fire from heaven and devours them. The Great White Throne Judgment is next where the Lord judges all non-believers for their works. Every one of them has evil deeds in their lives, and every single one of them is sent to the Lake of Fire for eternal judgment. The Lake of Fire is a horrible, terrible place of torment for these evil ones. It is dark and ugly, and the people are burning up in fire for eternity.

After this judgment is over, the New Jerusalem is brought down from the new heaven to the new earth. Although technically the beginning of eternity may be with the creation of the new heaven and earth, I think the celebration of the beginning of eternity will occur when the New Jerusalem comes down from heaven to earth. The New Jerusalem is our heavenly home on earth for all time. All believers throughout time will have a home in the New Jerusalem. It is a glorious city and probably the greatest creation (outside of humankind) of the Lord's. We will be able to go out and come in as we are led by the Lord. It will be a city where God the Father and God the Son will dwell. There will be no temple, with no need for sun or moon, but there will be the Lord's light, the Shekinah Glory, everywhere. We shall also drink from the River of Life and eat from the Tree of Life. God will provide for our every need—physical, emotional, and spiritual for eternity. And best of all we shall see the Lord Himself face to face!

Prayer

Lord, I pray for all the people of the world at this time for their salvation. I pray You will send them trustworthy people who will share with them the good news message of Yeshua, so they can be saved. Help them to see the truth of Yeshua and the truth of the final judgment of the Lake of Fire. Truly, no one wants to go to the hellfire of the Lake of Fire and be tormented forever. However, the only way to escape from this judgment is to believe and trust in Yeshua as our Messiah, Lord, and Savior. Help the Jewish and Gentile people of the world see this light before it is too late.

Thank you, Lord, for your Eternal Kingdom and the wonderful rewards you will give to all believers throughout time. Living with you in the New Jerusalem with definitely be awe-inspiring. Thank you for our eternal home existing on the new earth. And thank you for the blessings you will provide in eternity. I am looking forward to this time where there will be no sin, no curse, constant fellowship with you, and constant experience of your love, joy, and peace for all time. I pray in the mighty name of Yeshua HaMeshiach, Jesus the Messiah, Amen!

Chapter 19

SUMMARY

Israel in prophecy is perhaps the most misunderstood theology in the Body of Messiah. Most believers do not know that most prophecy revolves around the tiny nation of the Jewish people—Israel! God made many promises to the Jewish people a long time ago and still has to fulfill many of them. Ultimately, much of this Jewish prophecy will culminate in the Messianic Millennial Kingdom. However, before we summarize the future of Israel, we need to understand the past of Israel. Why? Knowing the past helps us to understand the why of the present and future.

Israel today has been greatly affected by Israel in the past. There has always been animosity against Israel even from the beginning when God called Abraham. God made promises to Abraham and the Jewish people, and HaSatan did not like it. This is the bigger picture of all the hatred toward the Jewish people. God loves the Jewish people, and HaSatan therefore hates them and empowers people to hate them as well. This is exactly what we see in Israel's history—many nations and people hating them and warring against them. We see in the Scriptures that most of the nations surrounding Israel throughout her history warred against her in some time or another.

Then Psalm 83 reveals Arab, Persian, and Muslim nations in a constant attack of war against Israel. This psalm not only reveals their intentions but their heart of hatred toward the Jewish people. These nations conspire together in their plans to completely wipe out the Jewish people. They not only want to destroy Israel, they also want to wipe out any memory of her! This evil desire to wipe out the Jewish people from existence continues through to the present day and will continue into the future. There is no biblical reason to think that any of these nations will change their worldview. Although this is true, we must remember that Scripture reveals that nations have a hatred toward Israel. It does not mean that every single citizen hates the Jewish people. When the Lord mentions nations, He is speaking about the leadership and most of the people, not all of the people. There are many folks around the world who do not hate the Jewish people.

This evil is not just confined to the Arab, Persian, and Muslim nations. It has spread around the world, fueled by HaSatan. This hatred will soon manifest in one of the world's superpowers—Russia.

The next Israeli prophetic event that I believe will occur is the Ezekiel War. This is where a confederate group of nations will attack Israel with the goal of stealing all of Israel's goods. Ezekiel identifies only five nations involved with this confederacy: Russia, Iran, Sudan, Libya, and Turkey. This Ezekiel War is not the Armageddon War many believers think will occur at the end of Jacob's Trouble. Nor is it the world war that occurs during the first half of Jacob's Trouble. Rather it is a war that the Bible clearly reveals could occur at any time in the present. It is interesting to note that the Lord says their goal is to plunder Israel, not necessarily to try to destroy and annihilate all the Jewish people (although many Jewish people will certainly die in this war).

The Ezekiel War does not end with human intervention. Scripture shows that neither the United States nor any other country will come to Israel's defense. This idea was highly expected and greatly feared under President Obama's administration, but is far less likely under President Trump. Only the Lord Himself, as He enters into human history, will bring an end to the war. The devastation to the confederacy armies will be massive, but the destruction of their homelands will be even more shocking.

The effects of the present Israel-Arab wars and the Ezekiel War will be fascinating to watch. I believe we'll see the world dramatically change its mind concerning Israel. Can you imagine the looks on people's faces around the world when they actually see the judgment cast by the Lord on these five nations? The judgment of God will probably help the world to usher in the one-world government. And why not? They may be thinking: "Israel's God just destroyed all who attacked her, and maybe this God wants to attack us, too. So we shall need to have a one-world government to appease Israel's God and bring peace to the world." The world will also be talking of having a peace treaty with Israel. I believe we shall also see an increase of the Jewish people making *aliyah* to Israel. They will certainly have a great desire and right to build the third Temple. Some of these effects will run right up to the middle of Jacob's Trouble.

After the Ezekiel War, the One-World Order will come about. The Bible does not give us a timeframe in how long it will take, but it certainly seems that it will not happen overnight! The wheels of the political system turn slowly. However, the demand from the people of the world will be great, and the politicians will have to act! Sometime after the one-world government is formed, it will be broken up into ten kingdoms. Daniel makes this abundantly clear that the ten kingdoms encompass the whole world, not just a small region like the European Union (EU). Many believers erroneously think that today's EU comprises the ten kingdoms of Daniel.

Once the ten kingdoms are created and thrive in the world, the Anti-messiah will begin to rise to power. The Anti-messiah may have already been involved with the world's political system, but his rise to power comes after the ten-kingdom system is in place. Sometime after the Ezekiel War and probably during the creation of the One-World Order and the ten kingdoms, the greatest event in the Body of Messiah's history occurs!

This event is the Pre-Trib Rapture where all believers in Yeshua will be snatched up from this Earth and will meet the Lord in the clouds. We shall then enter heaven with Yeshua, and thus we shall evermore be with Him. Wherever He goes, we shall go with Him. The Rapture will occur sometime before Jacob's Trouble begins. We do not know how long before, but we do know it is before. That's why it is called "pre," which means "before." The Pre-Trib Rapture also ends the age of the Body of Messiah. The Body of Messiah age began on the Feast of Shavuot (Pentecost) almost 2,000 years ago, and it will end at the Pre-Trib Rapture.

However, we must remember that although there are many spiritual connections between the Rapture and the Feast of Trumpets, the Rapture is most definitely imminent. This means the Rapture could occur at any time. When the Rapture does occur, the world will be in shock. Many millions of believers around the world will instantly vanish into thin air! Where did they go? Conspiracy theories will crop up all over the place, and the Anti-messiah, most likely, will have the answer the world is waiting for. Whatever his answer, the point to be made here is that some people of the world will not be duped by HaSatan and will know the truth. This truth will set them free! Instantly and around the world, people will be turning to Yeshua as their Messiah, Lord and Savior.

Sometime after the Pre-Trib Rapture, the Anti-messiah will sign a peace treaty with Israel on behalf of the world. Again, we do not know how many days after the Rapture it will take to sign this treaty. It is also possible, but highly improbable, that the Rapture will occur on the day of the signing. The signing of the peace treaty begins Daniel's final seventieth week, the last seven-year period for Israel, Jerusalem, and the Jewish people. Seven years to the day after the signing of the treaty will be the end. I know this sounds simplistic, but it needs to be stated. Many believers ask me when the end of the seven-year Tribulation Period occurs. It will be exactly seven Jewish years after the signing of the peace treaty between Anti-messiah and Israel. The Bible gives us no event that marks the ending of Jacob's Trouble other than the timing of this seven years!

Many believers think Jacob's Trouble is characterized by three and a half years of peace in the first half of the Tribulation and then three and a half years of God's judgment in the second half. This couldn't be further from biblical truth! God's judgment and wrath upon Israel and the world occurs throughout the entire seven-year period! By the fourth seal of Revelation 6, 25 percent of the world's population will die—that's one-fourth of the world's population. In numbers, that means about 2 billion people around the world will die in the first half of Jacob's Trouble. How can anyone think there will be peace in the first half or that this is not God's judgment upon humankind? In addition to all of this are all the wars, rumors of wars, famines and earthquakes. All of these will occur in great numbers around the world. Again, how can any believer think the Lord is not pouring out His wrath on the world in this whole timeframe?

Now, it is certainly possible that the nation of Israel has some pseudo-peace in the first half of Jacob's Trouble. This is the reason for signing the peace treaty in the first place. But, this peace is more a lack of war with Israel's enemies than true peace! However, we noted from our study that Jewish and Gentile believers around the world will die for their faith in Yeshua at the hands of the one-world religion during the first half of the Tribulation.

During the first half of Jacob's Trouble, God will work His plan for Israel. First, Israel will be regathered to the Land of Israel. This regathering process will continue through to "mid-trib." Second, the Lord will judge Israel. This judgment will be wrought at the hands of the one-world religion in the first half of the tribulation toward Messianic Jews and the Anti-messiah in the second half toward all Jewish people. Third, the Lord will save Israel. He will save the one-third of the Jewish people who make it through the Tribulation Period alive. They will all be saved toward the end of Jacob's Trouble. Fourth, the Lord will properly restore Israel back to the Land of Israel. This restoration process will occur after Yeshua's Second Coming.

God not only will work His salvation plan for the nation of Israel, He also will chose 144,000 individual Jewish people to be saved at the beginning of Jacob's Trouble. These 144,000 Jewish men will be miraculously saved, become sealed servants of the Lord, and preach the good news message of Yeshua to the world. Israel will also see the two Jewish witnesses preach in the city of Jerusalem. They will perform many miracles, signs, and wonders for the Lord in the three and a half years of their ministry. Just prior to the "mid-trib," the Anti-messiah will kill the two witnesses. Their bodies will lie dead on the street of Jerusalem for three and a half days. After the three and a half days, the Lord will bring them back to life and then rapture them to heaven in the sight of all their enemies. This will be a most impressive sight for the world to see, and yet, how many people, Jewish or Gentile, will believe in Yeshua because of it?

While all of this is happening in Israel, the Anti-messiah will war against three of the ten kingdoms of the world. He will dominate these three kingdoms, and the seven remaining kingdoms will surrender and submit to him as well. The Anti-messiah then shall take full control over the world and will be declared king of the world!

At the middle of the Tribulation is when all hell will break loose on Israel—literally! The Anti-messiah will unleash the worst holocaust ever against the Jewish people! Two-thirds of the Jewish population in the Land will die. Right before the holocaust, the Anti-messiah will have stopped the animal sacrifices and worship of God in the Temple. He will then set up the Abomination of Desolation with the help of the False Prophet and require worship from the Jewish and Gentile people of the world.

The statue that will be set up as part of the abomination will then require all people to receive the 666 mark. If anyone receives the mark, they will be able to buy and sell in the Anti-messiah's commercial system. Whoever receives the mark will obviously have to receive HaSatan as their god. Around the world, whoever does not receive the mark will be a wanted person and hunted down. Many believers of Yeshua who do not receive the mark will die for their faith. Many believers will also survive until the end of Jacob's Trouble. A group of Jewish believers will leave Jerusalem and the Land of Israel for the wilderness and mountains at the middle of Jacob's Trouble. They will stay in God's blessed location for three and a half years and wait for the Lord's return. The Lord will provide for their needs and protect them from the Anti-messiah's army. It is believed that this safe location will be Petra and the Paran Mountain range.

The second half of Jacob's Trouble will bring lots of trouble to Israel. The Anti-messiah will hunt the Jewish people down all around the world. Yeshua says it will be the worst holocaust in Israel's history! Two-thirds of the Jewish people in the Land will die. But the good news is that one-third of the Jewish people will be saved toward the end of Jacob's Trouble. They will then call upon Yeshua to return in His Second Coming and deliver them from the clutches of the Anti-messiah.

The Second Coming of Yeshua will actually occur right after Jacob's Trouble is over. When Yeshua comes back, He will not come back as Mister Nice Guy who says, "Go ahead and put me up on the tree!" No, He will come back as the conquering King and Messiah that He is. And conquer He certainly will! The Armageddon War will be the war to end all wars. Yeshua will come back and truly wipe out the evil ones of the world! This war shall be a complete decimation. The blood will flow across Israel for about 180 miles. Millions and possibly up to hundreds of millions of soldiers will die in this war. The devastation will be immense!

The typical belief about the location of Yeshua's return is the Mount of Olives. However, Scripture does not support this view. It is better to believe that Yeshua lands at Bozrah (Petra area) where many Jewish believers will have lived since the middle of Jacob's Trouble. It is from this location that Yeshua will begin the destruction of the evil ones and travel back to Israel.

After the war is over, the cleanup will be incredible! However, there are seventy-five days before the Messianic Millennial Kingdom will begin. In this time, Yeshua is to perform many good deeds that need to be completed before the Kingdom can begin. The Anti-messiah and the False Prophet will be sent to the Lake of Fire. HaSatan will be cast into the abyss for 1,000 years. Israel's geography will be transformed, the Land cleansed of its defilement, and the fourth Temple will be built and anointed for Kingdom worship.

The Messianic Millennial Kingdom will last for a literal 1,000 years. The Scriptures are quite clear in this revelation. Unfortunately, many believers have already accepted metaphorical teaching and the spiritualizing of texts when a more literal approach is demanded by the Lord. One reason we believe in a literal 1,000 years is because the Lord is fulfilling His promises to His Son. In the Abrahamic and Davidic covenants, the Lord promised the Jewish people that the Jewish Messiah will rule and reign over the Jewish people in the Land of Israel forever!

Although Yeshua will be the Jewish Messiah in the Messianic Millennial Kingdom, He will also be the King of the World. He will be King ruling from His Jewish throne in the Jewish Temple in the Jewish Land of Israel! As you can see, the Messianic Millennial Kingdom will definitely be Jewish. In actuality, life in the Kingdom will return to a Messianic Jewish lifestyle. Worship of the Lord will return to a Messianic Jewish system that will include animal sacrifices! The Kingdom will also be characterized by peace, justice, faithfulness, and righteousness. There will be dramatic changes in the world where people will live for the entire 1,000 years. The world will repopulate, and believers will be priests and kings, ruling with Messiah over the world. Sin will not be allowed to abound like it does in today's world. The Lord will rule with a rod of iron! The miraculous will occur in the Kingdom as living water will flow from the Temple, the Lord's fire will encircle the city of Jerusalem, the Shekinah Glory will be upon Yeshua shining forth from His Temple and the canopy *chuppah* over the Temple Mount area shall be a light in the darkness as well.

After the 1,000 years is ended, HaSatan will be released from the pit. He will gather the evil ones from around the world to perform the last war of the world. This war is called "Gog and Magog II." However, this is really not a war but a complete wipeout. HaSatan and his evil ones congregate outside the city of Jerusalem to attack the holy ones of the Lord. However, the Lord rains down fire from heaven upon them all and annihilates them. HaSatan will then be sent to the Lake of Fire, and the Lord will perform the Great White Throne Judgment.

Everything that everyone ever does in life is written down in God's scrolls. Most believers in Yeshua, let alone most people, do not realize this! These scrolls contain the lists of works that all people perform in their lives, and the Lord will judge each person according to these deeds. Unfortunately for all people who come before the throne, there will be no one who is acquitted. Without Yeshua in their lives, their works will be seen as filthy rags. All who come before the Great White Throne Judgment will be eternally judged to the Lake of Fire!

After the Great White Throne Judgment is over, the Lord will then cleanse creation. Actually, He will destroy all of His original creation: the heavens and the earth. Once all the evil is finally judged and dealt with, the Lord will then perform a new act of creation. He will create a new heaven and a new earth as the old ones will have passed away. With this new creation, the New Jerusalem is introduced. The holy city, where all believers will live forever, flies down from the new heaven to the new earth.

The New Jerusalem is the most beautiful city ever created by the Lord. The Shekinah Glory of the Lord will envelop it. The city will be the largest city ever built—about 1,363 miles long, wide, and deep. Our eternal home will be made completely of transparent pure gold. The River of Life will flow through it, and the Tree of Life will bear fruit and leaves for healthy living in it. It will certainly be a wonderful sight for all who see it! But the best idea concerning the city is not how it is made, but who is inside. Obviously, I am talking about the Father and the Son sitting on their throne! God the Father and God the Lamb will sit on their throne and rule their Eternal Kingdom forever! All believers shall serve and reign with them forever. And we shall see ADONAI Himself face to face. What a wonderful sight that will be! Are you going to be there to see the Lord?

Well, folks, I hope you have enjoyed reading and studying *Israel in Prophecy* as much as I have enjoyed writing it! I am looking forward to seeing how this book affects the minds and hearts of Messianic Jewish and Gentile believers around the world, and even the Jewish community as well. Shalom!

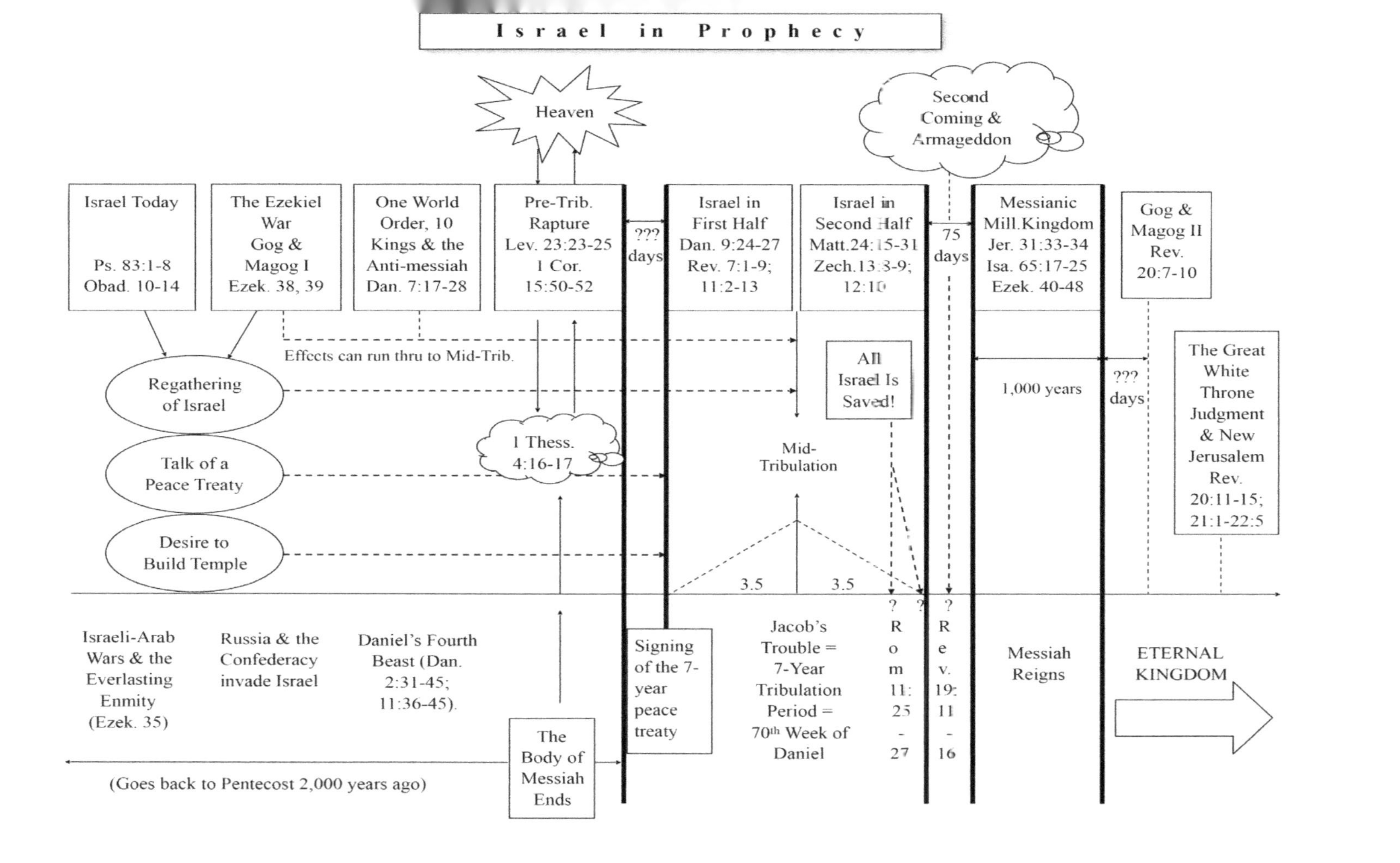
Israel in Prophecy
Heaven
Second Coming & Armageddon
Israel Today
Ps. 83:1-8
Obad. 10-14
The Ezekiel War Gog & Magog I Ezek. 38, 39
One World Order, 10 Kings & the Anti-messiah Dan. 7:17-28
Pre-Trib. Rapture Lev. 23:23-25 1 Cor. 15:50-52
??? days
Israel in First Half Dan. 9:24-27 Rev. 7:1-9; 11:2-13
Israel in Second Half Matt.24:15-31 Zech.13:3-9; 12:10
75 days
Messianic Mill.Kingdom Jer. 31:33-34 Isa. 65:17-25 Ezek. 40-48
Gog & Magog II Rev. 20:7-10
Effects can run thru to Mid-Trib.
Regathering of Israel
Talk of a Peace Treaty
Desire to Build Temple
1 Thess. 4:16-17
All Israel Is Saved!
Mid-Tribulation
1,000 years
??? days
The Great White Throne Judgment & New Jerusalem Rev. 20:11-15; 21:1-22:5
3.5
3.5
? Rom 11:25-27
? ? Rev. 19:11-16
Israeli-Arab Wars & the Everlasting Enmity (Ezek. 35)
Russia & the Confederacy invade Israel
Daniel's Fourth Beast (Dan. 2:31-45; 11:36-45).
Signing of the 7-year peace treaty
Jacob's Trouble = 7-Year Tribulation Period = 70th Week of Daniel
Messiah Reigns
ETERNAL KINGDOM
The Body of Messiah Ends
(Goes back to Pentecost 2,000 years ago)

Printed in the USA
CPSIA information can be obtained
at www.ICGtesting.com
CBHW051130191024
16129CB00011B/657

9 781545 642559